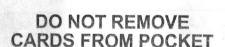

Highlights

Student Contact Book (SCB) provides invaluable help when an assignment or personal interest sends a student outside the library for information. It lists:

- over 800 organizations that answer inquiries and offer free or low-cost publications
- over 200 who's whos, professional rosters, and other directories that will connect the student to individual experts

The information and publications they provide should be nearly as current as the day's newspaper.

▶ Tied to the Curriculum...and to the Headlines

Teachers, students, and librarians guided the selection of topics represented in *SCB*. Its ten broad subject chapters represent all sides of some 150 topics under discussion in today's classrooms, including:

Acid rain
AIDS
Animal rights
Child abuse
Cults
Drunk driving
Earthquakes
Endangered species
Freedom of speech
Gun control
Homelessness
Literacy
Mental health
Native Americans
Nuclear energy
Political parties
Pollution
Pregnancy and birth technology
Substance abuse
Television
U.S. Supreme Court
and more!

▶ Features to Aid Fast Results

SCB has been designed to help the novice researcher working with tight deadlines and budgets:

- Toll-free and fax phone numbers in organization entries.
- Sample information-request letter and telephone interview script are included with tips for their use.
- Publications listed in organization entries cost no more than $25, with special emphasis on free publications.

ISSN 1066-2413

STUDENT CONTACT BOOK

How to Find Low-Cost, Expert Information on Today's Issues for:

Term Papers
•
Debates
•
Research Projects
•
and More!

ANNETTE NOVALLO, EDITOR

Joyce Jakubiak and Joseph M. Palmisano,
Associate Editors

Gale Research Inc.
DETROIT • LONDON • WASHINGTON D.C.

Annette Novallo, *Editor*
Karen Hill, *Contributing Editor*
Joyce Jakubiak and Joseph M. Palmisano, *Associate Editors*
Ned Burels and Diane Sawinski, *Assistant Editors*
Linda S. Hubbard, *Senior Editor*

Aided by: Pamela Dundas, Julia C. Furtaw,
Bradley J. Morgan, and Annette Piccirelli

Victoria B. Cariappa, *Research Manager*
Gary Oudersluys, *Research Supervisor*
Richard A. Lawson, *Editorial Associate*
Melissa Brown, Daniel L. Day, Charles Jewell, Colin McDonald,
Phyllis Shepherd, Patti Taraskiewicz, Tracie A. Wade,
and Elin Wong, *Editorial Assistants*

Benita L. Spight, *Data Entry Supervisor*
Gwendolyn Tucker, *Data Entry Group Leader*
Majorita Onyekuru, *Data Entry Associate*

Theresa Rocklin, *Supervisor of Systems and Programming*
Tom Potts and Tim Richardson, *Programmers*

Cynthia Baldwin, *Art Director*
Tracey Rowens, *Graphic Designer*
Barbara J. Yarrow, *Graphic Services Supervisor*
C.J. Jonik, *Keyliner*

ISBN 0-8103-8876-6
ISSN 1066-2413

Printed in the United States of America

Published simultaneously in the United Kingdom
by Gale Research International Limited
(An affiliated company of Gale Research Inc.)

Contents

Acknowledgments

Student Contact Book was compiled in consultation with teachers and librarians from across the United States. With advice from their own students, they helped assure that *SCB* is a good resource for the classroom assignments and personal interests of today's young people. The following individuals have earned special thanks for their participation throughout the development of the project:

Edna Boardman,
Minot High School, Minot, ND

John Bovberg,
Fountain Valley High School, Irvine, CA

Theresa Galvin,
Wootton High School, Rockville, MD

Dawn Ganss,
Westfield High School, Westfield, NJ

Judy Greco,
Ben Hill Junior High School, Tampa, FL

Janet Sarratt,
John E. Ewing Junior High School, Gaffney, SC

Introduction

Student Contact Book (SCB) connects young researchers to expert data and opinion on a wide spectrum of topics now being discussed in the classroom. It guides students to a wealth of information services and low-cost publications available from special interest organizations, clearinghouses, and agencies. It also helps them find experts to contact for personal insights into today's issues. Students from junior high to junior college will find invaluable assistance to enrich their:

- term papers
- debate preparation
- research projects
- and more

▶ *SCB* Adds New Dimensions to Research

Teachers often assign projects that require students to do original research. They can use *SCB* to:

- go beyond the library to locate up-to-the-minute information on today's hot topics
- reduce research time in writing term papers or preparing for debates
- gather diverse opinion on controversial issues and learn to weigh arguments
- identify free or low-cost publications to enhance their projects
- contact researchers, activists, and administrators associated with important concerns
- generate new ideas for resources or topics

▶ Advisory Board Helps Shape Contents

An advisory board of teachers, students, and librarians identified about 150 topics related to their curricula or of popular interest. They helped shape the chapter arrangement and consulted on page design. Their advice helped to assure that young people will find *SCB* both valuable and easy-to-use.

▶ Helps Students Tap Expert Resources

Student Contact Book identifies:

Organizations
More than 800 government agencies, nonprofit organizations, research centers, and information clearinghouses that answer inquiries and offer free or low-cost publications on their areas of interest. All listed organizations responded to our editors' requests for information, either on the telephone or by sending publications—so students can expect their research efforts to be successful. Organizations that did not reply or who issue only publications costing more than $25 are not included, no matter how well known.

Publications Listing People
More than 200 who's whos, biographical dictionaries, membership lists for professional associations, and other kinds of guides that will connect students to experts on the topics covered in *SCB*. Only sources published in 1989 or later and widely available are included. Each source provides contact information on the individuals listed. Because not all of the topics in *SCB* are covered by a specialized directory of individuals, guides to organizations are also included for some subjects so students can find an expert at the group's headquarters or get a referral through that office.

▶ Special Features Aid Student Research

Broad Subject Chapters. Entries in *SCB* are organized into ten broad subject chapters as listed on the "Contents" pages, making browsing easy. Each chapter includes a section on organizations and one on publications listing people.

Informative Chapter Opening Pages. Each chapter begins with: a complete list of the subjects covered in the chapter; references to other chapters with related subjects; and a list of possible research topics.

Balanced Coverage of Controversial Issues. Representatives of all viewpoints on controversial issues are included in *SCB*. For example, on the subject of animal rights there are groups that: oppose all animal testing; defend the use of animals in research; and work to assure that humane guidelines are followed in research laboratories.

"How to Contact Organizations and People." In a special section preceding the first subject chapter are samples of an information-request letter and a telephone interview script, along with tips on their use.

Alphabetical and Subject Index. Lists all the organizations and publications in *SCB* in one A-Z sequence by name and under all applicable subject terms to provide maximum access to entries.

See "How to Use This Book," following this introduction for details on these and other features.

▶ How *SCB* Was Compiled

Organizations. The editors scanned Gale Research's highly regarded *Encyclopedia of Associations, Research Centers Directory,* and *Clearinghouse Directory* for organizations that would be good resources for students on the topics selected by the *SCB* Advisory Board. Certain categories of entries, such as the company listings and those for foreign embassies and state tourist offices, were added to cover specific topics. Each organization was contacted to make sure that it would provide information to students and to get as many details as possible. An organization entry includes a brief description of the group's purpose or point-of-view and information activities, lists of publications available for free or for less than $25, and contact information.

Publications. Most entries for publications covering people were based on information in Gale's *Directories in Print*. As students are likely to consult these sources in a library, not to purchase them, only tips on use, frequency, and publisher name are provided.

▶ Your Suggestions and Comments Welcome

Questions, comments, and suggestions regarding *Student Contact Book* are welcomed, as are suggestions for additional organizations and publications not yet profiled. Please contact:

Student Contact Book
Gale Research Inc.
835 Penobscot Bldg.
Detroit, MI 48226-4094
Telephone: (313)961-2242
Toll-Free: 1-800-347-GALE
Fax: (313)961-6815

Annette Novallo

How to Use This Book

Whether you're still trying to choose a topic or have very specific information needs, *Student Contact Book (SCB)* will help solve your research problem. Its design supports both productive browsing and targeted investigations with these elements:

▶ List of Topics Covered

Use this alphabetical list of subjects to find the chapter to begin your search. It includes all the subjects, broad and narrow, for which the organizations and publications in *SCB* provide information. It also includes cross-references from alternate subject terms, for example: American Indians, see Native Americans. The number following the subject term refers to the chapter in which that subject is covered.

▶ Broad Subject Chapters Make Browsing Easy

SCB's ten chapters match broad subject groupings tied to school curricula and student interests at the junior high through junior college level. The specific topics covered within the chapter often relate to one another, so scanning the listings can help spark ideas or round out the scope of your project. There are separate sections in the chapter for organizations and for directories that will lead you to individual experts (see the sample entries later in this section). Each chapter opens with a list of the topics it covers.

▶ A List of Sample Research Topics Opens Each Chapter

The first page of each chapter lists dozens of ideas for specific research projects you could pursue with the resources in that chapter. Use one of the suggestions as is or brainstorm further to come up with your own ideas. Also on this page:

- a complete list of the subjects covered by the chapter
- a recommendation of other chapters that cover related topics

▶ Two Types of Resources in Each Chapter

Each *SCB* chapter is divided into two sections. The first section has entries for organizations, the second has directories that list people. You can get "live" information by talking to people at organizations or from individual experts. The organizations also have low-cost publications on their areas of interest. Organization entries appear in only one chapter, but are indexed under all subjects for which they provide significant information. Publications are listed in every chapter for which they are useful, so highly specialized sources appear just once, while *Who's Who in America* is cited in every chapter.

To Contact Organizations... Entries describe activist organizations, professional groups, research centers, information clearinghouses, and government agencies—all providing free or low-cost information to the public. Entries are arranged alphabetically by organization name. A typical listing includes:

- organization name
- a list of all subjects for which the group has significant information available for easy scanning. The list for an organization may include subjects covered in other chapters, since a group is only listed once in *SCB*. The entries can also be found under these subjects in the Alphabetical and Subject Index.
- a brief description of the organization, taking note of any special purpose or philosophy that might influence its viewpoint in the material it sends out.
- mention of pamphlets, special reports, bulletins, or other publications available without cost (a self-addressed, stamped envelope may be required since most of these are nonprofit groups).
- a list of books, booklets, and other materials available for less than $25.00. When known, listings include publication date, number of pages, price, and a brief description.
- contact information, including mailing address and phone number, with toll-free and fax telephone numbers when available.

To Contact People... Lists who's whos, membership lists of professional organizations, biographical guides, address books, and a variety of subject-specific directories. The sources may be arranged alphabetically, by geographic location, by subject specialty, or some other criterion; many will have indexes that offer an alternative way to find a listing. For instance, *Almanac of American Politics* is arranged by state, but has an alphabetical name index. All sources listed in these sections have contact information and were published in the past three years.

Editors have included widely held sources like *Who's Who in America,* but to help you contact experts in specialized fields some sources that may be too expensive or infrequently used to be in a small library are also included. You should still be able to consult them at a large library or through inter- library loan programs. Entries are arranged alphabetically by title. A typical entry includes:

- title
- a brief description of the types of people or organizations covered, what details a typical listing provides, and how the book is arranged and indexed
- how often the book is published
- publisher's name

▶ Index Pinpoints Entries by Name or Subject

If you are looking for a specific organization or publication by name, turn to the Alphabetical and Subject Index to find the page on which it appears. All the entries in *SCB* appear here in one A-Z sequence.

The same subject terms you see in the "List of Topics Covered" and in the "Provides information on" line in the organization entries are interfiled in this alphabetical sequence. Under each subject term you will find all the organizations and publications that pertain to it listed with their page numbers.

So, if you know you want to look up the National Association for the Advancement of Colored People (NAACP) and don't know whether to try "Government and Public Affairs" or "History and Heritage," turn to this index for the exact page reference. Look up the subject "African Americans" to find all the organizations and directories that could help research on this ethnic group.

▶ Making Contact

The section on "How to Contact Organizations and People" that follows this one includes a sample letter and phone script to help you make the most of the leads you find in *SCB.*

How to Contact Organizations and People

Here are some tips to get you started once you've identified the organization or person you want to contact.

To Contact Organizations...

All of the organizations, associations, research centers, and other groups in the *Student Contact Book* either provide information over the phone or send out brochures, magazines, and other publications. Some of the organizations request a self-addressed, stamped envelope (sometimes abbreviated SASE) so that they can mail out information without cost to them. Most government agencies and many clearinghouses will send volumes of information free of charge. The secret to getting what you want is to be specific:

- Specify the titles of the publications you want. Ask for a publications list so you find out about all they offer.
- Clearly write or type your name and address at the top of the letter or include it on an enclosed envelope.
- Enclose a self-addressed, stamped envelope, if required. Simply write your name and address on the outside of the envelope, and put a stamp on it.
- Enclose payment for publications, if they are not free. Use a check or money order; do not send cash.

▶ Sample Letter

Michael Smith
228 Blossom Ave.
Orchard, MI 48026

Stepfamily Foundation, Inc.
333 West End Ave.
New York, NY 10023

February 12, 1993

Dear Sirs,

I am researching the subject of step families as a term paper for senior English class at Valley High School. I am interested in receiving a free copy of the brochure The Step Family Foundation. Please also send any other free materials on step families and a complete list of your publications.

Enclosed is a stamped envelope with my home address.

Thank you for your cooperation.

Sincerely,

[Your Signature]

To Contact People...

Contacting an expert is a fast way to gather up-to-date information or to get an insider's view on your topic. If you have a specific person in mind, you can just look for the name in a who's who or professional directory listed in the "To Contact People" sections of *SCB* and find the phone number or address you need.

But you don't have to have an individual's name to locate an expert—*SCB* also lists directories of agencies and organizations, so that you can contact, for example, your state's solid waste administrator to find out what recycling programs are in place. You may also decide to use the "To Contact Organizations" listings and be connected with a group's spokesperson or recommended expert. And don't overlook the obvious: You can use your local yellow pages telephone directory to find organizations right in your own community that are active in your area of interest.

Before you place a call:

- Prepare questions to be asked in advance. Have several questions prepared on a sheet of paper in front of you. Be specific.
- Be prepared to take notes—have a pencil and paper next to the telephone.

- Place calls to a business address during business hours. Check time zones before you call, using the map in the front of your local telephone directory.

When placing a phone call to an expert:

- Ask for the person you are calling by name.
- Clearly state who you are.
- Clearly state your reason for calling and enlist the experts cooperation by asking if you can ask questions.
- Ask specific questions you have prepared in advance. If the responses are too technical, ask for an explanation.
- If the person you called is not helpful or does not provide the information you are seeking, ask if he or she can recommend another person for you to contact.
- Thank the contact.

► Sample Phone Script

Hello. My name is Laura Renee. I wish to speak to Mr. Ron Adams.

Hello Mr. Adams. I am Laura Renee and I'm calling from Northwood High School in North Dakota. I'm researching fitness among high school students for a social science term paper. Would you have a few minutes to talk with me about fitness issues?

(Ask specific questions:)
Have levels of fitness declined over the past 10 years?
What factors contribute to changes in fitness?
What can we do to improve fitness in the schools? At home?

Thanks for answering my questions. If I come across additional questions in my research, may I call you back?

Thank you. Good bye.

When the call is completed, review the answers you have jotted down. Fill in your notes while your memory of the call is still fresh. Send a brief thank you note acknowledging the expert's help.

Good luck.

List of Topics Covered

This list will guide you to **chapters** covering these topics and issues. Please use the Index at the back of the book to find specific **organizations** and **publications**.

STUDENT CONTACT BOOK

Government and Public Affairs

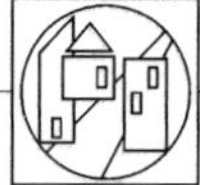

▶ Chapter 1 covers these topics:

Capital Punishment
Censorship
Civil Rights and Liberties
Computer Crime
Crime Prevention
Criminal Justice
Drunk Driving
Elections
Freedom of Speech
Government
Governors' Conferences
Gun Control
Hate Crimes
Juvenile Justice
Mayors' Conferences
Political Parties
Politics
Prisons
Rape
Sexual Harassment and Discrimination
Term Limitations for Public Officials
Terrorism
U.S. Presidents
U.S. Supreme Court
Victims

▶ Related topics appear in chapters on:

Arts and Entertainment; Family Connections and Concerns; History and Heritage; Social Issues

▶ Ideas for research topics:

Amnesty International's Efforts on Behalf of Political Prisoners
Appointment of the First Female Justice of the U.S. Supreme Court
Are Computers Threatening Our Privacy?
Can the Government Stop the Drug Trade?
The Case for Term Limitations on Federal Offices
Censorship in School Newspapers
City Government-Business Partnerships for Urban Renewal
Computer Crime by College Students
Crime Prevention in Schools
Crime Victim's Rights

▶ Ideas for research topics (continued):

Death Penalty's Effect on Crime Rates
Does the First Amendment Extend to Nazis?
Drunk Driving Penalties Nationwide
Effective Programs to Combat Drunk Driving
Elections—Incumbents' Advantage
How Political Campaign Spending Is Monitored
Federal vs. State Powers on Environmental Regulation
Firearms Accidents Involving Children
Freedom of Speech in Schools
Gang Violence
Governors' Conferences
Government Procurement—Do Purchasing Practices Invite Infractions?
Government's Role in Society
Handgun Control—Arguments For and Against
History of the Civil Rights Movement
How the Reagan and Bush Appointees Are Shifting the Balance of the U.S. Supreme Court
Human Rights Issues in Africa
Juvenile Justice—Successful Programs in Rehabilitating Young Offenders
The Kennedy Assassination—What the Kennedy Library Holdings Show
Landmark Cases in Equal Employment Opportunity
Lobbyists' Role in Clean Air Legislation
Mayors' Conferences—Enterprise Zones and Urban Renewal
Presidential Sites
Presidential Veto and the Balance of Power
Prison Reform—Are More Cells the Answer?
Public Figures and the Right to Privacy
Rape—Programs for Victims and for Repeat Offenders
Republican and Democratic Party Platforms—How Do They Compare?
Sexual Discrimination in the Workplace
State Death Penalty Laws
State Lotteries as Public Finance Tools
Successful Programs to Rehabilitate Youthful Offenders
Supreme Court Decisions That Shaped the Battle for Civil Rights
Terrorism in the 1990s
U.S. Presidents
U.S. Supreme Court Justices
U.S. Supreme Court's Role in Government

To Contact Organizations . . .

▶ AAA Foundation for Traffic Safety

Provides information on: *Drunk Driving*

The Foundation works to prevent traffic-related accidents by distributing films, videos, and related materials on safety to schools, libraries, police departments, and senior citizens. The Foundation provides grants to universities, colleges, and research agencies for traffic safety studies including such subjects as drunk driving, truck safety, and pedestrian and bicycle safety.

Information for free:

The Effects of Blood Alcohol Levels on Driving Simulator, Coordination, and Reaction Time Tests in a High Risk Population. 1992. Additional copies are $5 each. Research study involving young people and the effects of alcohol on driving ability.

To find out more, write or phone:

AAA Foundation for Traffic Safety
1730 M St., NW
Washington, DC 20036
Phone: (202)775-1456

▶ Academy for State and Local Government

Provides information on: *Government, Politics*

The Academy examines issues of concern to state and local governments and integration of solutions. Studies focus on tax legislation, preemption, legal issues before the U.S. Supreme Court, public finance, economic and community development, and international issues affecting state and local governments.

Information for free:

Access to Care for the Medically Indigent: A Resource Document for State and Local Officials. 1985. 248 pages. Includes an analysis of the medically indigent population, the legal obligations of state and local governments, and ten state and local case studies.

Contrasting Approaches to Economic Growth. 1984. 45 pages. Combination of two separate studies of development policies.

Economic Development Abroad. 1986. 48 pages. A collection of newsletters examining international economic development problems.

The Future of State and Local Government as Seen in the Futures Literature. 1985. 122 pages. Covers recurrent, emerging, and neglected issues in finance, economic development, the environment, education, and human resources.

Membership Directory. 1989. 113 pages.

National Scenic Byways Study. 1990. 30 pages. An overview of Canadian and overseas scenic highways and byways.

Salary and Fringe Benefits Survey. 1985. 26 pages. Provides an analysis of salaries and benefits of member organizations.

State and Local Implications of a Federal Value Added Tax. 1987. 42 pages. A study investigating the effects of a value added tax, a sales tax in which a product is taxed as it moves through the production-distribution process.

Symposium on Federalism: Issues Before the Supreme Court. 1986. 222 pages. A collection of articles.

Where Will the Money Come From? Finding Reliable Revenue for State and Local Governments in a Changing Economy. 1986. Examines the changing fiscal prospects of a service economy.

To find out more, write or phone:

Academy for State and Local Government
444 N. Capitol St. NW, Ste. 349
Washington, DC 20001
Phone: (202)434-4850 or *Fax:* (202)638-5109

▶ Alliance for Justice

Provides information on: *Civil Rights and Liberties*

The Alliance is a national association of environmental, civil rights, and consumer public interest organizations who focus on key issues that affect the impact and survival of the public interest movement. The group provides a forum for discussing critical issues and coordinates action by alerting members of key developments in the courts, Congress, and federal agencies.

Information for a fee:

Contempt for Law: Excluding the Public from the Rulemaking Process. 1983. 72 pages. $5. Provides 100 examples of regulations in violation of the public's legal right to participate in the regulatory process.

Directory of Public Interest Law Centers. 1991. 43 pages. $5. Lists 175 public interest law centers.

Liberty and Justice For All: Public Interest Law in the 1980s and Beyond. 1989. 165 pages. $9. Covers activities and developments of public interest law.

Pipeline. Quarterly. Price included in $20 Alliance for Justice membership dues. Newsletter containing articles on recent developments in the public interest sector.

To find out more, write or phone:
Alliance for Justice
1601 Connecticut Ave. NW, Ste. 600
Washington, DC 20009
Phone: (202)332-3224 or *Fax:* (202)265-2150

▶ American Bar Association Section of Individual Rights and Responsibilities

Provides information on: *Civil Rights and Liberties, Law, Human Rights*

This section of the American Bar Association concentrates on law and public policy as they relate to civil and constitutional rights, civil liberties, and human rights in the United States and internationally. SIRR projects include representation of the homeless, people with AIDS, and those facing capital sentences.

Information for a fee:
Human Rights Magazine. Quarterly. $17/year.

To find out more, write or phone:
American Bar Association
Section of Individual Rights and Responsibilities
1800 M St., NW, S. Lobby
Washington, DC 20036
Phone: (202)331-2280 or *Fax:* (202)331-2261

▶ American Civil Liberties Union (ACLU)

Provides information on: *Civil Rights and Liberties, Freedom of Speech*

The American Civil Liberties Union fights for the rights set forth in the Bill of Rights of the U.S. Constitution, including the freedom of speech, press, assembly, and religion, due process of law and fair trial, equality before the law regardless of race, color, sexual orientation, national origion, political opinion, or religious belief. Activities of the ACLU include advocacy and public education. It maintains a library, and sponsors projects on such topics as women's rights, gay and lesbian rights, and children's rights.

Information for free:
Center for National Security Studies. 1989. A summary of the group's functions and activities.
Civil Liberties Alert. A report on legislation concerning civil liberties.
Index of Materials. Includes press releases, testimony, legislative alerts, and other documents produced by the ACLU on current legislation.

Literature and Publications List/Order Form. Pamphlet.

Information for a fee:

1990 AIDS in Prison Bibliography. $5. Lists resources on AIDS in prisons, including corrections policies on AIDS, educational materials, medical and legal articles, and recent AIDS studies.

Civil Liberties. Price included in $20 ACLU membership fee. Newsletter.

In Defense of American Liberties. 1990. 479 pages. $24.95. A history of the ACLU.

Expanding the Right of Employees in America. 1988. $3.95.

Fighting Police Abuse. 1992. $5. A community action manual.

First Principles: National Security and Civil Liberties. Quarterly. $10 student rate. A journal covering the relationship between national security and civil liberties.

Immigration Reform Act: Employer Sanctions and Discrimination Prohibitions. 1988. $1. Pamphlet.

No Way Out: Young, Pregnant and Trapped by the Law. 1991. $2. Pamphlet.

Using the Freedom of Information Act: A Step by Step Guide. 1990. 16 pages. $3.

With Liberty and Justice for Women. $1. Information on the Women's Rights Project.

To find out more, write or phone:

American Civil Liberties Union
132 W. 43rd St.
New York, NY 10036
Phone: (212)944-9800

▶ American Correctional Association (ACA)

Provides information on: *Prisons, Juvenile Justice*

The American Correctional Association is comprised of correctional administrators, wardens, superintendents, members of prison and parole boards, probation officers, psychologists, educators, sociologists, and other individuals and institutions involved in the correctional field. The Association promotes improved correctional standards, develops adequate physical facilities, sponsors educational and training programs, and studies causes of juvenile crime and methods of prevention.

Information for free:

ACA Books Sale Catalog. 1992. Lists the various publications, audio- and video-tapes available through the Association.

Information for a fee:

AIDS: The Impact on the Criminal Justice System. 1990. 243 pages. $20. A collection of articles that looks at the public policy choices facing the criminal justice system as a result of AIDS.

American Jails Public Policy Issues. 1991. 288 pages. $17.95. A collection of articles that disucss the policy environment of the jail, health and safety, crowding and management, and the emerging social issues confronting today's jails.

Behind Bars. 1991. 93 pages. $12. A look at the people who live and work inside a correctional institution.

Causes, Preventive Measures, and Methods of Controlling Riots and Disturbances in Correctional Institutions. 1990. 96 pages. $22. Covers the three aspects of riots and disturbances - causes, prevention, and control.

The Cycle of Juvenile Justice. 1992. 195 pages. $12.95. Examines how juvenile justice policy has gone through cycles of reform resulting in little or no improvement in the treatment of delinquency.

Delinquent Gangs: A Psychological Perspective. 1991. 313 pages. $19.95. Helps explain what a gang is, and why gang-related violence is on the rise.

Delinquents on Delinquency. 1990. 205 pages. $15.95. Results of interviews with both professionals and youth that attempt to answer the following: What causes juvenile delinquency? Which intervention reduces it? How can it be prevented?

Girls, Delinquency, and Juvenile Justice. 1992. 249 pages. $16.95. Looks at the special problems of delinquent girls and the juvenile justice system's attempts to apply male-oriented solutions.

Guards Imprisoned: Correctional Officers at Work. Second edition, 1989. 250 pages. $19.95. Looks at the working environment of correctional officers through their perceptions and experiences.

Issues in Juvenile Delinquency. 1985. 104 pages. $18. Examines handling violent juveniles, teen court programs, and training juvenile detention officers.

To find out more, write or phone:

American Correctional Association
Anthony P. Travisono, Exec. Dir.
8025 Laurel Lakes Ct.
Laurel, MD 20707-5075
Toll-free: 1-800-ACA-JOIN or *Phone:* (301)206-5100 or *Fax:* (301)206-5061

▶ American Jail Association

Provides information on: *Prisons*

The American Jail Association is comprised of sheriffs, jail managers, supervisors, and officers. Goals of the Association include raising the standards of detention facilities, exchanging information on jail management techniques, and maintaining the professionalism of jail personnel.

Information for a fee:
The following publications are included with the $25 yearly membership price:

American Jails. Bimonthly magazine. Includes advertisers' index, book reviews, calendar of events, and state jail association news.
Jail Managers Bulletin. Monthly.
Jail Operations Bulletin. Monthly.
Product Directory. Annual.
Who's Who in Jail Management. Annual.

To find out more, write or phone:
American Jail Association
1000 Day Rd., Ste. 100
Hagerstown, MD 21740
Phone: (301)790-3930 or *Fax:* (301)790-2941

▶ American Justice Institute

Provides information on: *Crime Prevention*

The Institute helps institutions and individuals become more willing and able to reduce the occurrence of crime, delinquency, and related social problems. It conducts research and provides information.

To find out more, write or phone:
American Justice Institute
Lawrence A. Bennett Ph.D.
705 Merchant St.
Sacramento, CA 95814
Phone: (916)442-0707

▶ American League of Lobbyists (ALL)

Provides information on: *Politics, Political Action Committees*

Registered lobbyists and other professionals interested in the lobbying profession are members of the League. Lobbyists work to influence public officials, especially legislative bodies, to sway opinion on votes or leislation. ALL conducts professional development education programs, seminars, and programs to improve public understanding and recognition of the role of lobbyists in the legislative process.

Information for free:
ALL News. Monthly. Association and industry newsletter. Includes list of new members and calendar of events.

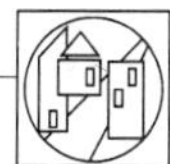

To find out more, write or phone:

American League of Lobbyists
PO Box 30005
Alexandria, VA 22310
Phone: (703)960-3011 or *Fax:* (703)960-4070

▶ American Restitution Association (ARA)

Provides information on: *Juvenile Justice*

Persons and organizations interested in the idea of accountability in the juvenile justice system work to promote the concept of juvenile restitution as a means of compensating victims of crime and to instill a sense of responsibility and accountability in youth. The ARA provides technical assistance to people and organizations and provides legal advice on issues affecting juvenile restitution policies and operations.

Information for a fee:

Accountability in Action. Semiannual. Available with $20 annual membership dues. Newsletter.
Directory of Restitution Programs. Available with $20 annual membership.
Guide to Juvenile Restitution. Quarterly. Available with $20 annual membership.

To find out more, write or phone:

American Restitution Association
Elizabeth Watson, Pres.
c/o 232 Horton Hall
Shippensburg University
Shippensburg, PA 17257
Phone: (803)744-3381 or *Fax:* (919)856-5815

▶ Anti-Repression Resource Team

Provides information on: *Civil Rights and Liberties, Hate Crimes, Terrorism*

The Team combats all forms of political repression, including police violence and misconduct, Ku Klux Klan and Nazi terrorism, and spying and covert action by secret police and intelligence agencies. The group focuses on research, writing, lecturing, and publishing. It conducts training workshops for church, labor, and community organizations. A library of materials on spying, repression, covert action, terrorism, and civil liberties is kept.

To find out more, write or phone:
Anti-Repression Resource Team
Ken Lawrence, Dir.
PO Box 122
Jackson, MS 39205
Phone: (601)969-2269

▶ Association for the Sexually Harassed (ASH)

Provides information on: *Sexual Harassment and Discrimination*

ASH seeks to eliminate sexual harassment, which ASH defines as the "unwelcomed exposure to physical contact, pornography, sexual jokes, requests for dates, and demeaning comments, made by male or female, which causes an individual's environment or work place to become intimidating, hostile, or offensive." Works to educate the public about the effects of sexual harassment and provides assistance to victims in outlining problems of sexual harassment. The Association conducts research on victims of sexual harassment and posttraumatic stress disorder and conducts studies relating sexual harassment to homelessness, crime, unemployment, and worker's compensation injuries.

To find out more, write or phone:
Association for the Sexually Harassed
PO Box 27235
Philadelphia, PA 19118
Phone: (215)952-8037

▶ Jimmy Carter Library

Provides information on: *U.S. Presidents*

The Library holds books written by and about Jimmy Carter, Mrs. Carter, and the Carter administration.

Information for free:
Jimmy Carter Library Resource List. 5 pages.
Museum of the Jimmy Carter Library Gift Catalog. Includes books, souvenirs, postcards, games, stationery, posters, videotapes, and educational materials.

Information for a fee:
Constitution. $5. This book traces the roots of our nation's history and tradition by following the Constitutional Convention for middle and high school students.
First Lady From Plains. $3.95. The memoirs of former First Lady Rosalynn Carter.

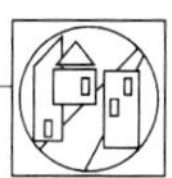

Getting to Know Jimmy Carter. A packet for upper elementary and middle school students providing an introduction to the early life of Jimmy Carter.

It's a Wide, Wild Interdependent World. $7. A book for middle and high school students to examine cultural differences and social, economic, and political needs of people throughout the world.

Keeping Faith: Memoirs of a President. $22.50. Jimmy Carter recounts his years in the White House.

Partner of the President. $7. Responsibilities and duties of the First Lady are explored in this publication for middle and high school students.

Peace in the Middle East. $5. Middle school students are introduced to the history , culture, and problems of the Middle East in this book.

Presidential Campaigns. $9.95. A "witty" publication about American politics.

Public Papers of the Presidents of the United States: Jimmy Carter. Annual. $17.95 each. A multi-volume series of statements and speeches made by President Carter from 1977 to 1981.

Race to the White House. In this publication, middle school students are introduced to the roles of political parties, qualifications for candidacy, and the requirements for becoming a voter.

To find out more, write or phone:

Jimmy Carter Library
1 Copenhill Ave.
Atlanta, GA 30307
Phone: (404)331-3942

▶ Center for Constitutional Rights (CCR)

Provides information on: *Civil Rights and Liberties*

The Center is a nonprofit organization aiming to advance and protect the rights guaranteed by the United States Constitution. Works in such areas as women's rights, civil rights, freedom of the press, racism, electronic surveillance, criminal trials, and affirmative action.

Information for free:

Birth Control Confidential. 1987. Provides information on the legal rights of teenagers to birth control, abortion, and sex education in Texas, Arkansas, Mississippi, Missouri, and Oklahoma.

A Splendid Body of Tigerish People. 1989. Describes the work of the Center for Constitutional Rights.

The U.S. Invasion of Panama. 1990.

Information for a fee:

And Before I'll be a Slave. 1990. $10. Guide to community-based voting rights.
If an Agent Knocks: Federal Investigators and Your Rights. 1989. $1.
Racially-Motivated Violence Litigation Strategies. 1984. 245 pages. $6 for students.
Stopping Sexual Assault in Marriage: A Guide for Women, Counselors and Advocates. 1990. $1.

To find out more, write or phone:

Center for Constitutional Rights
666 Broadway, 7th Fl.
New York, NY 10012
Phone: (212)614-6464 or *Fax:* (212)614-6499

▶ Center for Democratic Renewal (CDR)

Provides information on: *Civil Rights and Liberties, Hate Crimes*

CDR is a multi-racial, multi-ethnic, inter-faith, nonprofit organization that promotes opposition to hate group activity and bigoted violence through education, activism, and action. A national clearinghouse for efforts to counter hate group activity, the CDR also maintains a Midwest office in Kansas City, Missouri, and a Northwest office in Seattle, Washington. CDR also offers youth education programs.

Information for a fee:

The Invisible Empire: The Ku Klux Klan Impact on History. 166 pages. $12.00. Written for school age young people, it provides a general background of the Klan.
They Don't All Wear Sheets: A Chronology of Racist and Far Right Violence 1980-1986. 100 pages. $10.00. Addresses bigoted violence, and the nature of crimes against Blacks, Jews, and gay people.
Violence, Victimization, and Defamation. $4. An annual report documenting the nationwide epidemic of homophobic violence.
When Hate Groups Come to Town: A Handbook of Model Community Responses. 146 pages. $14. Provides suggested actions.

To find out more, write or phone:

Center for Democratic Renewal
PO Box 50469
Atlanta, GA 30302-0469
Phone: (404)221-0025 or *Fax:* (404)221-0045

▶ Center for the Study of Civil Rights

Provides information on: *Civil Rights and Liberties*

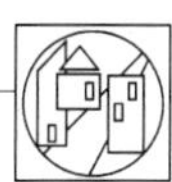

The Center coordinates cross-disciplinary research in civil rights studies and analyzes current public policy issues related to the civil rights of women as well as minority group members. It focuses on the civil rights movement from the late 1930s to the present. Research results can be obtained over the phone.

To find out more, write or phone:

Center for the Study of Civil Rights
Dr. Armstead L. Robinson, Dir.
University of Virginia
1512 Jefferson Park Ave.
Charlottesville, VA 22903
Phone: (804)924-3109

▶ Center for the Study of the Presidency

Provides information on: *U.S. Presidents*

The Center is devoted to the study of the American presidency, including constitutional principles, relations with Congress, and organization and staffing. The group analyzes the highest office in the nation through the study of history, economics, philosophy, political science, journalism, and rhetoric. The purpose of its studies is not only for the sake of good government but also for the quality of present and future leadership. The Center serves as a library and clearinghouse for information on the presidency, participates in program planning and research for television and radio, and serves in a counseling capacity for White House staff, congressional committees, and other governmental and nongovernmental agencies in the U.S. and abroad.

Information for a fee:

Command Decision and the Presidency. $16.
Proceedings Series, Volume I-VI:
The White House: Organization and Operations. $8.
The Presidency of the 1970's. $8.
Organizing and Staffing the Presidency. $8.
The Presidency and Information Policy. $8.
The Presidency and National Security Policy. $13.
The Presidency in Transition. $20.

To find out more, write or phone:

Center for the Study of the Presidency
208 E. 75th St.
New York, NY 10021
Phone: (212)249-1200 or *Fax:* (212)628-9503

▶ Center for Women Policy Studies

Provides information on: *Sexual Harassment and Discrimination*

The Center for Women Policy Studies is a politically active research institution dedicated to advancing women's equality. The Center's main areas of concern include educational equity, economic opportunity for low income women, work and family policies, women and AIDS, reproductive rights and health, and violence against women. The needs of women of color are of particular importance within the Center's programs. Research results are published in bibliographies, monographs, working documents, policy analysis reports, and books. The Center also publishes educational materials.

Information for free:
Center for Women Policy Studies. Brochure describing the Center.

To find out more, write or phone:
Center for Women Policy Studies
2000 P St., NW, Ste. 508
Washington, DC 20036
Phone: (202)872-1770 or *Fax:* (202)861-0691

▶ Center for Youth Research

Provides information on: *Juvenile Justice*

The Center is involved in community-based youth research primarily in the areas of delinquency, education, law, and cross-cultural development. Research on youth development in the community includes studies on planning for youth programs and facilities, social skills training for students, youth gangs, and delinquency prevention.

Information for free:
Research reports.

To find out more, write or phone:
Center for Youth Research
University of Hawaii at Manca
2500 Campus Rd.
Honolulu, HI 96822
Phone: (808)956-7517 or *Fax:* (808)956-5950

 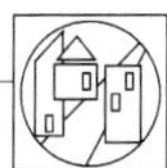

▶ Centre of Criminology

Provides information on: *Criminal Justice, Juvenile Justice, Civil Rights and Liberties*

The Centre deals with all aspects of criminology, including administration of criminal justice, sociology of law, public policing, private justice, sentencing, corrections, alternatives to imprisonment, juvenile justice, gender and social control, news media and social control, and public attitudes toward crime, sentencing, and civil liberties.

Information for a fee:

Crime Stoppers: A Study of the Organization of Community Policing. 1989. 114 pages. $8. Explains the community policing movement.

Criminology: A Reader's Guide. 1991. $17.95.

The Fitness Interview Test: A Method for Examining Fitness to Stand Trial 1984. 84 pages. $4.50. Describes the development of a structured interview and rating scale for assessing fitness/competence to stand trial.

News Accounts of Attacks on Women: A Comparison of Three Toronto Newspapers. 1984. 98 pages. $6.

Police Use of Deadly Force: Canadian Perspectives. 1985. $9. Research report.

Understanding Justices: A Study of Canadian Justices of the Peace. 1991. 280 pages. $19.95. Report examining various aspects of the role of the justice of the peace, their selection, training, and income.

Workshop on Collecting Race and Ethnicity Statistics in the Criminal Justice System. 1991. 29 pages. $3.50. A report of a workshop designed to discuss the topic of race and ethnicity statistics in the Canadian criminal justice system.

To find out more, write or phone:

Centre of Criminology
University of Toronto
130 George St., Rm. 8001
Toronto, ON, Canada M5S 1A1
Phone: (416)978-3720 or *Fax:* (416)978-4195

▶ Citizens' Commission on Civil Rights

Provides information on: *Civil Rights and Liberties*

The Commission is made up of bipartisan former federal cabinet officials concerned with achieving the goal of equality of opportunity. Its objectives are to monitor the federal government's enforcement of laws barring discrimination on the basis of race, sex, religion, ethnic background, age, or handicap, to foster public understanding of civil rights issues, and to make constructive policy recommendations.

Information for a fee:

Barriers to Registration and Voting: An Agenda for Reform. 1988. $10. A study of restrictive voter registration practices that adversely affect voter participation of minorities, low-income, and disabled people.

A Decent Home.A Report on the Continuing Failure of the Federal Government to Provide Equal Housing Opportunity. 1983. $10. A report examining fair housing laws, discrimination in the housing market, and the need for reform.

Lost Opportunities: The Civil Rights Record of the Bush Administration Mid-Term. 1991. $15. Looks at the status of civil rights policies and enforcement during the first two years of the Bush administration.

One Nation, Indivisible: The Civil Rights Challenge for the 1990s. 1989. $15. Analyzes the record of the enforcement by federal civil rights agencies during the 1980s and provides recommendations for change.

To find out more, write or phone:

Citizens' Commission on Civil Rights
2000 M St., NW, Ste. 400
Washington, DC 20036
Phone: (202)659-5565 or *Fax:* (202)293-2672

▶ Citizens Committee for the Right to Keep and Bear Arms

Provides information on: *Firearms, Gun Control*

The Committee is made up of individuals interested in defending the Second Amendment; more than 150 members of Congress serve on the advisory board. It conducts educational and political activities, weekend seminars, and in-depth studies on gun legislation.

Information for free:

Citizens Committee for the Right to Keep and Bear Arms and You. Describes the group's agenda and activities.

Information for a fee:

Point Blank. Monthly. Included in membership dues; $15/year for nonmembers. Newsletter fostering public awareness on the right of citizens to bear arms. Reports on gun control legislation, pro-gun candidates, committee activities, and news stories.

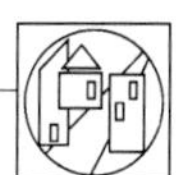

To find out more, write or phone:

Citizens Committee for the Right to Keep and Bear Arms
Liberty Park
12500 NE 10th Pl.
Bellevue, WA 98005
Phone: (206)454-4911 or *Fax:* (206)451-3959

▶ Claremont Institute for the Study of Statesmanship and Political Philosophy

Provides information on: *Government, Politics*

The Institute is designed to help recover and restore the original principles of America, focusing on Asian studies, American history, political philosophy, modern economics, and foreign policy. Contemporary issues of concern include economic growth, air quality, property rights, the environment, and public policy issues.

Information for a fee:

Endangered Species and Endangered Humanity. 14 pages. $5. Booklet addressing the danger of current environmental laws and regulations.

The Federal Government and Slavery. 26 pages. $3.50.

Freedom of Expression: Purpose as Limit. 181 pages. $9.95. Questions why the public has the freedom of speech.

Homosexuality and the Natural Law. 39 pages. $5. Addresses what the organization calls "the most radical threat to the American family today—the organized homosexual movement."

The High Costs and Poor Performance of the U.S. Postal Service Monopoly: Why Not Give Free Competition a Try? $2.50.

The Increasing Soviet Presence in the Pacific. $5.

The Media Elite: America's New Power Brokers—An Abridgement. 44 pages. $5.

Nuclear-Free-Zone Politics in Asia-Pacific. $5.

The Transformation of American Citizenship. 16 pages. $5.

The United States and the Republic of China: Democratic Friends, Strategic Allies, and Economic Partners. 176 pages. $18.95. A book of essays addressing the shared purpose between the U.S. and the Republic of China.

To find out more, write or phone:

Claremont Institute for the Study of Statesmanship and Political Philosophy
4650 Arrow Hwy., Ste. D-6
Montclair, CA 91763-1223
Phone: (714)621-6825 or *Fax:* (714)626-8724

▶ Coalition to Stop Gun Violence

Provides information on: *Firearms, Gun Control*

The Coalition is made up of educational, professional, and religious organizations united to seek a ban on the private sale and possession of handguns in America. Exceptions to the ban would include the police, active military personnel, federally licensed collectors, and target shooters whose handguns are used and kept only at shooting clubs. The group works to enact restrictive handgun controls at the national, state, and local levels and assists state and local handgun control organizations. The group conducts research and gathers statistics on subjects such as suicide, homicide, and accidents involving handguns; handguns and self-defense; and handgun production and the marketing tactics of manufacturers.

Information for a fee:
The Banner. Annual. Included in $25 membership dues.

To find out more, write or phone:
Coalition to Stop Gun Violence
100 Maryland Ave., NE
Washington, DC 20002-5625
Phone: (202)544-7190 or *Fax:* (202)544-7213

▶ Committee for Single Six-Year Presidential Term

Provides information on: *Term Limitations for Public Officials*

The Committee seeks a constitutional amendment allowing for a single six-year term for U.S presidents. It maintains a collection of historical material and research on related issues.

To find out more, write or phone:
Committee for Single Six-Year Presidential Term
1529 18th St., NW
Washington, DC 20036
Phone: (202)234-3681

▶ Committee for the Study of the American Electorate

Provides information on: *Elections*

The Committee is a research group that studies the decline of participation in the American political process. It conducts conferences with recognized authorities and compiles statistics.

Information for a fee:
Offers bimonthly reports on elections. $5/each.

To find out more, write or phone:
Committee for the Study of the American Electorate
421 New Jersey Ave., SE
Washington, DC 20003
Phone: (202)546-3221

▶ Communist Party of the United States of America (CPUSA)

Provides information on: *Political Parties*

A political party of the working class, CPUSA is "dedicated to the interests of all working and nationally oppressed peoples. Its aim is a socialist society." It maintains a speakers' bureau and biographical archives, and offers specialized education.

Information for a fee:
Jewish Affairs. 4/year. $7.50/year.
Political Affairs. Monthly. $20/year. Also publishes pamphlets.

To find out more, write or phone:
Communist Party of the United States of America
235 W. 23rd St., 7th Fl.
New York, NY 10011
Phone: (212)989-4994

▶ Computer Security Institute

Provides information on: *Computer Crime*

The objectives of the Institute are to advance the view that information is an important asset and must be protected; to keep members informed on computer issues; and to represent the interests of users and vendors in the electronic data processing field. Offers various publications and periodicals.

To find out more, write or phone:
Computer Security Institute
600 Harrison St.
San Francisco, CA 94107
Phone: (415)905-2370 or *Fax:* (415)905-2234

▶ Computer Virus Industry Association

Provides information on: *Computer Crime*

The Association offers help to companies involved in identifying and getting rid of computer viruses. (A computer virus is a program, usually hidden in normal software, that instructs a computer to alter or destroy information.) The group conducts research programs, and compiles statistics. It also publishes an informational packet and a periodical.

To find out more, write or phone:
Computer Virus Industry Association
PO Box 391703
Mountain View, CA 94039-1703
Phone: (408)727-4559

▶ Conference of Chief Justices

Provides information on: *U.S. Supreme Court*

The Conference is made up of chief justices of supreme courts of the United States, District of Columbia, American Samoa, Guam, Puerto Rico, the Mariana Islands, and the Virgin Islands.

Information for free:
National Center for State Courts Publications Catalog. 81 pages.

Information for a fee:
Adoption Information Improvement Feasibility Study: Final Report. 1986. 101 pages. $6.
Causal Analysis of the Relationship Between Learning Disabilities and Juvenile Delinquency. 1984. 103 pages. $6.18.
Child Support Guidelines Summary. 1990. 152 pages. $9.
Issues and Recommendations Concerning the Prohibition of Weapons in Courtrooms and Courthouse Buildings. 1984. 12 pages. $1.
Media in the Courts. 1981. 142 pages. $2.25.
Proceedings of the National Conference on Gender Bias in the Courts. 1990. 69 pages. $4.95.
State Court Journal. Quarterly. $24/year. Features articles by experts in the field of court improvement.
Student Litigation: A Compilation and Analysis of Civil Cases Involving Students, 1977-1981. 1982. 208 pages. $12.48.
Victims, Witnesses, and Courts. 1986. 122 pages. $8.
Women in the Judiciary: A Symposium for Women Judges. 1983. 116 pages. $8.
Also offers information on judicial selection, traffic courts, courtroom reporting, juries, plea bargaining, sentencing, and more.

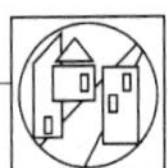

To find out more, write or phone:

Conference of Chief Justices
National Center for State Courts
300 Newport Ave.
Williamsburg, VA 23187
Phone: (804)253-2000

▶ Conservative Party

Provides information on: *Political Parties*

The Conservative Party is a political organization in New York State dedicated to what it defines as "individual liberty, limited constitutional government, and defense of the Republic against its enemies." The party's platform calls for reduction in federal controls and spending, a balanced federal budget and reduction of the federal debt, revision of tax laws and reduction of personal and corporate income tax rates, legislation to curb "coercive" practices by unions, elimination of rent control and opposition to government control of prices or wages, reliance on private institutions, programs, and physicians to meet the nation's medical needs, passage of a constitutional amendment to permit prayer in public schools, limitation of American foreign aid and military and technical assistance to nations opposing communism, elimination of the communist government in Cuba, repeal of laws permitting abortion, and opposition to the Equal Rights Amendment.

Information for free:

Legislative Platform. Annual.

To find out more, write or phone:

Conservative Party
Michael R. Long, State Chm.
486 78th St.
Ft. Hamilton Station, NY 11209
Phone: (718)921-2158 or *Fax:* (718)921-5268

▶ Calvin Coolidge Memorial Foundation

Provides information on: *U.S. Presidents*

The Foundation seeks to continue the memory of Calvin Coolidge (1872-1933) and to interpret his life, times, and presidential administration. It provides educational programs and maintains a library.

Information for free:
Educational Packet.

Information for a fee:
Calvin Coolidge Memorial Foundation Newsletter. Quarterly. Price included in $5 student membership fee.

To find out more, write or phone:
Calvin Coolidge Memorial Foundation
Box 97
Plymouth, VT 05056
Phone: (802)672-3389

▶ Correctional Education Association (CEA)

Provides information on: *Prisons, Juvenile Justice, Education*

The Association helps teachers and others who provide educational services to students in prisons or other correctional settings. They provide timely and practical information needed to run a successful program, and they help to increase the quality of existing programs. The Association also serves to represent the interests of prison education before government, media, and community groups. It also maintains biographical archives and compiles statistics.

Information for free:
Correctional Education Packet. Includes several informational brochures, a ten-page history of correctional education, and a keynote speech given at CEA's Annual Conference.
Lawyers for Literacy: A Bar Leadership Manual. A booklet detailing the problems of illiteracy and the efforts being made to combat it.
Trust for Insuring Educators (T.I.E.). Brochure.

Information for a fee:
Annual Directory for Correctional Educators. $25. Lists contact information of CEA members, including libraries and institutions.
Learning Behind Bars: Selected Educational Programs from Juvenile, Jail, and Prison Facilities. $5. A booklet providing information on 30 institutions, including what makes their program different and successful.
Standards for Adult and Juvenile Correctional Educational Programs. $10. The first standards specifically for use in correctional institutions.

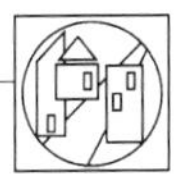

To find out more, write or phone:

Correctional Education Association
8025 Laurel Lakes Ct.
Laurel, MD 20707-5075
Toll-free: 1-800-783-1232 or *Phone:* (301)490-1440 or *Fax:* (301)206-5061

▶ Crime Control Institute & Crime Control Research Corporation

Provides information on: *Crime Prevention*

The Crime Control Institute is a research organization that seeks to improve public safety through alternative crime control strategies. The Institute conducts random clinical trials of social policies and issues reports.

Information for a fee:

Crime Control Reports:
Citizens Killed by Big City Police. $15. Statistical analysis from 1970-1984.
Contrasting Crime General and Crime Specific Theory: The Case of Hot Spots of Crime. $10. Examines the environment in which crimes occur.
Drunk Driving Tests in Fatal Accidents. $15.
Police Murdered in Drug-Related Situations, 1972-1988. $10.
Predicting Domestic Homicide: Prior Police Contact and Gun Threats. $15.
Stray Bullets and Mushrooms': Random Shootings of Bystanders in Four Cities, 1977-88. $10.

To find out more, write or phone:

Crime Control Institute & Crime Control Research Corporation
1063 Thomas Jefferson St., NW
Washington, DC 20007
Phone: (202)337-2700 or *Fax:* (202)337-8324

▶ Crime Victims Research and Treatment Center

Provides information on: *Rape, Victims, Acquaintance Rape, Marital Rape, Incest*

The Center studies the psychological effects of criminal victimization, including effects of rape on married, cohabitating, and dating relationships. It also studies the characteristics of incest victims and their families, and characteristics of criminal offenders. The Center provides evaluation and treatment services for victims and their families, works with police departments, consults with attorneys, and provides expert testimony in criminal and civil court cases involving rape, child molestation, and battering of women. Other activities include educational programs for professionals and the public.

Information for free:
Publications. 15 pages. Bibliographic listing of scientific articles.
Child Victims of Sexual Abuse. 1988.
Rape in America: A Report to the Nation. 1992.
Natural Disasters and Mental Health: Theory, Assessment and Intervention.
The Social Consequences of Divorce: Implications for Family Policy. 1983.

To find out more, write or phone:
Crime Victims Research and Treatment Center
Department of Psychiatry and Behavioral Sciences
Medical University of South Carolina
171 Ashley Ave.
Charleston, SC 29425
Phone: (803)792-2945 or *Fax:* (803)792-3388

▶ Death Row Support Project

Provides information on: *Capital Punishment, Prisons*

This project of the Church of the Brethren links concerned individuals with prisoners who have been sentenced to death. The Project founders believe correspondence is a way of serving Jesus and brightening the lives of prison inmates. The Project works to educate the public about prison life and offers information opposing the death penalty.

To find out more, write or phone:
Death Row Support Project
Rachel Gross, Coordinator
PO Box 600
Liberty Mills, IN 46946
Phone: (219)982-7480

▶ Democratic Governors Association (DGA)

Provides information on: *Political Parties*

Governors of the states and territories of the U.S. who are members of the Democratic Party make up the Democratic Governors Association.

Information for free:
Update. Quarterly newsletter.

To find out more, write or phone:
Democratic Governors Association
Mark Gearan, Exec.Dir.
430 S. Capitol St., SE
Washington, DC 20003
Phone: (202)479-5153

▶ Democratic National Committee (Democratic Party)

Provides information on: *Politics*

The Democratic National Committee is a political organization formed to promote and teach Democratic interests and beliefs. The committee serves as a link between the state democratic organizations and national administration. It organizes and sponsors national political activities, provides technical assistance to political candidates, assembles representative groups from home states to attend national functions, and sponsors Democratic candidate training seminars.

Information for free:
The following publications are periodically updated and are issued by request:
Delegate Selection Rules for Conventions;
Democratic Charter/By-Laws;
Final Calls to Conventions;
Get Out the Vote;
History of the Party;
Official Proceedings of National Convention;
Party Lines;
Platform of the Party;
Voter Registration Manual.

To find out more, write or phone:
Democratic National Committee (Democratic Party)
430 S. Capitol St. S.E.
Washington, DC 20003
Phone: (202)863-8000

▶ Educational Fund to End Handgun Violence

Provides information on: *Firearms, Gun Control*

The organization examines and offers public education on handgun violence in the U.S., particularly as it affects children. It participates in the development of materials and educational programs for schools in an effort to convince teenagers not to carry guns. The fund provides information on the illegal use of machine guns, firearm violence, and public health. It also conducts research on handgun violence, firearms marketing and production, and the design of firearms. It maintains the Firearms Litigation Clearinghouse, which collects and distributes information relating to handguns, particularly information on firearm liability suits.

Information for free:

Handgun Fact Sheet. Answers such questions as "Who is allowed to purchase handguns?" and "How many Americans are killed by handguns each year?"

Information for a fee:

Assault Weapons and Accessories in America. $5. Study on the use, marketing, and popularity of assault weapons.

Kids and Guns. 1989. 25 pages. $10. Gives information and statistics on youth suicide, homicide, and accidental fatalities involving firearms.

To find out more, write or phone:

Educational Fund to End Handgun Violence
110 Maryland Ave., NE
Box 72
Washington, DC 20002
Phone: (202)544-7227 or *Fax:* (202)544-7213

▶ Dwight D. Eisenhower Library

Provides information on: *U.S. Presidents*

The Dwight D. Eisenhower Library contains papers, books, manuscripts, government documents, items in VF drawers, photographs, recordings, and films on the life, presidency, and military career of Dwight D. Eisenhower and his associates.

Information for a fee:

Abilene Reflector Chronicle. $1.00. Local newspaper's memorial edition on the Eisenhowers.

Abilene's Favorite Son. 55 pages. $4.95. Centennial edition, 1890-1990.

At Ease, Stories I Tell to Friends. $7.95. Written by Dwight D. Eisenhower, this paperback recounts memorable moments in the President's early life and career.

Crusade in Europe. 559 pages. $14.95. Written by Dwight D. Eisenhower, this book serves as an account of the North African and Western European campaigns of World War II; a description of modern coalition warfare; and an account of the problems of military command in a democratic society.

Dwight D. Eisenhower, Hero and Politician. 207 pages. $9.95. Biography of Eisenhower's life through his presidency.

Eisenhower Center Booklet. 32 pages. Booklet describes the interior and exterior of the five buildings; includes a special section on Eisenhower at Abilene.

Eisenhower, Turning the World Toward Peace. $22.95. 438 pages. Book offers a behind-the-scenes view of Eisenhower and his policies.

The Eisenhowers. 508 pages. Chronicles the Eisenhower family from their arrival in the United States to 1984.

The Wisdom of Dwight D. Eisenhower. $8.50. Book contains quotations from Eisenhower's speeches and writings, 1939-1969.

To find out more, write or phone:

Dwight D. Eisenhower Library
SE Fourth St.
Abilene, KS 67410
Phone: (913)263-4751

▶ Elections Research Center (ERC)

Provides information on: *Elections*

The purpose of the Center is to collect data and statistics on state and national election returns.

To find out more, write or phone:

Elections Research Center
5508 Greystone St.
Chevy Chase, MD 20815
Phone: (301)654-3540

▶ Expansionist Party of the United States

The party consists of individuals interested in seeing the U.S. expand geographically. The Expansionist Party seeks annexation to the U.S. of any countries that are willing to abide by the Constitution, culminating in world union. It also urges a larger role in society for ethnic and sexual minorities. Special areas of interest include Australia, Canada, Guam, India, Latin America, Oceania, the Philippines, Puerto Rico, South Africa, the West Indies, and Europe.

Information for free:

Publishes periodic flyers.

To find out more, write or phone:
Expansionist Party of the United States
L. Craig Schoonmaker, Chm.
446 W. 46th St.
New York, NY 10036-3584
Phone: (212)265-1081

▶ Federal Election Commission National Clearinghouse on Election Administration

Provides information on: *Elections*

The objective of the Clearinghouse is to improve the efficiency of the federal election process by providing information and assistance to state legislatures, state and local election officials, and others on the conduct of federal elections. The Clearinghouse answers phone and mail questions from the public on the electoral process, and publishes reports on such topics as state campaign finance laws, voter registration systems, bilingual election services, and voting machine technology.

Information for a fee:
Election Directory. 1987/88. $3.50.
Managing Elections. $12.95.
Reducing Voter Wait Time. $14.50.
Voter Information and Education Programs 2: Voter Education Programs in the Schools. $14.50.

To find out more, write or phone:
Federal Election Commission
National Clearinghouse on Election Administration
999 E St., NW
Washington, DC 20463
Phone: (202)219-3670

▶ Gerald R. Ford Library

Provides information on: *U.S. Presidents*

The Gerald R. Ford Library contains papers, books, bound periodical volumes, archival/manuscripts collections, photographs, audiotapes, videotapes, and microfilm on the life and presidency of Gerald R. Ford.

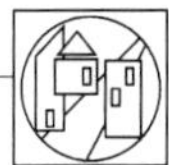

Information for free:

Gerald R. Ford Foundation Newsletter. Quarterly.

Historical Materials in Gerald Ford Library. 90 pages. Guide.

Also offers PRESNET, a database service that performs computerized searches on a variety of topics free of charge.

To find out more, write or phone:

Gerald R. Ford Library
1000 Beal Ave.
Ann Arbor, MI 48109
Phone: (313)668-2218 or *Fax:* (313)668-2341

▶ Freedom of Expression Foundation

Provides information on: *Freedom of Speech*

The purpose of the Foundation is to provide information to Congress and the public concerning freedom of speech as guaranteed by the First Amendment. It maintains the Education and Research Fund, which informs the public of issues surrounding the First Amendment.

Information for free:

Freedom of Expression Foundation Newsletter. Quarterly.

To find out more, write or phone:

Freedom of Expression Foundation
c/o Dr. Craig R. Smith, Pres.
5220 S. Marina Pacifica
Long Beach, CA 90803
Phone: (310)985-4301

▶ Freedom of Information Center (FOI Center)

Provides information on: *Censorship, Freedom of Speech, Freedom of Information*

The FOI Center serves as a clearinghouse for information on freedom of the press and free speech. It maintains files that document actions by government, media, and society affecting the movement and content of information. The FOI Center provides reference and research services (may involve nominal fees) and a referral service. The FOI Center houses files on freedom of the press and freedom of speech topics, including: academic freedom, censorship, fairness doctrine, Federal Freedom of Information Act, First Amendment cases, FOI hotlines, libel, literacy/illiteracy, minorities in the media, new world information order, pornography, shield legislation, state access laws, and student press.

Information for a fee:
Bibliographies. $1 each.

To find out more, write or phone:
Freedom of Information Center
Kathleen Edwards, Mgr.
20 Walter Williams Hall
University of Missouri
Columbia, MO 65211
Phone: (314)882-4856 or *Fax:* (314)882-9157

▶ Ulysses S. Grant Association

Provides information on: *U.S. Presidents*

The Association contains papers and documents of Ulysses S. Grant (1822-85), and distributes information about Grant.

Information for free:
Brochure.

Information for a fee:
Ulysses S. Grant: Essays and Documents. $19.95.
The Personal Memoirs of Julia Dent Grant. $12.95.

To find out more, write or phone:
Ulysses S. Grant Association
Southern Illinois University
Morris Library
Carbondale, IL 62901
Phone: (618)453-2773

▶ Green Committees of Correspondence

Provides information on: *Environmental Protection, Political Parties*

The group consists of green political organizations sharing what the group has adopted as ten key values: ecological wisdom, grass roots democracy, personal and social responsibility, nonviolence, decentralization, community-based economics, postpatriarchal values, respect for diversity, global responsibility, and future focus/ sustainability. It seeks to develop a politically significant Green movement in the United States and build a "grassroots democracy from the bottom up," and works

toward a "fundamental restructuring of our political and economic institutions." It operates Green Committees of Correspondence Clearinghouse, which distributes lists of local and regional Green movement contacts and makes available books and periodicals on the Green movement, ecological awareness, and grass roots politics.

Information for free:

Green Politics. Biweekly tabloid.
Groundworth. 3/year.
Reclaiming Our Future. 3/year. Newspaper.
Regeneration. 3/year. Periodical.

To find out more, write or phone:

Green Committees of Correspondence
PO Box 30208
Kansas City, MO 64112
Phone: (816)931-9366 or *Fax:* (816)531-2271

▶ Hand-gun Control, Inc.

Provides information on: *Firearms, Gun Control*

This public citizens' lobby works for legislative controls and governmental regulations on the manufacture, importation, sale, transfer, and civilian possession of handguns. The group compiles up-to-date information on the handgun issue, including approaches, statistics, legislation, and research.

Information for a fee:

Action Guide. Included in membership fee.
"Guns Don't Die—People Do". Book. Special legislative reports and pamphlets.

To find out more, write or phone:

Hand-gun Control, Inc.
Charles J. Orasin, Pres.
1225 I St. NW, Ste. 1100
Washington, DC 20005
Phone: (202)898-0792 or *Fax:* (202)371-9615

▶ President Benjamin Harrison Foundation

Provides information on: *U.S. Presidents*

The Foundation is made up of individuals and corporate supporters interested in the life and times of Benjamin Harrison (1833-1901). It works to preserve Harrison's memory and maintain artifacts of his life. The group operates Harrison's home in Indianapolis as a museum, offers educational programs, and maintains a library.

Information for free:
Information packet for students.

Information for a fee:
Statesman. Monthly. $15/year. Newsletter.

To find out more, write or phone:
President Benjamin Harrison Foundation
1230 N. Delaware St.
Indianapolis, IN 46202
Phone: (317)631-1898

▶ Rutherford B. Hayes Presidential Center (RBHPC)

Provides information on: *U.S. Presidents*

The Center commemorates the life of Rutherford B. Hayes (1822-93), 19th President of the United States, and serves as a center for the study of the Gilded Age (1865-1916). Tours of the Hayes Victorian residence are offered, and a museum features exhibits on Hayes and on turn-of-the-century life in America. The Center also operates a library containing 71,000 volumes and manuscripts, including Hayes' personal correspondence, scrapbooks, diaries, and photographs.

Information for free:
The Statesman. Quarterly. Newsletter that includes a calendar of events.

Information for a fee:
Hayes Historical Journal: A Journal of the Gilded Age. Quarterly. $20/year.

To find out more, write or phone:
Rutherford B. Hayes Presidential Center
1337 Hayes Ave.
Fremont, OH 43420-2796
Phone: (419)332-2081

▶ Hinckley Institute of Politics

Provides information on: *Politics, Political Parties*

The Institute encourages students to participate in major party activities and promotes careers in politics and public service. Maintains a small library.

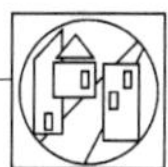

Information for free:
Politics at Hinckley. Annual newsletter.

To find out more, write or phone:
Hinckley Institute of Politics
University of Utah
253 Orson Spencer Hall
Salt Lake City, UT 84112
Phone: (801)581-8501 or *Fax:* (801)581-6277

▶ Hindelang Criminal Justice Research Center

Provides information on: *Prisons, Substance Abuse, Criminal Justice*

The Center studies the impact of imprisonment, correctional environments, uses and interpretation of crime statistics, parole and sentencing policy, and changes in the criminal justice system. Activities also include studies on bail decision-making, development of a casebook of materials on whistle-blowing, and analysis of the criminal careers of women in an experimental correctional treatment project in the 1960's.

Information for a fee:
Family Processes and Initiation of Delinquency and Drug Use: The Impact of Parent and Adolescent Perceptions. 1990. Working paper. $3.
Patterns of Adolescent Firearms Ownership and Use. 1991. Working paper. $2.50.
Patterns of Male and Female Gang Membership. 1992. Working paper. $2.50.
Peer Influence and Initiation to Drug Use. 1988. Working paper. $2.

To find out more, write or phone:
Hindelang Criminal Justice Research Center
State University of New York at Albany
135 Western Ave.
Albany, NY 12222
Phone: (518)442-5600

▶ Honest Ballot Association

Provides information on: *Elections*

The Association is a nonpartisan union of citizens organized to ensure clean elections, and to prevent honest votes from being offset by trickery and fraud. It investigates and prevents colonization of voters, fraudulent registrations, repetitious voting, intimidation of voters, and unsuitable polling places. The group conducts studies of the adequacy of existing election laws, instructs qualified persons to serve as watchers at polling places, and sponsors research, polling, and arbitration.

Information for free:
The Association brochure.

To find out more, write or phone:
Honest Ballot Association
Murray Schwartz, Pres.
North Shore Towers, Bldg. 3 Arcade
272-30 Grand Central Pkwy.
Floral Park, NY 11005
Phone: (516)466-4100

▶ Herbert Hoover Presidential Library

Provides information on: *U.S. Presidents*

The Library encourages original scholarship on the private and public career of Herbert Hoover (1874-1964), and national public policy during the Hoover period.

Information for a fee:
Newsletters, Hoover's writings, and research materials.

To find out more, write or phone:
Herbert Hoover Presidential Library
PO Box 696
West Branch, IA 52358
Phone: (319)643-5327

▶ Human Rights Watch

Provides information on: *Freedom of Speech, Human Rights*

Human Rights Watch is an international organization that monitors the human rights practices of about 60 governments around the world. This involves investigating cases of murder, disappearance, kidnapping, torture, imprisonment, exile, censorship, and other forms of punishment for nonviolent expression. The group puts pressure on governments primarily by publicizing human rights violations. Activities are carried out through five regional organizations including Africa Watch, Americas Watch, Asia Watch, Helsinki Watch, Middle East Watch, and the Fund for Free Expression.

Information for free:
Questions and Answers. Brochure. Provides description of the organization, areas of interest, and accomplishments.

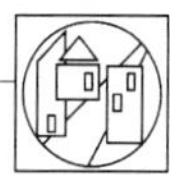

Summary of Membership Benefits. Brochure. Provides description of the organization, and membership costs.

A publications catalog and update list are also available.

Information for a fee:

Behind Closed Doors. Torture and Detention in Egypt. 1992. 144 pages. $10.

Brutality Unchecked. Human Rights Abuses Along the U.S. Border with Mexico. 1992. 88 pages. $7.

Defending the Earth. Abuses of Human Rights and the Environment. 1992. 128 pages. $10.

Double Jeopardy. Police Abuse of Women in Pakistan. 1992. 100 pages. $10.

Human Rights in Iraq. 1990. 170 pages. $19.95.

Human Rights in Northern Ireland. 1991. 200 pages. $15.

Human Rights Watch. Newsletter. Available with $20 introductory membership.

Political Murder and Reform in Colombia. The Violence Continues. 1992. 98 pages. $7.

Restricted Subjects. Freedom of Expression in the United Kingdom. 1991. 80 pages. $7.

Each division of Human Rights Watch offers numerous publications, many for under $5. Orders under $30 require a shipping charge.

To find out more, write or phone:

Human Rights Watch
485 5th Ave.
New York, NY 10017-6104
Phone: (212)972-8400 or *Fax:* (212)972-0905

▶ Information Systems Security Association

Provides information on: *Computer Crime*

The Association is made up of computer security and electronic data processing personnel, planners, consultants, and others in the banking, retail, insurance, aerospace, and publishing industries. The Association's purpose is to increase knowledge about information security, and sponsor educational programs, research, and discussion.

Information for a fee:

Access. Quarterly magazine. $4/issue; $16/year.

To find out more, write or phone:

Information Systems Security Association
Richard V. Rueb, Exec. Dir.
PO Box 9457
Newport Beach, CA 92658
Phone: (312)644-6610

▶ Institute of Bill of Rights Law

Provides information on: *Freedom of Speech*

The Institute of Bill of Rights Law focuses their studies on constitutional liberties, emphasizing the First Amendment and mass media issues.

Information for a fee:
Bill of Rights Journal. 2/year. $8/issue.
William and Mary Law Review. Quarterly. $7/issue.

To find out more, write or phone:
Institute of Bill of Rights Law
College of William and Mary
Marshall-Wythe School of Law
Williamsburg, VA 23185
Phone: (804)221-3808 or *Fax:* (804)221-3261

▶ Institute of Criminal Justice

Provides information on: *Substance Abuse, Criminal Justice, Alcoholism*

The Institute studies social drug and alcohol abuse, including legal issues in probation and parole, corrections data analysis systems, electronic monitoring, serial murder, and management by objective systems for correctional departments. It coordinates technical assistance requests from local and state criminal justice agencies throughout the nation. The Institute maintains a library, and will research and answer questions.

To find out more, write or phone:
Institute of Criminal Justice
Sam Houston State University
College of Criminal Justice
Huntsville, TX 77341
Phone: (409)294-1647 or *Fax:* (409)294-1653

▶ Institute of Governmental Studies

Provides information on: *Government, Politics*

The Institute studies such topics as American national, state, and local government and politics, public policy, public organization and administration, urban-metropolitan problems, federalism and intergovernmental relations.

Information for free:
IGS Press Books. Brochure listing publications and prices.

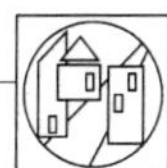

Information for a fee:

Across the Border: Rural Development in Mexico and Recent Migration to the United States. 1981. 198 pages. $4.50.

In the Interest of Earthquake Safety. 1971. 22 pages. $2.

North American and Comparative Federalism: Essays for the 1990s. 1992. 102 pages. $11.95.

Oil Pollution and the Public Interest: A Study of the Santa Barbara Oil Spill. 1972. 157 pages. $4.50.

Prison Population and Criminal Justice Policy in California. 1992. 72 pages. $7.95.

Race, Poverty and the Cities: Hyperinnovation in Complex Policy Systems. 1988. 73 pages. $6.95.

Scholarships for Children. 1992. 87 pages. $7.95.

Also available is a working paper list, which is published to provide quick analysis of reports and papers. $3.50 each.

To find out more, write or phone:

Institute of Governmental Studies
University of California
102 Moses Hall
Berkeley, CA 94720
Phone: (510)642-1474

▶ Institute of Strategic Studies on Terrorism

Provides information on: *Terrorism*

The Institutes's purpose is to collect and study all aspects of terrorism and to provide the most current information and expert training regarding counter-terrorism and executive protection tactics. The group conducts three-day seminars on threat analysis, risk assessment, terrorism, anti-terrorism, and counter-terrorism. The Institute compiles statistics and maintains a library of books, periodicals, congressional records, news articles, and official reports.

To find out more, write or phone:

Institute of Strategic Studies on Terrorism
Gene Gerringer, Dir.
PO Box 3372
Early, TX 76803
Phone: (915)643-1433

▶ International Association of Correctional Officers (IACO)

Provides information on: *Prisons*

The Association is comprised of correctional facility officers, sheriffs, and other employees in the corrections field. The group promotes the development of innovative services, evaluation, and high standards of training in an effort to increase the effectiveness of correctional facilities.

Information for a fee:
Keepers Voice Magazine. Quarterly. $25 included in membership fee.

To find out more, write or phone:

International Association of Correctional Officers
Tonya Mathews, Assoc. Dir.
1333 S. Wabash
PO Box 53
Chicago, IL 60605
Phone: (312)996-9267

▶ International Association of Justice Volunteerism (IAJV)

Provides information on: *Criminal Justice, Juvenile Justice, Voluntarism*

IAJV is a nonprofit association committed to the improvement of juvenile and criminal justice systems through citizen participation. It acts as a clearinghouse for information on justice volunteers through its newsletter, other publications, and library services.

Information for a fee:

The ABCs of Volunteer Recruitment, Selection and Training. 50 cents. Paper summarizing three volunteer management processes.

Fund Raising. $2.00. General guide to fund raising, including information proposals, presentations, and funding sources.

Principles of a Volunteer Program. 50 cents. Overview developed by ACTION covering the organizational issues and program concepts of a volunteer program.

Some Possible Sources of Volunteers. 50 cents. One page reference identifying 108 potential sources of volunteers.

Today's Volunteers: A Guide to Involvement. $1.00. Paper exploring self-motivation for volunteer involvement and agency variables needed to attract volunteers.

Volunteer Management: The Art of Recruiting Unpaid Staff. $2.00. Paper outlining recruitment of special groups such as the poor, rural residents, and minorities.

Volunteerism: A Workbook on How to Build or Improve a Volunteer Program. 60 pages. $6.95. Workbook covering development of volunteer programs.

Volunteers in Criminal Justice: A Historical Perspective of the Volunteer Movement. $4.00. Paper serving as a historical overview for volunteers and paid staff. Traces English and American antecedents to the movement.

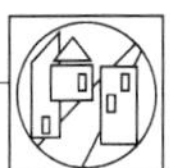

Volunteers in Justice: Observation on a Movement. 30 pages. $2.50. Booklet reviewing the effectiveness of using volunteers in juvenile justice, crime prevention, victim assistance, courts, prisons, and justice policies.

To find out more, write or phone:

International Association of Justice Volunteerism
William F. Winter, Exec.Dir.
University of Wisconsin-Milwaukee
Criminal Justice Institute
Box 786
Milwaukee, WI 53201
Phone: (414)229-6092 or *Fax:* (414)229-5311

▶ Inter-University Consortium for Political and Social Research (ICPSR)

Provides information on: *Politics, Criminal Justice*

ICPSR receives, processes, maintains, and distributes social, economic, and political data on national and international levels, including survey data, historical, demographic, and census data, international relations and cross national data, aging and aging process data, crime, deviance, and criminal justice data, and leisure activities data. ICPSR acts as a central information service for machine-readable social science data received from other data centers or from individual researchers.

Information for free:

ICPSR Annual Report. 1990-91.

Where to Turn for the Data You Need. Brochure giving general information about ICPSR, their data collections, and computing assistance and services.

Information for a fee:

ICPSR Bulletin. 4/year. $15/year. Provides information on recently released or updated ICPSR data collections, and U of M activities.

ICPSR Guide to Resources and Services, 1991-1992. 613 pages. $20.

To find out more, write or phone:

Inter-University Consortium for Political and Social Research
University of Michigan
Box 1248
Ann Arbor, MI 48106
Phone: (313)764-2570 or *Fax:* (313)764-8041

▶ Lyndon B. Johnson Library and Museum

Provides information on: *U.S. Presidents*

The Library contains information by and about Lyndon B. Johnson, his career, administration, and family. It includes a special collection of oral history interviews, and individual personal papers.

Information for free:

Historical Materials in the Lyndon Baines Johnson Library. A catalog of manuscripts, publications, and audiovisual materials available for research in the library.

To find out more, write or phone:

Lyndon B. Johnson Library and Museum
2313 Red River St.
Austin, TX 78705
Phone: (512)482-5137

▶ Juvenile Justice Clearinghouse

Provides information on: *Sexual Abuse, Juvenile Justice, Runaways, Child Abuse, Insanity Defense, Prisons, Missing Children*

The Clearinghouse gathers and exchanges information on juvenile justice and youth issues.

Information for free:

America's Missing and Exploited Children: Their Safety and Their Future.
Child Sexual Abuse Victims and Their Treatment.
Missing, Abducted, Runaway, and Throwaway Children in America: Executive Summary.
Missing Children: Found Facts.
Missing and Exploited Children: The Challenge Continues.
OJJDP Juvenile Justice Bulletin: National Youth Gang Suppression and Intervention Program.
OJJDP Update on Statistics: Juvenile Court Drug and Alcohol Cases: 1985-1988.
Sexual Exploitation of Missing Children: A Research Review.

Information for a fee:

Many bibliographies are offered for a fee of $17.50, including such topics as AIDS, adult female offenders, crowding in prisons and jails, prison violence, insanity defense, drug testing, juvenile gangs, sexual exploitation of children, community policing, terrorism, crime and the elderly, rape and sexual assault, and more.

To find out more, write or phone:

Juvenile Justice Clearinghouse
National Victims Resource Center
Office of Juvenile Justice and Delinquency Prevention
1600 Research Blvd.
Mailstop K-3
Rockville, MD 20850
Toll-free: 1-800-638-8736 or *Phone:* (301)251-5535 or *Fax:* (301)251-5747

▶ John F. Kennedy Library

Provides information on: *U.S. Presidents*

The library covers the subjects of John F. Kennedy, his administration, mid-20th century politics, and government.

Information for free:

Historical Materials in the John Fitzgerald Kennedy Library. 208 pages. A catalog of library holdings, research facilities, and application procedures.

John F. Kennedy: A Reading List. 39 pages. A booklet containing information on books written by Kennedy, books relating to his life, and studies on the Kennedy administration.

Information for a fee:

Encyclopedia of Presidents: John F. Kennedy. $6.95. A book for children ages 11-13.

John F. Kennedy, A Discovery Book. $2.95.

John F. Kennedy's Inaugural Address. $3.50.

The Kennedy Library. $9.95.

Kennedy, Young People's President. $14.95.

Let the Word Go Forth. $15. A treasury of JFK speeches, statements, and writings.

A Memoir, Robert F. Kennedy. $7.95.

Robert F. Kennedy. $9.95. A biography of RFK for young readers.

Robert F. Kennedy, In His Own Words. $16. RFK's comments on the Kennedy years taken from his oral history at the Kennedy library.

Timeline of Kennedy Years from the Library Museum. $3.

The Library also offers crafts, photos, posters, clothing, jewelry, and mugs.

To find out more, write or phone:

John F. Kennedy Library
Columbia Pt.
Boston, MA 02125
Phone: (617)929-4500

▶ Martin Luther King, Jr. Center for Nonviolent Social Change, Inc.

Provides information on: *Civil Rights and Liberties, African Americans, Poverty*

The Center seeks to build a permanent and living memorial to Dr. Martin Luther King Jr. (1929-68), American clergyman, civil rights leader, and 1964 Nobel Prize winner. Through study, education, training, research, and constructive action, the group is committed to seeking nonviolent solutions to world problems like poverty, racism, and violence.

Information for free:
Publishes a quarterly newsletter and a variety of brochures.

To find out more, write or phone:
Martin Luther King, Jr. Center for Nonviolent Social Change, Inc.
Coretta Scott King, Pres.
449 Auburn Ave., NE
Atlanta, GA 30312
Phone: (404)524-1956 or *Fax:* (404)522-6932

▶ La Raza Unida Party (LRUP)

Provides information on: *Political Parties*

The Party consists of individuals dedicated to achieving self-determination and greater government representation for Latinos through electoral processes. The group concentrates on political issues that involve Chicanos and Mexicans and the working classes. A library of slides, photos, and publications is maintained, and research programs are conducted.

Information for free:
El Sembrador. 4-6/year. Newspaper.
Also publishes free pamphlets, statistics, and research results.

Information for a fee:
La Semilla. 2/year. $3 each. Newspaper.

To find out more, write or phone:
La Raza Unida Party
483 5th St.
San Fernando, CA 91340
Phone: (818)365-6534

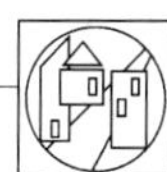

▶ League of Women Voters of the United States

Provides information on: *Politics, Social Welfare, Elections*

The League is a voluntary organization of men and women, 18 years old or older, that promotes political responsibility through informed and active participation of citizens in government. Members select and study public policy issues at local, state, and national levels and take political action on these issues. Leagues at all levels distribute information on candidates and issues and campaign to encourage registration and voting. National concerns include government, international relations, natural resources, and social policy.

Information for a fee:

How to Watch a Debate. 1986. $.75. Information targeted to high school students including what to watch and listen for in government debates.

In the Public Interest. 1989. 199 pages. $24.95. Covers the League of Women Voters founding and its first 50 years.

League Action Service (LAS): Report From the Hill and Action Alerts. $10. LAS keeps citizens informed through the periodic newsletter Report From the Hill and timed Action Alerts to let subscribers know when to act.

Meeting Basic Human Needs: A Crisis of Responsibility. 1987. 8 pages. $1.25. Explains the worsening crisis of Americans' need for food, housing, and health care.

Meeting the Employment Needs of Women: A Path Out of Poverty? 1984. 6 pages. $.85. A look at obstacles many women face in the workplace such as sex discrimination, day-care needs, education, and federal job-training programs.

The National Voter. $2.50/single issue, $12/year. Magazine that covers national issues and accounts of grassroots lobbying.

Recycling is More Than Collections: Questions and Concerns From the Ground Up. 1992. 36 pages. $5.95. Reviews challenges to expanding recycling markets and reports findings of a survey of solid waste officials and newspaper publishers.

Safety on Tap: A Citizen's Drinking Water Guide. 1987. 68 pages. $7.95. Examines issues of drinking water quality.

Thinking Globally.Acting Locally: A Citizen's Guide to Community Education on Global Issues. 1988. $5. Step-by-step handbook for bringing global issues home.

The Women's Vote: Beyond the Nineteenth Amendment. 1983. 24 pages. $1.75. Describes the voter registration and "get-out-the-vote" efforts of 1984, focusing on voting rates, and minorities and women.

Also publishes information on state and local government, the budget, nuclear waste, the Equal Rights Amendment, and how to be politically effective.

To find out more, write or phone:

League of Women Voters of the United States
1730 M St., NW
Washington, DC 20036
Phone: (202)429-1965 or *Fax:* (202)429-0854

▶ Libertarian Party

Provides information on: *Political Parties*

The Libertarian Party believes that "each individual has the absolute right to exercise sole dominion over his or her own life." It opposes censorship, the draft, victimless crime laws, and government regulation on personal matters; supports property rights, free trade, and eventual elimination of taxation.

Information for a fee:

Liberty Today. Updated 2/year. $1.
Libertarianism in One Lesson. 1991. $8.
LP News. Monthly. $1.

To find out more, write or phone:

Libertarian Party
1528 Pennsylvania Ave., SE
Washington, DC 20003
Toll-free: 1-800-682-1776 or *Phone:* (202)543-1988 or *Fax:* (202)546-6094

▶ Abraham Lincoln Association (ALA)

Provides information on: *U.S. Presidents*

The Association is made up of individuals and organizations interested in Abraham Lincoln (1809-65). It seeks to further the collection, preservation, and distribution of information on the life of Lincoln.

Information for a fee:

Abraham Lincoln Association Newsletter. Quarterly. Price included in $25 membership fee.

To find out more, write or phone:

Abraham Lincoln Association
Old State Capitol
Springfield, IL 62701
Phone: (217)782-4836

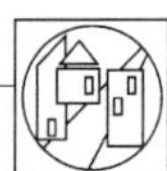

▶ Martin Institute for Peace Studies and Conflict Resolution

Provides information on: *Terrorism*

The Institute is interested in the research of economic, social, psychological, political, biological, and religious causes of terrorism, violence, and war. It also studies institutional and social conditions resulting in peace, and methods for resolving conflicts on the individual, group, and international level.

Information for free:
Newsletter. 2/year.

Information for a fee:
Research project results are available for under $10.

To find out more, write or phone:

Martin Institute for Peace Studies and Conflict Resolution
University of Idaho
Moscow, ID 83843
Phone: (208)885-6527 or *Fax:* (208)885-5757

▶ Meiklejohn Civil Liberties Institute

Provides information on: *Civil Rights and Liberties, Human Rights*

The Institute collects and documents material for attorneys and others on constitutional, international, U.N. Charter, First Amendment, and peace law. MCLI provides materials and assistance to help people in the exercise of their constitutional rights.

Information for free:
MCLI publications catalog and order form.

Information for a fee:
Enforcing the Hidden U.S. Equal Rights Law for Women. 1990. 90 pages. $10.
Human Rights Organizations and Periodicals Directory. 1990. $24. Lists 700 U.S. organizations, publications, and agencies.
MCLI Newsletter. 2/year. $1.
Missile Envy: The Arms Race and Nuclear War. 1986. $4.
New U.S. Law Making Genocide a Federal Crime. $2.
Peace Law Basics. 1991. $15. 130 pages. Excerpts from the Peace Law Almanac.
Peace Law Packet: Right to Education. $20. Includes briefs, motions, testimony, etc.
Peace Net Bulletins. Monthly. $1. Publishes such topics as the Rodney King/Police Acquittal cases, U.S. Troops to Saudi Arabia, and the Illegality of U.S. Invasion of Panama.
Prelude to War with Iraq: A Chronology of Crisis Mismanagement. 1991. $12.

To find out more, write or phone:

Meiklejohn Civil Liberties Institute
PO Box 673
Berkeley, CA 94701
Phone: (510)848-0599 or *Fax:* (510)848-6008

▶ White Burkett Miller Center of Public Affairs

Provides information on: *Government, U.S. Presidents, Politics*

Center topics are politics, government, and public affairs. It focuses on the American presidency, including its nature, purposes, and problems. The Center maintains a public library and will answer phone inquiries.

Information for free:
Imprimatur. 2-4/year. Papers and criticisms by scholars and observers.
Miller Center Report. Quarterly newsletter.

To find out more, write or phone:

White Burkett Miller Center of Public Affairs
University of Virginia
Box 5106
Charlottesville, VA 22905
Phone: (804)924-7236 or *Fax:* (804)982-2739

▶ MIS Clearinghouse/International City Management Association

Provides information on: *Government*

The Clearinghouse is an independent nonprofit organization that provides reports and videos on local government management topics. Selected topics include: AIDS policies, art in public places, computer mapping and design, day care services, disaster preparedness, employee public relations, fiscal fitness, identification and prevention of sexual harassment in the workplace, juvenile first offenders, loss prevention, microcomputer usage, modern law enforcement, neighborhood property maintenance, police patrol staffing, recycling, sewer access rights, street tree management, volunteer services, water pollution control, community development, and tourism promotion.

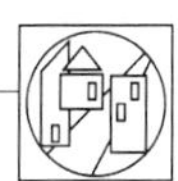

Information for free:

CMA Management Catalog. 1992. 44 pages. Lists hundreds of reports, books, videos, and training packages and courses on the broad topic of local government, the officials, concerns, and issues facing them.

Information for a fee:

Day Care Services. 26 pages. $13. A report covering day care needs, such as those of employers, and families.

Drug Testing, Sexual Harassment, Smoking: Employee Rights Issues. 1988. 21 pages. $12.95. Report covering local and federal governments' role in upholding employee rights in these three areas.

Fire Protection: A Review of Operations, Organization, and Effectiveness. 1990. 84 pages. $17. A review of the effectiveness and organization of a volunteer fire company.

Local Initiatives for Child Care. 1989. 16 pages. $12.95. Report presenting case studies of four local government initiatives in child care.

Managing Resort Communities. 1985 $12.95. Offers information on problems facing resort communities, such as financial improvements and managing rapid growth.*Police and Fire Fitness Testing*. 1988. 16 pages. $12.95. Explains how to set up a physical fitness program for public safety employees.

State, Local, and Council Relations: Managers' Perspectives. 1992. $16.50. Report covering such topics as council effectiveness, local authority, state mandates, and state financial assistance.

Strategies for Reducing Homelessness. 1990. $12.95. Describes a comprehensive approach to homelessness, including day shelter, prevention, and transitional programs.

To find out more, write or phone:

MIS Clearinghouse/International City Management Association
777 N. Capitol St., NE, Ste. 500
Washington, DC 20002-4201
Phone: (202)962-3596 or *Fax:* (202)962-3500

▶ Mississippi Alcohol Safety Education Program (MASEP)

Provides information on: *Drunk Driving*

The MASEP studies substance abuse and traffic safety, including the effects of ethyl alcohol in the body, blood alcohol concentration, the Implied Consent Law, the effect of alcohol and other drugs on driving skills, the nature of problem drinking, and alcoholism treatment centers. The program maintains data files, and publishes research results in its own publications and scholarly journals.

Information for free:

Classifying the DUI Offender: A Cluster Analysis of Arrest Histories. 1985.

A Comparison of DWI Repeaters and Non-Repeaters Who Attended a Level I Rehabilitation Program. 1981.

Drinking Reasons, Drinking Locations, and Automobile Accident Involvement Among Collegians. 1989.

The Effect of Alcohol Consumption on Risk-Taking While Driving. 1987.

Life Problems Experienced from Drinking: Factors Associated with Level of Problem Drinking Among Youthful DWI Offenders. 1985.

A publication list is also available listing additional articles, reports and working papers. 11 pages.

To find out more, write or phone:

Mississippi Alcohol Safety Education Program
Social Science Research Center
Mississippi State University
100 Research Blvd.
PO Box 5287
Mississippi State, MS 39762
Phone: (601)325-7127

▶ James Monroe Museum and Library

Provides information on: *U.S. Presidents*

The organization has a collection of books, periodicals, artwork, and journals covering James Monroe, the Monroe Doctrine, 18th-20th century politics, and presidents.

Information for a fee:

Discover James Monroe. $3.95.

Encyclopedia of Presidents: James Monroe. $12.

Images of a President: Portraits of James Monroe. $4.95.

James Monroe and the Constitution. $3.

James Monroe: Quest for National Identity. $18.95. A biography of Monroe.

James Monroe: Young Patriot. $2.50.

Monroe Family Recipes. $3.

Monroe On. $3.

Monroe, the People, the Sovereigns. $16.95.

Monroe U.S.A. $6.

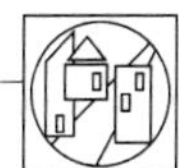

To find out more, write or phone:
James Monroe Museum and Library
908 Charles St.
Fredericksburg, VA 22401
Phone: (703)899-4559

▶ Mothers Against Drunk Driving (MADD)

Provides information on: *Drunk Driving, Victims*

Mothers Against Drunk Driving works to stop drunk driving and support victims of drunk driving crashes. MADD supports law enforcement programs and state and federal legislation for reform of laws on drunk driving. It also provides public education programs for encouraging more strict laws requiring mandatory minimum punishment. MADD provides victim assistance by supplying information for victims and their families on bereavement groups, the judicial system, and other assistance groups. It also operates a Victim Outreach Program, which aids victims by taking them through the court process step by step.

Information for free:

MADD Publications Catalog. 1992. Catalog of publications, cassette tapes, bumper stickers, key chains, posters, and other promotional items.

Information for a fee:

About Drinking and Driving. $.55. Pamphlet
Alcohol and Health. $.55. Pamphlet.
Children of Alcoholics. $.55. Pamphlet.
Choosing Not to Drink. $.55. Pamphlet.
No Time for Goodbyes. 178 pages. $7. Helps those coping with sudden and violent death.
Preventing Teenage Alcohol Abuse. $.55. Pamphlet.
Student Library. Annual newsletter. Addresses issues of interest to students, such as myths about alcohol, fake IDs, and law enforcement.
Victim Information Pamphlet. $.55. Pamphlet.
Why You Should Say "No!" to Alcohol/Other Drugs and Driving. $.55. Pamphlet.

To find out more, write or phone:
Mothers Against Drunk Driving
511 E. John Carpenter Fwy., No. 700
Irving, TX 75062
Toll-free: 1-800-GET-MADD or *Phone:* (214)744-6233 or *Fax:* (214)869-2206

▶ National Alliance Against Racist and Political Repression (NAARPR)

Provides information on: *Civil Rights and Liberties*

The Alliance is a coalition of political, labor, church, civic, student, and community organizations and individuals dedicated to protecting people's right to organize. It seeks to mobilize millions of people to unite in word and action against many forms of repression of human rights in the U.S. This includes persecution and jailing of political activists; attempts to suppress prisoners' rights movements and use of behavior control against prisoners and the poor; assaults on labor's right to organize, strike, and act effectively; police crimes against the people, especially non-whites; legislation and court decisions repressing basic rights; and the death penalty.

Information for free:
The Organizer. Quarterly. Newsletter.
Also publishes pamphlets.

To find out more, write or phone:
National Alliance Against Racist and Political Repression
11 John St., Rm. 702
New York, NY 10038
Phone: (212)406-3330 or *Fax:* (212)406-3542

▶ National Association of Juvenile Correctional Agencies (NAJCA)

Provides information on: *Juvenile Justice*

The National Association of Juvenile Correctional Agencies is comprised of institutions and agencies involved with the study, care, training, and treatment of children in the juvenile justice system. Also included are personnel of residential centers for delinquent children. Activities of the Association include providing ideas on the function and goals of the juvenile correctional field, promoting research and progressive legislation, encouraging recruitment of qualified personnel, and examining the issues of training and working conditions.

Information for a fee:
NAJCA News. Quarterly newsletter. $25. Price includes membership dues.
Proceedings. Annual. Included in $25 membership price. Includes minutes of annual meeting and position papers.

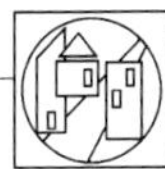

To find out more, write or phone:

National Association of Juvenile Correctional Agencies
55 Albin Rd.
Bow, NH 03304-3703
Phone: (603)271-5945

▶ National Center for Computer Crime Data (NCCCD)

Provides information on: *Computer Crime*

The Institute helps to prevent, investigate, and prosecute computer crime by distributing documents and other data to those in need of this information. NCCCD sponsors speakers, seminars, and publications for the education of both the professional communities and the public, conducts research, compiles statistics, and maintains a library consisting of the case histories of computer crimes, indexes to experts in the field, and other publications.

Information for a fee:

Computer/Law Journal. Quarterly. $20/single issue.
The Defense of a Computer Crime Case. 197 pages. $25. Covers the current law of computer crime.
Also offers articles from the publication Introduction to Computer Crime.
Computer Crime, Career of the Future? $2.
Computer Crime Update. $4.
Cracking Down on Computer Crime. $3.
Lobbying for Computer Legislation. $3.
A Security Manager's Guide to Hacking. $4.

To find out more, write or phone:

National Center for Computer Crime Data
1222 17th Ave., Ste. B
Santa Cruz, CA 95062
Phone: (408)475-4457 or *Fax:* (408)475-5336

▶ National Center on Institutions and Alternatives

Provides information on: *Prisons, Juvenile Justice*

The Center serves as a clearinghouse on decarceration and aids in developing and promoting strategies to reduce the number of people involuntarily institutionalized. Its goals include finding alternatives to mental hospitals, developing and promoting alternatives to prison programs, eliminating unnecessary lockup in "massive, impersonal" prisons and juvenile training schools. The group has completed statistics on the regional differences in the number of imprisoned young people and a national study of jail suicides.

Information for free:
Newsletter. Quarterly.

Information for a fee:
Darkness Closes In: National Study of Jail Suicides. 65 pages. $15.

To find out more, write or phone:
National Center on Institutions and Alternatives
635 Slaters Ln., Ste. G-100
Alexandria, VA 22314
Phone: (703)684-0373

▶ National Center for Juvenile Justice (NCJJ)

Provides information on: *Juvenile Justice*

The Center is dedicated to quality research in the juvenile justice field, and the improvement of how youth are handled by the system. The Center collects juvenile court statistics, hosts visiting scholars, provides technical assistance to juvenile courts, assesses juvenile justice services, and designs programs and facilities.

Information for free:
National Center for Juvenile Justice Annual Report.
National Center for Juvenile Justice Publications List.

Information for a fee:
Guide to the Data Sets in the National Juvenile Court Data Archive. 1989. Catalog that describes case-level data files submitted to the Archive by states and jurisdictions across the country. It also presents a brief history of the Archive and the procedures for accessing the data files.
Kindex Bibliographies. $25. Custom-tailored bibliographic searches available from Kindex, a database containing information on materials listed in the publication Kindex: An Index to Legal Periodical Literature Concerning Children.
Organization and Administration of Juvenile Services: Probation, Aftercase, and State Delinquent Institutions. 1991. $12.
Parental Responsibility for Delinquent Acts of Children: Selected Legislative Provisions. 1990. $15. Covers legislation that indicates whether parents may be held responsible for the delinquent acts of their children.
Rights of Victims of Juvenile Crimes. 1990. $15.
Today's Delinquent. Annual publications of a review of an issue in the field of juvenile delinquency. Titles, available for $12 each, include:

Drugs. 1984.
Family. 1985.
Parents. 1986.
Schools. 1987.
The Mind and Matter of Delinquency. 1988.

To find out more, write or phone:
National Center for Juvenile Justice
701 Forbes Ave.
Pittsburgh, PA 15219
Phone: (412)227-6950 or *Fax:* (412)227-6955

▶ National Committee for an Effective Congress

Provides information on: *Politics, Elections*

The organization is an independent political action committee that raises funds from private citizens and gives them to its endorsed candidates for the U.S. Senate and House of Representatives. It provides both support and professional technical campaign assistance to progressive Democrats and Republicans who are genuinely committed to preserving and advancing the liberties and rights of all Americans. Recent research and educational programs of the Committee include election finance reform, congressional procedures, and military vs. domestic items in national budget.

Information for free:
Profile of the Candidates. Booklet.

Information for a fee:
Election Update. 10/year. Newsletter. Available for a donation.

To find out more, write or phone:
National Committee for an Effective Congress
10 E. 39th St., Ste. 601
New York, NY 10016
Phone: (212)686-4905 or *Fax:* (212)686-4908

▶ National Conference of Black Mayors

Provides information on: *Mayors*

The National Conference of Black Mayors is dedicated to helping its membership to improve the delivery of city services, and to create a foundation for new growth, stable populations, and a decrease in outward migration.

Information for free:
Mayors Roster. Annual.
Municipal Watch. Quarterly.

To find out more, write or phone:

National Conference of Black Mayors
1430 W. Peachtree St. NW, Ste. 700
Atlanta, GA 30309
Phone: (404)892-0127 or *Fax:* (404)876-4597

▶ National Crime Prevention Council (NCPC)

Provides information on: *Crime Prevention*

The National Crime Prevention Council seeks to educate the public on how to prevent crime and build safer, more caring communities. The Council accomplishes this task through public service advertising, providing training and technical assistance to crime prevention community and youth groups, and developing crime prevention/child protection curricula. The Council also coordinates the activities of the Crime Prevention Coalition, an alliance of over 100 citizens groups, government agencies, labor and law enforcement bodies, and state and national crime prevention and social service organizations.

Information for free:

Catalyst Newsletter. 10 issues per year. Reports on what's happening in crime prevention and offers in-depth profiles on innovative programs.

NCPC Introductory Packet. Includes a variety of NCPC brochures and pamphlets.

Your Inside Look at Crime Prevention. Full-color booklet that covers issues ranging from home security and assault prevention to child protection and community action against drug abuse.

Information for a fee:

Changing Perspectives: Youth As Resources. 85 pages. $16.95. A project shifts the perspective to young people, viewing youth as resources in helping solve community problems.

Charting Success: A Workbook for Developing Crime Prevention and Other Community Service Projects. 52 pages. $4.95. Assists in developing projects to reduce crime and the fear of crime, assist victims, and strengthen communities.

Crime and Crime Prevention Statistics-1991 Edition. $8.95. Survey of facts about crime and its prevention, and the criminal justice system.

Given the Opportunity: How Three Communities Engaged Teens as Resources in Drug Abuse Prevention. 56 pages. $6.95. Describes community supports, projects undertaken, results achieved, and lessons learned when teens coordinate drug prevention.

Making a Difference: Young People in Community Crime Prevention. 132 pages. $14.95. Offers tips on starting and running successful programs.

Violence, Youth, and a Way Out. $5.95. Gives ideas for reducing delinquency.

Young People in Crime Prevention Programs. $4.95. Examples of programs where teens have become part of the solution and both community and teens benefit.

To find out more, write or phone:

National Crime Prevention Council
1700 K St., NW, 2nd Fl.
Washington, DC 20006
Phone: (202)466-6272 or *Fax:* (202)296-1356

▶ National Crime Prevention Institute

Provides information on: *Crime Prevention*

The Institute trains police officers, criminal justice planners, security personnel in the private sector, and community representatives in crime prevention for the establishment of crime prevention programs. Provides information and technical assistance to these groups and conducts seminars and schools in the areas of crime prevention theory, practice and management, and security for private industry.

Information for a fee:

Loss Prevention Through Crime Analysis. 1989. 104 pages. $18.95. Explains the methodology of crime analysis and shows how it enhances policy decisions.

The Use of Locks in Physical Crime Prevention. 1987. 104 pages. $17.95. A reference manual examining different types of locks and how easily they can be broken.

To find out more, write or phone:

National Crime Prevention Institute
University of Louisville, Shelby Campus
School of Justice Admin.
Louisville, KY 40292
Phone: (502)588-6987 or *Fax:* (502)588-6990

▶ National Criminal Justice Association (NCJA)

Provides information on: *Criminal Justice, Substance Abuse, Narcotics Control*

The Association promotes innovation in the criminal justice system through a coordinated efforts by law enforcement, the courts, corrections, and juvenile justice. NCJA work has focused on issues surrounding criminal justice-related concerns, such as prison crowding and drug laws enforcement. It also works with the states and federal government on such public safety issues as community-based fire prevention.

Information for a fee:

Directory of State-Identified Intervention/Treatment Programs for Drug-Dependent Offenders. $2.

Executive Summary of States' Policies and Practices in Developing and Providing Treatment for Drug-Dependent Offenders. $2.

A Guide to State Controlled Substances Acts. 1991. $25.

A Roundtable Discussion on the Use of the Military in the Control of Illegal Drugs. 1984. $14.

States Laws and Procedures Affecting Drug Trafficking Control: A National Overview. 1985. $20.

Treatment Options for Drug-Dependent Offenders: A Review of the Literature for State and Local Decision Makers. $2.

To find out more, write or phone:

National Criminal Justice Association
444 N. Capitol St. NW, Ste. 608
Washington, DC 20001
Phone: (202)347-4900 or *Fax:* (202)347-2862

▶ National Criminal Justice Reference Service (NCJRS)

Provides information on: *Victims, Narcotics Control, Criminal Justice, Juvenile Justice*

NCJRS is an international information clearinghouse of criminal justice information. Reference specialists are available Monday through Friday 8:30 a.m. to 7:00 p.m. EST, to search the NCJRS database or to use other research techniques to answer questions about criminal justice issues, including AIDS information, law enforcement, drugs and crime, courts, corrections, juvenile justice, statistics, criminology, victims, and corrections construction. Topical bibliographies and topical searches are available on specific subjects. In addition to the following materials, NCJRS offers a microfiche program for access to nearly 30,000 documents.

Information for free:

Arresting the Demand for Drugs: Police and School Partnerships. 1987. 33 pages.

The Armed Criminal in America. 1986. 5 pages.

The Cause, Transmission, and Incidence of AIDS. 1987. 4 pages.

HIV Antibody Testing: Procedures, Interpretation, and Reliability of Results. 1988. 8 pages.

Project DARE: Teaching Kids to Say "No" to Drugs and Alcohol. 1986. 4 pages.

Prosecution of Child Sexual Abuse: Innovations in Practice. 1985. 7 pages.

TV and Violence. 1985. 4 pages. Crime file study guide.

Violence in Schools. 1983. 4 pages.

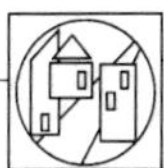

Information for a fee:

Evaluation of Urban Crime Prevention Programs: Executive Summary. 1984. 22 pages. $4.60

Guardian Angels: An Assessment of Citizen Response to Crime. 1986. 31 pages. $4.60

Helping Crime Victims: Executive Summary. 1987. 18 pages. $4.60.

Keeping the Peace: Parameters of Police Discretion. 1986. 39 pages. $5.20.

The Nature and Patterns of American Homicide. 1985. 74 pages. $8.40.

To find out more, write or phone:

National Criminal Justice Reference Service
Box 6000
Rockville, MD 20850
Toll-free: 1-800-851-3420 or *Phone:* (202)862-2900

▶ National Governors' Association

Provides information on: *Governors*

The Association is made up of governors of the 50 states, Guam, American Samoa, the Virgin Islands, the Northern Mariana Islands, and Puerto Rico. NGA serves as a vehicle through which governors influence the development and implementation of national policy and apply creative leadership to state problems. It keeps the federal establishment informed of the needs and perceptions of states, serves as a source of information on new state programs, and provides technical assistance to governors on a wide range of issues. The group maintains a library and biographical archives, and compiles statistics.

Information for free:

National Governors' Association Publications Catalog.

Information for a fee:

America in Transition, The International Frontier: Report of the Task Force on Children. 1989. 38 pages. $10.95. Covers the role of the states in the international economy.

Curbing Waste in a Throwaway World: Report of the Task Force on Solid Waste Management. 1990. 68 pages. $15. A report on solid waste issues.

Decent and Affordable Housing for All. 1986. 28 pages. $7.50. Discusses the availability of safe, sanitary, and adequate housing.

Every Child Ready for School: Report of the Action Team on School Readiness. $16.95. A report based on the premise that education and school readiness are everyone's business, and an early investment should be made in children.

From Homes to Classrooms to Workrooms: State Initiates to Meet the Needs of the Changing American Family. 1992. $15. Outlines state strategies to support families in balancing work and family.

A Healthy America: The Challenge for the States. 1991. 200 pages. $18.75. Explores solutions to the nation's health care problems, and the role of states in finding them.

Keys to Changing the System: Report of the Action Team on the School Years. 1992. $16.95. Looks at action initiates in 11 states, with an emphasis on what lessons can be learned when using systemic educational reform.

Kids in Trouble: Coordinating Correctional and Social Service Systems for Youth . 1991. 32 pages. $15. Looks at improving government intervention strategies by coordinating juvenile justice services with child welfare, education, mental health, and vocational training services.

New Alliances for Rural America. 1988. 70 pages. $15. Report on rural economic development, health, education, and transportation.

Recruiting Minority Classroom Teachers: A National Challenge. 1988. 40 pages. $7.50. Summary of a 15-state survey of minority teacher supply and demand.

To find out more, write or phone:

National Governors' Association
Hall of States
444 N. Capitol St.
Washington, DC 20001
Phone: (202)624-5300 or *Fax:* (202)624-5313

▶ National Judicial Education Program to Promote Equality for Women and Men in the Courts

Provides information on: *Sexual Harassment and Discrimination*

The Program is a nonprofit organization that provides information on gender bias in the courts and materials for judicial and legal education in the area.

Information for free:

Myths of Equality. Factsheets giving statistics on issues such as sexual harassment on the job, education, child sexual abuse, and separation and divorce.

State Index of Women's Legal Rights. 1987.

Subject Publications List. A listing of various information resources offered by the organization.

Information for a fee:

Black Women in a High Tech World. $2.

Computer Equity Report No. 1: Sex Bias at the Computer Terminal and How Schools Program Girls. $3.

In Their Own Voices: Young Women Talk About Dropping Out. $6.95.

Like She Owns the Earth: Women and Sports. $3.

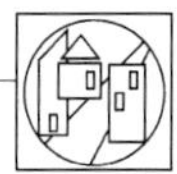

Protecting Young Women's Right to Abortion: A Guide to Parental Notification and Consent Laws. 1990. $3.50.
The Report Card on Educating Hispanic Women. $2.
The State-by-State Guide to Women's Legal Rights. $12.95.

To find out more, write or phone:

National Judicial Education Program to Promote Equality for Women and Men in the Courts
99 Hudson St., 12th Fl.
New York, NY 10013
Phone: (212)925-6635 or *Fax:* (212)226-1066

▶ National Rainbow Coalition, Inc.

Provides information on: *Civil Rights and Liberties*

The National Rainbow Coalition, Inc. promotes the creation of a better nation and world by lifting the hope of all Americans and assuring economic justice, peace, human rights, and dignity for all. Areas of concentration include civil rights, government, politics, labor, education, religion, the environment, and health care.

Information for free:
Brochures are available upon request.

To find out more, write or phone:

National Rainbow Coalition, Inc.
Rev. Jesse L. Jackson Sr., Pres.
1700 K St., NW, Ste. 800
Washington, DC 20006
Phone: (202)728-1180 or *Fax:* (202)728-1192

▶ National School Safety Center (NSSC)

Provides information on: *Crime Prevention, Victims*

The Center serves as a national clearinghouse for school safety programs and activities related to campus security, school law, community relations, student discipline and attendance, and the prevention of drug abuse, gangs, and bullying. The Center's purpose is to focus national attention on the importance of providing safe and effective schools. It provides training, technical assistance, and resources on school safety and school crime prevention.

Information for free:
NSSC Resources List.

Safe Schools and Quality Schooling.
High Risk Youth/At the Crossroads. Pamphlet.
Set Straight on Bullies. Pamphlet.
What's Wrong With This Picture? Pamphlet.

Information for a fee:

Gangs in Schools: Breaking Up is Hard to Do. 1988. 48 pages. $5. Offers an introduction to various types of gangs—including ethnic gangs and satanic cults—and gives practical advice on preventing or reducing gang encroachment in schools.

The Need to Know: Juvenile Record Sharing. 1989. 88 pages. $12. Book deals with the confidentiality of juvenile records and why those who work with offenders need to share information in them.

NSSC Resource Papers. $4 each. Individual topics include:
Safe Schools Overview;
Increasing School Attendance;
Drug Traffic and Abuse in Schools;
School Bullying and Victimization;
Weapons in Schools;
Role Models, Sports and Youth;
Corporal Punishment in Schools.

School Crime and Violence: Victims' Rights. 1986. 106 pages. $16. Text on school safety law offering an overview of victims' rights, treatment in our laws and courts, and its effect on America's schools.

School Safety. 3/year. 36 pages. $12/year. News journal.

School Safety Checkbook. 1988. 219 pages. $15. Text on crime and violence prevention in schools.

Set Straight on Bullies. 1989. $10. Examines the myths and realities about schoolyard bullying and the characteristics of bullies and bullying victims. Provides strategies for educators, parents, and students to better prevent and respond to schoolyard bullying.

To find out more, write or phone:

National School Safety Center
4165 Thousand Oaks Blvd., Ste. 290
Westlake Village, CA 91362
Phone: (805)373-9977 or *Fax:* (805)373-9277

▶ National Victim Center

Provides information on: *Victims, Child Abuse, Criminal Justice, Domestic Violence*

The National Victim Center gathers and distributes information on victims' rights and criminal justice issues. The Center focuses on victims of violent crime, including sexual assault, homicide, drunk driving, child abuse, family violence, elder abuse, hate and racial violence, and drug-related violence. It connects crime victims with care providers, services, and assistance. The Center also supports child abuse research, and helps grassroots organizations develop programs to help victims.

Information for free:

Crime, Safety & You. National Victim Center quarterly newsletter. Sample copy free. Examines violent crime issues and prevention techniques.

Rape in America. Brochure containing facts and myths about rape.

Victims' Rights and the Media. Brochure.

Information for a fee:

America Speaks Out: Citizens' Attitudes about Victims' Rights and Violence. 1991. $2.50. Presents survey results.

Overview of Crime and Victimization in America. Annual. $3.00. Statistical update on U.S. crime.

Rape in America: A Report to the Nation. 1992. $20. Research and statistical update.

To find out more, write or phone:

National Victim Center
309 W. 7th St., Ste. 705
Fort Worth, TX 76102
Phone: (817)877-3355 or *Fax:* (817)877-3396

▶ National Victims Resource Center (NVRC)

Provides information on: *Victims, Rape, Domestic Violence*

NVRC provides victim-related information and offers information about national, state, and local victim-related organizations and state programs that receive funds authorized by the Victims of Crime Act. It provides national victimization statistics; federally-sponsored victim related research studies; names, addresses, and telephone numbers of people to contact for information and assistance; and information on state victims compensation programs funded by the Office for Victims of Crime.

Information for free:

Black Victims.

Female Victims of Violent Crime.

Forensic Use of Hypnosis.

Hate Crimes.

Missing, Abducted, Runaway, and Throwaway Children in America.

Robbery Victims.

School Crime.
Teenage Victims. Violence in Schools.
Women in Prison. The above are bulletins, special reports, summaries, or full reports of criminal justice data.

Information for a fee:
Battered Women. $5. Topical search.
Child Sexual Exploitation. $5. Topical search.
Crime and the Elderly. $17.50. Bibliography.
Effects of Violence on Children. $5. Topical search.
Homicide Victims. $5. Topical search.
Marital Rape and Date/Acquaintance Rape. $5. Topical search.
National Victims Resource Directory. $20.50. Listings of data or organizations to contact for more information.
Rape. $5. Topical search.
Victims: Family Violence. $17.50. Topical bibliography.

To find out more, write or phone:
National Victims Resource Center
Dept. F
PO Box 6000
Rockville, MD 20850
Toll-free: 1-800-627-NVRC or *Fax:* (301)251-5212

▶ Operation PUSH

Provides information on: *Civil Rights and Liberties, Human Rights*

Operation PUSH is an international human rights organization and movement directed toward educational and economic equality for all, particularly Black, Hispanic, and poor people. The group uses research, education, negotiation, and direct action to achieve its goal of self and community motivation and social responsibility. PUSH stands for People United to Serve Humanity.

Information for a fee:
PUSH Magazine. Quarterly. $3.

To find out more, write or phone:
Operation PUSH
930 E. 50th St.
Chicago, IL 60615
Phone: (312)373-3366

▶ Peace and Freedom Party (PFP)

Provides information on: *Political Parties*

PFP is a political party whose members include union workers, professionals, laypersons, students, environmental activists, women, teenagers, minorities, homosexuals, and other activists who work for world socialism. The party's objectives are to reduce the Pentagon budget by 50 percent, lower the full-time work week to 30 hours with no reduction in pay, create 20 million jobs that the party believes will end poverty, racism, and sexism, fight organized crime, abolish individual taxes and the IRS, lower present voting age to 13, distribute condoms to young people as a disease-prevention measure, legalize most street drugs and allow doctors to distribute free drugs so those addicted will not have to "deal, steal, or sell their bodies just to satisfy their habit," create a free education system, and free all political prisoners. The party works to eliminate oppression and discrimination based on sex and sexual preference, class, race, age, or nationality.

Information for a fee:
Publishes leaflets and newspapers periodically for a donation.

To find out more, write or phone:

Peace and Freedom Party
Paul Kangas, Contact
PO Box 422644
San Francisco, CA 94142
Phone: (415)897-0153

▶ People Against Rape

Provides information on: *Rape, Acquaintance Rape*

People Against Rape works to help teens and children avoid becoming the victims of sexual assault and rape by providing instruction in the basic principles of self-defense. The group promotes self-esteem and motivation in teens through educational programs, offers substance abuse prevention programs, and teacher/parent training programs.

Information for a fee:
Defend: Preventing Date Rape and Other Sexual Assaults. 1992. $4.95.
My Power Book. $12. A motivational workbook.
Also offers an informational packet, including the "Hands Off, I'm Special" booklet, brochures, and pamphlet for $5.

To find out more, write or phone:

People Against Rape
401 William St.
PO Box 5318
River Forest, IL 60305
Toll-free: 1-800-877-7252 or *Phone:* (708)452-0737

▶ People for the American Way

Provides information on: *Civil Rights and Liberties, Censorship*

A nonpartisan constitutional liberties organization committed to reaffirming the American values of pluralism, diversity, and freedom of expression and religion. The group is engaged in a mass media campaign to create a positive climate of tolerance and respect for diverse peoples, religions, and values. It operates the National Resource Center, a collection of printed and visual materials.

Information for a fee:

Attacks on the Freedom to Learn. 1990-91. 125 pages. $8.95. The group's ninth annual report on state censorship attempts to restrict what public schools teach.

Betraying Our Trust: A Status Report on First Amendment Rights with Preface. 1988. 128 pages. $11.95. A study that traces Reagan-era challenges to First Amendment rights, revealing "a slow but steady disregard for democratic principles."

Church-State Separation in America: The Tradition Nobody Knows. 1984. 11 pages. $4.95. Examines issues surrounding the relationship between politics and religion.

Democracy's Next Generation: A Study of Youth and Teachers. 1989. 204 pages. $11.95. A study exploring the attitudes and values of today's youth on voting, politics, and government.

Government Secrecy: Decisions Without Democracy. 1987. 104 pages. $10.95. Report exposing government secrecy, from the censorship of government employees, to the Iran-Contra scandal.

Hate in the Ivory Tower: A Survey of Intolerance on College Campuses and Academia's Response. 1991. 80 pages. $10.95. A survey of 128 colleges and universities.

Looking at History: A Review of Major U.S. History Textbooks. 1986. 198 pages. $10.95. Examines school books for objectivity and accuracy.

Protecting the Freedom to Learn: A Citizen's Guide. 1989. 56 pages. $5.95. A guide describing threats to public education. Includes guidelines to help communities avoid or combat censorship in their schools.

Religion, Politics, and the Media. 1988. 48 pages. $5.95. Examines the issue of how religion should influence politics and public life.

The Vanishing Voter and the Crisis in American Democracy: New Strategies for Reversing the Decline in Voter Participation. 1988. 33 pages. $5.95. A study of voter participation and trends.

To find out more, write or phone:

People for the American Way
2000 M St. NW, Ste. 400
Washington, DC 20036
Phone: (202)467-4999 or *Fax:* (202)293-2672

▶ POPS, Preserve Our Presidential Sites

Provides information on: *U.S. Presidents*

The organization seeks to promote, preserve, and upgrade gravesites of deceased American presidents and encourages restoration and maintenance of these monuments. Other activities include educating youth concerning their American heritage and history and conducting lectures with slide presentations.

Information for free:

Portraits of the Presidents. Brochure.
The Presidents' Ladies. Flyers.

To find out more, write or phone:

POPS, Preserve Our Presidential Sites
201 Bernhardt Dr.
Buffalo, NY 14226
Phone: (716)839-4494

▶ Populist Party of America

Provides information on: *Political Parties*

The Populist Party believes in the idea that "values and beliefs of the middle class majority should rule, rather than special interests and minority pressure groups." Its objective is to become an alternative choice for Americans. The Party believes in the nationalist philosophy of "America First."

Information for a fee:

Are You A Populist? $.07. Pamphlet listing the party's major issues.
The Populist Observer. Monthly. $21/year. Newspaper covering news of interest to the Party.
The Populist Party Platform. $.07. Pamphlet providing the party platform.
Presenting the Populist Platform. $.07. A pamphlet giving an introduction to the Party.

Stand up for Your Right to Keep and Bear Arms. $.06. Pamphlet concerning gun control.
Vote Populist Party. $.07. Pamphlet giving a ten-point program to "help return America to greatness."

To find out more, write or phone:

Populist Party of America
Donald B. Wassall, Chm.
PO Box 1989
Ford City, PA 16226
Phone: (412)763-1225 or *Fax:* (412)763-3175

▶ Project Censored

Provides information on: *Censorship, Freedom of Information*

Project Censored seeks to explore and publicize the extent of censorship by locating stories on significant issues of which the public is unaware. It recognizes and promotes good investigative journalism and encourages the public to demand coverage of controversial issues or to seek information from other sources.

Information for free:
The 10 Best Censored Stories. Pamphlet.
The Top 10 Junk Food News Stories of the Year. Press release.

Information for a fee:
The Top 25 Censored News Stories of the Year. Annual book. $15.

To find out more, write or phone:

Project Censored
Sonoma State University
Dept. of Communications Studies
Rohnert Park, CA 94928
Phone: (707)664-2500

▶ Project on Government Procurement

Provides information on: *Government*

The Project conducts investigations to expose corruption in federal agencies and Congress. It acts as a clearinghouse for sources who want to expose wrongdoing in government while remaining anonymous.

Information for a fee:
The Brooks Act: Environmental Uses Could Waste Taxpayers' Billions. 1991. $5.

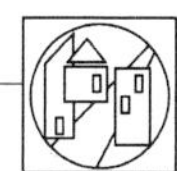

Cleaning up Nuclear Waste: Why is D.O.E. Five Years Behind and Billions over Budget? 1991. $5.
Courage without Martyrdom: A Survival Guide for Whistleblowers. 1989. 44 pages. $5.
Defense Procurement Papers. 1988. 108 pages. $5.
High Tech Weapons in Desert Storm: Hype or Reality? 1991. $5.
More Bucks Less Bang: How the Pentagon Buys Ineffective Weapons. 1983. 341 pages. $5.
U.S. Weapons Unit Costs: Dramatic Increases in Current and Future Weapons Systems. 1990. $5.

To find out more, write or phone:
Project on Government Procurement
2025 Eye St., NW, Ste. 1117
Washington, DC 20006-1903
Phone: (202)466-5539 or *Fax:* (202)466-5596

▶ Ronald Reagan Library

Provides information on: *U.S. Presidents*

The Library holds personal papers and financial records relating to Ronald Reagan.

Information for a fee:
Gift Shop Catalog. $4.50.

To find out more, write or phone:
Ronald Reagan Library
40 Presidential Dr.
Simi Valley, CA 93065
Phone: (805)522-8444

▶ Republican Governors Association (RGA)

Provides information on: *Political Parties*

The Association provides contact with governors' offices, and coordinates with other Republican Party organizations working directly with candidates for governorships.

To find out more, write or phone:
Republican Governors Association
310 1st St. SE
Washington, DC 20003
Phone: (202)863-8587 or *Fax:* (202)863-8659

▶ Republican National Committee

Provides information on: *Political Parties*

The Republican National Committee provides support activities to Republican administrators, members of Congress, governors, state and local office holders, and Republic campaigns. The group conducts research on current issues, maintains a library of books, periodicals, newspapers, and videotapes relating to political history, leaders, organizations, issues, and events. It also keeps files of biographies of major party leaders, historical information, and election statistics.

To find out more, write or phone:
Republican National Committee
310 1st St., SE
Washington, DC 20003
Phone: (202)863-8500

▶ RID - U.S.A.

Provides information on: *Drunk Driving*

RID is a group working to heighten public awareness of the effects drunk drivers have on society. The group promotes passage of more effective laws dealing with drunk drivers, provides victim support, and works to increase public involvement. RID provides background information on driving records and court procedures and acts as liaison between victims and agencies, courts, coroners, district attorneys, and police. The group maintains biographical archives and a library of pamphlets, manuals, and books.

Information for a fee:
Drunk Drivers Victims' Rights. $1 plus $2 shipping and handling. Manual.
Drunk Driving—Its Impact, Its Victims. $1 plus $2 shipping and handling. Manual.
RID National Newsletter. Quarterly. $10. Includes chapter and national news.
Also available is a chapter information kit including both manuals listed above and several issues of the RID Newsletter. $20.

To find out more, write or phone:
RID - U.S.A.
PO Box 520
Schenectady, NY 12301
Phone: (518)372-0034 or *Fax:* (518)370-4917

▶ Theodore Roosevelt Association

Provides information on: *U.S. Presidents*

The Association is made up of persons interested in the life and principles of Theodore Roosevelt (1858-1919). It maintains bibliographical archives and will respond to students' questions on relevant topics.

Information for free:
Theodore Roosevelt Association Journal. Quarterly.

To find out more, write or phone:

Theodore Roosevelt Association
Box 720
Oyster Bay, NY 11771
Phone: (516)922-1221

▶ Franklin D. Roosevelt Library

Provides information on: *U.S. Presidents*

The Franklin D. Roosevelt Library contains papers, books, pamphlets and serials, manuscripts, photographs, museum objects, films, records, and audiotapes on the life and presidency of Franklin D. Roosevelt; also houses other special collections.

Information for a fee:

Before the Trumpet. 390 pages. $17.95. Book depicts Roosevelt's family, early years, and private life.

A First Class Temperament—The Emergence of Franklin Roosevelt. 840 pages. $14.95. Book depicts FDR's private life, personal ordeals, and public triumphs.

FDR's Fireside Chats. $24.95. Book provides an overview of Roosevelt's concerns and his oratorical style.

Franklin D. Roosevelt—His Life and Times: An Encyclopedic View. 472 pages. Book covers over 320 topics on FDR's life and times.

Franklin Delano Roosevelt. 196 pages. $16.95. Biography of FDR.

Franklin D. Roosevelt's Inaugural Address of 1933. $2.50.

On War Against Japan: Franklin D. Roosevelt's "Day of Infamy" Address of 1941. $2.50.

To find out more, write or phone:

Franklin D. Roosevelt Library
511 Albany Post Rd.
Hyde Park, NY 12538
Phone: (914)229-8114

▶ Roper Center for Public Opinion Research, Inc.

Provides information on: *Politics*

The Center focuses on social and political attitudes and behavior. This involves studying public affairs, public policy, and communication and mass media. The Center maintains an archive of public opinion information, which includes actual survey response data. Information can be accessed online by users. The Center also performs customized searches.

To find out more, write or phone:

Roper Center for Public Opinion Research, Inc.
PO Box 440
Storrs, CT 06268
Phone: (203)486-4440 or *Fax:* (203)486-6308

▶ Second Amendment Foundation

Provides information on: *Firearms, Gun Control*

The Foundation is an association that supports the "constitutional right to privately own and possess firearms." SAF carries on many educational and legal action programs designed to inform the public about the gun control debate, produces a weekly pro-gun radio program distributed to 400 stations nationwide, and provides public service announcements through the media. The group maintains a library and biographical archives and compiles statistics.

Information for a fee:
Armed and Female. $4.50 paperback.
The Good Side of Guns. $3.
In the Gravest Extreme. $7.95.
Realistic Defense Tactics. $9.95.
The Gun Control Debate You Decide. $16.95.
The Gun Safety Handbook. $4.95.
The Street Smart Gun Book. $11.95.
Women and Guns. Monthly. $24.95/year.
Women's Views on Self Defense. $5.50.

To find out more, write or phone:

Second Amendment Foundation
James Madison Bldg.
12500 NE 10th Pl.
Bellevue, WA 98005
Phone: (206)454-7012 or *Fax:* (206)451-3959

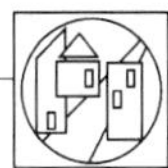

▶ Socialist Labor Party of America (SLP)

Provides information on: *Political Parties*

SLP is a political group whose party platform aims to establish a classless, socialist, industrial democracy in which the political state is abolished and the industries and services are under social ownership and rank-and-file control. The party sponsors study classes, discussion groups, speakers, and local organizers.

Information for a fee:

The Abortion Issue: A Socialist View. 4 pages. $10. Pamphlet.
Bourgeois Socialism: Its Rise and Collapse in America. 208 pages. $2.50.
Capitalism: Breeder of Race Prejudice. 46 pages. $.50.
Capitalism and Unemployment. 61 pages. $.50.
Democracy: Past, Present, and Future. 80 pages. $.50.
Marxian Science and the Colleges. 96 pages. $.75.
The Middle East Conflict. 8 pages. $.20.
The People. Biweekly. $4/year. The official journal of the Socialist Labor Party. Covers such topics as militarism, strikes, nuclear power, and other issues and articles on labor history and socialism.
The Truth About Inflation. 32 pages. $.50.

To find out more, write or phone:

Socialist Labor Party of America
PO Box 50218
Palo Alto, CA 94303-0218
Phone: (415)494-1532

▶ Socialist Party U.S.A. (SP-USA)

Provides information on: *Political Parties*

SP-USA defines itself as a democratic socialist political party encompassing a wide range of opinions within its ranks instead of a rigid "party line." The party seeks radical and fundamental change in the structure and quality of economic, political, and social relationships in America, through education, grass roots organizing, and electoral action.

Information for a fee:

The Socialist. 10/year. $8. Newsletter covering social and political issues from a socialist perspective.

To find out more, write or phone:
Socialist Party U.S.A.
516 W. 25th St., Rm. 404
New York, NY 10001
Phone: (212)691-0776

▶ Socialist Workers Party (SWP)

Provides information on: *Political Parties*

SWP is a political party whose stated goal is to educate and organize the working class in order to establish a "workers' and farmers' government," which will "abolish capitalism in the the U.S. and join in the worldwide struggle for socialism." The party strives to advance the unity of working people by participating in activities that call for jobs through reducing the workweek with no cut in pay, equality in employment and education for Blacks, Latinos, and women through affirmative action, cancellation of the foreign debt of semicolonial countries, and an end to farm foreclosures and guaranteed income to working farmers. The Party promotes and supports defense of the Cuban revolution, elimination of apartheid in South Africa, unilateral nuclear disarmament, an immediate shutdown of all nuclear power plants, and a halt to environmental destruction.

Information for a fee:
The Militant. Weekly. $1.50.

To find out more, write or phone:
Socialist Workers Party
406 West St.
New York, NY 10014
Phone: (212)242-5530 or *Fax:* (212)727-3107

▶ Sons of Liberty

Provides information on: *Gun Control, Firearms*

Sons of Liberty is made up of politically conservative individuals seeking to defend the U.S. Constitution. The group concentrates efforts on the right to keep and bear arms, and opposes gun control, including restrictions on semiautomatic weapons. It claims that less than one percent of registered guns are used for illegal purposes, therefore gun control would constitute harassment of 99 percent of gun owners. The group provides information on the right to bear arms, and compiles statistics.

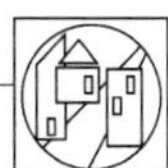

To find out more, write or phone:

Sons of Liberty
Joseph W. Kerska, Pres.
PO Box 503
Brisbane, CA 94005
Phone: (415)468-2402

▶ Special Interest Group on Security, Audit and Control

Provides information on: *Computer Crime*

The purpose of the Group is to maintain high levels of skill and awareness regarding technology and practice in the fields of computer security, audit, and control. It examines issues including control of access to resources, identity verification, risk analysis, logging of transactions, data reduction, and architectural foundations for security systems.

To find out more, write or phone:

Special Interest Group on Security, Audit and Control
c/o Assn. for Computing Machinery
1515 Broadway
New York, NY 10036
Phone: (212)869-7440

▶ Students Against Driving Drunk (SADD)

Provides information on: *Drunk Driving*

SADD works to increase public awareness of and urge students to take action against drunken driving, drug abuse, and consumption of alcohol by minors.

Information for a fee:

Celebrate Life—Prom and Graduation Activities Guide. $2. Describes dri-hi parties and other prom and graduation activities.

College Program Manual. $2. A "how-to" manual for a SADD college chapter.

The Contract for Life. $4.95. A book telling the SADD story.

High School SADD Chapter Handbook and Curriculum Guide. $2. A SADD guide for high schools.

How to Start Your SADD Chapter and New Ideas for Existing SADD Chapters. $2. A manual to assist in starting a new chapter.

Middle School SADD Chapter Handbook and Curriculum Guide. $2.

Student Athletes Detest Drugs Manual. $2. Describes the process of starting a drug-free program for college and high school athletes.
Also offers SADD kits, contracts, and promotional items.

To find out more, write or phone:
Students Against Driving Drunk
Robert Anastas, Exec.Dir.
PO Box 800
Marlborough, MA 01752
Phone: (508)481-3568 or *Fax:* (508)481-5759

▶ Supreme Court Historical Society

Provides information on: *U.S. Supreme Court*

The Society is made up of students, people, and libraries engaged in historical research and gathering of memorabilia and artifacts on the history of the Supreme Court. It distributes information to scholars, historians, and the public. The Society sponsors special research projects, including the Index of Opinions by Justice, which indexes each justice's written opinions and statements.

To find out more, write or phone:
Supreme Court Historical Society
111 2nd St., NE
Washington, DC 20002
Phone: (202)543-0400

▶ Harry S. Truman Library Institute for National and International Affairs

Provides information on: *U.S. Presidents*

The Institute was formed to support the Truman Library and promote its interests as a research center.

Information for a fee:
Newsletter. Quarterly. Price included in $25 membership fee.

To find out more, write or phone:
Harry S. Truman Library Institute for National and International Affairs
24 Highway & Delaware
Independence, MO 64050
Phone: (816)833-1400

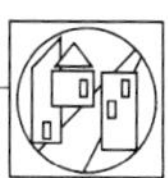

▶ United States Conference of Mayors (USCM)

Provides information on: *Mayors*

Cities with populations of over 30,000 are members of the Conference. It provides educational information, technical assistance, and legislative services to cities.

Information for a fee:

AIDS: The Second Wave—The Impact of the AIDS Epidemic in 5 Cities. 1992. $15.
Drug and Alcohol Abuse in the Workplace: Testing, Employee Assistance, and Discipline. 1986. $25.
The Federal Budget and the Cities. Annual. $15.
Impact of AIDS on America's Cities: A 26-City Report. 1990. $5.
Impact of the National Recession on America's Cities. 1991. $10.
Mentally Ill and Homeless: A 22-City Survey. November 1991. $10.
Recycling in America: Profiles of the Nation's Resourceful Cities. 1991. $10.
Recycling in Schools: How to Develop Your Own Program. 1992. Prices vary according to amount ordered.
A Status Report on Hunger and Homelessness in America's Cities: 1991 (A 28-City Survey). 1991. $10.

To find out more, write or phone:

United States Conference of Mayors
1620 Eye St., NW
Washington, DC 20006
Phone: (202)293-7330 or *Fax:* (202)293-7330

▶ U.S. Presidential Museum—Library of Presidents

Provides information on: *U.S. Presidents*

The Library contains information on U.S. Presidents, presidential candidates, Vice Presidents, First Ladies, political parties, and campaigns. It is open to the public for reference use by appointment only.

To find out more, write or phone:

U.S. Presidential Museum—Library of Presidents
622 N. Lee St.
Odessa, TX 79761
Phone: (915)332-7123

▶ Woodrow Wilson Birthplace Foundation (WWBF)

Provides information on: *U.S. Presidents*

The WWBF supports the preservation, restoration, maintenance, and interpretation of the birthplace of Woodrow Wilson (1856-1924), 28th President of the United States, 1913-21. WWBF conducts research and interprets the life and times of President Wilson, and maintains a research library and archives. The Foundation also manages a historic house and museum.

Information for a fee:
The Woodrow Wilson Birthplace Foundation Newsletter. Quarterly. Included in $20 membership dues. Covers activities of the presidential museum.

To find out more, write or phone:
Woodrow Wilson Birthplace Foundation
PO Box 24
Staunton, VA 24401
Phone: (703)885-0897 or *Fax:* (703)886-9874

▶ Women Against Rape (WAR)

Provides information on: *Rape*

The organization works toward the prevention of rape. WAR sponsors crisis intervention services, including a rape crisis hotline for support and referrals and rape survivor support groups, and offers rape prevention training including self-defense classes for women.

Information for a fee:
W.A.R. Newsletter. Quarterly. $15 donation. Covers current information on rape issues.

To find out more, write or phone:
Women Against Rape
Box 02084
Columbus, OH 43202
Phone: (614)291-9751

▶ Women in Municipal Government

Provides information on: *Government*

The organization is made up of women who are elected and appointed city officials including mayors, council members, and commissioners. The group seeks to encourage active participation of women officials in the organizational and policy-making processes and programs of the National League of Cities and state municipal leagues,

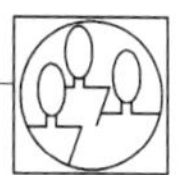

identify qualified women for service in the NLC and other national positions, and promote issues of interest to women and the status of women in the nation's cities.

Information for free:

Constituency Report. Quarterly newsletter. Requires only the cost of postage.

To find out more, write or phone:

Women in Municipal Government
Kathryn Shane McCarty, Coordinator
National League of Cities
1301 Pennsylvania Ave., NW
Washington, DC 20004
Phone: (202)626-3000 or *Fax:* (202)626-3043

To Contact People . . .

These books identify individual experts or organizations that can direct you to one.

▶ *The Address Book: How to Reach Anyone Who Is Anyone*

This book can be used to contact more than 3,500 prominent persons including political leaders, business executives, athletes, actors and actresses, artists, musicians, and writers. The book lists name and address. Names are listed alphabetically.
Biennial. Perigee Books.

▶ *Almanac of American Politics*

Organized by state, this book presents profiles of the current state governors, U.S. senators, and members of the U.S. House of Representatives. Entries include name, biographical data, voting records on major issues, and other relevant information.
Biennial. National Journal.

▶ *The American Bench*

This source lists more than 18,000 judges sitting in local, state, and federal courts, and the courts themselves. Entries for judges include name, personal and professional data, jurisdiction, important cases ruled on, memberships, previous judgeships, and office phone. Information is arranged geographically.
Biennial. Forster-Long, Inc.

▶ *American Political Science Association Membership Directory*

This directory can be used to contact members of the American Political Science Association. The book lists name, address, title, affiliation, highest degree, and specialty. Names are arranged alphabetically.
Triennial. American Political Science Association.

▶ *Books on Trial: A Survey of Recent Cases*

This book lists some 25 attorneys who have participated in school district book censorship litigation. Attorney name, firm name, and address are listed. The publication is arranged geographically.
1987; 1991 update. National Coalition Against Censorship.

▶ *Canadian Who's Who*

This book lists about 12,000 notable Canadians in Canada and abroad based on position or achievement. Entries include name, address, personal and career data.
Annual. University of Toronto Press.

▶ *Criminal Justice Information Exchange Directory*

The directory covers about 100 criminal justice-related organizations (mostly libraries) that form an information exchange network. Entries include name, address, phone, name and title of contact, holdings, services (interlibrary loan, microfiche, online searches), restrictions on users, and special interest areas. Arrangement of the publication is geographical and alphabetical.
Annual. U.S. National Criminal Justice Reference Service (NCJRS).

▶ *Directory of Criminal Justice Issues in the States*

The publication includes a listing of nearly 50 state Statistical Analysis Centers that sponsor about 420 criminal justice policy research studies. Entries include center name, address, phone, and name and title of contact. Arrangement of the book is geographical.
Annual. Justice Research and Statistics Association.

▶ *Directory of Election Officials*

Use this book to contact state election agencies and election officials and federal officials with election-related responsibilities. Information includes agency name,

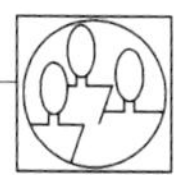

address, phone, and names and titles of officials. The book is arranged geographically.
Biennial. Clearinghouse on Election Administration, Federal Election Commission.

▶ *Directory of the Governors of the American States, Commonwealths and Territories*

The source covers governors of the 50 states, American Samoa, Guam, the Northern Mariana Islands, Puerto Rico, and the Virgin Islands. Entries include name, biographical data, photograph, and spouse name and photograph. Arrangement of the book is geographical.
Annual. National Governors' Association.

▶ *Directory of Information Resources on Victimization of Women*

The directory covers special libraries, clearinghouses, and online databases offering resource information on women and children as victims of abuse.
Response.

▶ *Directory of International Networking Resources on Violence Against Women*

Use this directory to locate nongovernmental organizations, United Nations offices, United States organizations with international activities, and international periodicals in the field of violence against women.
Response.

▶ *Directory of Jail and Prison Ministries in America*

The directory covers 400 Christian ministries in prisons. Entries include name, address, phone, names and titles of key personnel, and description of services. Arrangement of the book is geographical.
1991. Institute for Prison Ministries.

▶ *Directory of Judges with Juvenile/Family Law Jurisdiction*

The publication covers 1,400 judges who have juvenile, family, or domestic relations jurisdiction, and includes an additional 700 non-judicial associate members. The entries include name, office address, phone and fax, and are arranged alphabetically and geographically.
Biennial. National Council of Juvenile and Family Court Judges.

▶ *Directory of Juvenile and Adult Correctional Departments, Institutions, Agencies and Paroling Authorities*

This book gives contact information for some 4,000 juvenile and adult correctional departments and related authorities. For each agency, the book lists location, phone, name of contact person, how long in operation, average number and types of inmates, cost of care, degree of security, and number of staff. The book is arranged primarily in geographic order within sections (federal, states, military Canada, etc).
Annual. American Correctional Association.

▶ *First Amendment Lawyers Association—Directory*

This directory covers approximately 125 member lawyers who support and defend cases involving the First Amendment to the U.S. Constitution.
Annual. First Amendment Lawyers Association.

▶ *Governors' Staff Directory*

Use this book to contact key staff members in each of the 55 governor's offices. The book contains name of governor, addresses and phone numbers of governor's main, district, and Washington offices, and names and titles of key staff members. Information is arranged geographically.
Semiannual. Publication Department, National Governors' Association.

▶ *Guns Illustrated*

Publication includes national and international firearms associations, manufacturers, importers, and distributors of firearms, shooting equipment, and services. Entries include name, address, phone, area of interest, or product or service provided. Arrangement of the book is alphabetical.
Annual. DBI Books, Inc.

▶ *International Who's Who*

This book covers 20,000 prominent persons worldwide. Entries include name, nationality, personal and career information, honors, awards, writings, address, and phone. Names are arranged alphabetically.
Annual. Europa Publications Ltd.

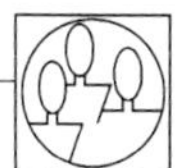

▶ *Judicial Staff Directory*

This directory lists contact information for about 12,000 members and staff of the federal judicial system, including judges, court executives, clerks, magistrates, United States attorneys, and United States marshals, including 1,800 biographies. Entries include name, title, address, phone, and biographical data. Information is arranged by type of court and district.
Annual. Staff Directories Ltd.

▶ *Law Firms Yellow Book: Who's Who in the Management of the Leading U.S. Law Firms*

Use this source to locate approximately 620 large law firms and over 13,000 attorneys and administrators in the U.S. Entries are arranged alphabetically by firm name.
Semiannual. Monitor Publishing Co.

▶ *Martindale-Hubbell Law Directory*

This directory lists law firms in the United States, Canada, and leading law firms worldwide. It also includes a biographical section by firm, and a separate list of patent lawyers, attorneys in government service, and in-house counsel. Entries are arranged geographically.
Annual. Martindale-Hubbell, Inc.

▶ *Mayors of America's Principal Cities*

This book lists about 900 mayors of all United States cities belonging to the United States Conference of Mayors. It also includes all other cities with populations of 30,000 or more. Mayors' names are listed along with city hall address, phone, date term expired, city name, and population. The book is arranged in geographic order.
Semiannual. United States Conference of Mayors.

▶ *National Court Appointed Special Advocate Association Directory*

The directory covers about 475 state and local programs and members of the Court Appointed Special Advocate Association who speak for abused and neglected children in court. Entries include the name, address, phone, name of director, and programs. Arrangement of the book is geographical.
Semiannual. National Court Appointed Special Advocate Association.

▶ *The National Directory of Courts of Law*

Use the directory to locate information on 20,130 federal, state, county, local, territorial, tribal, and specialized law courts. Entries include court name, address, phone, geographical area served, county affiliation. The book is divided into four sections: Federal Courts, State Courts, Territorial Courts, and Courts of the Native American Tribes. Each is classified by level of jurisdiction.
Biennial. Information Resources Press.

▶ *National Directory of Law Enforcement Administrators and Correctional Institutions*

This directory covers police departments and police chiefs in cities and towns with populations of more than 1,600; sheriffs and criminal prosecutors in all counties in the nation; state law enforcement and criminal investigation agencies; federal criminal investigation and related agencies; state and federal correctional institutions; campus law enforcement departments; airport and harbor police; Bureau of Indian Affairs officials, and Canadian law enforcement personnel. Entries are arranged in separate geographical sections for sheriffs and prosecutors, city police chiefs, and state criminal investigation agencies. There also are separate sections for federal agencies and miscellaneous law enforcement and related agencies.
Annual. National Police Chiefs and Sheriffs Information Bureau.

▶ *National Directory of Prosecuting Attorneys*

This directory lists about 2,800 elected or appointed local prosecuting attorneys. Entries are arranged geographically.
Biennial. National District Attorneys Association.

▶ *PACs Americana: The Directory of Political Action Committees and Their Interests*

This source covers about 4,200 political action committees (PACs) registered with the Federal Election Commission, and their sponsoring organizations. The entries include for sponsors: company name, headquarters address and phone, affiliated organizations, political/economic interests, and names, acronyms, and alternative names of sponsored political action committees; for PACs: name, sponsor name, and names, titles, addresses, and phone numbers of treasurer and other officials. The book is arranged alphabetically in separate sections.
1991. Sunshine Services Corporation.

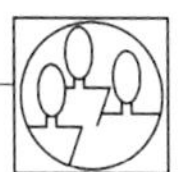

▶ *Prisoner Project Resource List*

This list provides contact information for about 30 organizations or publications that support gay prisoners. Entries include name of group or publication, address, phone, and contact. Names are arranged alphabetically.
Annual. Updated in quarterly "RFD Journal" in section titled "Brothers Behind Bars." RFD Journal.

▶ *Records of the Presidency: Presidential Papers and Libraries from Washington to Reagan*

The publication includes a list of presidential archives and historic sites. The entries are arranged chronologically.
1989. Oryx Press.

▶ *Recovering from Rape*

The publication includes a listing of rape crisis centers in the United States.
1989. Henry Holt & Co.

▶ *Taylor's Encyclopedia of Government Officials: Federal and State*

Use this book to contact over 20,000 federal and state government officials. The entries include name, title, address, and phone, and are arranged by agency, department, or by state.
Biennial, with monthly updates. Political Research, Inc.

▶ *Who's Who in America*

This book contains information on 79,000 people, primarily in the U.S., considered to be of current national interest because of achievement or position. Entries include name, address, personal data, career data, memberships, special achievements, and publications. Names are listed alphabetically; a separate volume indexes people by profession and location.
Biennial. Updated quarterly. Marquis Who's Who.

▶ *Who's Who in American Law*

Listed are over 27,650 lawyers, judges, law school deans and professors, and other legal professionals. Entries are arranged alphabetically.
Biennial. Marquis Who's Who.

▶ *Who's Who in American Law Enforcement*

Use this source to locate persons in supervisory or command positions in law enforcement agencies. Entries are arranged alphabetically.
Triennial. National Association of Chiefs of Police.

▶ *Who's Who in American Politics*

This book can be used to contact more than 25,000 people involved in politics, ranging from principal local, state, and federal officials to men and women active and influential behind the scenes. Entries include name; legal and mailing addresses; birthplace and date; party affiliation; present and previous political, governmental, and business positions; family data; voting residence; achievements; memberships; and writings. Names are arranged in geographic order.
Biennial. R. R. Bowker Co.

▶ *Who's Who of American Women*

This book contains information on more than 30,000 high-profile women in all fields. Entries include name, address, personal, educational, and career data, professional association membership, special achievements, awards, and writings. Names are arranged alphabetically.
Biennial. Marquis Who's Who.

▶ *Who's Who in the World*

This directory covers more than 31,000 people of current international interest because of their achievement or position. Entries include name, address, biographical data, civic activities, awards, writings, and other information. Names are arranged alphabetically.
Biennial. Marquis Who's Who.

2

Family Connections and Concerns

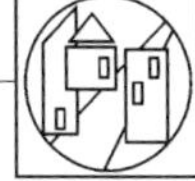

▶ Chapter 2 covers these topics:

Child Abuse
Child Custody
Child Protection
Divorce
Domestic Violence
Incest
Latchkey Children
Marriage
Missing Children
Parental Kidnapping
Parenting
Runaways
Single Parents
Step Families

▶ Related topics appear in chapters on:

Beliefs, Cults, and Sects; Careers and Work; Government and Public Affairs; Health and Personal Concerns; Social Issues

▶ Ideas for research topics:

Alcohol and Drug Abuse among Runaways and At-Risk Youth
The Breakdown of the Traditional American Family
Child Custody Issues in Divorce
Childcare in the U.S. and in Other Countries
Children's Adjustment in Joint Custody Arrangements
The Church's Influence on Marriage and Family Values in the 90s
Divorce Rates in "No Fault" States
Do Intervention Programs Threaten Family Privacy?
The Effects of Child Abuse Laws on the Rates of Child Abuse and Neglect
The Effects of Divorce or Separation on Children
The Family Cycle of Abusive and Violent Relationships
The Foster Care System
Future Families—What Will They Be Like?

▶ Ideas for research topics (continued):

The Government's Role in Child Abuse Intervention
Homicide Rates and Family Violence
How Are "Family Values" Expressed in My Community
Incest and the Psychosexual Development of the Child
The Impact of the Changing Roles of Husband and Wife on the Socialization of Children
The Impact of the Working Woman on the Traditional Family
Is One Parent Enough—The Increased Burden on the Single Parent
Latchkey Children—Their Personal Development and Impact on the Community
Parental Kidnapping
The Role of the Educator in Gender Development of Children
Runaways and Prostitution
School Dropout Rates and Teenage Parents
The School's Role in Child Abuse Detection and Intervention
Stepfamilies and the Socialization of Children
Successful Programs in Rehabilitating Spouse Abusers
What Rights Do Children Have?
Why Do Men Batter Their Wives?

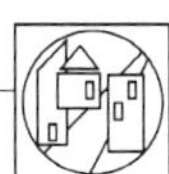

To Contact Organizations . . .

▶ ABA Center on Children and the Law (ACCL)

Provides information on: *Family Law, Child Abuse, Foster Families, Adoption, Learning Disabled Students and Learning Disabilities, Parental Kidnapping*

The ABA Center was established to conduct research and distribute information on law, policy, and related practice affecting children and families. The Center maintains resources on child abuse and neglect, foster care, adoption, parental kidnapping of children, child support, grandparents' rights, development disabled children's rights, and child exploitation. Conferences and educational programs are sponsored by the Center.

Information for a fee:

Child Abuse: A Policy Guide. $3.00.

Criminals and Civil Liability in Child Welfare Work: The Growing Trend. 1984; 1986 case law supplement. 152 pages. $6.50. Analysis, with case descriptions, of grounds for holding agencies and workers liable.

Grandparent Visitation Disputes: A Legal Resource Manual. 1989. 129 pages. $19.95. Intended for attorneys and judges handling grandparent visitation cases.

How We Make Decisions in Child Protective Services Intake and Investigations. $4.50.

Legal Remedies in Parental Kidnapping Cases: A Collection of Materials. $15.

Representing Learning Disabled Children: A Manual for Attorneys. $10.

The Rights of Foster Parents. $6.

To find out more, write or phone:

ABA Center on Children and the Law
1800 M St., NW, Ste. 200, South Lobby
Washington, DC 20036
Phone: (202)331-2250 or *Fax:* (202)331-2220

▶ Academy of Family Mediators

Provides information on: *Divorce, Domestic Violence*

The Academy is devoted to professional and public education about mediation. It promotes mediation as an alternative in family and divorce disputes.

Information for a fee:

Mediation News. Quarterly. $20. Newsletter of the Academy of Family Mediators.

Mediation and Spouse Abuse. $21. Special issue of "Mediation Quarterly" exploring the use of mediation and domestic violence.

To find out more, write or phone:
Academy of Family Mediators
PO Box 10501
Eugene, OR 97440
Phone: (503)345-1205 or *Fax:* (503)345-4024

▶ American Association for Protecting Children (AAPC)

Provides information on: *Child Abuse, Domestic Violence, Sexual Abuse, Child Protection*

Individuals and agencies who seek to protect children from neglect and abuse are members of the Association. They work to increase effective and responsive community child protective services.

Information for free:

Child Abuse and Neglect: A Shared Community Concern. 1991. 32 pages.
Child Protection: The Role of the Courts. 1980. 73 pages.
The Role of Law Enforcement in the Prevention and Treatment of Child Abuse and Neglect. 1984. 69 pages.
Study of the National Incidence and Prevalence of Child Abuse and Neglect: Study Findings. 1988. 148 pages.

Information for a fee:

Adolescent Abuse/Neglect: Intervention Strategies. 1980. 68 pages. $6.80.
Child Abuse and Neglect Public Awareness Materials for Adults and Children. 1991. $7.
Child Fatalities Resulting From Abuse and Neglect: A Selected Annotated Bibliography. 1989. 41 pages. $4.
Early Childhood Programs and the Prevention and Treatment of Child Abuse and Neglect. 1979. 84 pages. $8.
Family Violence. 1980. 101 pages. $10.
Protecting Children. Quarterly. $25/year. Magazine covering programs, research, state activities, legislation, and conferences in the child welfare field.
National Incidence and Prevalence of Child Abuse and Neglect: 1988. Revised report. 1991. 158 pages. $16.50.
Responding to Child Neglect and Abuse. 1989. $3. Offers answers to common questions asked about child maltreatment.
Sexual Abuse of Children: Implications for Treatment. 1980. $7.50. Provides easily applied answers to common practice issues.
Treatment for Abused and Neglected Children. 1979. 86 pages. $8.60.

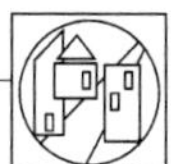

To find out more, write or phone:

American Association for Protecting Children
American Humane Association
63 Inverness Dr., E.
Englewood, CO 80112-5117
Toll-free: 1-800-2ASK-AHA or *Phone:* (303)792-9900 or *Fax:* (303)792-5333

▶ Believe the Children (BTC)

Provides information on: *Child Abuse, Family Law*

BTC seeks to heighten public and professional awareness of child abuse inflicted by people from outside the child's family. The group conducts research, distributes information, offers support to victimized families, and lobbies for criminal justice and professional support.

Information for free:

Believe the Children. Annual. Newsletter containing research studies and publication list.

Also publishes brochures.

To find out more, write or phone:

Believe the Children
Leslie Floberg, Pres.
PO Box 77
Hermosa Beach, CA 90254
Phone: (310)379-3514

▶ Canadian Council on Social Development (CCSD)

Provides information on: *Domestic Violence, Poverty, Victims, Employment, Homelessness, Step Families, Healthcare*

The Council is an independent, nonprofit organization that takes a look at social policies in the areas of health, poverty, housing, employment, and justice. It works to develop original programs that are responsive to current and future needs on social issues, especially the field of family violence. The Council serves the self-help community by providing current information and articles on events, resources, and groups.

Information for free:

A Guide to the Charter for Equality-Seeking Groups. 1987. 48 pages. Guidebook for individuals or groups working on equality issues.

Mental Health Assistance to Victims of Crime and Their Families. 1985. 72 pages. Report on the proceedings of the Crime Victims Trauma Conference, which focused on the emotional trauma of victimization and the mental health needs of victims.

Rights and Services for Crime Victims. 1981. 28 pages. General information on the needs, rights, and services for crime victims.

Social Development Publications Catalogue.

Information for a fee:

Crime Prevention Through Social Development: An Overview With Sources. 1984. 63 pages. $7. Examines examples of Canadian social programs that reduce violence by addressing the social causes of crime.

Employment and Social Development in a Changing Economy. 1986. 86 pages. $7. This publication looks at local economic initiatives and their potential to combat high rates of unemployment.

Homelessness in Canada: The Report of the National Inquiry. 1987. 16 pages. $2. Report summarizing a study of homelessness in Canada.

Organizing for the Homeless. 1989. 134 pages. $15. A resource to those interested in effectively organizing the homeless.

Perception. 4/year. $21/year, $5/single copy. A bilingual magazine that examines developments in the areas of income security, health, housing, social planning, legal aid, and education.

Self-Help in Canada. 1989. 175 pages. $15. Examines the state of development of self-help/mutual aid in Canada.

So You Want to Find a Job? 1987. 18 pages. $1. Booklet written for youth that provides tips on using employment services.

Stepmothers: Exploring the Myth—A Survival Guide to Stepfamilies. 1986. 145 pages. $10.95. A practical guide to the stepmother role and her relationships with stepchildren, the stepfather, and relatives.

Tapping the Untapped Potential: Towards a National Policy on Volunteerism. 1977. 75 pages. $4. Report on problems in developing voluntary resources.

Vis-a-Vis. 4/year. Included in $20 CCDS membership dues. Newsletter that explores developments in the field of family violence.

To find out more, write or phone:

Canadian Council on Social Development
55 Parkdale Ave.
Ottawa, ON, Canada K1Y 4G1
Phone: (613)728-1865 or *Fax:* (613)728-9387

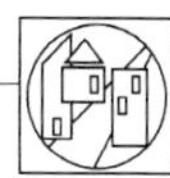

▶ Center for Early Adolescence (CEA)

Provides information on: *Latchkey Children, Youth, Parenting, Literacy, Sexuality, Teenage Pregnancy, Substance Abuse, Dropouts*

CEA is a national center dedicated to promoting the healthy growth and development of 10- to 15-year-olds. Staff members identify, observe, and document high-quality after-school programs for young adolescents. CEA focuses on many issues relating to adolescence including school improvement, literacy, responsive community services for young adolescents, parent education, leadership education, and health and sexuality. The Center attempts to strengthen prevention efforts to combat adolescent pregnancy, substance abuse, and school dropout problems, and assists schools and other organizations by providing staff development, program planning, individualized consultation, and other services.

Information for free:

Center for Early Adolescence Catalog. Talks about the Center and describes publications.

Information for a fee:

Adolescents in Need: An Approach for Helping Rural At-Risk Youth. 65 pages. $12.

After School: Young Adolescents on Their Own. 1986. 86 pages. $10. Report examines the policy implications of the latchkey issue and its effects on the early adolescent age group. Also discusses public policy initiatives for adolescent socialization, government policies that relate to adolescents, and possible options for the future.

Before It's Too Late: Dropout Prevention in the Middle Grades. 1988. 87 pp. $12. Explores how middle-grades schools can strengthen their holding power for drop-out prone youngsters.

Early Adolescence and Religion: A Status Study. 1982. $5. Reviews research on religious development, reports on successful programs for youth, and provides a resource list.

Early Adolescence: A Resource Directory. 1987. 58 pp. $7. Annual listing of organizations and journals that focus on early adolescent education, adolescent development, religion, family community, health, and sexuality.

Early Adolescence: What Parents Need to Know. 1982. 37 pp. $5. Answers questions regarding the physical, intellectual, and social development of young adolescents, and covers religion, discipline, and when parents need to worry.

Early Adolescent Sexuality: Resources for Professionals, Parents, and Young Adolescents. 1989. 58 pp. $7. Resource list of books films and videos, journals, curricula, pamphlets, and organizations that address AIDS, decision-making, homosexuality, menstruation, parent-teen communication, puberty, and pregnancy prevention.

Educating Young Adolescents: A Resource List. 27 pp. $7. Listing of books, articles, journals, and organizations for the educator.

A Portrait of Young Adolescents in the 1990s. $15.

Programs for Young Adolescents. 1986. 173 pages. $17. Covers planning, fundraising, publicity, inservice training, facilities, program evaluation, and staffing.

3:00 to 6:00 P.M.: Young Adolescents at Home and in the Community. 1982. 92 pages. $7. Essays on the need for services that respond to adolescents, including effective after school programs.

To find out more, write or phone:

Center for Early Adolescence
University of North Carolina at Chapel Hill
School of Medicine
D-2 Carr Mill Town Center
Carrboro, NC 27510
Phone: (919)966-1148 or *Fax:* (919)966-7657

▶ Center on the Family in America

Provides information on: *Marriage, Divorce*

Center on the Family in America researches family-related issues, including marriage and divorce, family wage, advocacy of child-bearing, and family policy and health. The Center publishes research results in its own publications, and in articles for publications with similar ideals and viewpoints.

Information for a fee:

Chronicles: A Magazine of American Culture. Monthly. $24/year.
The Family in America. Monthly. $21/year. Newsletter.
Religion and Society Report. Monthly. $24.

To find out more, write or phone:

Center on the Family in America
The Rockford Institute
934 N. Main St.
Rockford, IL 61103-7061
Phone: (815)964-5053 or *Fax:* (815)965-1826

▶ Center for Family Research

Provides information on: *Latchkey Children, Incest, Child Abuse, Divorce, Poverty, Senior Citizens*

The Center concentrates on the study of family issues, including divorce rates, working women, child abuse, incest, governmental family welfare programs, daycare, and elderly care.

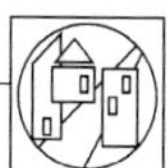

Information for free:
Research reports.

To find out more, write or phone:

Center for Family Research
University of Georgia
Institute for Behavioral Research
548 Boyd Graduate Studies Research Center
Athens, GA 30602
Phone: (706)542-1806

▶ Center for the Family in Transition

Provides information on: *Step Families, Divorce, Domestic Violence*

A nonprofit, clinical, educational and research center focusing on families in separation, divorce, and remarriage, including preventive interventions, high conflict, and violent families.

Information for free:
Center for the Family in Transition Resource List.

Information for a fee:
Offers over 60 reprints from previously published resources on the effects of divorce and separation on children for $4 each.

To find out more, write or phone:

Center for the Family in Transition
Bldg. B, Ste. 300
5725 Paradise Dr.
Corte Madera, CA 94925
Phone: (415)924-5750

▶ Center for the Study of Parental Acceptance and Rejection

Provides information on: *Child Abuse, Parenting*

The Center conducts comparative and interdisciplinary studies of the causes, consequences, and conditions of parental acceptance and rejection, including child abuse and neglect. It serves as an umbrella organization for independent research projects nationally and internationally, including those conducted in Czechoslovakia, Greece, Mexico, Puerto Rico, Egypt, U.S., Pakistan, Nigeria, India, Newfoundland, and Malaysia.

Information for free:
Parental Acceptance-Rejection Bibliography. 1992. 20 pages. Includes books, monographs, articles, directories, theses, and dissertations.

Information for a fee:
Handbook for the Study of Parental Acceptance and Rejection. 1990. 181 pages. $15. A book designed to facilitate research on parental acceptance-rejection.

To find out more, write or phone:
Center for the Study of Parental Acceptance and Rejection
University of Connecticut
Box U-158
Storrs, CT 06269-2158
Phone: (203)486-0073 or *Fax:* (203)486-4865

▶ Child Welfare League of America

Provides information on: *Child Abuse, Victims, Youth, Learning Disabled Students and Learning Disabilities, Teenage Pregnancy, Homelessness, Child Protection*

The League works to improve care and services for abused or neglected children, youth, and their families. They operate the Child Welfare League of America Children's Campaign, a grass roots network of people committed to acting on behalf of children. Other League activities include consultation, research, agency and community surveys, and a library and information service.

Information for free:
Child Welfare League of America Catalog. A listing of available standards, bibliographies, books, monographs, video resources, newsletters, and magazines.

Information for a fee:
Careless to Caring for Troubled Youth. 1983. 109 pages. $12.95. Describes what has gone wrong with the youth care system and what needs to be done to create change.
Courage to Care: Responding to the Crisis of Children with AIDS. 1990. 416 pages. $15.95 paperback. Reviews the implications of AIDS on individuals, families, and society, offering a range of care, services, training, education, and prevention strategies.
Facing Teenage Pregnancy: A Handbook for the Pregnant Teen. 1990. 123 pages. $12.95. Guides adolescents through the various options in dealing with pregnancy.
Homelessness: The Impact on Child Welfare in the '90s. 1991. $6.95. Report summarizing the importance of linking child welfare with housing service.
Independence: A Life Skills Guide for Teens. 1988. 96 pages. $14.95. Reviews topics to guide teenagers in their pursuit of responsible independence.

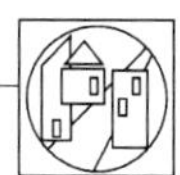

Serving Gay and Lesbian Youths: The Role of Child Welfare Agencies. 1991. $6.95.
Discusses barriers that child welfare agencies must overcome in order to meet the needs of this particular client group.

To find out more, write or phone:

Child Welfare League of America
440 1st St. NW, Ste. 310
Washington, DC 20001-2085
Phone: (202)638-2952 or *Fax:* (202)638-4004

▶ Children of the Night

Provides information on: *Runaways*

The purpose of Children of the Night is to provide protection and support for street children, usually runaways ages 8-17, who are involved in pornography or prostitution. It provides shelter, a 24 hour hotline, and a street outreach program. CN places street children with drug programs, counselors, and in independent living situations.

Information for free:

Children of the Night 1991 Statistics. 3 pages.
Children of the Night Newsletter. Monthly.
Also publishes articles and a brochure.

To find out more, write or phone:

Children of the Night
Dr. Lois Lee, Exec.Dir.
14530 Sylvan St.
Van Nuys, CA 91411
Phone: (818)908-4474 or *Fax:* (818)908-1468

▶ Children's Defense Fund

Provides information on: *Child Abuse, Education, Employment, Mental Health, Parenting, Teenage Pregnancy*

The Children's Defense Fund is involved in research, public education, assistance to state and local groups, and community organizing in areas of child welfare, child health, adolescent pregnancy prevention, child care and development, family services, and child mental health. It works with people and groups to change policies and practices resulting in neglect or maltreatment of children.

Information for a fee:

Adolescent and Young Adult Fact Book. Annual. $12.95.

CDF Child, Youth, and Family Futures Clearinghouse. Bimonthly. A monograph series of about 30 reports (most are $4.50) on aspects of the teen pregnancy problem and efforts to prevent it, and child poverty, health, and education.

The Health of America's Children: Maternal and Child Health Data Book. $12.95.

A Measure of Our Success: A Letter to My Children and Yours. $15. 24 questions and answers on how to raise children.

The State of America's Children. Annual. $12.95. Examines the status of America's children, youth, and families. It emphasizes the ways that advocates, communities, states, and the federal government can work together to improve maternal and child health, child care, child welfare, youth employment, education, housing, and more.

To find out more, write or phone:

Children's Defense Fund
122 C St., NW
Washington, DC 20001
Phone: (202)628-8787 or *Fax:* (202)783-7324

▶ Clearinghouse on Child Abuse and Neglect and Family Violence Information

Provides information on: *Child Abuse, Domestic Violence, Victims, Sexual Abuse*

The Clearinghouse provides information services to prevent child abuse and family violence and provides assistance to victims. It develops publications and services from its computerized databases of documents, audiovisuals, program directories, public awareness materials, and national organizations, as well as from many other resources. Information specialists are available to answer questions, make referrals, and suggest publications.

Information for free:

Child Abuse and Neglect: A Shared Community Concern. 1991. 32 pages.

Child Abuse Prevention, Adoption and Family Services Act of 1988. 1988. 13 pages. Text of Public Law 100-294.

Child Protection in Military Communities. 1980. 90 pages.

Child Protection: The Role of the Courts. 1980. 73 pages.

Child Sexual Abuse Prevention: Tips to Parents. Brochure.

National Center on Child Abuse and Neglect Catalog.

National Center on Child Abuse and Neglect Research Symposium on Child Neglect. 1989. 173 pages.

National Center on Child Abuse and Neglect Research Symposium on Child Sexual Abuse. 1989. 110 pages.

Preventing Child Abuse and Neglect: A Guide for Staff in Residential Institutions. 1980. 71 pages.
A Report to Congress: Joining Together to Fight Child Abuse. 1986. 50 pages.
The Role of Law Enforcement in the Prevention and Treatment of Child Abuse and Neglect. 1984. 69 pages.
Study of the National Incidence and Prevalence of Child Abuse and Neglect: Study Findings (Executive Summary and Final Report). 1988. 148 pages.
Supervising Child Protective Workers. 1979. 61 pages.

Information for a fee:
Adolescent Abuse/Neglect: Intervention Strategies. 1980. 68 pages. $6.80
Adolescent Maltreatment: Issues and Program Models. 1984. 116 pages. $11.60.
Adolescent Sex Offenders. $4.50. Bibliography.
Anti-social Behavior Resulting from Abuse. $3.50 Bibliography.
Child Abuse and Neglect Audiovisual Catalog. 1991. 60 pages. $6.
Child Abuse and Neglect Film and Video Catalog. 1991. 160 pages $16.
Characteristics of Abused Children. $4.50. Bibliography.
Characteristics of Abusive Parents. $5.50. Bibliography.
Child Fatalities Resulting from Abuse and Neglect: A Selected Annotated Bibliography. 1989. 41 pages. $4.
Emotional Maltreatment. $3.50. Bibliography.
Generational Cycle of Abuse. $2. Bibliography.
Organizations Concerned with Child Abuse and Neglect and Family Violence Issues. 1990. $5.50.
Runaway, Throwaway, and Homeless Children. $5. Bibliography of 1965-91 publications.

To find out more, write or phone:

Clearinghouse on Child Abuse and Neglect and Family Violence Information
U.S. Department of Health and Human Services
National Center on Child Abuse and Neglect
PO Box 1182
Washington, DC 20013
Toll-free: 1-800-394-3366 or *Phone:* (703)385-7565 or *Fax:* (703)385-3206

▶ Committee for Mother and Child Rights

Provides information on: *Divorce, Family Law, Child Custody*

Members of the Committee are people concerned about mother and child rights; many members are mothers who have lost custody, have been faced with contested custody of their children, or have other custody-related problems. The group works to help mothers and children who are going through the trauma of contested custody or who have been through it, or have custody but fear losing it. The Committee seeks to educate the public about the injustices that they believe can happen to mothers and children. It also aims to improve the status of mothers.

To find out more, write or phone:
Committee for Mother and Child Rights
Rte. 1, Box 256A
Clear Brook, VA 22624
Phone: (703)722-3652

▶ Dads Against Discrimination (DADS)

Provides information on: *Divorce*

DADS provides a forum for fathers to discuss family problems. It offers a shelter service for fathers who are restrained from their homes by court order. The organization produces programs for cable television, provides legal and medical referrals, and offers guidance in understanding laws on domestic relations.

To find out more, write or phone:
Dads Against Discrimination
Victor Smith, Pres.
PO Box 8525
Portland, OR 97207
Phone: (503)222-1111

▶ Denver Center for Marital and Family Studies

Provides information on: *Marriage, Parenting*

The Center analyzes marital and family relationships in various stages of development. These states include courtship, engagement, marriage, birth of children, child-rearing, children leaving home, and marriage in the later years. Individual studies concentrate on families at risk for psychopathology, and prevention of family problems. The Center provides training to clinical psychology graduate students, maintains a videotape library, and responds to questions regarding the Center's research.

To find out more, write or phone:

Denver Center for Marital and Family Studies
Dr. Howard J. Markman, Dir.
Department of Psychology
University of Denver
Denver, CO 80208
Toll-free: 1-800-366-0166 or *Phone:* (303)871-3829 or *Fax:* (303)871-4747

▶ Emerge: A Men's Counseling Service on Domestic Violence

Provides information on: *Domestic Violence, Counseling*

Emerge offers counseling for men who have abused a woman in a relationship. The group conducts training programs on counseling techniques, and serves as an information and telephone referral service. Emerge also offers a preventive education program for teenagers and young adults on issues of violence and abuse in their own relationships.

Information for a fee:

Men Unlearning Violence: A Group Approach Based on a Collective Model. 20-page article. $3. Examines negative male socialization and how this behavior can be changed.

Stages of Anti-Sexist Awareness and Change for Abusive Men. 30-page article. $3.50. Describes three stages of attitude and behavior change in abusive men. Includes interviews.

Violent and Controlling Behaviors Check-List. 1-page worksheet. $.10 each. Lists various abusive behaviors and serves as a self-analysis tool for men.

What You Should Know About Your Violent Husband. Pamphlet. $.25 each. Addresses common questions of battered women whose partners are in couseling.

Why do Men Batter Their Wives? 32-page article. $3.50. Contains testimonies of 18 abusers and examines patterns of behavior.

Emerge also offers a bibliography of writings on wife abuse, and additional articles, many under $5.

To find out more, write or phone:

Emerge: A Men's Counseling Service on Domestic Violence
18 Hurley St., Ste. 23
Cambridge, MA 02141
Phone: (617)422-1550

▶ Family Research Laboratory (FRL)

Provides information on: *Domestic Violence, Marital Rape, Incest, Child Abuse, Sexual Abuse, Pornography, Parental Kidnapping*

The Family Research Laboratory is dedicated to the study of all aspects of family violence. Areas of study include abuse of elderly family members, marital rape, parental abductions, characteristics of fathers who commit incest, physical and sexual abuse of children, and pornography. FRL is concerned with the interrelation of various types of family violence. The group carries out its research through national and local surveys, interviews, data analysis, and other methods.

Information for free:

Family Research Laboratory. Brochure. Explains the purpose of FRL, areas of interest, staff and facilities.

A three-part packet including bibliography, program description, and library recommendation form is also available.

Information for a fee:

The following research papers are a sample of the information available from FRL.

Alcohol Abuse and Family Violence. 1983. $1.

Child Abuse in Stepfamilies. 1984. $1.

Corporal Punishment, Child Abuse, and Wife Beating: What Do They Have in Common? 1983. $1.

The Cost of Family Violence: Preliminary Results From a National Survey. 1987. $.50.

Elder Abuse: Its Relationship to Other Forms of Domestic Violence. 1984. $1.

Psychological, Cultural and Family Factors in Incest and Family Sexual Abuse. 1978. $.50.

Rape in Marriage: A Sociological View. 1983. $1.

Resources, Power, and Husband-Wife Violence. 1980. $1.

Sexual Socialization in America: High Risk for Sexual Abuse. 1980. $.50.

Violence as a Strategy of the Weak Against the Strong: The Case of Siblings. 1988. $1.50.

To find out more, write or phone:

Family Research Laboratory
University of New Hampshire
126 Horton Social Science Center
Durham, NH 03824-3586
Phone: (603)862-1888 or *Fax:* (603)862-1122

▶ Fatherhood Project

Provides information on: *Parenting*

The Project is a research organization dedicated to examining the future of fatherhood and ways to support men's involvement in childrearing. The project serves as a clearinghouse, providing information on fatherhood-related topics and referral to resources for and about fathers. It conducts research on working fathers and the work/family dilemma as it affects men. It also conducts corporate-wide programs, and provides consultation.

Information for free:
Fact sheets outlining the project's mission and activities.

To find out more, write or phone:
Fatherhood Project
Families and Work Institute
330 Seventh Ave.
New York, NY 10001
Phone: (212)268-4846 or *Fax:* (212)465-8637

▶ Institute for Children, Youth, and Families

Provides information on: *Parenting, Teenage Pregnancy, Youth, Senior Citizens*

The Institute concentrates on family, child, and youth studies, including community support for positive youth development, social support program development for teenage parents and parents at risk for parent-child dysfunction, prevention of child abuse through early intervention with first-time parents, and consultation on family and human development issues. It assesses the impact of psychosocial, environmental, and nutritional aspects of the family on the quality of life of the elderly. The Institute maintains a collection of its own publications, papers, and reports.

Information for free:
Research reports.

To find out more, write or phone:
Institute for Children, Youth, and Families
Michigan State University
Pablucci Bldg. 2
East Lansing, MI 48824
Phone: (517)353-6617 or *Fax:* (517)336-2022

▶ International Child Resource Institute (ICRI)

Provides information on: *Latchkey Children, Child Abuse, Healthcare*

The Institute is a group of individuals interested in issues regarding day care for children, including health, abuse and neglect, and legal advocacy. It gathers information on techniques and practices involved in innovative forms of child care and child health, provides technical assistance to individuals, corporations, and government agencies that wish to establish and maintain day care centers. ICRI serves as a clearinghouse for information on children's issues.

Information for free:
Pamphlet describing ICRI and its services.

Information for a fee:
ICRI's World Child Report. Quarterly. Included in $25 membership fee. Newsletter covering international child care issues.

To find out more, write or phone:
International Child Resource Institute
1810 Hopkins
Berkeley, CA 94707
Phone: (510)644-1000 or *Fax:* (510)525-4106

▶ Joint Custody Association

Provides information on: *Divorce, Child Custody*

Psychologists, psychiatrists, physicians, social workers, marital and family counselors, concerned parents, and others concerned with joint custody of children and related divorce issues form the Association. It offers information on joint custody for the children of divorce, surveys court decisions and their consequences, and assists children, parents, attorneys, counselors, and jurists with implementation of joint custody practices. The Association maintains bibliographical archives of joint custody and other materials.

To find out more, write or phone:
Joint Custody Association
10606 Wilkins Ave.
Los Angeles, CA 90024
Phone: (310)475-5352

▶ C. Henry Kempe National Center for the Prevention and Treatment of Child Abuse and Neglect

Provides information on: *Child Abuse, Foster Families, Parenting*

The Kempe Center provides a resource for training, consultation, program development, evaluation, and research in all forms of child abuse and neglect. It offers a therapeutic preschool, a statewide outreach program, and a communication link for those working with pre-school-aged abused children.

Information for a fee:

Child Abuse and Neglect: Cross-Cultural Perspectives. 1981. 217 pages. $16. Examines child-raising practices and child maltreatment in the context of nine different cultures around the world.

The Layperson's Role in the Prevention and Treatment of Child Abuse and Neglect. Written for and by the layperson working with abusive or neglecting families. Covers treatment methods, foster parenting, child care work, and the involvement of support staff.

Recognizing Child Abuse: A Guide for the Concerned. 1990. 270 pages. $16. Addresses child abuse issues including intervention in child protection efforts.

Think Twice: The Medical Effects of Physical Punishment. 1985. 60 pages. $8.50. Describes forms of physical punishment and its physical effects, complete with medical illustrations. Includes case studies, and disciplinary and child-raising alternatives for corporal punishment.

To find out more, write or phone:

C. Henry Kempe National Center for the Prevention and Treatment of Child Abuse and Neglect
University of Colorado Health Sciences Center
Department of Pediatrics
1205 Oneida
Denver, CO 80220-2944
Phone: (303)321-3963 or *Fax:* (303)329-3523

▶ Mothers Without Custody

Provides information on: *Child Custody, Parental Kidnapping, Single Parents, Divorce, Self-Help Groups*

The organization provides support to women living apart from one or more of their minor children for any reason, including court decisions, exchange of custody with an ex-spouse, intervention by a state agency, or childnapping by an ex-spouse. The group provides support to women currently exploring their child custody options during and after divorce. It helps establish local self-help groups and organize social events for mothers alone and mothers visiting their children.

Information for a fee:

Mother-to-Mother. Bimonthly. $20/year. Newsletter.

To find out more, write or phone:
Mothers Without Custody
Jennifer Isham, Pres.
PO Box 27418
Houston, TX 77256
Phone: (713)840-1622

▶ National Assault Prevention Center

Provides information on: *Domestic Violence, Learning Disabled Students and Learning Disabilities*

The Center's purpose is to prevent violence against vulnerable populations through education, prevention training, and research. It conducts research on the causes, consequences, and prevention of interpersonal violence. The Center also provides services to children aged two and one half years through adolescence, children and adults with mental retardation and developmental disabilities, and older citizens.

Information for a fee:
Increasing Safety for People Receiving Mental Health Services. $22.95.
Patient Assault Prevention Escape Training in a State Psychiatric Institute.
Planning to Prevent Abuse. $.60.
Preventing Assaults Against Older Adults. $2.
Strategies for Free Children. $21.25.
Technical Assistance Bulletin. $2.

To find out more, write or phone:
National Assault Prevention Center
PO Box 02005
Columbus, OH 43202
Phone: (614)291-2540

▶ National Center for Missing and Exploited Children (NCMEC)

Provides information on: *Runaways, Missing Children, Parental Kidnapping, Sexual Abuse, Child Protection*

The Center aids parents and law enforcement agencies in preventing child exploitation and in locating missing children. It serves as a national clearinghouse of information on effective state and federal legislation directed at the protection of children. NCMEC provides technical assistance to individuals, parents, groups, agencies, and state and local governments involved in locating and returning children

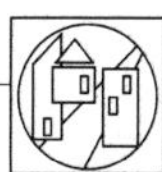

and in cases of child exploitation through cooperation with the Adam Walsh Child Resource Center.

Information for free:

The following brochures are available up to 50 copies each.

Child Protection. Prevention information for parents and children.

Just in Case.Parental Guidelines in Case You Need a Babysitter.

KIDS AND COMPANY: Together for Safety. A brochure that provides children with skills and information necessary to help prevent abduction and abuse.

National Center for Missing and Exploited Children. A general information brochure that contains a list of all NCMEC publications, and information on the missing and exploited child issue.

Single copies of the following books are available free of charge.

Children Traumatized in Sex Rings. 56 pages. Offers an overview of child sexual abuse and exploitation, and descriptions of different kinds of sex rings.

Parental Kidnapping. 90 pages. Explains laws, outlines prevention methods, and provides suggestions for care following abductions.

Youth at Risk. 56 pages. Examines the profiles of runaways, explores directions for system reform, and offers prevention measures.

To find out more, write or phone:

National Center for Missing and Exploited Children
2101 Wilson Blvd., Ste. 550
Arlington, VA 22201-3052
Toll-free: 1-800-843-5678 or *Phone:* (703)235-3900 or *Fax:* (703)235-4067

▶ National Center on Women and Family Law

Provides information on: *Poverty, Domestic Violence, Family Law, Child Custody, Rape, Sexual Harassment and Discrimination, Sexual Abuse*

The Center provides assistance to lawyers and women's advocates to help them deal more effectively with the legal problems of poor women and children. Efforts are focused on such problems as family violence, child custody, sex discrimination, and rape.

Information for free:

Battered Women's Resource List. A complete list of the Center's materials on battered women.

Child Custody Cover Sheet and Child Sexual Abuse Resource List. A complete listing of all the Center's materials with respect to custody.

Child Support Cover Sheet. A complete list of the Center's materials with respect to child support.

Publications of the National Center on Women and Family Law, Inc.

Information for a fee:
Battered Women: The Facts. $20.
Child Custody Resource List. $5.
Child Support Resource List. $5.
Custody, Visitation and Child Support. $10.
Disabled Battered Women. $7.
The Effect of Women Abuse on Children: Psychology and Legal Authority. 140 pp. $25. Addresses the idea that physical abuse of the mother has severe developmental, emotional, social and intellectual effects on the child and that battery should be a determinative factor in child custody decisions.
Resources on Gender Bias in the Courts. $1.
Woman Battering: A Major Cause of Homelessness. $3.

To find out more, write or phone:
National Center on Women and Family Law
799 Broadway, Rm. 402
New York, NY 10003
Phone: (212)674-8200 or *Fax:* (212)533-5104

▶ National Coalition Against Domestic Violence (NCADV)

Provides information on: *Domestic Violence*

NCADV is a grass roots coalition of battered women's service organizations and shelters working to help battered women and their children. Supplies technical assistance and makes referrals on issues of domestic violence.

Information for a fee:
A Current Analysis of the Battered Women's Movement. 1992. $8.
Domestic Violence Awareness Month Packet. 1992. $15.
1991 National Directory of Domestic Violence Programs. $25.
NCADV Update. Included in $20 membership fee, $5 for youth. An information bulletin.
NCADV Voice. Quarterly. Included in $20 membership fee, $5 for youth. Newsletter.
Rural Resource Packet. $10.

To find out more, write or phone:
National Coalition Against Domestic Violence
PO Box 34103
Washington, DC 20043-4103
Phone: (202)638-6388

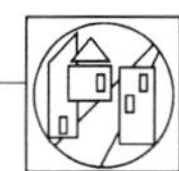

▶ National Council on Family Relations Family Resources Database

Provides information on: *Marriage, Teenage Pregnancy, Rape*

The Council accesses the Family Resources Database to find references to resource centers on marriage and the family. It also provides expert banks, curriculum, research, technical assistance, online search services, audiovisual, educational documents index, educational documents abstracts, and referrals. The resources available include reports, speeches, curriculum materials, newsletters, directories, fact sheets, and monographs.

Information for a fee:

2001: Preparing Families for the Future. 1990. 41 pages $8. Principal trends, theoretical research, program suggestions, and public policy concerns by family experts on family issues.

Contemporary Families: Looking Forward, Looking Back. 1991. 481 pages. $23.95. A decade's worth of research on families with forecast trends.

Families in Rural America: Stress, Adaptation and Revitalization. 1988. 297 pages. $18.50. Describes hardships faced by rural American families, their coping strategies and resources for their support.

Family Relations: Adolescent Pregnancy and Parenting. 1991. 120 pages. $17.00. Special journal issue that examines interventions, evaluations, and needs. Considers adoption, social support, and stress for pregnant adolescents.

Family Relations: Courtship Aggression. 1991. 120 pages. $17. Special journal issue. Topics include acquaintance rape within the college social scene, assessing the contribution of fraternity membership in sexual coercion and aggression, adult attachment patterns, and courtship violence.

To find out more, write or phone:

National Council on Family Relations
Family Resources Database
3989 Central Ave., NE, Ste. 550
Minneapolis, MN 55421
Phone: (612)781-9331 or *Fax:* (612)781-9348

▶ National Network of Runaway and Youth Services

Provides information on: *Homelessness, Runaways, Youth, AIDS, Substance Abuse, Alcoholism*

The National Network of Runaway and Youth Services is made up of human service agencies, programs, and coalitions dealing with the concerns of runaway, homeless, and other at-risk youth. The Network promotes development of responsive local services for youth and families, acts as an information clearinghouse, and sponsors educational programs for policymakers and the public. It also maintains the National Fund for Runaway Children to increase public awareness of the situation American runaway youths face and to encourage state and local governments, private agencies, and private citizens to address and work to solve these problems. The Network operates Safe Choices Project, an AIDS/HIV education and prevention project, and Youth-Reaching-Youth, a substance abuse prevention project.

Information for a fee:

Alcohol and Other Drug Use Among Runaway, Homeless, and Other Youth in High-Risk Situations: Strategies for Prevention, Intervention and Treatment. 1992. Report. $10.

Doing What We Do Best: A Guide to Replication of an Independent Living Project. 1986. Report. $4.

Helping Them Do Their Best: A Guide to Using Volunteers in Runaway Centers. 1986. $4.

Network News. Quarterly. $25/year. Provides updates on youth issues, a column written by youth, and a resource listing.

Policy Reporter. 8 issues/year. $25/year. Reports on legislative issues and court decisions that impact services to youth.

Sounds From the Streets: A Collection of Poems, Stories, and Art Work. 1991. $10.

To Whom Do They Belong? Homeless, Runaway and Other Youth in High-Risk Situations in the 1990s. 1991. $10. Report containing information about runaway and homeless youth.

A series of seven fact sheets containing information on the National Network and youth in high-risk situations are also available for under $5.

To find out more, write or phone:

National Network of Runaway and Youth Services
1319 F St. NW, Ste. 401
Washington, DC 20004
Phone: (202)783-7949 or *Fax:* (202)289-1933

▶ National Organization for Men

Provides information on: *Divorce, Family Law*

The Organization is made up of people interested in having "antiquated divorce and alimony laws changed." The group believes in adequate child support with both parents contributing and equal visitation and responsibility for each parent, and supports a standard and uniform divorce code in every state. It maintains extensive files of pertinent material, newspapers, and periodicals, and provides personal assistance to those involved in marital difficulties.

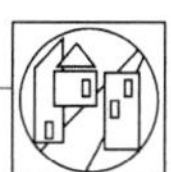

Information for a fee:
Newsletter. Monthly. $25.

To find out more, write or phone:
National Organization for Men
11 Park Pl., Ste. 1116
New York, NY 10007
Phone: (212)766-4030

▶ National Resource Center on Child Sexual Abuse

Provides information on: *Incest, Sexual Abuse, Child Protection*

The Center is an information, training, and technical assistance unit of the National Center on Child Abuse and Neglect and the Children's Bureau designed to advance knowledge and improve skills in investigating and managing child sexual abuse cases. Activities of the Center include offering a toll-free information service and sponsoring training sessions that explore practical methods of investigating, managing, treating, and prosecuting child sexual abuse cases.

Information for a fee:
The Center publishes reports, magazines, and bibliographies, including the following:
Building Blocks. $12.00. A history of the National Children's Advocacy Center and explanation of their current procedures in cases of child sexual and physical abuse.
Child Protective Services: A System in Crisis. $12.00. A report examining child protective service systems, including national standards for services, and legislative and policy reform.
Enhancing Child Sexual Abuse Services to Minority Cultures. $12.00. Looks at child welfare issues in minority communities.
A Judicial Response to Child Sexual Abuse. $12.00. Examines judicial authority in child abuse cases.
On Adult Female Perpetrators of Child Sexual Abuse. $2.00.
On Child Sexual Abuse and Spirituality. $2.00.
On Children as Witnesses (from legal sources). $2.00.
On the Effects of Sexual Abuse on Children. $2.00.
On Examinations for Possible Child Sexual Abuse. $2.00.

To find out more, write or phone:
National Resource Center on Child Sexual Abuse
107 Lincoln St.
Huntsville, AL 35801
Toll-free: 1-800-543-7006 or *Phone:* (205)534-6868 or *Fax:* (205)534-6883

▶ National Runaway Switchboard (NRS)

Provides information on: *Runaways*

The Switchboard is a confidential, 24-hour, toll-free national switchboard for runaways, families of runaways, and other troubled youth. NRS provides names, addresses, and phone numbers of centers for shelter and other social services across the country, including counseling centers, referral lines, drug treatment facilities, and family planning services. Messages between young people and their families can be set up if desired, as can conferences between youths and parents or agencies.

Information for free:
FrontLine. Quarterly. Newsletter containing statistical data and reports on activities. Also publishes free brochures.

To find out more, write or phone:
National Runaway Switchboard
3080 N. Lincoln Ave.
Chicago, IL 60657
Toll-free: 1-800-621-4000 or *Phone:* (312)880-9860

▶ Parents' Choice Foundation

Provides information on: *Parenting, Consumer Affairs*

The Foundation provides parents and professionals with a source of information about the videos, books, toys, games, music, television programs, movies, and computer software selections made by parents, children, teachers, librarians, and other professionals.

Information for free:
What Kids Who Don't Like to Read Like to Read.

Information for a fee:
Parents' Choice. Quarterly. $18/year.

To find out more, write or phone:
Parents' Choice Foundation
Diana Huss Green, Editor-in-Chief
PO Box 185
Newton, MA 02168
Phone: (617)965-5913 or *Fax:* (617)963-4516

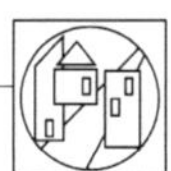

▶ Parents of Down Syndrome Children

Provides information on: *Parenting, Learning Disabled Students and Learning Disabilities*

Activities of the association include formal and informal meetings, parent-to-parent counseling between parents of children with Down Syndrome. The group works to contact new parents of Down Syndrome children to offer support and information on community resources, provide information on doctors, hospitals, and professionals, and promote membership in the Association for Retarded Citizens.

Information for a fee:
Parent Information Kit. $1.50.

To find out more, write or phone:
Parents of Down Syndrome Children
c/o Montgomery Co. Association for Retarded Citizens
11600 Nebel St.
Rockville, MD 20852
Phone: (301)984-5792

▶ Parents of Murdered Children

Provides information on: *Self-Help Groups, Parenting, Criminal Justice, Death and Dying*

Parents of Murdered Children is a self-help organization of parents whose children have been murdered and for relatives of homicide victims. It offers support and friendship to parents who have experienced the violent death of a son or daughter, and to others who have experienced the violent death of a family member. The group works to heighten society's awareness of the problems faced by those who survive a homicide victim and provides information about the grieving process and the criminal justice system as it pertains to survivors of a homicide victim. It also distributes literature and provides guest speakers.

Information for a fee:
Survivors. 3/year. $10. Newsletter that includes a schedule of parole hearings for prisoners serving homicide sentences.

To find out more, write or phone:
Parents of Murdered Children
100 E. 8th St., B-41
Cincinnati, OH 45202
Phone: (513)721-5683

▶ Parents United

Provides information on: *Incest, Sexual Abuse, Counseling*

Parents United is an organization of individuals and families who have experienced child sexual molestation. PU provides assistance to families affected by incest and other types of child sexual abuse by providing crisis and long-term support. PU also provides weekly counseling and conducts self-help therapy groups, and promotes self-awareness and responsibility to self, family, and community. The group compiles information and arranges medical, vocational, and legal counseling for families.

Information for a fee:
The Pun. Quarterly. $8/year. Newsletter.

To find out more, write or phone:
Parents United
Henry Giarretto Ph.D., Exec.Dir.
c/o Institute for Community as Extended Family
232 E. Gish Rd.
San Jose, CA 95112
Phone: (408)453-7616 or *Fax:* (408)280-6368

▶ Parents Without Partners (PWP)

Provides information on: *Single Parents, Self-Help Groups, Divorce, Death and Dying, Child Custody*

PWP promotes the study of and helps with the parenting problems of single parents in relation to the welfare and upbringing of their children. The group participates in research of single parent topics and operates the Single Parent Clearinghouse. It maintains a library on divorce, death, single parenting, custody, and related topics.

Information for free:
Information packet of brochures, manuals, etc; free with a self-addressed, stamped envelope.

Information for a fee:
The Single Parent. Bimonthly. $3/single copy, $15/year.

To find out more, write or phone:
Parents Without Partners
8807 Colesville Rd.
Silver Spring, MD 20910
Toll-free: 1-800-637-7974 or *Phone:* (301)588-9354 or *Fax:* (301)588-9216

▶ Runaway Hotline

Provides information on: *Runaways*

The Runaway Hotline is a 24-hour, toll-free national hot line for runaways. It serves as a means for runaways to contact their parents or relatives to let them know they are safe and well, without the risk of having their location revealed. No attempt is made to discover the location of the caller, and no information is given to relatives other than that which the caller wishes. The Hotline maintains a referral service for callers in need of shelter, counseling, medical help, legal assistance, transportation, or related services. The Hotline also compiles statistics.

Information for free:

Runaways. Brochure. Explains history of the Hotline, how it works, and services it provides.

Youth at Risk. 1986. Excerpt from a report profiling runaways, their family situations, and characteristics of potential runaways.

The Hotline also provides fact sheets containing statistics and a bibliography of books and articles about runaways.

To find out more, write or phone:

Runaway Hotline
Jill Gardner, Dir.
Governor's Office
PO Box 12428
Austin, TX 78711
Toll-free: 1-800-231-6946 or *Phone:* (512)463-1980

▶ Search Institute

Provides information on: *Parenting, Teenage Pregnancy, Youth, Sexuality, Senior Citizens*

The Search Institute concentrates on the social welfare of children, adolescents, families, and the elderly, including their needs, concerns, values, and beliefs. It studies schools, churches, youth-serving organizations, religious beliefs and behaviors, prevention of adolescent chemical abuse, peer pressure, limited resources of the elderly, parents coping with the stress of work and home, parent-child communications on sexuality, adult influence on youth, and teen pregnancy.

Information for free:

Source. Quarterly. Tells when reports will be released.

Information for a fee:
Research reports are available; costs range from $5 to $20.

To find out more, write or phone:

Search Institute
122 W. Franklin Ave., Ste. 525
Minneapolis, MN 55404-9990
Phone: (612)870-9511 or *Fax:* (612)870-4602

▶ Single Mothers By Choice (SMC)

Provides information on: *Single Parents, Adoption*

SMC is a group primarily made up of single professional women in their 30s and 40s who have either decided to, have, or are considering having children outside of marriage and women who are considering adoption as single parents (does not include mothers who are widowed or divorced). SMC provides support for single mothers, and offers information to women who choose to be single parents.

Information for a fee:
Highlights of the Newsletter. $10. A compilation of newsletters.
SMC Newsletter. Quarterly. $20/year.
Also publishes an SMC brochure and a list of newsletter back issues.

To find out more, write or phone:

Single Mothers By Choice
Jane Mattes, Chairperson
PO Box 1642, Gracie Square Sta.
New York, NY 10028
Phone: (212)988-0993

▶ Society's League Against Molestation (SLAM)

Provides information on: *Child Abuse, Sexual Abuse*

The League works to prevent sexual abuse and exploitation of children. SLAM counsels and assists victims and their families, researches the social, psychological, and legal aspects of child molestation, and monitors court cases and verdicts. It also offers tips for prevention and awareness of child molestation.

Information for free:
Offers brochures, fact sheets, and coloring books.

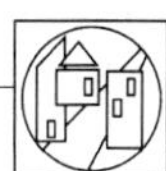

To find out more, write or phone:

Society's League Against Molestation
Joan McKenna, Dir.
c/o Women Against Rape/Childwatch
PO Box 346
Collingswood, NJ 08108
Phone: (609)858-7800 or *Fax:* (609)858-7063

▶ Stepfamily Foundation, Inc.

Provides information on: *Step Families, Divorce*

The Foundation works with such situations as stepfamilies, divorce, and counseling of stepfamilies, including remarital adjustment of stepmothers. Its purpose is to create awareness of the patterns and problems of stepfamilies, to educate and counsel those who live in a step relationship, and to act as a clearinghouse of information.

Information for free:

How We Work at the Stepfamily Foundation. Fact sheet. Explains step relationships and the counseling methods used by the Foundation.

Resources. Brochure. A guide to available literature, books, audiotapes, and videotapes.

The Step Family Foundation. Brochure. Explains the Foundation's purpose, cites statistics, and contains membership information.

Information for a fee:

Living in Step. $8. A book acknowledging step relationships "as having their own dynamics requiring unique care and solutions to make them work."

Stepparenting. $3. Contains techniques and tools developed from many years of counseling.

To find out more, write or phone:

Stepfamily Foundation, Inc.
333 West End Ave.
New York, NY 10023
Phone: (212)877-3244 or *Fax:* (212)362-7030

▶ Unwed Parents Anonymous (UPA)

Provides information on: *Single Parents, Self-Help Groups*

UPA is a support group based on the Twelve Steps and Twelve Traditions of Alcoholics Anonymous World Services. The group provides spiritual and emotional support for unwed parents during and after the pregnancy. UPA offers guidance in making the decision to keep a baby or to place a child in an adoptive home. It provides information and advice about relationships, child care, dating problems, finances, housing, child rearing, and other issues affecting parent and child.

Information for a fee:
Brochures available for $5.75 per 25. Titles include:
Advice to Grandparents;
Dating Guidelines from Unwed Mothers;
One Date at a Time!;
Should I Keep or Relinguish My Baby?;
Unwed Fathers;
Unwed Parents Anonymous;
UPA Twelve Steps and Twelve Traditions.
Not Again—Avoiding a Second Out-of-Wedlock Pregnancy. $2. Booklet.

To find out more, write or phone:
Unwed Parents Anonymous
Margot Sheahan, Exec. Officer
PO Box 44556
Phoenix, AZ 85064
Phone: (602)952-1463

▶ Women on Their Own (WOTO)

Provides information on: *Single Parents, Self-Help Groups*

An association of single, divorced, separated, or widowed women raising children on their own, the group links participants together to help each other and offer support and advocacy.

Information for a fee:
Networking Directory. Included in $15 membership dues.
WOTO Works. Quarterly newsletter. Included in $15 membership dues. Will send a complimentary copy upon request.
Also publishes a brochure.

To find out more, write or phone:
Women on Their Own
PO Box 1026
Willingboro, NJ 08046
Phone: (609)871-1499

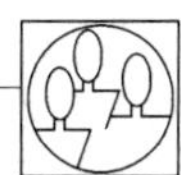

To Contact People . . .

These books identify individual experts or organizations that can direct you to one.

▶ *Canadian Who's Who*

This book lists about 12,000 notable Canadians in Canada and abroad based on position or achievement. Entries include name, address, personal and career data.
Annual. University of Toronto Press.

▶ *Child Welfare League of America Directory of Member Agencies*

Use this directory to contact members and associates of the Child Welfare League of America. Entries include agency name, address, phone number, name of executive director, list of services, and whether public or voluntary. Information is arranged geographically, then alphabetically.
Semiannual. ABC-CLIO.

▶ *Family Service America Directory of Member Agencies*

Use this directory to contact more than 290 accredited, provisional, and affiliated member agencies in the U.S. and Canada. Entries include agency name, address, phone, name of executive director, geographic territory covered, and services provided. Agencies are arranged in geographical order.
Annual. Family Service America.

▶ *International Who's Who*

This book covers 20,000 prominent persons worldwide. Entries include name, nationality, personal and career information, honors, awards, writings, address, and phone. Names are arranged alphabetically.
Annual. Europa Publications Ltd.

▶ *National Directory of Child Abuse Prosecutors*

This directory provides contact information for more than 800 prosecutors and district attorneys specializing in child abuse cases. Entries include district attorney name, assistant district attorney name, address, phone, and jurisdiction size. Information is arranged in geographical order.
1989. National Center for Prosecution of Child Abuse.

▶ *North American Directory of Programs for Runaways, Homeless Youth and Missing Children*

The directory covers over 450 organizations offering programs or providing resources for youth workers and other professionals concerned with either runaway or homeless teenagers or missing children. Entries include organization name, address, phone, telex, name and title of contact, names and titles of key personnel, geographical area served, financial data, description of services. Arrangement of book is geographical.
Biennial. American Youth Work Center.

▶ *Parental Kidnapping: An International Resource Directory*

This directory can be used to contact about 45 government agencies, missing child organizations, and other groups concerned with the kidnapping of children by their parents. The book lists organization name, address, and name and title of contact. Entries are arranged alphabetically.
Annual. Rainbow Books.

▶ *Programs to Strengthen Families: A Resource Guide*

Use this guide to identify more than 60 family support programs providing a variety of service models for working with families of varied economic and ethnic backgrounds in different geographic (urban, rural, etc.) settings. The guide covers parent education, prevention of child abuse and neglect, day care, neighborhood-based self-help and information support programs, statewide initiatives, and others. Entries include organization name, address, phone, program name, description, goals, history, community served, services, participants, staff, evaluation (by program or independent evaluator), source of funding, and materials available. Information is classified by type of program.
1992. Family Resource Coalition.

▶ *Register of Marriage & Family Therapy Providers*

Use this book to contact 12,000 members of the American Association for Marriage and Family Therapy. Coverage includes the United States and Canada, plus national and international affiliates. Entries include name, office address, phone, and highest degree held. Information is arranged in both alphabetical and geographical lists.
Biennial. American Association for Marriage and Family Therapy.

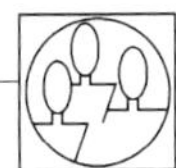

▶ *Solo Parenting: Your Essential Guide*

This guide contains a list of resources intended to aid the single parent.

1990. Penguin USA.

▶ *Who to Call: The Parent's Source Book*

Turn to the publication for information covering organizations, services, and other sources in the U.S. and Canada for agencies and personnel that deal with the recreational, educational, social, medical, psychological, and other needs of children, single parent groups, and adoption agencies. Entries include organization or agency name, address, phone, and description of services.

1992. William Morrow & Co., Inc.

▶ *Who's Who in America*

This book contains information on 79,000 people, primarily in the U.S., considered to be of current national interest because of achievement or position. Entries include name, address, personal data, career data, memberships, special achievements, and publications. Names are listed alphabetically; a separate volume indexes people by profession and location.

Biennial. Updated quarterly. Marquis Who's Who.

▶ *Who's Who of American Women*

This book contains information on more than 30,000 high-profile women in all fields. Entries include name, address, personal, educational, and career data, professional association membership, special achievements, awards, and writings. Names are arranged alphabetically.

Biennial. Marquis Who's Who.

▶ *Who's Who in the World*

This directory covers more than 31,000 people of current international interest because of their achievement or position. Entries include name, address, biographical data, civic activities, awards, writings, and other information. Names are arranged alphabetically.

Biennial. Marquis Who's Who.

3

History and Heritage

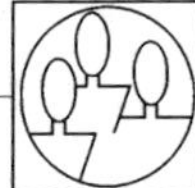

▶ Chapter 3 covers these topics:

Africa
African Americans
Apartheid
Asian Americans
Bilingual/Multilingual Education
Central America
Commonwealth of Independent States
Countries
Eastern Europe
Embassies
Ethnic Americans
Hispanic Americans
Immigration and Naturalization
International Development
International Relief
Middle East
Native Americans
Political Prisoners
Popular Culture
Refugees and Illegal Aliens
South America
Southeast Asia
State Tourism
Western Europe
World Affairs
World Regions

▶ Related topics appear in chapters on:

Beliefs, Cults, and Sects; Education; Government and Public Affairs

▶ Ideas for research topics:

African Symbolism in America
Alcoholism and Drug Abuse on American Indian Reservations
Asian Americans—The "Successful" Immigrants?
The Changing Status of African Americans in America
A Comparison of the Experiences of Cuban, Haitian, and Southeast Asian Refugee Immigrants
Events Leading to the Commonwealth of Independent States
The Effectiveness of Boycotts of American Companies in South Africa

▶ Ideas for research topics (continued):

Famine Aid—Programs with Lasting Success
Governmental Efforts to Improve the Status of American Indians
The Gulf War—Is It Really Over?
Has U.S. Immigration Reform Stemmed the Tide of Illegal Aliens?
How Much Has Legalized Gambling Helped Raised Income Levels on Indian Reservations?
The Impact of Bilingual Education on Dropout Rates
Legal Rights of Illegal Aliens
The Legalization of Peyote and Other Ritual Drugs on Indian Reservations
The Legend of Martin Luther King, Jr.
The Meaning of Affirmative Action
Minorities in Government
NAACP Efforts in Removing Racial Prejudice in American Institutions
Negative Stereotypes of Refugees
Not a Minority Anymore: Hispanics in America
POW/MIAs and Their Families
Protecting American Indian Lands and Resources
Racial Discrimination in the Workplace
Racial Violence
The Role of Schools in Cultural Awareness
Should English Be the Official U.S. Language?
Should Third World Development Repeat the History of Industrialization in North America and Europe?
Strong Ethnic Identity or Ethnocentrism?
The UN's International Pressure to End Apartheid
A United Europe: Arguments For and Against
U.S. Foreign Policy Goals after the Demise of the Soviet Union
What Happened to the Great Society?
What Is the Government Hiding about POW/MIAs and the Vietnam War?

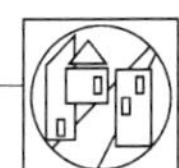

To Contact Organizations . . .

▶ ACCESS: A Security Information Service

Provides information on: *World Affairs, Terrorism, Commonwealth of Independent States*

ACCESS gathers and distributes information on international security and peace issues such as arms control, regional conflicts, and military spending. ACCESS responds to specific questions on a broad range of security issues and provides information and referrals on such topics as U.S. and the former Soviet Union defense budgets, peace studies programs in U.S. colleges and universities, and the value of Russian arms transfers to other countries.

Information for a fee:

The ACCESS Guide to the Persian Gulf Crisis. 1991. 60 pages. $7.50. A guide to background, resources, information, and organizations on the Persian Gulf crisis. Includes map, timeline of events, and issues for discussion.

The Access Resource Guide: An International Directory of Information on War, Peace, and Security. 1988. 238 pages. $14.95. Directory of over 650 sources of information and analysis, nationwide and worldwide.

One Nation Becomes Many: The ACCESS Guide to the Former Soviet Union. 1992. 126 pages. $17.95. A guide to the new nations formed by the dissolution of the Soviet Union. Includes maps, a timeline of key events, and issues for discussion.

Peace Research in Western Europe: A Directory Guide. 1989. $4. Directory reports staffing and programs of 81 peace research institutes in 15 West European countries.

Resource Brief. 8/year. $3. One page summary of timely subjects like terrorism or chemical and biological weapons. Includes survey of available resources.

Security Spectrum. 2-3/year. $5. Four-page overview of the major positions in the U.S. debate on a controversial subject like the Middle East, treaty compliance, or U.S. foreign policy.

To find out more, write or phone:

ACCESS: A Security Information Service
1730 M St., NW, Ste. 605
Washington, DC 20036
Phone: (202)785-6630 or *Fax:* (202)223-2737

▶ Alabama Bureau of Tourism and Travel

Provides information on: *Travel and Recreation, State Tourism*

The Bureau provides information on Alabama points of interest, including state parks, national landmarks and forests within the state, and cultural centers located within major cities. The Bureau will also provide general travel and tourism information, including hotel and motel lists, maps, general economic information, and major resort/activity brochures.

To find out more, write or phone:

Alabama Bureau of Tourism and Travel
532 S. Perry St.
Montgomery, AL 36104
Toll-free: 1-800-ALA-BAMA or *Phone:* (205)261-4169 or *Fax:* (205)264-7060

▶ Alaska Division of Tourism

Provides information on: *Travel and Recreation, State Tourism*

The Division provides information on state points of interest, including state parks; national wildlife refuges, forests, and parks within the state; and cultural centers located within major cities. The Division will also provide general travel and tourism information, including hotel and motel lists, maps, general economic information, and major resort/activity brochures.

To find out more, write or phone:

Alaska Division of Tourism
PO Box E
Juneau, AK 99811-0800
Phone: (907)465-2010 or *Fax:* (907)586-8399

▶ Alaska Federation of Natives (AFN)

Provides information on: *Native Americans*

Alaska Federation of Natives serves as an advocate for Alaskan Eskimos, Indians, and Aleuts before Congress, the Alaska state legislature, and other federal and state agencies.

Information for free:

AFN Newsletter. Quarterly. Includes president's report, information on winners of awards, and convention schedule.
Annual Report.

To find out more, write or phone:

Alaska Federation of Natives
1577 C St., Ste. 100
Anchorage, AK 99501
Phone: (907)274-3611

▶ American-Arab Anti-Discrimination Committee

Provides information on: *Ethnic Americans, Civil Rights and Liberties*

The Committee is a grass roots organization representing Arab-Americans. The Committee seeks to protect the rights of people of Arab descent, promote and defend the Arab-American heritage, and serve the needs of the Arab-American community. It works to end the stereotyping of Arabs in the media and discrimination against Arab-Americans in employment, education, and politics. The group organizes protests against racist advertisements and other media.

Information for a fee:

ABSCAM: Arabiaphobia in America. $1. An issue paper.
Arab Contributions to Civilization. $1. An issue paper.
The Arab Image in American Film and TV. $3. Book.
The Image of Arabs in American Fiction. $3. An issue paper.
Influence of the Arab Stereotype on Children. $1. An issue paper.
Social and Political Attitudes of Arab-Americans. $3. An issue paper.
The TV Arab. $5. Book.

To find out more, write or phone:

American-Arab Anti-Discrimination Committee
4201 Connecticut Ave., NW, Ste. 500
Washington, DC 20008
Phone: (202)244-2990 or *Fax:* (202)244-3196

▶ American Association for the Advancement of Science (AAAS) Science and Human Rights Program

Provides information on: *Scientists, Human Rights, Political Prisoners*

The Science and Human Rights Program collects information about scientists, engineers, and health professionals from various countries who are victims of human rights abuses or who have restrictions placed on them because of their professions. Once information on a human rights abuse is compiled, the program committee organizes action on behalf of the scientist, which can involve letter-writing to government officials, preparing statements of AAAS concern, and publishing reports of human rights abuses to broaden public awareness.

Information for free:

AAAS Science and Human Rights Program Publications List. Lists books, reports, and numerous journal articles on torture, political killings, and other human rights abuses.

Apartheid Medicine: Health and Human Rights in South Africa. 1990.

Directory of Persecuted Scientists, Engineers, and Health Professionals. 1992.

Report on Science and Human Rights. Newsletter.

Taking up the Challenge: The Promotion of Human Rights.

Information for a fee:

Scientists and Human Rights: Present and Future Directions. 1985. $4.50.

To find out more, write or phone:

American Association for the Advancement of Science
Science and Human Rights Program
Kari Hannibal, Sr. Prog. Assoc.
1333 H Street, N.W.
Washington, DC 20005
Phone: (202)326-6600 or *Fax:* (202)289-4950

▶ American Council for Nationalities Service

Provides information on: *Immigration and Naturalization, Refugees and Illegal Aliens*

The American Council for Nationalities Service is an organization that promotes cultural pluralism and assists refugees and immigrants in adjusting to American life and becoming fully participating citizens. The Council has member agencies, usually called International Institutes, in 34 cities that act as centers of service and fellowship for all nationalities. It advises its affiliated agencies on program and policy developments affecting the foreign born, provides local agencies working with immigrants with information on and technical assistance in immigration, language training, social casework, and related service issues, and works to improve immigration and naturalization laws and practices.

Information for a fee:

World Refugee Survey. Annual. $10.

To find out more, write or phone:
American Council for Nationalities Service
95 Madison Ave., 3rd Fl.
New York, NY 10016
Phone: (212)532-5858 or *Fax:* (212)532-8558

▶ Americans for Human Rights in Ukraine (AHRU)

Provides information on: *Human Rights, Political Prisoners*

AHRU works to pursue, expose, and combat violations of human rights and racial and ethnic prejudice in the Ukraine. It distributes information among U.S. officials, governmental agencies, and concerned citizens regarding what the AHRU calls the non-observance of human rights in the region. The AHRU promotes the welfare of political prisoners and their families both in the Ukraine and in exile, and supports individuals who defend religious, national, and human rights in the Ukraine.

To find out more, write or phone:
Americans for Human Rights in Ukraine
43 Midland Pl.
Newark, NJ 07106
Phone: (201)373-9729 or *Fax:* (201)373-4755

▶ Amnesty International of the U.S.A. (AIUSA)

Provides information on: *Political Prisoners, Human Rights*

The group works for the release of men and women imprisoned for their beliefs, color, ethnic origin, sex, religion, or language, provided they have neither used nor supported violence. AIUSA opposes torture and the death penalty and supports fair and prompt trials for all political prisoners.

Information for a fee:
Amnesty Action. Quarterly newsletter. Included in $15 student membership fee.
Amnesty International Report. Annual. $15/copy. Covers human rights abuses in 141 countries.
Also publishes country briefing papers, mission reports, and other special reports.

To find out more, write or phone:
Amnesty International of the U.S.A.
322 8th Ave.
New York, NY 10001
Phone: (212)807-8400 or *Fax:* (212)627-1451

▶ Argentina—Embassy

Provides information on: *Embassies, Immigration and Naturalization, Travel and Recreation*

The Embassy acts as the diplomatic representative abroad for Argentina. The Embassy provides the following types of information: business and economics, government and politics, immigration policies, law and legal issues, population and culture, student exchange programs, and travel and tourism.

To find out more, write or phone:
Argentina—Embassy
1600 New Hampshire Ave., NW
Washington, DC 20009
Phone: (202)939-6400 or *Fax:* (202)332-3171

▶ Arizona Office of Tourism

Provides information on: *Travel and Recreation, State Tourism*

The Office of Tourism provides information on state points of interest, including state parks; national landmarks, forests, and parks within the state, including the Grand Canyon and Petrified Forest National Parks; and cultural centers located within major cities. The Office will also provide general travel and tourism information, including hotel and motel lists, maps, general economic information, and major resort/activity brochures.

To find out more, write or phone:
Arizona Office of Tourism
1100 W. Washington
Phoenix, AZ 85007
Phone: (602)542-8687 or *Fax:* (602)238-6800

▶ Arkansas Department of Parks and Tourism

Provides information on: *Travel and Recreation, State Tourism*

The Department provides information on state points of interest, including state parks; national landmarks, forests, and parks within the state; and cultural centers located within major state cities. The Department will also provide general travel and tourism information, including hotel and motel lists, maps, general economic information, and major resort/activity brochures.

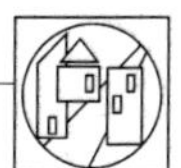

To find out more, write or phone:

Arkansas Department of Parks and Tourism
1 Capitol Mall
Little Rock, AR 72201
Toll-free: 1-800-643-8383 or *Phone:* (501)682-7777

▶ ARROW, Incorporated

Provides information on: *Native Americans*

ARROW (Americans for Restitution and Righting of Old Wrongs) is dedicated to the advancement of the American Indian. The group seeks to help the American Indian achieve a better educational, cultural, and economic standard and provide needy individuals with health care. ARROW works to improve tribal law and justice, and provides programs on drug and child abuse prevention.

Information for free:

Available to associate members.
American Indian Courtline. Periodic.
Adolescence—A Tough Time for Indian Youth. A Collection of six pamphlets.

To find out more, write or phone:

ARROW, Incorporated
1000 Connecticut Ave., NW, Ste. 1206
Washington, DC 20036
Phone: (202)296-0685

▶ Artists and Athletes Against Apartheid (AAAA)

Provides information on: *Apartheid, Athletes, Entertainers*

AAAA is made up of celebrities in the arts and sports who vow not to perform in South Africa because of its apartheid policy of racial segregation. The group's objective is to implement an international sports and cultural boycott of South Africa until apartheid is no longer imposed. It seeks to educate others in sports and the performing arts about apartheid and to dissuade them from performing. It also monitors the decline in the number of art and sports celebrities working in and traveling to South Africa.

To find out more, write or phone:

Artists and Athletes Against Apartheid
Arthur Ashe, Co-Chm.
545 8th St. SE, Ste. 200
Washington, DC 20003
Phone: (202)547-2550 or *Fax:* (202)547-7687

▶ The Asia Society (TAS)

Provides information on: *Asian Americans*

TAS works to increase American understanding of Asia and its role in world relations. It serves as a consultant on curriculum development and multimedia materials, and offers special services to educators on new ways to teach about Asian people and culture.

Information for a fee:
China Briefing. Annual. $14.95.
India Briefing. Annual. $14.95.
Korea Briefing. Annual. $14.95.
Also publishes performing arts monographs, books, educational guides and videotapes, brochures, study reports, media briefings, and catalogues of TAS exhibitions.

To find out more, write or phone:

The Asia Society
725 Park Ave.
New York, NY 10021
Phone: (212)288-6400 or *Fax:* (212)517-8315

▶ Asian American Legal Defense and Education Fund

Provides information on: *Asian Americans, Immigration and Naturalization, Employment, Civil Rights and Liberties*

The Asian American Legal Defense and Education Fund provides bilingual legal counseling and representation for people who cannot obtain access to legal assistance. Areas of concern include immigration, employment, housing, voting rights, and racially-motivated violence against Asian Americans. It monitors and reports on incidents of racial discrimination against Asian Americans. The group publishes a newsletter and pamphlets.

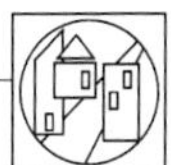

To find out more, write or phone:
Asian American Legal Defense and Education Fund
99 Hudson St.
New York, NY 10013
Phone: (212)966-5932

▶ ASPIRA Association

Provides information on: *Hispanic Americans, Healthcare Careers*

ASPIRA Association provides leadership development and educational assistance to the Hispanic community. Specific programs include the National Health Careers Program which improves the quality of health care delivered to the Hispanic community by increasing the number of Hispanic health care providers through counseling, tutoring, and internships. The Association also sponsors the Aspira Public Policy Research Program which develops and supports the leadership potential of Latino high school youth via workshops, seminars, and internships.

Information for free:
Annual Report/Newsletter.

Information for a fee:
Communities Count. 2-3/year. $4.
Parent Guide. 2-3/year. $4.

To find out more, write or phone:
ASPIRA Association
1112 16th St., NW, Ste. 340
Washington, DC 20036
Phone: (202)835-3600 or *Fax:* (202)223-1253

▶ Association for the Advancement of Policy, Research and Development in the Third World

Provides information on: *Developing Countries, International Development*

The Association promotes science, technology, and development through exchange and generation of practical solutions to problems facing governments in developing countries. It encourages the effective and improved utilization of resources, including human development and planning institutions. The group distributes information on policy management practices and current research in the field, and operates a small library on science, technology, and economic development.

To find out more, write or phone:

Association for the Advancement of Policy, Research and Development in the Third World
Dr. Mekki Mtewa, Exec.Dir.
PO Box 70257
Washington, DC 20024-0257
Phone: (202)723-7010 or *Fax:* (202)723-7010

▶ Association for the Study of Afro-American Life and History

Provides information on: *African Americans*

The Association is comprised of historians, scholars, and students interested in the research and study of Blacks as a contributing factor in civilization. The group promotes and collects historical research and writings relating to Blacks throughout the world, and attempts to bring about harmony among the races. The Association also encourages the study of Black history and training in the social sciences, history and other disciplines, and cooperates with governmental agencies, foundations, and others in designing future projects to advance the study of ethnic history.

Information for a fee:
Journal of Negro History. Quarterly. $25/year or $6.50 per issue.

To find out more, write or phone:

Association for the Study of Afro-American Life and History
1407 14th St., NW
Washington, DC 20005
Phone: (202)667-2822

▶ Association of Third World Studies

Provides information on: *Developing Countries, International Development*

The Association is made up of development specialists and other individuals interested in economic and social issues affecting Third World countries. The group promotes interest in the Western influence of developing countries.

Information for a fee:
Journal of Third World Studies. 2/year. Included in $20.00 membership dues. Analyzes Third World problems and issues.

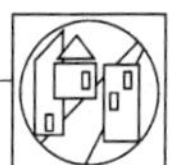

To find out more, write or phone:

Association of Third World Studies
Zia H. Hashmi, Pres.
PO Box 1232
Americus, GA 31709
Phone: (912)681-5668

▶ Australia—Embassy

Provides information on: *Embassies, Immigration and Naturalization, Travel and Recreation*

The Embassy acts as the diplomatic representative abroad for Australia. The Embassy provides the following types of information: business and economics, government and politics, immigration policies, law and legal issues, population and culture, student exchange programs, and travel and tourism.

To find out more, write or phone:

Australia—Embassy
1601 Massachusetts Ave., NW
Washington, DC 20036-2273
Phone: (202)797-3000 or *Fax:* (202)797-3168

▶ Balch Institute for Ethnic Studies

Provides information on: *Ethnic Americans, Immigration and Naturalization*

The Balch Institute for Ethnic Studies deals with immigration and ethnicity. The Institute's activities focus on documenting and interpreting the American multicultural experience. Also included are displays of clothing, household goods, and other artifacts representative of immigrant life.

Information for a fee:

New Dimensions. Semianually. $25. Price includes membership.

Also publishes research results and monographs on the history of immigration and ethnic groups in North America.

To find out more, write or phone:

Balch Institute for Ethnic Studies
18 S. 7th St.
Philadelphia, PA 19106
Phone: (215)925-8090

▶ Belgium—Embassy

Provides information on: *Embassies, Immigration and Naturalization, Travel and Recreation*

The Embassy acts as the diplomatic representative abroad for Belgium. The Embassy provides the following types of information: business and economics, government and politics, immigration policies, law and legal issues, population and culture, student exchange programs, and travel and tourism.

To find out more, write or phone:
Belgium—Embassy
3330 Garfield St., NW
Washington, DC 20008
Phone: (202)333-6900

▶ Black World Foundation

Provides information on: *African Americans*

The Foundation is made up of Black persons united to develop and distribute Black educational materials and to develop Black cultural and political thought. It maintains a Prisoner Fund to supply free copies of foundation publications to prisoners. It also offers books in the areas of Black literature, history, fiction, essays, political anaylsis, social science, poetry, and art.

Information for a fee:
Jesse Jackson. $11.95.

To find out more, write or phone:
Black World Foundation
Robert Chrisman, Pres.
PO Box 2869
Oakland, CA 94609
Phone: (510)547-6633

▶ Brazil—Embassy

Provides information on: *Embassies, Immigration and Naturalization, Travel and Recreation*

The Embassy acts as the diplomatic representative abroad for Brazil. The Embassy provides the following types of information: business and economics, government

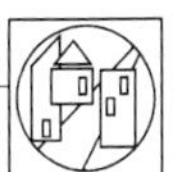

and politics, immigration policies, law and legal issues, population and culture, student exchange programs, and travel and tourism.

To find out more, write or phone:
Brazil—Embassy
3006 Massachusetts Ave., NW
Washington, DC 20008-3699
Phone: (202)745-2700 or *Fax:* (202)745-2827

▶ British Embassy

Provides information on: *Embassies, Immigration and Naturalization, Travel and Recreation*

The Embassy acts as the diplomatic representative abroad for Great Britain. The Embassy provides the following types of information: business and economics, government and politics, immigration policies, law and legal issues, population and culture, student exchange programs, and travel and tourism.

To find out more, write or phone:
British Embassy
3100 Massachusetts Ave., NW
Washington, DC 20008
Phone: (202)462-1340

▶ Brother to Brother International (BBI)

Provides information on: *International Development, International Relief*

Brother to Brother International is a nonprofit clearinghouse of information responding to appeals from the needy worldwide. BBI's goal is to identify sources of food, medical supplies, agricultural products, and assist in the distribution through local, regional, and international relief organizations. BBI responds to requests for information on sources of food, medical supplies, agricultural products, and other commodities available for charitable use.

To find out more, write or phone:
Brother to Brother International
4025 S. McClintock No. 210
Tempe, AZ 85285-7634
Toll-free: 1-800-642-1616 or *Phone:* (602)345-9200 or *Fax:* (602)345-2747

▶ Bureau of Indian Affairs

Provides information on: *Native Americans, Government*

The Bureau of Indian Affairs is the federal agency responsible for working with federally-recognized Indian tribal governments, relating to tribes on a "government-to-government" basis. The Bureau's main goal is to support tribal efforts to govern their own reservation communities by providing them with technical assistance, as well as programs and services. This support includes managing millions of acres of land held in trust by the U.S. for Indians, providing educational funding, and assisting tribes with local governmental services such as road construction, police protection, and economic development.

Information for free:
American Indians Today: Answers to Your Questions. Published every 1-2 years.

To find out more, write or phone:
Bureau of Indian Affairs
U.S. Department of the Interior
1849 C St., NW
Washington, DC 20240
Phone: (202)208-7163 or *Fax:* (202)208-6334

▶ California Office of Tourism

Provides information on: *Travel and Recreation, State Tourism*

The Office provides public information on points of interest in California, including state parks; national landmarks, forests, and parks within the state, including Redwood National Park and Sequoia National Forest; and cultural centers located within major cities. The Office will also provide general travel and tourism information (including hotel and motel lists, maps, general economic information, and major resort/activity brochures).

To find out more, write or phone:
California Office of Tourism
1121 L St., Ste. 103
Sacramento, CA 95814
Toll-free: 1-800-862-2543 or *Phone:* (916)322-2881 or *Fax:* (916)322-3204

▶ Canada—Embassy

Provides information on: *Embassies, Immigration and Naturalization, Travel and Recreation*

The Embassy acts as the diplomatic representative for Canada in the United States. It provides the following types of information: business and economics, government and politics, law and legal issues, population and culture, student exchange programs, and travel and tourism.

To find out more, write or phone:

Canada—Embassy
501 Pennsylvania Ave.
Washington, DC 20001
Phone: (202)682-1740 or *Fax:* (202)682-7726

▶ Center for Immigrants Rights

Provides information on: *Immigration and Naturalization, Civil Rights and Liberties*

The Center offers information to immigrants on their rights under law. It provides documentation and intervention in employer discrimination against immigrants, and provides paralegal training and educational programs in immigration law for church, community, and labor organizations.

Information for free:
CRI Report.

To find out more, write or phone:

Center for Immigrants Rights
48 St. Marks Pl., 4th Fl.
New York, NY 10003
Phone: (212)505-6890 or *Fax:* (212)995-5876

▶ Center for Studies of Ethnicity and Race in America (CSERA)

Provides information on: *Ethnic Americans, African Americans, Asian Americans, Hispanic Americans, Native Americans*

The Center studies race and ethnicity, including Afro-American, American Indian, Asian-American, and Chicano issues.

Information for free:
CSERA Newsletter. Bimonthly.

To find out more, write or phone:

Center for Studies of Ethnicity and Race in America
University of Colorado, Boulder
Ketchum 30
Campus Box 339
Boulder, CO 80309-0339
Phone: (303)492-8852

▶ Center for the Study of Ethnic Publications and Cultural Institutions

Provides information on: *Ethnic Americans*

The Center promotes research on ethnic publications and cultural institutions in the U.S. in cooperation with various scholarly, professional, and governmental organizations and agencies. It surveys ethnic press as well as ethnic serials, books, libraries, archives, and museums. Activities focus on developing a curriculum for library schools, emphasizing library services to ethnic communities and ethnic publications.

Information for a fee:

Ethnic Forum Journal of Ethnic Studies and Ethnic Bibliography. Annual. 200 pages. $25.

To find out more, write or phone:

Center for the Study of Ethnic Publications and Cultural Institutions
Kent State University
School of Library Science
Kent, OH 44242-0001
Phone: (216)672-2782

▶ Center for Teaching About China

Provides information on: *Asia*

The Center serves as a nonprofit national clearinghouse for instructional materials on China. The Center provides children's services and maintains a library.

Information for free:

China in the Classroom. Catalog of resources offered by the Center. Offers hundreds of titles from and about the Peoples Republic of China, including those from literature, history, biographies, arts, teaching guides, festival information books, language, health and religion, and more. Also offers audio-visual materials.

Information for a fee:

America's Response to China. 1980. 169 pages. $7.50.

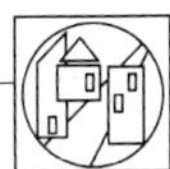

China Pushing Toward the Year 2000. 1981. 160 pages. $8.
Chinese Folk Art. 22 pages. $3.50.
Chinese New Year Celebration. 1988. 23 pages. $2.50.
Environmental Protection in China. 1986. 50 pages. $1.50.
Values and Religion in China Today. 1987. 120 pages. $12.
Women in Traditional China. 1980. 113 pages. $7.95.

To find out more, write or phone:
Center for Teaching About China
1214 W. Schwartz
Carbondale, IL 62901
Phone: (618)549-1555

▶ Central America Information Center (CAIC)

Provides information on: *Central America*

The Center acts as a catalyst for public debate on Central American issues, encourages individual action and the development of public policy, and serves as a clearinghouse of information on work, study, and travel in the region. CAIC develops training and resources for organizations participating in the Central American peace movement and monitors related legislative developments. The Center maintains a library and answers the public's questions about Central America.

To find out more, write or phone:
Central America Information Center
Dana Hohn, Dir.
PO Box 50211
San Diego, CA 92165
Phone: (619)583-2925

▶ Central American Refugee Center

Provides information on: *Human Rights, Immigration and Naturalization*

Central American Refugee Center is concerned with the plight of undocumented Central American refugees in the U.S. The Center provides refugees with emergency legal assistance to deal with immigration proceedings and applications for political asylum. The group also researches human rights violations in El Salvador.

Information for free:
Short documents and pamphlets on refugees and legal matters.

To find out more, write or phone:
Central American Refugee Center
3112 Mt. Pleasant St., NW
Washington, DC 20010
Phone: (202)328-9799

▶ Centre Against Apartheid

Provides information on: *Apartheid, Political Prisoners*

The Centre works toward the peaceful transformation of South Africa to a non-racial, democratic society. It administers a program to help political prisoners and returned exiles and their dependents in South Africa. Two additional programs provide young South Africans with assistance for study and training, and promote public awareness about apartheid issues.

Information for free:

Notes and Documents. Series of packets, organized by date, that contain lengthy statements on apartheid, and summaries of United Nations business. Others contain lists of available publications, leaflets, special issues, and posters. Some titles in the series include:

Ethical Principles of Conduct for Companies in a New Democratic South Africa. 1992. 6 pages.

Future Role of the United Nations System in Helping Address South Africa's Socio-Economic Problems. 1992. 29 pages.

Observance of International Day for the Elimination of Racial Discrimination. 1992. 17 pages.

Special Committee Against Apartheid Outlines Framework for International Support of the Peace Process in South Africa. 1992. 10 pages.

United Nations Educational and Training Programme for Southern Africa: An Overview. 1992. 14 pages.

To find out more, write or phone:
Centre Against Apartheid
United Nations
Rm. S-3275
New York, NY 10017
Phone: (212)963-5511 or *Fax:* (212)963-5305

▶ Centre for Russian and East European Studies

Provides information on: *Eastern Europe, Commonwealth of Independent States*

The Centre conducts research on Russia and Eastern Europe and supports projects in economics, geography, history, political science, sociology, and Slavic languages and literature.

Information for a fee:
Bulletin on Current Research. 3/year. $9/year. $15/2years.
Working Papers Series. Monthly. $9.

To find out more, write or phone:
Centre for Russian and East European Studies
University of Toronto
100 George St.
Toronto, ON, Canada M5S 1A1
Phone: (416)978-3330

▶ China Institute in America

Provides information on: *Asia*

The Institute is made up of individuals and corporations interested in The People's Republic of China and in furthering Chinese-U.S. understanding. It offers courses and lectures about China, and holds a weekly open house for visiting Chinese and American students and scholars. The Institute produces educational materials, organizes recreational programs, and conducts cultural and medical exchanges.

Information for free:
Semester brochure listing courses, symposia, and programs offered by the Institute.

To find out more, write or phone:
China Institute in America
125 E. 65th St.
New York, NY 10021
Phone: (212)744-8181 or *Fax:* (212)628-4159

▶ Colorado Tourism Board

Provides information on: *Travel and Recreation, State Tourism*

The Board provides information on state points of interest, including state parks; the many national wildlife refuges, forests, and parks within the state, including Rocky Mountain National Park and the Arapaho National Forest; and cultural centers located within major cities. The Board will also provide general travel and tourism information, including hotel and motel lists, maps, general economic information, and major resort/activity brochures.

To find out more, write or phone:
Colorado Tourism Board
1625 Broadway, Ste. 1700
PO Box 38700
Denver, CO 80202
Toll-free: 1-800-433-2656 or *Phone:* (303)592-5410 or *Fax:* (303)592-5406

▶ Committee of 21

Provides information on: *Political Prisoners, Human Rights*

The Committee is made up of congresswomen, women senators, and wives of congressmen who share a concern for victims of human rights abuses worldwide. The group sends letters of support to prisoners of conscience and their families, and makes appeals to the leaders of countries that are involved in human rights abuse. It operates a school outreach program enabling high school classes in the U.S. to "adopt" a prisoner of conscience.

Information for free:
Publishes periodic press releases.

To find out more, write or phone:
Committee of 21
Alexandra Arriaga, Co-Dir.
c/o Congressional Human Rights Caucus
Ford House Office Bldg., Rm. H2-590
Washington, DC 20515
Phone: (202)226-4040

▶ Committee on Health and Human Rights

Provides information on: *Human Rights*

The Committee supports and defends health professionals and groups working to combat human rights abuses. It works to identify and increase public and professional awareness of health-related human rights abuses worldwide such as torture, imprisonment of health professionals without a fair trial, health professionals and their skills in the torture of others, abuses of psychiatry for political purposes, and breach of confidentiality and falsification of medical information.

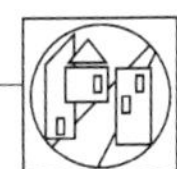

To find out more, write or phone:

Committee on Health and Human Rights
Institute of Medicine
2101 Constitution Ave., NW
Washington, DC 20418
Phone: (202)334-1717 or *Fax:* (202)334-2158

▶ Congress of Racial Equality (CORE)

Provides information on: *African Americans*

Congress of Racial Equality is a Black nationalist organization that bases its philosophy on the ideas of Marcus Garvey (1887-1940), the Jamaican-born Black nationalist leader. CORE looks to Africa for inspiration, and seeks the right of Blacks to govern themselves in those areas that immediately impact them. The group also sponsors CORE Community School, a private alternative school for grades one through eight in the Bronx, NY and Memphis, TN.

Information for a fee:

CORE Magazine. $3 per issue.
Equal Opportunity Journal. $6.

To find out more, write or phone:

Congress of Racial Equality
2111 Nostrand Ave.
Brooklyn, NY 11210
Phone: (212)598-4000

▶ Congressional Human Rights Caucus (CHRC)

Provides information on: *Human Rights, Political Prisoners*

CHRC is a bipartisan faction of the House of Representatives concerned with human rights abuses around the world. The Caucus coordinates efforts of Congress to end these abuses and to secure freedom from religious, ethnic, cultural, or political persecution for all people. It provides information on specific human rights cases. Members write letters to heads of state protesting the imprisonment of people around the world for their political beliefs, religious practices, or ethnic origins.

Information for free:

Congressional Human Rights Caucus Newsletter. Quarterly.

To find out more, write or phone:

Congressional Human Rights Caucus
c/o Alexandra Arriaga
H2-590, Ford House Office Bldg.
Washington, DC 20515
Phone: (202)226-4040

▶ Cuba Interests Section

Provides information on: *Embassies*

The Cuba Interests Section acts as a representative abroad for Cuba in the United States. It provides the following types of information: business and economics, government and politics, law and legal issues, population, and culture.

To find out more, write or phone:

Cuba Interests Section
2630 & 2639 16th St., NW
Washington, DC 20009
Phone: (202)797-8518

▶ Czech and Slovak Federative Republic—Embassy

Provides information on: *Embassies, Immigration and Naturalization, Travel and Recreation*

The Embassy acts as the diplomatic representative abroad for Czechoslovakia. The Embassy can answer general information questions and guide the public to information on business and economics, government and politics, immigration policies, law and legal issues, population and culture, and travel and tourism.

To find out more, write or phone:

Czech and Slovak Federative Republic—Embassy
3900 Linnean Ave., NW
Washington, DC 20008-3897
Phone: (202)363-6315

▶ Delaware Tourism Office

Provides information on: *Travel and Recreation, State Tourism*

The Tourism Office provides information on Delaware points of interest, including state parks; national landmarks and wildlife refuges located within the state; and cultural centers located within major cities. The Office also provides information on

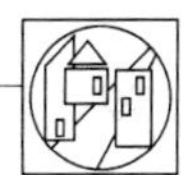

tourism and travel in Delaware, including hotel and motel lists, maps, and resort/activity brochures.

To find out more, write or phone:

Delaware Tourism Office
99 Kings Hwy.
PO Box 1401
Dover, DE 19903
Toll-free: 1-800-441-8846 or *Phone:* (302)736-4271 or *Fax:* (302)736-5749

▶ Denmark—Embassy

Provides information on: *Embassies, Immigration and Naturalization, Travel and Recreation*

The Embassy acts as the diplomatic representative abroad for Denmark. The Embassy provides the following types of information: business and economics, government and politics, immigration policies, law and legal issues, population and culture, student exchange programs, and travel and tourism.

To find out more, write or phone:

Denmark—Embassy
3200 Whitehaven St., NW
Washington, DC 20008
Phone: (202)234-4300

▶ Department of Commerce Michigan Travel Bureau

Provides information on: *Travel and Recreation, State Tourism*

The Travel Bureau provides information on state points of interest, including state parks; national landmarks, forests, and parks within the state, including Sleeping Bear Dunes National Lakeshore on Lake Michigan; and cultural centers located within major cities. The Bureau also provides general travel and tourism information, including hotel and motel lists, maps, general economic information, and major resort/activity brochures.

To find out more, write or phone:
Department of Commerce
Michigan Travel Bureau
PO Box 30226
Lansing, MI 48909
Toll-free: 1-800-543-2YES or *Phone:* (517)373-0670 or *Fax:* (517)373-7873

▶ Egypt—Embassy

Provides information on: *Embassies, Immigration and Naturalization, Travel and Recreation*

The Embassy acts as the diplomatic representative abroad for Egypt. The Embassy provides the following types of information: business and economics, government and politics, immigration policies, law and legal issues, population and culture, student exchange programs, and travel and tourism.

To find out more, write or phone:
Egypt—Embassy
2300 Decatur Plaza, NW
Washington, DC 20008
Phone: (202)232-5400 or *Fax:* (202)332-7894

▶ El Salvador—Embassy

Provides information on: *Embassies, Immigration and Naturalization, Travel and Recreation*

The Embassy acts as the diplomatic representative abroad for El Salvador. The Embassy provides the following types of information: business and economics, government and politics, immigration policies, law and legal issues, population and culture, student exchange programs, and travel and tourism.

To find out more, write or phone:
El Salvador—Embassy
2308 California St., NW
Washington, DC 20008
Phone: (202)265-3480 or *Fax:* (202)332-5103

▶ Ethiopia—Embassy

Provides information on: *Embassies, Immigration and Naturalization, Travel and Recreation*

The Embassy acts as the diplomatic representative abroad for Ethiopia. The Embassy provides the following types of information: business and economics, government and politics, immigration policies, law and legal issues, population and culture, student exchange programs, and travel and tourism.

To find out more, write or phone:
Ethiopia—Embassy
2134 Kalorama Rd., NW
Washington, DC 20008
Phone: (202)234-2281

▶ European Community Information Service

Provides information on: *Europe*

The Service is an information and public affairs office in the United States for the European communities. It distributes official documents and information brochures of the European communities. The group also maintains a library.

Information for a fee:
Europe. 10/year. $19.95. Magazine.

To find out more, write or phone:
European Community Information Service
2100 M St., NW, Ste. 707
Washington, DC 20037
Phone: (202)862-9500 or *Fax:* (202)429-1766

▶ Florida Department of Commerce Division of Tourism

Provides information on: *Travel and Recreation, State Tourism*

The Department of Commerce's Division on Tourism provides information on state points of interest, including state parks; national landmarks, forests, and parks within Florida, including the Everglades; and cultural centers located within major cities. The Division will also provide general travel and tourism information (hotel and motel lists, maps, general economic information, and major resort/activity brochures).

To find out more, write or phone:
Florida Department of Commerce
Division of Tourism
Collins Bldg., No. 530
Tallahassee, FL 32399-2000
Phone: (904)487-1462 or *Fax:* (904)487-0134

▶ Forum International: International Ecosystems University

Provides information on: *Poverty, World Affairs, Education, Environmental Protection*

The Forum promotes education, research, and action to deal with problems such as environmental deterioration, socioeconomic change, poverty, overpopulation, and lack of educational opportunity. It sponsors ecosystems field studies in Africa, Europe, Latin America, and North America.

Information for a fee:
Ecosphere. Bimonthly. $18/year. Tabloid describing theory and practice of "ecosystemic, whole-world-oriented, transdisciplinary, value-based education, research, and action programs."

To find out more, write or phone:
Forum International: International Ecosystems University
91 Gregory Ln., No. 21
Pleasant Hill, CA 94523
Phone: (510)671-2900 or *Fax:* (510)946-1500

▶ France—Embassy

Provides information on: *Embassies, Immigration and Naturalization, Travel and Recreation*

The Embassy acts as the diplomatic representative abroad for France. The Embassy provides the following types of information: business and economics, government and politics, immigration policies, law and legal issues, population and culture, student exchange programs, and travel and tourism.

To find out more, write or phone:
France—Embassy
4101 Reservoir Rd., NW
Washington, DC 20007
Phone: (202)944-6000 or *Fax:* (202)944-6072

▶ Georgia Division of Tourism Department of Industry and Trade

Provides information on: *Travel and Recreation, State Tourism*

The Division provides information on Georgia, including state parks; national wildlife refuges, forests, and parks within the state; and cultural centers located within major cities. The Department will also provide general travel and tourism information, including hotel and motel lists, maps, general economic information, and major resort/activity brochures.

To find out more, write or phone:

Georgia Division of Tourism
Department of Industry and Trade
PO Box 1776
Atlanta, GA 30301
Toll-free: 1-800-VIS-ITGA or *Phone:* (404)656-3590 or *Fax:* (404)656-3567

▶ Germany—Embassy

Provides information on: *Embassies, Immigration and Naturalization, Travel and Recreation*

The Embassy acts as the diplomatic representative abroad for Germany. The Embassy can answer questions or direct the public to information or resources on business and economics, government and politics, immigration policies, law and legal issues, population and culture, student exchange programs, and travel and tourism.

To find out more, write or phone:

Germany—Embassy
4645 Reservoir Rd. NW
Washington, DC 20007-1918
Phone: (202)298-4000 or *Fax:* (202)298-4249

▶ Ghana—Embassy

Provides information on: *Embassies, Immigration and Naturalization, Travel and Recreation*

The Embassy acts as the diplomatic representative abroad for Ghana. The Embassy provides the following types of information: business and economics, government and politics, immigration policies, law and legal issues, population and culture, student programs, and travel and tourism.

To find out more, write or phone:
Ghana—Embassy
3512 International Dr., NW
Washington, DC 20008
Phone: (202)686-4500

▶ Greece—Embassy

Provides information on: *Embassies, Immigration and Naturalization, Travel and Recreation*

The Embassy acts as the diplomatic representative abroad for Greece. The Embassy provides the following types of information: business and economics, government and politics, immigration policies, law and legal issues, population and culture, student exchange programs, and travel and tourism.

To find out more, write or phone:
Greece—Embassy
2221 Massachusetts Ave., NW
Washington, DC 20008-2873
Phone: (202)667-3168 or *Fax:* (202)939-5824

▶ Haiti—Embassy

Provides information on: *Embassies, Immigration and Naturalization, Travel and Recreation*

The Embassy acts as the diplomatic representative abroad for Haiti. The Embassy provides the following types of information: business and economics, government and politics, immigration policies, law and legal issues, population and culture, student exchange programs, and travel and tourism.

To find out more, write or phone:
Haiti—Embassy
2311 Massachusetts Ave., NW
Washington, DC 20008
Phone: (202)322-4090 or *Fax:* (202)745-7210

▶ Hawaiian Vistors Bureau

Provides information on: *Travel and Recreation, State Tourism*

The Visitor's Bureau provides information on state points of interest, including national parks and wildlife refuges located on the various islands that make up the

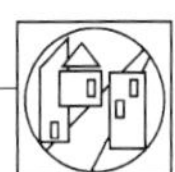

state; and cultural centers located within major cities. The Bureau will also provide general travel and tourism information, including hotel and motel lists, maps, general economic information, and major resort/activity brochures.

To find out more, write or phone:

Hawaiian Vistors Bureau
2270 Kalakaua Ave., Ste. 801
PO Box 8527
Honolulu, HI 96815
Phone: (808)923-1811 or *Fax:* (808)922-8991

▶ Hispanic Society of America

Provides information on: *Hispanic Americans*

Members of the Society are people who have made distinguished contributions to the fields of Hispanic art, literature, history, and general culture, which includes music, social customs, costumes, and bullfighting. The research institute maintains a museum that represents Hispanic development from prehistoric days to the present. It includes collections of paintings, sculpture, furniture, metalwork, pottery, glass, lace, and textiles. The reference library contains manuscripts and books printed before 1701 and later books on art, history, literature, and culture of Spain, Portugal, and colonial Hispanic America. Also available is a file of photographs on the fine and decorative arts and costumes of Spain and Portugal.

Information for free:

Publications catalog.

Information for a fee:

Audubon Park: The History of the Site of The Hispanic Society of America and Neighbouring Institutions. 1986 reprint. 30 pages. $2.

The Hispanic Society of America. Handbook: Museum and Library Collections. 1938. 443 pages. $5. Illustrated book of artifacts.

A History of The Hispanic Society of America, Museum and Library, 1904-1954, with a Survey of the Collections. 1954. 569 pages. $10. Illustrated book containing history of the society, museum and library collections, and appendices.

Many other books on art, ceramics, costume, history, language, and literature, as well as other topics are also available.

To find out more, write or phone:

Hispanic Society of America
613 W. 155th St.
New York, NY 10032
Phone: (212)926-2234

▶ Hong Kong Government Office—British Embassy

Provides information on: *Embassies, Immigration and Naturalization, Travel and Recreation*

The Embassy acts as the diplomatic representative abroad for the British colony of Hong Kong. The Embassy provides the following types of information: business and economics, government and politics, immigration policies, law and legal issues, population and culture, student exchange programs, and travel and tourism.

To find out more, write or phone:

Hong Kong Government Office—British Embassy
1233 20th St., NW, #504
Washington, DC 20038
Phone: (202)331-8947 or *Fax:* (202)462-2612

▶ Human Rights Internet (HRI)

Provides information on: *Human Rights*

HRI is a non-partisan educational and international communications network and clearinghouse on human rights. HRI maintains a documentation center containing publications on human rights organizations and resources for teaching and research.

Information for a fee:

Diverse Partners—Non-Governmental Organizations in the Human Rights Movement. $5.
Double Jeopardy.Discrimination Against Persons with AIDS. 1990. $8.
Human Rights Research and Education Bulletin. Quarterly. $18/year. A bulletin of information, contracts, and bibliography on topical issues.
Human Rights Tribune. Quarterly. $3.95/single issue; $20/year. Covers news and information on international human rights issues.
Master List. Annual. $20. A worldwide listing of human rights organizations and publications.

To find out more, write or phone:

Human Rights Internet
c/o Harvard Law School
1563 Massachusetts Ave.
Pound Hall, Rm. 401
Cambridge, MA 02138
Phone: (617)495-9362 or *Fax:* (617)496-5251

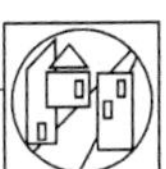

▶ Idaho Division of Travel Promotion

Provides information on: *Travel and Recreation, State Tourism*

Idaho's Division of Travel Promotion provides information on the culture and geography of Idaho, including national forests and wildlife refuges located within the state and cultural centers located within major cities. The Division also provides information on tourism and travel, including hotel and motel lists, maps, and general economic information.

To find out more, write or phone:

Idaho Division of Travel Promotion
700 W. State St.
Boise, ID 83720
Toll-free: 1-800-635-7820 or *Phone:* (208)334-2470 or *Fax:* (208)334-2631

▶ Illinois Department of Commerce & Community Affairs Division of Tourism

Provides information on: *Travel and Recreation, State Tourism*

The Department of Commerce & Community Affairs' Division of Tourism provides information on state points of interest, including state parks; national landmarks and wildlife refuges within the state; and cultural centers located within major cities. The Division also provides general travel and tourism information, including hotel and motel lists, maps, general economic information, and major resort/activity brochures.

To find out more, write or phone:

Illinois Department of Commerce & Community Affairs
Division of Tourism
620 E. Adams
Springfield, IL 62701
Toll-free: 1-800-223-0121 or *Phone:* (217)782-7139

▶ Immigration History Society (IHS)

Provides information on: *Immigration and Naturalization*

IHS is a society of scholars interested in the study of human migration, particularly immigration to the United States and Canada. IHS also provides a way for historians, sociologists, economists, and others engaged in researching this field to communicate with each other. The Society offers information on current research projects and available publications.

To find out more, write or phone:
Immigration History Society
Indiana University
Dept. of History
Bloomington, IN 47405
Phone: (812)855-0002

▶ India—Embassy

Provides information on: *Embassies, Immigration and Naturalization, Travel and Recreation*

The Embassy acts as the diplomatic representative abroad for India. The Embassy provides the following types of information: business and economics, government and politics, immigration policies, law and legal issues, population and culture, student exchange programs, and travel and tourism.

To find out more, write or phone:
India—Embassy
2107 Massachusetts Ave., NW
Washington, DC 20008-2811
Phone: (202)939-7000 or *Fax:* (202)939-7027

▶ Indian Heritage Council (IHC)

Provides information on: *Native Americans*

The Council promotes and supports Indian endeavors, and seeks a deeper understanding between Indians and non-Indians of the cultural, educational, spiritual, and historical aspects of Native Americans. IHC also conducts research and educational programs.

Information for free:
Offers a single copy of the membership newsletter for free.

Information for a fee:
Great American Indian Bible. $10, plus $2 shipping and handling.
Newsletter is available with $10 membership dues.

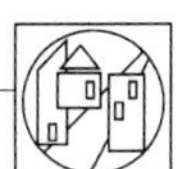

To find out more, write or phone:

Indian Heritage Council
Louis Hooban, CEO
Henry St.
Box 2302
Morristown, TN 37816
Phone: (615)581-5714

▶ Indiana Division of Tourism

Provides information on: *Travel and Recreation, State Tourism*

The Division provides information on Indiana points of interest, including state parks; national forests and parks within the state; and cultural centers located within major cities. The Division also provides general travel and tourism information, including hotel and motel lists, maps, general economic information, and major resort/activity brochures.

To find out more, write or phone:

Indiana Division of Tourism
1 N. Capitol, Ste. 700
Indianapolis, IN 46205-2288
Toll-free: 1-800-289-6646 or *Phone:* (317)232-8860 or *Fax:* (317)232-4146

▶ International Networks in Education and Development

Provides information on: *Education, Developing Countries, International Development*

The Network provides information on formal and nonformal education in developing nations, including information in the areas of concepts and issues in education, communication, economics and planning of education, literacy and numeracy, industrial and vocational education, health, agriculture, community development and leadership, home economics and human ecology, adult education, integrated development, children's education, relief organizations, environment and natural resources, and religious education.

Information for a fee:

Women in Development. $5.
Literacy and Basic Education. $4.
Non-formal Education and Health. $4.
Financial Resources for Non-formal Education. $3.

To find out more, write or phone:

International Networks in Education and Development
Michigan State University
College of Education
237 Erickson Hall
East Lansing, MI 48224-1034
Phone: (517)355-5522 or *Fax:* (517)336-2352

▶ Iowa Department of Economic Development Bureau of Tourism & Visitors

Provides information on: *Travel and Recreation, State Tourism*

The Bureau provides information on Iowa points of interest, including state parks; national landmarks and wildlife refuges within the state; and cultural centers located within major cities. The Bureau also provides general travel and tourism information, including hotel and motel lists, maps, general economic information, and major resort/activity brochures.

To find out more, write or phone:

Iowa Department of Economic Development
Bureau of Tourism & Visitors
200 E. Grand Ave.
Des Moines, IA 50309
Toll-free: 1-800-345-4692 or *Phone:* (515)281-3100 or *Fax:* (515)281-7276

▶ Iraq—Embassy

Provides information on: *Embassies*

The Embassy acts as the diplomatic representative abroad for Iraq. The Embassy provides the following types of information: business and economics, government and politics, law and legal issues, and population and culture.

To find out more, write or phone:

Iraq—Embassy
1801 P St., NW
Washington, DC 20036
Phone: (202)483-7500 or *Fax:* (202)462-5066

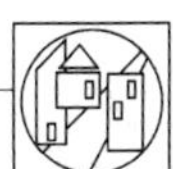

▶ Ireland—Embassy

Provides information on: *Embassies, Immigration and Naturalization, Travel and Recreation*

The Embassy acts as the diplomatic representative abroad for Ireland. The Embassy can answer general information questions or direct the public to resources on business and economics, government and politics, immigration policies, law and legal issues, population and culture, student exchange programs, and travel and tourism.

To find out more, write or phone:

Ireland—Embassy
2234 Massachusetts Ave., NW
Washington, DC 20008
Phone: (202)462-3939 or *Fax:* (202)232-5993

▶ Israel—Embassy

Provides information on: *Embassies, Immigration and Naturalization, Travel and Recreation*

The Embassy acts as the diplomatic representative abroad for Israel. The Embassy provides the following types of information: business and economics, government and politics, immigration policies, law and legal issues, population and culture, student exchange programs, and travel and tourism.

To find out more, write or phone:

Israel—Embassy
3514 International Dr., NW
Washington, DC 20008-3099
Phone: (202)364-5500

▶ Italy—Embassy

Provides information on: *Embassies, Immigration and Naturalization, Travel and Recreation*

The Embassy acts as the diplomatic representative abroad for Italy. It can answer general information questions relating to Italy or direct the public to information on business and economics, government and politics, immigration policies, law and legal issues, population and culture, student exchange programs, and travel and tourism.

To find out more, write or phone:
Italy—Embassy
1601 Fuller St. NW
Washington, DC 20009
Phone: (202)328-5500 or *Fax:* (202)328-5542

▶ Jamaica—Embassy

Provides information on: *Embassies, Immigration and Naturalization, Travel and Recreation*

The Embassy acts as the diplomatic representative abroad for Jamaica. The Embassy provides the following types of information: business and economics, government and politics, immigration policies, law and legal issues, population and culture, student exchange programs, and travel and tourism.

To find out more, write or phone:
Jamaica—Embassy
1850 K St., NW, No. 355
International Square Bldg.
Washington, DC 20006
Phone: (202)452-0660 or *Fax:* (202)452-0081

▶ Japan—Embassy

Provides information on: *Embassies, Immigration and Naturalization, Travel and Recreation*

The Embassy acts as the diplomatic representative abroad for Japan. The Embassy provides the following types of information: business and economics, government and politics, immigration policies, law and legal issues, population and culture, student exchange programs, and travel and tourism.

To find out more, write or phone:
Japan—Embassy
2520 Massachusetts Ave., NW
Washington, DC 20008
Phone: (202)939-6700 or *Fax:* (202)939-6788

▶ Japan Society

Provides information on: *Asian Americans*

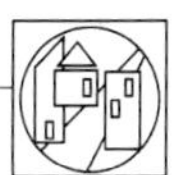

The Society is made up of individuals, institutions, and corporations representing the business, professional, and academic worlds in Japan and the United States. The Society promotes the exchange of ideas between Americans and Japanese, organizes exchange programs, offers courses in Japanese and English, and conducts lectures, art exhibitions, conferences, performances, and concerts.

Information for a fee:

Japan Society—Newsletter. 11/year. Included in $20 membership fee. Presents information on art, culture, sociology, economics, history, and film as they relate to Japan and U.S.-Japanese relations.

To find out more, write or phone:

Japan Society
333 E. 47th St.
New York, NY 10017
Phone: (213)832-1155

▶ Japanese American Citizens League

Provides information on: *Asian Americans, Civil Rights and Liberties*

The League is an organization that works to defend the civil and human rights of all peoples, particularly Japanese Americans. The group maintains the Japanese American Citizens League Legislative Education Committee, which conducts lobbying activities for the enactment of legislation that protects the civil and human rights of Japanese Americans, including the World War II detainment of Japanese Americans.

Information for a fee:

Pacific Citizen. Weekly. $25/year.

To find out more, write or phone:

Japanese American Citizens League
1765 Sutter St.
San Francisco, CA 94115
Phone: (415)921-5225

▶ Kansas Travel & Tourism Development

Provides information on: *Travel and Recreation, State Tourism*

Kansas Travel & Tourism Development provides information on state points of interest, including national landmarks and wildlife refuges within the state; and cultural centers located within major cities. It also provides general travel and tourism information, including hotel and motel lists, maps, general economic information, and major resort/activity brochures.

To find out more, write or phone:
Kansas Travel & Tourism Development
400 W. 8th St., No. 500
Topeka, KS 66603
Toll-free: 1-800-2KA-NSAS or *Phone:* (913)296-2009

▶ Kentucky Tourism Cabinet

Provides information on: *Travel and Recreation, State Tourism*

The Cabinet provides information on state points of interest, including state parks; national landmarks, forests, and parks within the state, including Mammoth Cave National Park; and cultural centers located within major cities. The Cabinet also provides general travel and tourism information, including hotel and motel lists, maps, general economic information, and major resort/activity brochures.

To find out more, write or phone:
Kentucky Tourism Cabinet
2400 Capital Plaza Tower
Frankfort, KY 40601
Toll-free: 1-800-225-TRIP or *Phone:* (502)564-4270

▶ Kenya—Embassy

Provides information on: *Embassies, Immigration and Naturalization, Travel and Recreation*

The Embassy acts as the diplomatic representative abroad for Kenya. The Embassy provides the following types of information: business and economics, government and politics, immigration policies, law and legal issues, population and culture, student exchange programs, and travel and tourism.

To find out more, write or phone:
Kenya—Embassy
2249 R St., NW
Washington, DC 20008
Phone: (202)387-6101

▶ Kuwait—Embassy

Provides information on: *Embassies, Immigration and Naturalization, Travel and Recreation*

The Embassy acts as the diplomatic representative abroad for Kuwait. The Embassy provides the following types of information: business and economics, government and politics, immigration policies, law and legal issues, population and culture, student exchange programs, and travel and tourism.

To find out more, write or phone:
Kuwait—Embassy
2940 Tilden St., NW
Washington, DC 20008
Phone: (202)966-0702 or *Fax:* (202)966-0517

▶ Lebanon—Embassy

Provides information on: *Embassies, Immigration and Naturalization*

The Embassy acts as the diplomatic representative abroad for Lebanon. The Embassy provides the following types of information: business and economics, government and politics, immigration policies, law and legal issues, and population and culture.

To find out more, write or phone:
Lebanon—Embassy
2560 28th St., NW
Washington, DC 20008-2744
Phone: (202)939-6300

▶ Louisiana Office of Tourism

Provides information on: *Travel and Recreation, State Tourism*

The Office provides information on state points of interest, including state parks; national landmarks, forests, and parks within the state, including the Jean Lafitte National Historical Park and Preserve; and cultural centers located within major cities. The Office also provides general travel and tourism information, including hotel and motel lists, maps, general economic information, and major resort/activity brochures.

To find out more, write or phone:
Louisiana Office of Tourism
90 Riverside N.
PO Box 94291
Baton Rouge, LA 70804-4291
Toll-free: 1-800-227-4386 or *Phone:* (504)342-8146

▶ Maine Office of Tourism

Provides information on: *Travel and Recreation, State Tourism*

The Maine Office of Tourism provides information on state points of interest, including state parks; national landmarks and wildlife refuges located within the state; and cultural centers located within major cities. The Office will also provide general travel and tourism information, including hotel and motel lists, maps, general economic information, and major resort/activity brochures.

To find out more, write or phone:
Maine Office of Tourism
State House Sta. 59
189 State St.
Augusta, ME 04333
Toll-free: 1-800-533-9595 or *Phone:* (207)289-5710

▶ Maryland Office of Tourism

Provides information on: *Travel and Recreation, State Tourism*

The Office of Tourism provides information on state points of interest, including state parks; national landmarks and wildlife refuges within Maryland; and cultural centers located within major cities. The Department will also provide general travel and tourism information, including hotel and motel lists, maps, general economic information, and major resort/activity brochures.

To find out more, write or phone:
Maryland Office of Tourism
45 Calvert St.
Annapolis, MD 21401
Toll-free: 1-800-543-1036 or *Phone:* (410)333-6611

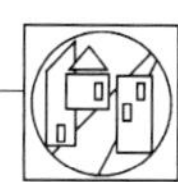

▶ Massachusetts Department of Commerce Division of Tourism

Provides information on: *Travel and Recreation, State Tourism*

The Department of Commerce's Division of Tourism provides information on state points of interest, including national sites and wildlife refuges located within Massachusetts, including the Cape Cod National Seashore; and cultural centers located within major cities. The Division also provides general travel and tourism information, including hotel and motel lists, maps, general economic information, and major resort/activity brochures.

To find out more, write or phone:
Massachusetts Department of Commerce
Division of Tourism
Levere H. Saltonstall Bldg., 13th Fl.
100 Cambridge St.
Boston, MA 02202
Toll-free: 1-800-447-MASS or *Phone:* (617)727-3201 or *Fax:* (617)727-6825

▶ Mexican American Legal Defense and Educational Fund

Provides information on: *Hispanic Americans, Civil Rights and Liberties, Law*

The purpose of the Mexican American Legal Defense and Educational Fund is to protect the civil rights of Hispanics, including Mexican-Americans. The group maintains litigation departments in the areas of education, employment, immigration, and voting rights. The Fund also maintains a Law School Scholarship Program to help promising and committed students enter the legal profession.

Information for free:
Annual Report.
Leadership Program Newsletter. 3/year.

To find out more, write or phone:
Mexican American Legal Defense and Educational Fund
634 S. Spring St., 12th Fl.
Los Angeles, CA 90014
Phone: (213)629-2512 or *Fax:* (213)629-8016

▶ Mexico—Embassy

Provides information on: *Embassies, Immigration and Naturalization, Travel and Recreation*

The Embassy acts as the diplomatic representative for Mexico in the United States. The Embassy provides the following types of information: business and economics, government and politics, immigration policies, law and legal issues, population and culture, student exchange programs, and travel and tourism.

To find out more, write or phone:

Mexico—Embassy
1911 Pennsylvania Ave., NW
Washington, DC 20007
Phone: (202)728-1600

▶ Middle East Institute

Provides information on: *Middle East*

The Institute promotes interest in the history, culture, politics, economy, and languages of the Middle East by providing information and sponsoring workshops for those who wish to learn more about Islam. It maintains a research library containing 20,000 books and audiovisual aids and a data bank on Middle Eastern countries. The Institute also sponsors the Sultan Qaboos bin Said Research Center, which works to promote understanding among Americans and peoples of the Persian Gulf.

Information for free:

The Middle East Institute Publications and Resources. Catalog listing books, audiovisuals, and other information.

Information for a fee:

Arab American Almanac. 1984. $2.
Crosscurrents in the Gulf: Arab, Regional and Global Interests. 1988. $24.95.
Journal. Quarterly. $9/issue. Contains major articles on contemporary political, economic, and social issues, a chronology of quarterly events, documents, article and book reviews, and a bibliography of periodical literature.
Middle East Organizations in Washington. 1989. $9.
Western Interests and U.S. Policy in the Middle East. 1988. $6.

To find out more, write or phone:

Middle East Institute
1761 N St. NW
Washington, DC 20036-0162
Phone: (202)785-1141 or *Fax:* (202)331-8861

▶ Minnesota Office of Tourism

Provides information on: *Travel and Recreation, State Tourism*

The Office of Tourism provides information on state points of interest, including state parks; the many national wildlife refuges, forests, and parks within Minnesota; and cultural centers located within major cities. The Office also provides general travel and tourism information, including hotel and motel lists, maps, general economic information, and major resort/activity brochures.

To find out more, write or phone:

Minnesota Office of Tourism
375 Jackson St.
250 Skyway Level
St. Paul, MN 55101
Toll-free: 1-800-652-9747 or *Phone:* (612)297-2333 or *Fax:* (612)296-7095

▶ Mississippi Division of Tourism

Provides information on: *Travel and Recreation, State Tourism*

The Division of Tourism provides information on state points of interest, including state parks; national landmarks, forests, and wildlife refuges within the state; and cultural centers located within major cities. The Division will also provide general travel and tourism information, including hotel and motel lists, maps, general economic information, and major resort/activity brochures.

To find out more, write or phone:

Mississippi Division of Tourism
1200 Walter Sillers Bldg.
PO Box 849
Jackson, MS 39205
Toll-free: 1-800-647-2290 or *Phone:* (601)359-3297 or *Fax:* (601)359-2832

▶ Missouri Division of Tourism

Provides information on: *Travel and Recreation, State Tourism*

The Division provides information on state points of interest, including state parks; national landmarks, scenic riverways, and wildlife refuges located within the state; and cultural centers located within major cities. The Division also provides general travel and tourism information, including hotel and motel lists, maps, general economic information, and major resort/activity brochures.

To find out more, write or phone:
Missouri Division of Tourism
Truman State Office Bldg.
301 W. High St.
PO Box 1055
Jefferson City, MO 65102
Phone: (314)751-4133 or *Fax:* (314)751-5160

▶ Mozambique—Embassy

Provides information on: *Embassies, Immigration and Naturalization, Travel and Recreation*

The Embassy acts as the diplomatic representative abroad for Mozambique. The Embassy provides the following types of information: business and economics, government and politics, immigration policies, law and legal issues, population and culture, student exchange programs, and travel and tourism.

To find out more, write or phone:
Mozambique—Embassy
1990 M St., NW, #570
Washington, DC
Phone: (202)293-7146 or *Fax:* (202)835-0245

▶ National Association for the Advancement of Colored People (NAACP)

Provides information on: *African Americans, Civil Rights and Liberties*

The Association is made up of persons who believe in the objectives and methods of the NAACP to achieve equal rights through the democratic process and eliminate racial prejudice by removing racial discrimination in housing, employment, voting, schools, the courts, transportation, recreation, prisons, and businesses. It offers referral services, and maintains a law library.

Information for free:
Offers pamphlets and brochures.

Information for a fee:
Crisis. 10/year. Price included in $15 membership fee. Magazine.

To find out more, write or phone:

National Association for the Advancement of Colored People
4805 Mt. Hope Dr.
Baltimore, MD 21215
Phone: (212)481-4100

▶ National Black Child Development Institute (NBCDI)

Provides information on: *African Americans, Child Protection, Healthcare, Child Abuse, Education, Latchkey Children*

NBCDI's purpose is to improve the quality of life for Black youth and to conduct direct services and advocacy campaigns aimed at both national and local issues of health, child welfare, education, and childcare. Program topics include Black leadership, child abuse, child neglect, child welfare, children's legal and human rights, counseling, early childhood education, health education, minority groups, and youth programs.

Information for a fee:

Selecting Child Care: A Checklist. 1990. 8 pages. $3. A practical checklist to ensure the quality of an early childhood program.

Child Care in the Public Schools: Incubator for Inequality? 1986. 28 pages. $5. A report reissued because of the 1990 passage of national child care legislation. Analyzes the national trend toward placing child care programs in the public schools and its potential impact on African American preschoolers.

To find out more, write or phone:

National Black Child Development Institute
1023 15th St., NW, Ste. 600
Washington, DC 20005
Phone: (202)387-1281 or *Fax:* (202)234-1738

▶ National Center for Bilingual Education

Provides information on: *Bilingual/Multilingual Education, Education*

The Association's purposes are to recognize, promote, and publicize bilingual education. It works to increase public understanding of the importance of language and culture, ensures equal opportunities in bilingual education for language-minority students, and promotes research in language education, linguistics, and multicultural education.

To find out more, write or phone:
National Center for Bilingual Education
Union Center Plaza
810 1st St., NE, 3rd Fl.
Washington, DC 20002
Phone: (202)898-1829

▶ National Coalition for Haitian Refugees

Provides information on: *Refugees and Illegal Aliens, Human Rights*

The Coalition is made up of Haitian, labor, civil rights, human rights, trade union, and religious organizations. Its goals are to ensure that Haitians receive fair treatment in their quest for asylum, convince the public of the need for legal status for the refugees, end U.S. Coast Guard interdiction of Haitian boats on the high seas, and deepen the public's understanding of the social, economic, and political causes of Haitian flight from Haiti.

Information for a fee:
Haiti: The Birth of a Democracy. 1991. $6. Report on the general elections held in Haiti in 1990.
Haiti Insight. Bimonthly. Back issues, $1. A newsletter on refugee and human rights affairs in Haiti.
Harvesting Oppression: Forced Haitian Labor in the Dominican Sugar Industry. 1990. $7.
In the Army's Hands: Human Rights in Haiti on the Eve of the Elections. 1990. $10.
Injustice on the High Seas: U.S. Interdiction of Haitian Boat People. 1989. $3.
Return to the Darkest Days: Human Rights in Haiti Since the Coup. 1991. $3.

To find out more, write or phone:
National Coalition for Haitian Refugees
16 E. 42nd St., 3rd Fl.
New York, NY 10017
Phone: (212)867-0020 or *Fax:* (212)867-1668

▶ National Congress of American Indians

Provides information on: *Native Americans*

National Congress of American Indians, seeks to protect, conserve, and develop Indian natural and human services. This is partly accomplished by serving the legislative interests of Indian tribes, and improving health, education, and economic conditions.

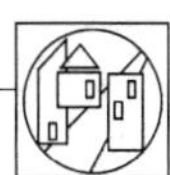

Information for a fee:

Sentinel. Monthly. $25. Price includes yearly membership fee. Provides information on political and legislative news. Includes survey results, calendar of events, and federal register notices.

To find out more, write or phone:

National Congress of American Indians
900 Pennsylvania Ave., SE
Washington, DC 20003
Phone: (202)546-9404

▶ National Council on Public History

Provides information on: *Careers, History*

The Council is a nonprofit membership organization that works to increase and improve the use of history in all sectors of society, support and speak for public history interests, and strengthen and expand the professional development of public historians.

Information for a fee:

Careers for Students of History. $6. Guide to career options open to historians in the academic, public, and private sectors.

Directory of Historical Consultants. $10. Guide to specialities, qualifications, and past experience of 43 historical consulting firms and independent consultants.

A Guide to Graduate Programs in Public History. $10. Contains detailed information on more than fifty programs in the U.S. and Canada.

To find out more, write or phone:

National Council on Public History
301 Cavanaugh Hall - IUPUI
425 University Blvd.
Indianapolis, IN 46202-5140
Phone: (317)274-2716 or *Fax:* (317)274-2347

▶ National Immigration Law Center (NILC)

Provides information on: *Immigration and Naturalization, Civil Rights and Liberties*

NILC provides information on immigration, immigrant's rights including immigration-related employment discrimination, the rights of amnesty aliens who have obtained permanent residence, and other immigration and legal issues.

Information for a fee:
Memoranda and documents are available with a $.05/page contribution.
Guide to Immigration and Naturalization Service Documents. 12 pages.
Highlights of the Immigration Act of 1990. 13 pages.
Immigrating Family Members. 23 pages.
Outline of Immigration Law. 18 pages.
Update on the Amnesty Program. 54 pages.

To find out more, write or phone:
National Immigration Law Center
1636 W. 8th St., Ste. 205
Los Angeles, CA 90017
Phone: (213)487-2531 or *Fax:* (213)384-4899

▶ National Immigration Project of the National Lawyers Guild

Provides information on: *Immigration and Naturalization, Law*

The Project brings together immigration lawyers, law students, and legal workers who work to correct practices and policies that discriminate against immigrants. The Project seeks to protect, defend, and expand the civil and human rights of all immigrants, regardless of their status in the U.S. It helps lawyers and community groups throughout the U.S. and collects documents on a wide variety of immigration issues.

Information for a fee:
Publishes an organization newsletter and manuals on immigration law and practice.

To find out more, write or phone:
National Immigration Project of the National Lawyers Guild
14 Beacon St., Ste. 506
Boston, MA 02108
Phone: (617)227-9727 or *Fax:* (617)227-5495

▶ National Immigration, Refugee and Citizenship Forum

Provides information on: *Immigration and Naturalization, Refugees and Illegal Aliens*

The Forum examines policies on immigration, refugee, and citizenship issues, and coordinates policy-focused working relationships and information networks.

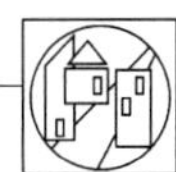

Information for a fee:
Epic Events. Bimonthly. $18/year. Newsletter.

To find out more, write or phone:
National Immigration, Refugee and Citizenship Forum
220 I St., Ste. 220
Washington, DC 20002
Phone: (202)544-0004

▶ National League of Families of American Prisoners and Missing in Southeast Asia

Provides information on: *Prisoners of War*

The League is made up of returned prisoners of war and family members of American servicemen who are missing and/or prisoners in Southeast Asia as a result of the Vietnam War. The League works to determine the status of servicemen still listed as missing-in-action in Southeast Asia, secure the release and return of all POWs, secure the return of the remains of American servicemen who died during the Vietnam War, and educate the public on these issues. It also acts as liaison among the families of POW/MIAs and the U.S. government.

Information for free:
National League of Families of American Prisoners and Missing in Southeast Asia-Newsletter. Bimonthly. Provides current status updates on all efforts and activities.
POW-MIA Fact Book. 1992. 46 pages. Facts from the Department of Defense.
Seeking Answers. Brochure. General overview of action being taken to locate those missing.
Also issues brochures, flyers, bibliographic listing, and educational materials.

To find out more, write or phone:
National League of Families of American Prisoners and Missing in Southeast Asia
Ann Mills Griffiths, Exec.Dir.
1001 Connecticut Ave. NW, Ste. 219
Washington, DC 20036
Phone: (202)223-6846

▶ National Puerto Rican Coalition (NPRC)

Provides information on: *Hispanic Americans*

The National Puerto Rican Coalition is composed of local and national Puerto Rican organizations and other individuals interested in programs and issues affecting the Puerto Rican community. The Coalition attempts to improve the social, economic, and political well-being of Puerto Ricans. The group evaluates the impact of governmental proposals, represents the interests of Puerto Ricans to the public and private sectors, develops a network of Puerto Rican organizations, and conducts research and community development.

Information for free:
Annual Report/Bulletin. Periodic.
NPRC Reports. 10/year.
Policy Agenda. Semiannual.
Also publishes reports and research findings.

To find out more, write or phone:

National Puerto Rican Coalition
1700 K St., NW, Ste. 500
Washington, DC 20006
Phone: (202)223-3915 or *Fax:* (202)429-2223

▶ National Urban League

Provides information on: *African Americans, Civil Rights and Liberties*

The National Urban League is a community service agency that works to eliminate racial segregation and discrimination in the U.S. and achieve equality for Blacks and other minorities in every phase of American life. The league provides direct service to minorities in the areas of employment and labor affairs, housing, education, social welfare, physical and mental health, family planning, law and consumer affairs, youth and student affairs, veterans' affairs, and community and minority business development. The League is made up of civic, professional, business, labor, and religious leaders, and has a staff of trained social workers and other professionals.

Information for a fee:
African American Issues of the Nineties: Cause for Alarm and Action. $12.
Beyond the Margin: Toward Economic Well-Being for Black Americans. $7.
THE PRICE: A Study of the Costs of Racism in America. $14.
Racially Motivated Violence: An Empirical Analysis of a Growing Social Problem. $5.
Stalling Out: The Relative Progress of African Americans. $12.
The State of Black America 1992. $24.95.
Strategies to Alleviate Teenage Pregnancy in the Twenty-First Century. Double edition. $19.
Youth Employment in American Industry. $8.95.

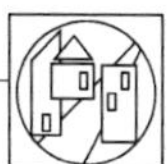

To find out more, write or phone:

National Urban League
500 E. 62nd St.
New York, NY 10021
Phone: (212)310-9000

▶ Near East Foundation

Provides information on: *International Relief, Africa, Middle East, International Development*

The Foundation works in the Middle East and Africa on projects to increase food production, to improve rural and community development and primary health care, and to provide start-up funds for projects until support is available from local sources. The Near East Foundation assigns qualified specialists overseas to assist with technical skills and human resources development. Countries and areas of operation include Botswana, Egypt, Eritrea, Jordan, Lebanon, Lesotho, Mali, Morocco, Nigeria, Sudan, Swaziland, Syria, and West Bank/Gaza.

Information for free:
Near East Foundation—Annual Report.

To find out more, write or phone:

Near East Foundation
342 Madison Ave., Ste. 1030
New York, NY 10173
Phone: (212)867-0064 or *Fax:* (212)867-0169

▶ Nebraska Department of Economic Development Division of Travel and Tourism

Provides information on: *Travel and Recreation, State Tourism*

The Division of Travel and Tourism provides information on state points of interest, including state parks; national landmarks and wildlife refuges within the state; and cultural centers located within major cities. The Division also provides general travel and tourism information, including hotel and motel lists, maps, general economic information, and major resort/activity brochures.

To find out more, write or phone:
Nebraska Department of Economic Development
Division of Travel and Tourism
301 Centennial Mall S.
PO Box 94666
Lincoln, NE 68509-4666
Toll-free: 1-800-228-4307 or *Phone:* (402)471-3794 or *Fax:* (402)471-3778

▶ Netherlands—Embassy

Provides information on: *Embassies, Immigration and Naturalization, Travel and Recreation*

The Embassy acts as the diplomatic representative abroad for the Netherlands. The Embassy can answer general information questions and provide information on business and economics, government and politics, immigration policies, law and legal issues, population and culture, student exchange programs, and travel and tourism.

To find out more, write or phone:
Netherlands—Embassy
4200 Linnean Ave., NW
Washington, DC 20008
Phone: (202)244-5300

▶ Nevada Commission of Tourism

Provides information on: *Travel and Recreation, State Tourism*

The Commission provides information on state points of interest, including state parks; national landmarks, forests, and parks within the state, including the Great Basin National Park; and cultural centers located within major cities. The Commission provides general travel and tourism information, including hotel and motel lists, maps, general economic information, and major resort/activity brochures.

To find out more, write or phone:
Nevada Commission of Tourism
State Capitol Complex
Carson City, NV 89710
Toll-free: 1-800-237-0774 or *Phone:* (702)885-4322 or *Fax:* (702)885-4450

▶ New Hampshire Office of Vacation Travel

Provides information on: *Travel and Recreation, State Tourism*

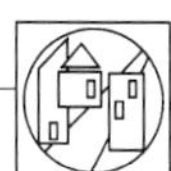

The Office of Vacation Travel can provide information on state points of interest, including state parks, national landmarks, and other sites within New Hampshire; and cultural centers located within major cities. The Office also provides general travel and tourism information, including hotel and motel lists, maps, general economic information, and major resort/activity brochures.

To find out more, write or phone:

New Hampshire Office of Vacation Travel
105 Loudon Rd.
PO Box 856
Concord, NH 03301
Toll-free: 1-800-258-3608 or *Phone:* (603)271-2666 or *Fax:* (603)271-2629

▶ New Jersey Division of Travel and Tourism

Provides information on: *Travel and Recreation, State Tourism*

The Division provides information on state points of interest, including state parks; national landmarks and wildlife refuges located within the state; and cultural centers located within major cities. The Division also provides general travel and tourism information, including hotel and motel lists, maps, general economic information, and major resort/activity brochures.

To find out more, write or phone:

New Jersey Division of Travel and Tourism
20 W. State St., CN 826
Trenton, NJ 08625-0826
Toll-free: 1-800-JER-SEY7 or *Phone:* (609)292-2470 or *Fax:* (609)633-7418

▶ New Mexico Economic Development Department Tourism Division

Provides information on: *Travel and Recreation, State Tourism*

The Division provides information on state points of interest, including state parks; the many national landmarks, forests, wildlife refuges, and parks within New Mexico, including Carlsbad Caverns National Park; and cultural and historical centers located within major cities. The Division also provides general travel and tourism information, including hotel and motel lists, maps, general economic information, and major resort/activity brochures.

To find out more, write or phone:

New Mexico Economic Development Department
Tourism Division
1100 St. Francis Dr., Rm. 8900
Santa Fe, NM 87503
Toll-free: 1-800-545-2040 or *Phone:* (505)827-0291 or *Fax:* (505)983-1565

▶ New York State Department of Economic Development Division of Tourism

Provides information on: *Travel and Recreation, State Tourism*

The Division of Tourism provides information on state points of interest, including state parks; national landmarks, wildlife refuges, and parks within the state; and cultural centers located within major cities. The Division also provides general travel and tourism information, including hotel and motel lists, maps, general economic information, and major resort/activity brochures.

To find out more, write or phone:

New York State Department of Economic Development
Division of Tourism
1 Commerce Plaza
Albany, NY 12245
Toll-free: 1-800-CAL-LNYS or *Phone:* (518)473-0715 or *Fax:* (518)474-6416

▶ Nicaragua—Embassy

Provides information on: *Embassies, Immigration and Naturalization, Travel and Recreation*

The Embassy acts as the diplomatic representative abroad for Nicaragua. The Embassy provides the following types of information: business and economics, government and politics, immigration policies, law and legal issues, population and culture, student exchange programs, and travel and tourism.

To find out more, write or phone:

Nicaragua—Embassy
1627 New Hampshire Ave., NW
Washington, DC 20009
Phone: (202)387-4371

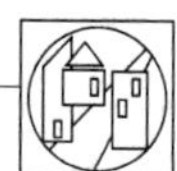

▶ Nigeria—Embassy

Provides information on: *Embassies, Immigration and Naturalization, Travel and Recreation*

The Embassy acts as the diplomatic representative abroad for Nigeria. The Embassy provides the following types of information: business and economics, government and politics, immigration policies, law and legal issues, population and culture, student exchange programs, and travel and tourism.

To find out more, write or phone:
Nigeria—Embassy
2201 M St.
Washington, DC 20037
Phone: (202)822-1500

▶ North American Congress on Latin America

Provides information on: *World Affairs, Central America*

The Congress is an independent research organization that looks at Latin American and U.S. foreign policy. It maintains a library and an extensive data bank.

Information for a fee:
Report on the Americas. 5/year. $4/single issue, $22/year. Journal covering U.S. foreign policy and developments in Latin America and the Caribbean.

To find out more, write or phone:
North American Congress on Latin America
475 Riverside Dr., Rm. 454
New York, NY 10115
Phone: (212)870-3146

▶ North Carolina Department of Commerce Division of Travel & Tourism

Provides information on: *Travel and Recreation, State Tourism*

The Division provides information on state points of interest, including state parks; national seashores, parks, and wildlife refuges located within the state; and cultural centers located within major cities. The Division also provides general travel and tourism information, including hotel and motel lists, maps, general economic information, and major resort/activity brochures.

To find out more, write or phone:
North Carolina Department of Commerce
Division of Travel & Tourism
430 N. Salisbury St.
PO Box 25249
Raleigh, NC 27603
Toll-free: 1-800-847-4862 or *Phone:* (919)733-4171 or *Fax:* (919)733-0110

▶ North Dakota Tourism Promotion

Provides information on: *Travel and Recreation, State Tourism*

North Dakota Tourism Promotion provides information on state points of interest, including state parks; national landmarks and wildlife refuges within the state; and cultural centers located within major cities. It also provides general travel and tourism information, including hotel and motel lists, maps, general economic information, and major resort/activity brochures.

To find out more, write or phone:
North Dakota Tourism Promotion
Liberty Memorial Bldg.
600 East Blvd.
Bismark, ND 58505
Phone: (701)224-2525

▶ Norwegian Embassy

Provides information on: *Embassies, Immigration and Naturalization, Travel and Recreation*

The Embassy acts as the diplomatic representative abroad for Norway. The Embassy provides the following types of information: business and economics, government and politics, immigration policies, law and legal issues, population and culture, student exchange programs, and travel and tourism.

To find out more, write or phone:
Norwegian Embassy
2720 34th St., NW
Washington, DC 20008
Phone: (202)333-6000

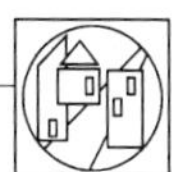

▶ Ohio Department of Development Division of Travel & Tourism

Provides information on: *Travel and Recreation, State Tourism*

The Division provides information on state points of interest, including cultural centers located within major cities. The Division also provides general travel and tourism information, including hotel and motel lists, maps, general economic information, and major resort/activity brochures.

To find out more, write or phone:

Ohio Department of Development
Division of Travel & Tourism
77 S. High St., 29th Fl.
PO Box 1001
Columbus, OH 43266-0101
Toll-free: 1-800-BUC-KEYE or *Phone:* (614)466-8844 or *Fax:* (614)463-1540

▶ Oklahoma Tourism & Recreation Department

Provides information on: *Travel and Recreation, State Tourism*

The Department provides information on state points of interest, including state parks; national landmarks and wildlife refuges within the state; and cultural centers located within major cities. The Department will also provide general travel and tourism information, including hotel and motel lists, maps, general economic information, and major resort/activity brochures.

To find out more, write or phone:

Oklahoma Tourism & Recreation Department
500 Will Rogers Bldg.
Oklahoma City, OK 73105
Toll-free: 1-800-652-6552 or *Phone:* (405)521-2406 or *Fax:* (405)521-3089

▶ Operation Crossroads Africa

Provides information on: *Africa, International Development*

Operation Crossroads Africa is an association of students and professionals, mostly from the U.S., who live and work with African counterparts during July and August on self-help community development projects in Africa. Opportunities are provided for interaction with village elders, educators, and political and other community leaders. Operation Crossroads Africa encourages community growth that comes from an African culture base rather than growth based on Western styles and practices.

Information for free:
Annual Report.
Crossroads Communique. Quarterly.
Also publishes brochures.

To find out more, write or phone:
Operation Crossroads Africa
475 Riverside Dr., Rm. 242
New York, NY 10115
Phone: (212)870-2106

▶ Order Sons of Italy in America (OSIA) Commission for Social Justice

Provides information on: *Ethnic Americans*

OSIA works to keep alive the cultural heritage of Italy and Italian people. The Commission is the anti-defamation arm of OSIA and the Italian-American movement. It works to gain positive recognition for the contributions of Italians and Italian-Americans.

Information for a fee:
Capitol Notes. Quarterly. Price included in $25 membership dues. Newsletter.
OSIA News Includes the Justice Update. 10/year. Price included in $25 membership dues.

To find out more, write or phone:
Order Sons of Italy in America
Commission for Social Justice
219 E St., NE
Washington, DC 20002
Phone: (202)547-2900

▶ Oregon Economic Development Department Division of Tourism

Provides information on: *Travel and Recreation, State Tourism*

The Division of Tourism provides information on state points of interest, including state parks; national landmarks, forests, and wildlife refuges within the state; and cultural centers located within major cities. The Division also provides general travel and tourism information, including hotel and motel lists, maps, general economic information, and major resort/activity brochures.

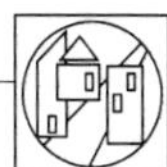

To find out more, write or phone:
Oregon Economic Development Department
Division of Tourism
775 Summer St., NE
Salem, OR 97310
Toll-free: 1-800-547-7842 or *Phone:* (503)378-3451 or *Fax:* (503)581-5115

▶ Organization of American States (OAS)

Provides information on: *World Regions*

OAS is an international organization created to achieve peace and justice among the American nations, to promote their solidarity, and to defend their independence. The group operates through agencies and institutions throughout the hemisphere. It maintains a museum of modern Latin American art, and a library of publications, documents, monographs, and periodicals.

To find out more, write or phone:
Organization of American States
17th St. and Constitution Ave. NW
Washington, DC 20006
Phone: (202)458-6046

▶ Organization of Chinese Americans

Provides information on: *Asian Americans, Civil Rights and Liberties*

Organization of Chinese Americans is made up of U.S. citizens and permanent residents over age 18, most of whom are Chinese-Americans. The Organization's objectives are to foster public awareness of the needs and concerns of Chinese-Americans, advance equal rights, responsibilities and opportunities, and to unite Chinese-Americans. These objectives are accomplished by creating closer ties to industry, sponsoring cultural exhibitions and festivals, and conducting cultural, educational, and political seminars.

Information for a fee:
IMAGE. Bimonthly newsletter. Price included in $25 single membership.

To find out more, write or phone:
Organization of Chinese Americans
1001 Connecticut Ave., NW, Ste. 707
Washington, DC 20036
Phone: (202)223-5500

▶ Panama—Embassy

Provides information on: *Embassies, Immigration and Naturalization, Travel and Recreation*

The Embassy acts as the diplomatic representative abroad for Panama. The Embassy provides the following types of information: business and economics, government and politics, immigration policies, law and legal issues, population and culture, student exchange programs, and travel and tourism.

To find out more, write or phone:
Panama—Embassy
2862 McGill Ter., NW
Washington, DC 20008
Phone: (202)483-1407 or *Fax:* (202)483-6132

▶ Pennsylvania Department of Commerce Bureau of Travel Marketing

Provides information on: *Travel and Recreation, State Tourism*

The Bureau provides information on state points of interest, including state parks; national landmarks and wildlife refuges within the state; and cultural centers located within major cities. The Bureau also provides general travel and tourism information, including hotel and motel lists, maps, general economic information, and major resort/activity brochures.

To find out more, write or phone:
Pennsylvania Department of Commerce
Bureau of Travel Marketing
Forum Bldg., Rm 453
Harrisburg, PA 17120
Toll-free: 1-800-847-4872 or *Phone:* (717)787-5453 or *Fax:* (717)234-4560

▶ People's Republic of China—Embassy

Provides information on: *Embassies, Immigration and Naturalization, Travel and Recreation*

The Embassy acts as the diplomatic representative abroad for the People's Republic of China. The Embassy provides the following types of information: business and economics, government and politics, immigration policies, law and legal issues, population and culture, student exchange programs, and travel and tourism.

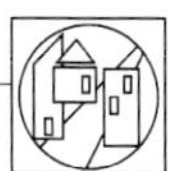

To find out more, write or phone:

People's Republic of China—Embassy
2300 Connecticut Ave., NW
Washington, DC 20008
Phone: (202)328-2517

▶ Philippines—Embassy

Provides information on: *Embassies, Immigration and Naturalization, Travel and Recreation*

The Embassy acts as the diplomatic representative abroad for the Philippines. The Embassy provides the following types of information: business and economics, government and politics, immigration policies, law and legal issues, population and culture, student exchange programs, and travel and tourism.

To find out more, write or phone:

Philippines—Embassy
1617 Massachusetts Ave., NW
Washington, DC 20036
Phone: (202)483-1414

▶ Poland—Embassy

Provides information on: *Embassies, Immigration and Naturalization, Travel and Recreation*

The Embassy acts as the diplomatic representative abroad for Poland. The Embassy provides the following types of information: business and economics, government and politics, immigration policies, law and legal issues, population and culture, student exchange programs, and travel and tourism.

To find out more, write or phone:

Poland—Embassy
2640 16th St., NW
Washington, DC 20009-4202
Phone: (202)234-3800

▶ Popular Culture Association (PCA)

Provides information on: *Popular Culture*

The Association's study topics include television, motion pictures, editorial cartoons, pulp fiction, underground culture, folklore, American humor, popular and protest music, Black culture, Indian and Chicano popular culture, and the social significance of soap opera. PCA compiles statistics and maintains a library.

Information for free:
Bowling Green State University Popular Press Catalog. 44 pages.

Information for a fee:
Advertising and Popular Culture: Studies in Variety and Versatility. 1992. 168 pages. $14.95. Contains 15 articles that focus on the role advertising plays in culture.
Dress and Popular Culture. 1991. 156 pages. $15.95. Examines the part clothing plays in our lives.
Journal of American Culture. Quarterly. $25/year. Covers "the American experience."
Journal of Popular Culture. Quarterly. $25/year. Concentrates on the study of culture in various areas and forms, including the arts, sciences, and print and electronic media.
Journal of Popular Literature. 2/year. $12.50.
Politics and Popular Culture in America Today. 184 pages. $19.95. A look at the history and future of politics and popular culture.
Popular Culture and Curricula. $6.95. Examines popular culture in the classroom.
Popular Music and Society. Quarterly. $20/year. A journal covering music in general.
Reflections of Faith: Religious Folklife in America. 1992. 186 pages. $19.95. Looks at expressions of religious folk culture and its effects on the American environment, and the nature of religious objects.

To find out more, write or phone:
Popular Culture Association
Bowling Green State University
Popular Culture Center
Bowling Green, OH 43403
Phone: (419)372-7861 or *Fax:* (419)372-8095

▶ Portugal—Embassy

Provides information on: *Embassies, Immigration and Naturalization, Travel and Recreation*

The Embassy acts as the diplomatic representative abroad for Portugal. The Embassy provides the following types of information: business and economics, government and politics, immigration policies, law and legal issues, population and culture, student exchange programs, and travel and tourism.

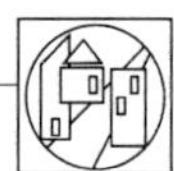

To find out more, write or phone:

Portugal—Embassy
2125 Kalorama Rd., NW
Washington, DC 20008
Phone: (202)328-8610

▶ Reebok International Ltd.

Provides information on: *Human Rights*

Reebok International Ltd. is one of the largest producers of athletic shoes and sports apparel in the U.S. To help spread the message of human rights, the company created the Reebok Human Rights Award. This award recognizes people on the front lines of human rights work who have significantly improved the human rights conditions of people in their communities. To support the work of the award recipients, Reebok distributes $25,000 to a human rights organization designated by each winner. In 1992, Reebok helped create the "Witness" project. This project supplies human rights workers with equipment such as video cameras and computers to help the workers better report on the abuses they observe.

To find out more, write or phone:

Reebok International Ltd.
Paula Van Gelder, Manager of Human Rights Programs
Reebok Human Rights Programs
100 Technology Center Dr.
Stoughton, MA 02072
Phone: (617)341-5000 or *Fax:* (617)341-5087

▶ Refugee Policy Group

Provides information on: *International Relief, Refugees and Illegal Aliens, AIDS, Immigration and Naturalization, Human Rights*

The Group increases domestic and international awareness of refugee issues and their relationship to concerns such as immigration, human rights, relief and development, foreign policy, and security. It gathers and catalogs refugee-related information and improves communications and interaction between public and private sectors by linking those involved in refugee programs with policy and decision-makers.

Information for a fee:

Current Trends and Developments—Contagious Disease and Refugee Protection: AIDS Policy in the United States. 1990. 5 pages. $5.50.

Future Directions in the U.S. Resettlement Program. 1987. 122 pages. $10.50.

Improving International Response to Humanitarian Situations. 1990. 39 pages. $9.50.
Minors in Immigration Proceedings: Problem of Child Welfare and Immigration Enforcement. 1987. 74 pages. $10.50.
Promoting Mental Health Services for Refugees: A Handbook on Model Practices. 1991. 125 pages. $16.
Refugees and Human Rights: A Research and Policy Agenda. 1989. 16 pages. $7.50.
Refugee Issues: Current Status and Directions for the Future. 1983. 36 pages. $9.50.
Refugee Women and Economic Self Reliance. 1992. 22 pages. $5.
Unaccompanied Refugee Children: The Evolution of U.S. Policies 1939-1984. 1984. 84 pages. $10.50.
U.S. Immigration and Refugee Policy: Entering the 1990's. 1989. 33 pages. $5.50. Also offers information on refugees from such regions as Africa, Southeast Asia, Latin America, and Mexico.

To find out more, write or phone:
Refugee Policy Group
1424 16th St. NW, Ste. 401
Washington, DC 20036
Phone: (202)387-3015 or *Fax:* (202)667-5034

▶ Refugee Voices, A Ministry with Uprooted Peoples (RV)

Provides information on: *Refugees and Illegal Aliens, Migrant Workers*

RV is an organization engaged in a national campaign to educate Americans about the plight of uprooted peoples such as refugees, undocumented aliens, and economic migrants. The group hopes to eliminate myths concerning refugees by acknowledging their contributions to society, inform U.S. religious groups about refugees, and educate voters about legislation affecting uprooted peoples. RV acts as an information clearinghouse for groups aiding refugees.

Information for free:
Refugee Voices. Quarterly Newsletter.
Also publishes brochure.

To find out more, write or phone:
Refugee Voices, A Ministry with Uprooted Peoples
c/o Fr. Frank Moan, SJ
3041 4th St., NE
Washington, DC 20017
Toll-free: 1-800-728-0284 or *Phone:* (202)832-0020 or *Fax:* (202)832-5616

▶ Religious Task Force on Central America

Provides information on: *World Affairs, Human Rights, Central America*

Task Force objectives are to influence a change in U.S. foreign policy in Central American and to publicize events taking place in Central America in the hopes that public action will occur concerning human rights violations and other issues. It serves as a resource center for people seeking accurate information about the war in Central America. The group provides national coordination of religious-based Central American campaigns.

Information for a fee:

Action Alerts for Organizations and Communities. Periodic. 6-12/year. $15/year. Issued when current events or pending laws warrant publishing.

Central America Report. Bimonthly. $7/year. Newsletter.

Like Grains of Wheat. $6.95 plus $1.50 shipping and handling. Book.

To find out more, write or phone:

Religious Task Force on Central America
1747 Connecticut Ave. NW
Washington, DC 20009
Phone: (202)387-7652

▶ Republic of Afghanistan—Embassy

Provides information on: *Embassies*

The Embassy acts as the diplomatic representative abroad for Afghanistan. It can answer inquiries from the public or direct people to resources on business and economics, government and politics, immigration policies, law and legal issues, and population and culture.

To find out more, write or phone:

Republic of Afghanistan—Embassy
2341 Wyoming Ave., NW
Washington, DC 20008-1683
Phone: (202)234-3770

▶ Resource Center of The Americas

Provides information on: *Central America, Refugees and Illegal Aliens*

Resource Center of The Americas provides information, educational resources, and news publications from and about Central America. The Center's goals are to build awareness and understanding of Central American society, history, and politics; to coordinate and develop the resources of people concerned about Central America; and contribute to the development of U.S. policies toward Central America that respect its history and culture. It also works to protect the human and legal rights of Central American refugees who seek asylum in the United States. The Center responds to up to 1,000 calls per month pertaining to everything from travel plans in Central America to land reform in El Salvador.

Information for a fee:

Centroamerica: The Month in Review. 10 pages. $2/sample copy. Summary of news compiled from national and international sources and first-hand journalistic reports.

El Salvador: Conflict and Change. $12.95. Resource for high school students covering land reform, labor, human rights, the role of the U.S., and responsibilities of individuals.

To find out more, write or phone:

Resource Center of The Americas
317 17th Ave., SE
Minneapolis, MN 55414
Phone: (612)627-9445 or *Fax:* (612)627-9450

▶ Rhode Island Tourism Division

Provides information on: *Travel and Recreation, State Tourism*

The Division provides information on state points of interest, including cultural centers located within major cities. The Division also provides general travel and tourism information, including hotel and motel lists, maps, general economic information, and major resort/activity brochures.

To find out more, write or phone:

Rhode Island Tourism Division
7 Jackson Walkway
Providence, RI 02903
Toll-free: 1-800-556-2484 or *Phone:* (401)277-2601 or *Fax:* (401)277-2102

▶ Russia—Embassy

Provides information on: *Embassies, Immigration and Naturalization, Travel and Recreation*

The Embassy acts as the diplomatic representative abroad for the Russian Republic. The Embassy provides the following types of information: business and economics,

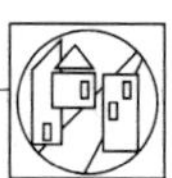

government and politics, immigration policies, law and legal issues, population and culture, student exchange programs, and travel and tourism.

To find out more, write or phone:

Russia—Embassy
1125 16th St., NW
Washington, DC 20036-4801
Phone: (202)628-7551

▶ South Africa—Embassy

Provides information on: *Embassies, Immigration and Naturalization, Travel and Recreation*

The Embassy acts as the diplomatic representative abroad for South Africa. The Embassy provides the following types of information: business and economics, government and politics, immigration policies, law and legal issues, population and culture, student exchange programs, and travel and tourism.

To find out more, write or phone:

South Africa—Embassy
3051 Massachusetts Ave., NW
Washington, DC 20008-3693
Phone: (202)232-4400 or *Fax:* (202)265-1607

▶ South American Explorers Club

Provides information on: *Travel and Recreation, South America*

The Club seeks to further the exchange of information among scientists, adventurers, and travelers with the purpose of encouraging exploration throughout Latin America. It supports all forms of scientific field exploration research in such areas as biology, geography, anthropology, and archeology, as well as field sports, including backpacking, hiking, mountaineering, and whitewater rafting. The group focuses on environmental and ecological concerns, and makes available information on organizations in Latin America that offer services to travelers, scientists, and outdoorsmen. It also maintains a library and bibliographical archives.

Information for a fee:

South American Explorer. Quarterly. $18/year. Magazine covering Latin American exploration.

To find out more, write or phone:
South American Explorers Club
126 Indian Creek Rd.
Ithaca, NY 14850
Phone: (607)277-0488

▶ South Carolina Department of Parks, Recreation & Tourism Division of Tourism

Provides information on: *Travel and Recreation, State Tourism*

The Division of Tourism provides information on state points of interest, including state parks, national landmarks, and cultural centers located within major cities. The Division will also provide general travel and tourism information, including hotel and motel lists, maps, general economic information, and major resort/activity brochures.

To find out more, write or phone:
South Carolina Department of Parks, Recreation & Tourism
Division of Tourism
1205 Pendleton St., Ste. 113
PO Box 71
Columbia, SC 29201
Phone: (803)734-0122

▶ South Dakota Division of Tourism

Provides information on: *Travel and Recreation, State Tourism*

The Division provides information on state points of interest, including state parks; national landmarks, forests, and parks within the state, including Badlands National Park; and cultural centers located within major cities. The Division will also provide general travel and tourism information, including hotel and motel lists, maps, general economic information, and major resort/activity brochures.

To find out more, write or phone:
South Dakota Division of Tourism
711 Wells Ave.
PO Box 1000
Capitol Lake Plaza
Pierre, SD 57501
Toll-free: 1-800-843-1930 or *Phone:* (605)773-3301

▶ South-East Asia Center

Provides information on: *Refugees and Illegal Aliens, Immigration and Naturalization*

The South-East Asia Center is a grassroots organization seeking to assist Lao, Hmong, Cambodian, Vietnamese, and Chinese refugees from Indochina. It promotes the independence and well-being of Indochinese refugees and immigrants and encourages cooperation and mutual understanding among all minorities. The Center strives to sensitize people to the plight of refugees who do not speak English.

Information for free:
New Life News. Periodic.
South-East Asia Center. Pamphlet giving general information on the Center.

To find out more, write or phone:
South-East Asia Center
1124-1128 W. Ainslie
Chicago, IL 60640
Phone: (312)989-6927

▶ Southern Christian Leadership Conference (SCLC)

Provides information on: *African Americans, Civil Rights and Liberties*

The Southern Christian Leadership Conference is a nonsectarian agency that works primarily in the southern states to improve civic, religious, economic, and cultural conditions. It fosters nonviolent resistance to all forms of racial injustice, including state and local laws and practices. It conducts leadership training programs that address such subjects as registration and voting, social protest, use of the boycott, picketing, nature of prejudice, and understanding politics. It sponsors citizenship education schools to teach reading and writing, help people pass literacy tests for voting, and provide information about income tax forms, tax-supported resources, aid to handicapped children, public health facilities, how government is run, and social security. The group also conducts Crusade for the Ballot, which aims to double the Black vote in the South through increased voter registrations.

Information for a fee:
SCLC Magazine. Bimonthly. $20.

To find out more, write or phone:
Southern Christian Leadership Conference
334 Auburn Ave., NE
Atlanta, GA 30312
Toll-free: 1-800-421-0472 or *Phone:* (404)522-1420

▶ Spain—Embassy

Provides information on: *Embassies, Immigration and Naturalization, Travel and Recreation*

The Embassy acts as the diplomatic representative abroad for Spain. The Embassy provides information on business and economics, government and politics, immigration policies, law and legal issues, population and culture, student exchange programs, and travel and tourism.

To find out more, write or phone:
Spain—Embassy
2700 15th St., NW
Washington, DC 20009
Phone: (202)265-0190 or *Fax:* (202)328-3212

▶ Sweden—Embassy

Provides information on: *Embassies, Immigration and Naturalization, Travel and Recreation*

The Embassy acts as the diplomatic representative in the United States for Sweden. The Embassy provides the following types of information: business and economics, government and politics, immigration policies, law and legal issues, population and culture, student exchange programs, and travel and tourism.

To find out more, write or phone:
Sweden—Embassy
600 New Hampshire Ave., NW, #1200
Washington, DC 20008
Phone: (202)944-5600 or *Fax:* (202)342-1319

▶ Switzerland—Embassy

Provides information on: *Embassies, Immigration and Naturalization, Travel and Recreation*

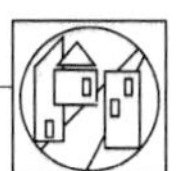

The Embassy acts as the diplomatic representative abroad for Switzerland. The Embassy generally answers questions and can provide information on business and economics, government and politics, immigration policies, law and legal issues, population and culture, student exchange programs, and travel and tourism in Switzerland.

To find out more, write or phone:
Switzerland—Embassy
2900 Cathedral Ave., NW
Washington, DC 20008-3405
Phone: (202)745-7900 or *Fax:* (202)387-2564

▶ Tennessee Department of Tourism Development

Provides information on: *Travel and Recreation, State Tourism*

The Department provides information on state points of interest, including state parks; national landmarks, forests, and parks within the state; and cultural centers located within major cities. The Department will also provide general travel and tourism information, including hotel and motel lists, maps, general economic information, and major resort/activity brochures.

To find out more, write or phone:
Tennessee Department of Tourism Development
PO Box 23170
Nashville, TN 37202
Phone: (615)741-2158

▶ Texas Department of Commerce Division of Tourism

Provides information on: *Travel and Recreation, State Tourism*

The Division provides information on state points of interest, including state parks; national landmarks, forests, and parks within the state; and cultural centers located within major cities. The Division will also provide general travel and tourism information, including hotel and motel lists, maps, general economic information, and major resort/activity brochures.

To find out more, write or phone:
Texas Department of Commerce
Division of Tourism
First City Centre
816 Congress Ave.
PO Box 12728
Austin, TX 78711
Toll-free: 1-800-888-8TEX or *Phone:* (512)462-9191 or *Fax:* (512)320-9456

▶ Thailand—Embassy

Provides information on: *Embassies, Immigration and Naturalization, Travel and Recreation*

The Embassy acts as the diplomatic representative for Thailand in the United States. The Embassy provides the following types of information: business and economics, government and politics, immigration policies, law and legal issues, population and culture, student exchange programs, and travel and tourism.

To find out more, write or phone:
Thailand—Embassy
2300 Kalorama Rd., NW
Washington, DC 20008
Phone: (202)483-7200

▶ Third World Resources

Provides information on: *Developing Countries, International Development*

Third World Resources serves as a clearinghouse for print and audiovisual resources on Third World regions and issues. The group assists social change activists and educators in the Third World in locating sources of Third World-related information from industrialized nations. Third World Resources operates a data center with a library, search service, information service, and more.

Information for a fee:
For $14.95 each, the following directories offer a list of organizations, books, periodicals, pamphlets and audiovisual resources:
Asia and Pacific. 1986. 160 pages.
Food, Hunger, Agribusiness. 1987. 160 pages.
Human Rights. 1989. 160 pages.
Latin America and Caribbean. 1986. 160 pages.
Middle East. 1987.

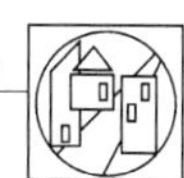

Third World Struggle for Peace With Justice. 1990. 180 pages.
Women in the Third World. 1987. 160 pages.
Also publishes books and brochures.

To find out more, write or phone:
Third World Resources
464 19th St.
Oakland, CA 94612-2297
Toll-free: 1-800-735-3741 or *Phone:* (510)835-4692 or *Fax:* (510)835-3017

▶ Travel Montana Department of Commerce

Provides information on: *Travel and Recreation, State Tourism*

Travel Montana provides tourism and travel information, including information on the cultural and geographical highlights of the state. The organization also provides hotel and motel lists, maps, general economic information, and major resort/activity brochures.

To find out more, write or phone:
Travel Montana
Department of Commerce
1424 9th Ave.
Helena, MT 59620-0411
Toll-free: 1-800-541-1447 or *Phone:* (406)444-2654 or *Fax:* (406)444-2808

▶ Turkish Embassy

Provides information on: *Immigration and Naturalization, Travel and Recreation, Embassies*

The Embassy acts as the diplomatic representative abroad for Turkey. The Embassy provides the following types of information: business and economics, government and politics, immigration policies, law and legal issues, population and culture, student exchange programs, and travel and tourism.

To find out more, write or phone:
Turkish Embassy
1606 23rd St., NW
Washington, DC 20008
Phone: (202)387-3200 or *Fax:* (202)387-0201

▶ Uganda—Embassy

Provides information on: *Embassies, Immigration and Naturalization, Travel and Recreation*

The Embassy acts as the diplomatic representative abroad for Uganda. The Embassy provides the following types of information: business and economics, government and politics, immigration policies, law and legal issues, population and culture, student exchange programs, and travel and tourism.

To find out more, write or phone:
Uganda—Embassy
5909 16th St., NW
Washington, DC 20011-2816
Phone: (202)726-7100

▶ Ukraine—Embassy

Provides information on: *Embassies, Immigration and Naturalization, Travel and Recreation*

The Embassy acts as the diplomatic representative abroad for the Ukraine. The Embassy provides the following types of information: business and economics, government and politics, immigration policies, law and legal issues, population and culture, student exchange programs, and travel and tourism.

To find out more, write or phone:
Ukraine—Embassy
1828 L St., NW, Ste. 711
Washington, DC 20036
Phone: (202)628-7551

▶ United Indians of All Tribes Foundation

Provides information on: *Native Americans*

The Foundation promotes the interests of Native Americans by developing and expanding Native American economic self-sufficiency, education, and arts. It sponsors the National Indian Cultural-Educational Center, which houses a variety of ongoing programs such as model educational programs, community educational services, technical assistance, adult career education, and employment assistance. The group operates Daybreak Star Press, maintains a 300-volume library, media center, museum, and Native American dinner theatre. The Foundation also conducts cultural symposia and rotating art exhibits.

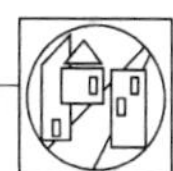

Information for a fee:
Daybreak Star Reader. 8/year. $5.75/year.

To find out more, write or phone:
United Indians of All Tribes Foundation
Bernie Whitebear, Exec.Dir.
Daybreak Star Arts Center
Discovery Park
PO Box 99100
Seattle, WA 98199
Phone: (206)285-4425

▶ U.S.-Asia Institute

Provides information on: *Asian Americans*

The purpose of the Institute is to strengthen ties between the East and the West and foster communication, cooperation, and cultural exchange between the U.S. and Asia. The group promotes an understanding in Asia of the issues important to the development of American domestic and foreign policies through research and special programs.

Information for free:
Offers a newsletter, conference proceedings, booklets, and brochures.

To find out more, write or phone:
U.S.-Asia Institute
232 E. Capitol St., NE
Washington, DC 20003
Phone: (202)544-3181

▶ United States Committee for Refugees (USCR)

Provides information on: *Refugees and Illegal Aliens*

United States Committee for Refugees serves as an information and advocacy center seeking to communicate the plight of the world's millions of refugees to the American people and to provide a nongovernmental focal point for humanitarian concern in meeting the needs of a changing world refugee situation. USCR consults with national and international leaders, maintains a close working relationship with voluntary organizations, and supports specialized United Nations agencies working to alleviate refugee problems. It also monitors hearings and legislation of the U.S. Congress and policies of the U.S. government on refugee affairs.

Information for free:
Refugee Reports. A sample copy of the monthly USCR newsletter is available without charge.

Information for a fee:
USCR Issue Paper Series. $4 each. Includes such titles as
Peace or Terror: A Crossroads for Southern Africa's Uprooted. 1989.
Refugees at Our Border: The U.S. Response to Asylum Seekers. 1989.
Uncertain Harbors: The Plight of Vietnamese Boat People. 1987.
The U.S. Government, Humanitarian Assistance, and the New World Order: A Call for a New Approach. 1991.
The World Refugee Survey. 1992. $10. An annual report on refugee situations around the world.
Also offers titles on such areas as Iran, Sudan, Central America, Uganda, Laos, Ethiopia, Tibet, and more.

To find out more, write or phone:
United States Committee for Refugees
1025 Vermont Ave. NW, Ste. 920
Washington, DC 20005
Phone: (202)347-3507

▶ United States Naturalized Citizen Association

Provides information on: *Immigration and Naturalization, Ethnic Americans*

The Association promotes general welfare of persons from Europe, Asia, Latin America, and Africa who have become U.S. citizens. It helps find employment for newly naturalized citizens, supports homes for the aged, hospitals, orphanages, and schools for handicapped children, and works for adoptions, employment of minorities, and relief for refugees.

To find out more, write or phone:
United States Naturalized Citizen Association
Rev.Dr. Peter P. S. Ching, Pres.
PO Box 19822
Alexandria, VA 22320
Phone: (703)549-2962

▶ United States Virgin Islands Department of Tourism

Provides information on: *Travel and Recreation, State Tourism*

The Department provides information on the Virgin Islands, including historical sites and cultural centers. The Department will also provide general travel and tourism information, including hotel and motel lists, maps, general economic information, and major resort/activity brochures.

To find out more, write or phone:

United States Virgin Islands Department of Tourism
Emancipation Sq.
Charlotte Amalie
PO Box 6400
St. Thomas, VI 00801
Toll-free: 1-800-USV-INFO or *Phone:* (809)774-8784 or *Fax:* (809)774-4390

▶ University of Wisconsin Center for Southeast Asian Studies

Provides information on: *Southeast Asia*

The Center researches, teaches, and provides information in the areas of southeast Asian studies. It offers courses on Southeast Asia in such areas as language and literature, theater and drama, political science, and urban and regional planning. The Center maintains a substantial library collection on Southeast Asia and is collecting political and labor tracts, popular literature, religious pamphlets, videotapes, and other materials to add to its collection on modern culture.

Information for a fee:

Aesthetic Tradition and Cultural Transition in Java and Bali. 1984. 331 pages. $14.00. Examines the aesthetics of traditional Javanese culture, and looks at the new aesthetics that have developed in response to social change.

Anthropology Goes to War: Professional Ethics and Counterinsurgency in Thailand. 1992. 325 pages. $14.95.

Between Two Coups: The Continuing Institutionalization of Democracy in Thailand. 1989. 60 pages. $6.50.

Bomb: Indonesian Short Stories by Putu Wijaya. 1988. 251 pages. $12.00.

A Complete Account of the Peasants' Uprising in the Central Region. 1983. 140 pages. $8.

Gender, Power, and the Construction of the Moral Order: Studies from the Thai Periphery. 1988. 106 pages. $8.00.

Interpretive Accounts of the Khmer Rouge Years: Personal Experience in Cambodian Peasant World View. 1989. 86 pages. $6.00.

To find out more, write or phone:
University of Wisconsin
Center for Southeast Asian Studies
4115 Helen C. White
600 N. Park St.
Madison, WI 53706
Phone: (608)263-1755

▶ Utah Travel Council

Provides information on: *Travel and Recreation, State Tourism*

The Council provides information on state points of interest, including state parks; national landmarks, forests, and parks within Utah, including Bryce Canyon National Park; and cultural centers located within major cities. The Council will also provide general travel and tourism information, including hotel and motel lists, maps, general economic information, and major resort/activity brochures.

To find out more, write or phone:
Utah Travel Council
Council Hall, Capitol Hill
300 N. State St.
Salt Lake City, UT 84114
Phone: (801)538-1030 or *Fax:* (801)538-1399

▶ Venezuela—Embassy

Provides information on: *Embassies, Immigration and Naturalization, Travel and Recreation*

The Embassy acts as the diplomatic representative in the United States for Venezuela. The Embassy provides the following types of information: business and economics, government and politics, immigration policies, law and legal issues, population and culture, student exchange programs, and travel and tourism.

To find out more, write or phone:
Venezuela—Embassy
2445 Massachusetts Ave., NW
Washington, DC 20008
Phone: (202)797-3800

▶ Vermont Travel Division

Provides information on: *Travel and Recreation, State Tourism*

The Division provides information on state points of interest, including cultural centers located within major cities. The Division will also provide general travel and tourism information, including hotel and motel lists, maps, general economic information, and major resort/activity brochures.

To find out more, write or phone:
Vermont Travel Division
134 State St.
Montpelier, VT 05602
Phone: (802)828-3236 or *Fax:* (802)828-3233

▶ Virginia Division of Tourism

Provides information on: *Travel and Recreation, State Tourism*

The Division provides information on state points of interest, including state parks and cultural centers located within major cities. The Division will also provide general travel and tourism information, including hotel and motel lists, maps, general economic information, and major resort/activity brochures.

To find out more, write or phone:
Virginia Division of Tourism
202 N. 9th St., Ste. 500
Richmond, VA 23219
Toll-free: 1-800-VIS-ITVA or *Phone:* (804)786-2051 or *Fax:* (804)786-5374

▶ Washington Convention & Visitors Bureau

Provides information on: *Travel and Recreation, State Tourism*

The Bureau provides information on Washington, DC, including landmarks and monuments located throughout the nation's Capitol as well as cultural centers and other sites of public interest. The Bureau will also provide general travel and tourism information, including hotel and motel lists, maps, general economic information, and major resort/activity brochures.

To find out more, write or phone:

Washington Convention & Visitors Bureau
1212 New York Ave., NW
Washington, DC 20005
Phone: (202)789-7000 or *Fax:* (202)789-7007

▶ Washington Department of Trade and Economic Development Tourism Promotion and Development Division

Provides information on: *Travel and Recreation, State Tourism*

The Division provides information on state points of interest, including state parks; the many national landmarks, forests, and parks within the state, including Olympic National Forest; and cultural centers located within major cities. The Division will also provide general travel and tourism information, including hotel and motel lists, maps, general economic information, and major resort/activity brochures.

To find out more, write or phone:

Washington Department of Trade and Economic Development
Tourism Promotion and Development Division
101 General Administration Bldg.
Olympia, WA 98504-0613
Phone: (206)753-5600 or *Fax:* (206)586-1850

▶ West Virginia Travel Development Division

Provides information on: *Travel and Recreation, State Tourism*

The Division provides information on state points of interest, including state parks; national landmarks, forests, and scenic rivers within West Virginia; and cultural centers located within major cities. The Division also provides general travel and tourism information, including hotel and motel lists, maps, general economic information, and major resort/activity brochures.

To find out more, write or phone:

West Virginia Travel Development Division
2101 Washington St., E.
Charleston, WV 25305
Toll-free: 1-800-CAL-LWVA or *Phone:* (304)558-2286

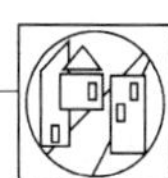

▶ Wisconsin Tourism Development

Provides information on: *Travel and Recreation, State Tourism*

Wisconsin Tourism Development provides information on state points of interest, including state parks; national parks and wildlife refuges within the state; and cultural centers located within major cities. It also provides general travel and tourism information, including hotel and motel lists, maps, general economic information, and major resort/activity brochures.

To find out more, write or phone:

Wisconsin Tourism Development
123 W. Washington Ave.
PO Box 7970
Madison, WI 53707
Toll-free: 1-800-372-2737 or *Phone:* (608)266-2161 or *Fax:* (608)267-2829

▶ The World Bank

Provides information on: *Developing Countries, International Development*

The objective of the World Bank and its affiliate associations is to help raise the standard of living in developing countries. World Bank provides various forms of financial assistance such as extending credits on easier terms than are normally available. The organization makes loans for projects aimed at strengthening the economies of developing countries in Asia, the Middle East, Africa, and the Western Hemisphere.

Information for free:

Index of Publications and Guide to Information Products and Services. Updated annually. 96 pages. Lists some 750 World Bank publications.

The World Bank Annual Report.

Information for a fee:

Developing Agricultural Extension for Women Farmers. 1992. 124 pages. $7.95. Discussion paper. Contains guidelines on how to prepare and implement programs that target women farmers.

Education in Asia. 1992. 224 pages. $12.95. Study showing the importance of basic education.

Global Economic Prospects and the Developing Countries 1992. 80 pages. $10.95. A survey of the long-term prospects for the global economy.

The Greenhouse Effect. 26 pages. $6.95. Describes how countries can cooperate to reduce negative climate change.

Organizing and Managing Tropical Disease Control Programs. 1992. 131 pages. $8.95. Technical paper. Reviews successful disease control programs.

People and Trees. 1992. 288 pages. $17.95. Shows how forestry can help meet basic national goals when managed properly by local people.

Trends in Private Investment in Developing Countries. 1992. 55 pages. $6.95. Discussion paper. Presents statistical data on private investment trends in 40 developing countries.

To find out more, write or phone:

The World Bank
1818 H St. NW, Rm. E1227
Washington, DC 20433
Phone: (202)473-1155 or *Fax:* (202)477-6391

▶ Worldwatch Institute

Provides information on: *World Affairs, Environmental Protection*

The Institute is a research organization that encourages a reflective and deliberate approach to global problem-solving. It works to anticipate global problems and social trends and to focus attention on emerging global issues. Recent projects include technology, agriculture, local community action, current global trends in population growth and family planning, renewable energy options, and economic, political, and demographic problems facing the world in the last quarter of this century.

Information for a fee:

How Much is Enough? The Consumer Society and the Future of the Earth. $8.95. A look at the effects of the consumer lifestyle, such as car driving and beef eating, on the earth.

Saving the Planet: How to Shape an Environmentally Sustainable Global Economy. $8.95. Gives advice on how to help the global economy.

State of the World. $10.95. Annual. Worldwatch Institute report on the state of the world's natural resources.

Worldwatch Magazine. Bimonthly. Covers worldwide issues that deal with problems and solutions in the effort to save the planet.

The Worldwatch Paper Series, reports published 6-8 times a year covering such issues as recycling, energy, population, and transportation. $5. Some titles include: Air Pollution, Acid Rain, and the Future of Forests; Alternatives to the Automobile: Transport for Livable Cities; Banishing Tobacco; The Global Politics of Abortion; Poverty and the Environment; Reforesting the Earth; and Slowing Global Warming.

The Worldwatch Reader on Global Environmental Issues. $10.95, paperback. An introduction to the environment.

To find out more, write or phone:

Worldwatch Institute
1776 Massachusetts Ave., NW
Washington, DC 20036
Phone: (202)452-1999 or *Fax:* (202)296-7365

▶ Wyoming Travel Commission

Provides information on: *Travel and Recreation, State Tourism*

The Commission provides information on state points of interest, including state parks; national landmarks, forests, and parks within the state, including Grand Teton and Yellowstone National Parks; and cultural centers located within major cities. The Commission will also provide general travel and tourism information, including hotel and motel lists, maps, general economic information, and major resort/activity brochures.

To find out more, write or phone:

Wyoming Travel Commission
I-25 at College Dr.
Cheyenne, WY 82002-0660
Toll-free: 1-800-225-5996 or *Phone:* (307)777-7777 or *Fax:* (307)777-6904

▶ Yugoslavia—Embassy

Provides information on: *Embassies*

The Embassy acts as the diplomatic representative abroad for the Serbia-Montenegro Republic. The Embassy provides information on the Republic's business and economics, government and politics, immigration policies, law and legal issues, population, and culture.

To find out more, write or phone:

Yugoslavia—Embassy
2410 California St., NW
Washington, DC 20008-1697
Phone: (202)462-6566

To Contact People . . .

These books identify individual experts or organizations that can direct you to one.

▶ *The Address Book: How to Reach Anyone Who Is Anyone*

This book can be used to contact more than 3,500 prominent persons including political leaders, business executives, athletes, actors and actresses, artists, musicians, and writers. The book lists name and address. Names are listed alphabetically.
Biennial. Perigee Books.

▶ *African-American Blackbook International Reference Guide*

The reference guide covers about 5,000 African-American businesses and organizations, including local affiliates, African-Americans on boards of major corporations, in the food, beverage, and tobacco industries, and elected officials. Entries include firm name, address, phone, key personnel, and history.
Annual. National Publications Sales Agency, Inc.

▶ *American Association for the Advancement of Slavic Studies Directory of Programs in Soviet and East European Studies*

Coverage includes approximately 300 educational institutions in the U.S. and Canada with Soviet and East European programs, departments, and centers. Entries include institution name, address, phone, description of programs and activities, faculty research interests, and degrees offered.
Triennial. American Association for the Advancement of Slavic Studies.

▶ *Asian Americans Information Directory*

The directory covers 5,200 sources of information on Asian American life and culture, including national, state, and local organizations; newspapers, newsletters, journals, directories, and videos, television and radio stations, research and study centers, university area studies programs, library and museum collections, and government agencies. Entries include name, address, phone, name and title of contact, and description. The book is classified by nationality or ethnic group, then by type of organization, publication, etc.
First edition. 1991. Gale Research Inc.

▶ *Black Americans Information Directory*

The directory covers sources of information on a variety of aspects of Black American life and culture, including national, state, and local organizations, publishers of newspapers, periodicals, newsletters, and other publications and videos, television and radio stations, traditionally Black colleges and universities, library collections, museums and other cultural institutions, Black studies programs and research centers, federal and state government agencies, Black religious organizations, and awards, honors, and prizes. Entries in book include, name, address, phone, name and title of contact, description of services, activities, etc. The publication is classified by type of organization, activity, service, etc.
Biennial. Gale Research Inc.

▶ *Canadian Who's Who*

This book lists about 12,000 notable Canadians in Canada and abroad based on position or achievement. Entries include name, address, personal and career data.
Annual. University of Toronto Press.

▶ *Directory of Bilingual Speech-Language Pathologists and Audiologists*

This book lists more than 900 members who have speaking proficiency in English and at least one other language. Entries include personal name, address, phone, area of certification (i.e. speech-language pathology, audiology, or both). Information is arranged by foreign language spoken, then geographical.
Biennial. American Speech-Language-Hearing Association.

▶ *Directory of Caribbeanists*

Coverage includes about 850 people and 25 institutions that share an interest in Caribbean studies. Entries include name, address, descipline, affiliation, and area of interest. Same information is listed alphabetically, classified by subject, and geographical.
1989. Caribbean Studies Association, Department of Social Services, Interamerican University of Puerto Rico.

▶ *Directory of Federal Historical Programs and Activities*

Coverage includes about 1,700 federally employed historians and federal government agencies operating historical programs. For historians, entries include name, phone, area of expertise, and historical program. Program entries include name, address, and

functions of historians.
Triennial. American Historical Association, and the Society for History in the Federal Government.

▶ *Directory of Graduate and Undergraduate Programs and Courses in Middle East Studies in the United States, Canada, and Abroad*

Use this directory to contact more than 180 educational institutions. Entries include name of school; department name, address, and phone; degrees offered; courses; names of faculty members; graduate student support available, etc. The book is arranged in separate alphabetical sections for the U.S., Canada, and overseas.
Biennial. Middle East Studies Association of North America.

▶ *Directory of Historical Organizations in the United States and Canada*

Coverage includes about 13,000 historical and genealogical societies. The book also lists and describes the more than 175 historical properties maintained by the National Park Service. Entries include organization name, address, phone, type of agency, founding date, name of one official, number of members and staff, publications, brief note on major programs and period of interest.
Biennial. American Association for State and Local History.

▶ *Directory of National Organizations Dealing with Central America*

Use the directory to locate over 30 of the most influential organizations active in the Central America debate. Entries include organization name, address, phone, and description of history and activities. Entries are arranged alphabetically.
1990. World Without War Council.

▶ *Directory of Popular Culture Collections*

Use this book to locate more than 600 collections of print and nonprint materials on popular culture, primarily in the United States. The book lists institution, address, phone, hours of operation, special services, fees, and name of curator or librarian. Information is arranged alphabetically.
1989. Oryx Press.

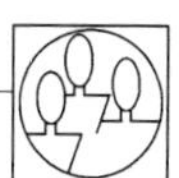

▶ *Ebony—100 Most Influential Black Americans Issue*

Entries include name, profession, and brief career notes.
Annual. Johnson Publishing Company, Inc.

▶ *Foreign Consular Offices in the United States*

Use this book to contact foreign consular offices in the U.S. and key personnel. Consular offices represent the foreign country in the United States. Information includes name of country, addresses of consulates, phone numbers, names of consuls and other personnel, and jurisdictions. The book is arranged geographically.
Annual. Bureau of Public Affairs, U.S. Department of State.

▶ *Hispanic Resource Directory*

Find more than 6,200 local, regional, and national Hispanic organizations, associations, research centers, academic programs, foundations, chambers of commerce, government agencies, and other bodies of interest to the Hispanic American community. The book is arranged geographically.
1991. Triennial. Denali Press.

▶ *How and Where to Research Your Ethnic-American Cultural Heritage*

This book provides information on historical societies, cultural institutes, libraries, archives, publishers, and other sources for genealogical research into German, Russian, Native American, Polish, Black, Japanese, Jewish, Irish, Mexican, Italian, Chinese, and Scandinavian backgrounds. Twelve separate volumes cover each ethnic group. Entries include institution name, address, and phone.
Most volumes first published 1979. Robert D. Reed.

▶ *Human Rights: A Reference Handbook*

Coverage includes a list of organizations in the United States related to human rights. Entries include name, address, phone, contacts, description of services, and list of services provided. Entries are arranged alphabetically by subject.
1990. ABC-CLIO.

▶ *Human Rights Organizations and Periodicals Directory*

Coverage includes over 700 U.S. organizations and periodicals dedicated to improving human rights. Entries for organizations provide name, address, phone, name and

title of contact, geographical area served, and description of projects/services. For periodicals, entries include publication title, publisher name, address, phone, and description of publication. Entries are arranged alphabetically.
Biennial. Meiklejohn Civil Liberties Institute.

▶ *International Rural Sociology Association Membership Directory*

Use this directory to identify 1,600 professionals and paraprofessionals working in rural communities in both developed and developing countries.
Annual. International Rural Sociology Association.

▶ *International Who's Who*

This book covers 20,000 prominent persons worldwide. Entries include name, nationality, personal and career information, honors, awards, writings, address, and phone. Names are arranged alphabetically.
Annual. Europa Publications Ltd.

▶ *Japanese Studies in the United States—Part II: Directory of Japan Specialists and Japanese Studies Institutions in the U.S. and Canada*

Coverage includes approximately 1,400 academic specialists and 120 Japanese studies programs in the United States and Canada. For academic specialists, entries include personal name, address, phone, biographical data, research interests, and major publications. For institutions, entries include organization name, address, phone, courses, academic and research programs, library collections, publications, and outreach activities. Entries are arranged alphabetically.
1989. Association for Asian Studies, Inc.

▶ *Latin American Studies Association—Handbook & Membership Directory*

Coverage includes 3,200 people and institutions with scholarly interests in Latin America. Entries include name, address, phone, and fax. The book is arranged alphabetically.
1991. Latin American Studies Association.

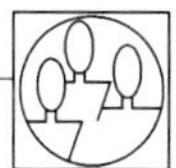

▶ *Middle East: A Directory of Resources*

This book contains contact information for organizations and publishers of books, periodicals, audiovisuals, and other materials from and about Middle Eastern countries. Entries include organization or company name, address, phone, and materials available. Entries are arranged alphabetically by resource.
1988. Updated quarterly. Third World Resources.

▶ *Minority Organizations: A National Directory*

This book lists over 7,700 groups composed of or intended to serve members of minority groups, including Alaska Natives, American Indians, African Americans, Hispanic Americans, and Asian Americans. Entries include organization name, address, description of activities, purpose, publications, and more. The publication is arranged by minority group.
1992. Garrett Park Press.

▶ *Native American Directory: Alaska, Canada, United States*

Use this directory to find information on Native American performing arts groups, craft materials suppliers, stores and galleries, Indian-owned motels and resorts; tribal offices, museums, and cultural centers; associations, schools; newspapers, radio and television programs and stations operated, owned, or specifically for Native Americans; calendar of events, including officially sanctioned powwows, conventions, arts and crafts shows, all-Indian rodeos, and Navajo rug auctions. Generally, entries include organization or company name, address, descriptive comments, and dates (for shows or events). Information is arranged geographically by state.
1992. National Native American Cooperative.

▶ *Native Americans Information Directory*

The directory covers approximately 4,000 sources of information on aspects of Native American, Native Canadian, Native Alaskan, and Native Hawaiian life and culture. This includes federally recognized tribes, national, state, and local organizations, publishers of newspapers, periodicals, newsletters, and other publications and videos, broadcast media, museum collections, federal government agencies; research centers; educational and studies programs, and library collections. Entries include organization or publication name, address, phone, name and title of contact, description of services, activities, etc. The book is classified by group (Native American, Canadian, Alaskan, or Hawaiian), then by type of resource.
1992. Gale Research Inc.

▶ *North American Human Rights Directory*

Use this directory to contact about 710 organizations based in the United States and Canada engaged in work in international human rights and social justice. The book lists organization name, address, phone, names of principal staff members, publications, whether tax exempt or registered with United Nations, and brief description of origin, purposes, and programs. Organizations are arranged in alphabetical order.
1991. Human Rights Internet.

▶ *Raising the Curtain: A Guide to Independent Organizations and Contacts in Eastern Europe*

Use this guide to find information on 200 organizations and contacts in Eastern Europe interested in exchange with other countries. Entries include name, address, phone, descriptions, names and addresses of organizational contacts. The book is arranged both alphabetically and geographically.
World Without War Council.

▶ *Refugee and Immigrant Resource Directory*

Use this directory to contact some 2,000 organizations offering assistance to refugees and immigrants. The directory lists organization name and address, phone, fax, number of employees, geographical area served, financial data, name and title of contact, hours of operation, description of services, publications, U.S. Board of Immigration Appeals recognition, date of establishment, statement of purpose, and coded list of activities. Information is arranged geographically by state.
Approximately triennial. Denali Press.

▶ *Refugee Resettlement Program—Annual Report to the Congress*

This report can be used to locate state refugee coordinators. Principle content includes a report on the activities of the Refugee Resettlement Program, including federal, state, and private refugee programs in placement, education, job training, health, and social services; and a list of grants awarded by the Refugee Health Program of the Centers for Disease Control.
Annual. U.S. Family Support Administration, Office of Refugee Resettlement.

▶ *Research Centers Directory*

Coverage includes over 13,000 university-related and other nonprofit research organizations that carry on continuing research programs in all areas of study. This includes research institutes, laboratories, experiment stations, computing centers, research parks, technology transfer centers, and other facilities and activities in the U.S. and Canada. Entries include unit name, name of parent institution, address, phone, fax, principal fields of research, name of director, year founded, and related information. Information is classified by broad subjects, then alphabetical by unit name.
Annual. Gale Research Inc.

▶ *Who's Who in America*

This book contains information on 79,000 people, primarily in the U.S., considered to be of current national interest because of achievement or position. Entries include name, address, personal data, career data, memberships, special achievements, and publications. Names are listed alphabetically; a separate volume indexes people by profession and location.
Biennial. Updated quarterly. Marquis Who's Who.

▶ *Who's Who of American Women*

This book contains information on more than 30,000 high-profile women in all fields. Entries include name, address, personal, educational, and career data, professional association membership, special achievements, awards, and writings. Names are arranged alphabetically.
Biennial. Marquis Who's Who.

▶ *Who's Who among Black Americans*

Use this book to identify some 19,000 African-American leaders in government, business, education, religion, communications, civic affairs, the arts, law, medicine, science, sports, and entertainment. The book provides name, home and/or business address (at listees' discretion), education, career, and personal data; organizational affiliations; honors, awards, and special achievements. Names are listed in alphabetical order.
Biennial. Gale Research Inc.

▶ *Who's Who among Hispanic Americans*

Coverage includes over 9,000 notable contemporary Hispanic Americans. Entries provide name, address, biographical data, educational background, career history,

awards and honors, noteworthy achievements, and related information. Names are arranged alphabetically.
Biennial. Gale Research Inc.

▶ *Who's Who in International Affairs*

Coverage includes 7,000 people involved in all aspects of international politics, economics, and cultural affairs. Entries provide name, biographical data, education, position held and years appointed, current post, publications, address, telephone, telex, and fax.
Triennial. Europa Publications Ltd.

▶ *Who's Who in the World*

This directory covers more than 31,000 people of current international interest because of their achievement or position. Entries include name, address, biographical data, civic activities, awards, writings, and other information. Names are arranged alphabetically.
Biennial. Marquis Who's Who.

▶ *World Directory of Human Rights Teaching & Research Institutions*

The directory lists over 330 institutions dedicated to human rights training, research, development, and education. Entries list institution name, address, type and level of course, target group, admission requirements, length of course, language used in course, costs, name of instructor, scholarships available. Entries are arranged geographically by country.
Social and Human Services Documentation Centre, United Nations Educational, Scientific and Cultural Organization (UNESCO).

4

Careers and Work

▶ Chapter 4 covers these topics:

Career Choices | Career Development | Employment

▶ Related topics appear in chapters on:

Education; Family Connections and Concerns; Health and Personal Concerns

▶ Ideas for research topics:

The Best and Worst Jobs—Factors to Consider
Career Choices for Teenaged Parents
Career Education
Companies as Members of the Community
The Changing Labor Market
Changing Roles of Men and Women in the Workplace
Drug Tests, Lie Detectors, Background Checks—How Far Should a Company Be Allowed to Go in Screening Potential Employees
Employee Benefits: An Important Part of Compensation
Environmental Careers
Equity in the Workplace
Handicapped Persons in the Work Force
How Does the American Work Force Compare to Other Industrialized Nations?
How National Economic Trends Are Reflected in (Your State)?
Impact of an MBA on Lifetime Earnings
The Impact of the Recession on Young Career Seekers
Internships and On-the-Job Training
Job Hunting Strategies
Matching Personal Skills and Interests to a Career
Nontraditional Occupations
Occupational Trends in America
The Pluses and Minuses of Holding a Job While in High School
Should Re-Training Programs Be Part of Our Unemployment Benefits?

▶ Ideas for research topics (continued):

Small Businesses vs. Large Corporations as Employers

Wage Differences Between Men and Women in the Same Jobs

What's It Like to Work For (Company Name)?

To Contact Organizations . . .

▶ American College Admissions and Career Counseling Center

Provides information on: *College Testing and Entrance Requirements, Counseling, Careers*

The Center provides educational and career counseling to young people and adults. It maintains an educational and career resource library, and provides information on college admissions and career counseling to the national media.

To find out more, write or phone:
American College Admissions and Career Counseling Center
2401 Pennsylvania Ave., Ste. 10-C-51
Philadelphia, PA 19130
Phone: (215)232-5225

▶ Arthur Andersen & Co., S.C.

Provides information on: *Business and Finance Careers*

Arthur Anderson is one of the top accounting firms in the world. The company provides services related to auditing, taxes, and consulting. A large share of the company's business is conducted in locations around the world. Arthur Anderson has training centers for its employees in the U.S., the Netherlands, Spain, and Asia/Pacific. More than 50,000 people attended the company's training courses in 1990.

Information for free:
Accelerate Your Career. 1991. 30 pages. Booklet. Presents profiles of first-year employees, description of employee programs, professional services, training centers, financial highlights, and global update.

To find out more, write or phone:
Arthur Andersen & Co., S.C.
Recruiting and College Relations
33 W. Monroe St.
Chicago, IL 60603
Phone: (312)580-0069

▶ Apple Computer, Inc.

Provides information on: *Computer Careers, Marketing and Sales Careers, Business and Finance Careers, Human Resources Careers*

Established in 1977, Apple Computer, Inc. is one of the world's largest makers of personal computers. Apple is noted for its desktop publishing system and user-friendly Macintosh computers. In addition to U.S. locations, Apple has operations in Ireland, Singapore, the United Kingdom, Belgium, the Netherlands, Italy, and Australia. Career opportunities for people with bachelor's or graduate degrees exist in hardware/software engineering, manufacturing, sales and marketing, information systems and technology, finance, and human resources.

Information for free:
Fact sheets providing overview of company and related career opportunities.

To find out more, write or phone:
Apple Computer, Inc.
College Relations Department
20525 Mariani Ave.
Cupertino, CA 95014
Toll-free: 1-800-331-4496 or *Phone:* (408)974-3010

▶ Armstrong World Industries, Inc.

Provides information on: *Engineering Careers, Business and Finance Careers, Marketing and Sales Careers*

Armstrong World Industries, Inc. is a primary manufacturer of interior furnishings such as linoleum, furniture, and building products. The company employs more than 25,000 people in 90 manufacturing plants worldwide.

Information for free:
Brochures describing specific career areas are available in business information services, engineering, management accounting, industrial engineering, marketing, production planning, and research and development.

To find out more, write or phone:
Armstrong World Industries, Inc.
Bing G. Spitler, Manager, College Relations
College Relations Dept.
PO Box 3001
Lancaster, PA 17604
Phone: (717)396-2541

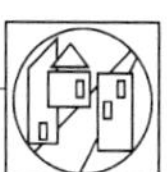

▶ Center on Education and Work

Provides information on: *Vocational Education, Careers*

The Center on Education and Work is dedicated to strengthening the vocational and technical education of youth and adults. Research areas include the labor market, occupational trends, gender equity, high school dropouts, youth unemployment, guidance information systems, follow-up, performance standards, and programs and services for students with disabilities. The Center is also involved in organizing vocational education programs and apprenticeship programs for training workers.

Information for a fee:

Career Planning Workbook: Astronaut to Zoologist. $12.50. Geared toward teen parents planning for the future.

Exploring New Worlds: A Workbook on Trades and Technology for Women. $7. Encourages women to consider higher paying occupations.

Going to Work. $5. Gives tips on identifying interests and getting a job.

Life Skills Workbook: A Guide to Personal Growth. $12.50. Teaches practical life skills, such as stress management, self-awareness, and child care. Geared toward teen parents.

Personal Choices, Personal Power. $6.50. Focuses on sexual rights and responsibilities.

Prep Sr. $3. Activity book that helps identify skills and interests.

Replicating Jobs in Business and Industry for Persons with Disabilities. 5 volumes. $15 each. Describes jobs performed by persons with disabilities. Contains additional job and company information.

Resource Directory for Single Parents. $6.50. Contains educational information, financial aid resources, employment programs, and social services.

Successful Single Parenting: A Guide to Building Teamwork and Communication with Your Children. $15. Provides tips on being a single parent.

Women in Higher Wage Occupations Resource Manual. $12. Contains activities and worksheets to help students understand the importance of career choices.

To find out more, write or phone:

Center on Education and Work
University of Wisconsin
964 Educational Sciences
1025 W. Johnson
Madison, WI 53706
Phone: (608)263-3696 or *Fax:* (608)262-9197

▶ Chrysler Corp.

Provides information on: *Engineering Careers, Marketing and Sales Careers, Business and Finance Careers, Human Resources Careers*

Founded in 1925, Chrysler Corporation is one of the world's top 10 car manufacturers. With an annual production of 2 million vehicles, Chrysler's sales total about $27 billion per year. Numerous and varied job opportunities at Chrysler are related to vehicle design and engineering, manufacturing, procurement and supplier operations, sales and service, marketing, finance, management, and human resources. College graduates enter Chrysler by direct-assignment to a specific area or through training programs. Chrysler employs about 120,000 people in operations located in the U.S., Canada, Mexico, Europe, Africa, Latin America, the Middle East and the Orient. Chrysler is based in Detroit, Michigan, and nearly half of all Chrysler employees live and work in the Detroit metropolitan area.

Information for free:

Expand Your Horizons with Chrysler Corporation. 16 pages. College recruiting booklet describing various department functions within Chrysler and the appropriate training or degree requirements for available positions.

To find out more, write or phone:

Chrysler Corp.
Bernard Baker
12000 Chrysler Dr.
Highland Park, MI 48288
Phone: (313)956-1268

▶ Citibank

Provides information on: *Business and Finance Careers*

Citibank provides banking and financial services on an international scale. Citibank employees work in more than 90 countries around the world. Employees are hired as summer associates and management associates.

Information for free:

More Than a Citibank. 1991. Brochure. Contains company overview and 42 employee profiles.

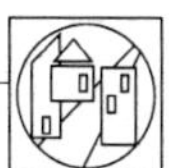

To find out more, write or phone:

Citibank
399 Park Ave.
New York, NY 10043
Toll-free: 1-800-248-4636 or *Phone:* (212)559-1000 or *Fax:* (212)527-3277

▶ Coca-Cola USA Division of the Coca-Cola Co.

Provides information on: *Marketing and Sales Careers, Business and Finance Careers, Engineering Careers, Computer Careers, Human Resources Careers*

Coca-Cola is known throughout the world as a maker of soft drinks. Coca-Cola products are sold in more than 160 countries and account for about 41 percent of all soft drinks sold. In the U.S. alone, there are 10 syrup production facilities, more than 165 bottling plants, and more than 2 million retail locations. Career areas at Coca-Cola exist in marketing, sales, quality assurance, finance, communications, manufacturing, engineering, information systems, operations, purchasing, and human resources.

Information for free:

Refreshing Opportunities. 1991. Brochure. Provides company overview, and lists career areas, products, and benefits of employment.

To find out more, write or phone:

Coca-Cola USA
Division of the Coca-Cola Co.
Staffing Department
PO Drawer 1734
Atlanta, GA 30301
Toll-free: 1-800-GET-COKE or *Phone:* (404)676-2121 or *Fax:* (404)676-6792

▶ Colgate-Palmolive Co.

Provides information on: *Marketing and Sales Careers, Engineering Careers, Computer Careers, Human Resources Careers*

Colgate-Palmolive is internationally known for making products such as toothpaste, dishsoap, household cleaners, and pet food. More than two-thirds of the company's sales come from outside the U.S. The company employs 24,000 people worldwide in a variety of career areas such as marketing, sales, human resources, research and development, manufacturing and engineering, business systems, and finance.

Information for free:

Careers with Colgate-Palmolive. 12 pages. Booklet. Describes global operations and career opportunities. Lists alternate address for opportunities with Corporate Technology Group: Manager, Technology Staffing, Colgate-Palmolive Corporate Technology Center, 909 River Rd., PO Box 1343, Piscataway, NJ 08855-1343.

The Colgate-Palmolive Company. 24 pages. Booklet. Provides overview of company products.

To find out more, write or phone:

Colgate-Palmolive Co.
Manager, Recruitment and Development
300 Park Ave.
New York, NY 10022
Phone: (212)310-2000 or *Fax:* (212)310-3284

▶ Coopers & Lybrand

Provides information on: *Business and Finance Careers*

Coopers & Lybrand is one of the top accounting firms in the nation. The firm employs 61,000 people in 107 countries. Career opportunities exist in four areas including accounting and auditing, tax services, management consulting, and actuarial, benefits and compensation consulting.

Information for free:

Why Choose C&L? 20 pages. Booklet and fact sheets presenting company policy, services offered, and career prospects.

To find out more, write or phone:

Coopers & Lybrand
1251 Avenue of the Americas
New York, NY 10020
Phone: (212)536-2000 or *Fax:* (212)642-7328

▶ Council on Career Development for Minorities

Provides information on: *Counseling*

The Council works to heighten the awareness and employability of minority college students and to improve career counseling and referral services offered to them. It provides programs to help minority students improve test-taking and learning skills, promotes the inclusion of career education into college curricula, and serves as a consultant to colleges involving government grants. The group conducts a corporate orientation program, which provides sophomore-level minority students with the

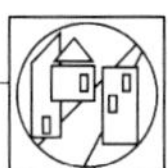

opportunity to study actual business activities and the factors that affect their employability and chances for promotion in the corporate business world. It also maintains a database on historically Black colleges and universities and other educational institutions with large numbers of minority students.

To find out more, write or phone:

Council on Career Development for Minorities
1341 W. Mockingbird Ln., Ste. 412-E
Dallas, TX 75247
Phone: (214)631-3677

▶ Deloitte & Touche

Provides information on: *Business and Finance Careers*

Deloitte & Touche is one of the top accounting firms in the nation. Some of the firm's clients are Dow Chemical, General Motors, The New York Times, Rockwell, and Toys "R" Us. The firm provides services that include accounting and auditing, management consulting, mergers and acquisitions consulting, and tax advice. More than 60,000 employees work for Deloitte & Touche, under the umbrella DRT International, in more than 100 countries.

Information for free:

Momentum. Professionals on the Move. 24 pages. Booklet highlighting employees, college internship program, educational possibilities, career paths, community involvement, international opportunities, and clients.

To find out more, write or phone:

Deloitte & Touche
Karen Graci, Recruitment/College Relations
10 Westport Rd.
PO Box 820
Wilton, CT 06897-0820
Phone: (203)761-3179 or *Fax:* (203)834-2231

▶ Dow Chemical Co.

Provides information on: *Business and Finance Careers, Engineering Careers, Science Careers, Radio and Television Careers, Computer Careers, Marketing and Sales Careers*

Dow Chemical is one of the largest chemical manufacturers in the nation. Dow's products range from plastics and consumer products to pharmaceuticals and agricultural products. Dow employs 55,000 people in the U.S., Canada, Latin America, Europe, and the Pacific.

Information for free:

Student Employees Can Do Great Things at Dow. 12 pages. Describes work options for student employees and provides contact information.

You Can Do Great Things at Dow. 24 pages. Provides overview of company and products and describes career opportunities. Separate booklets in the series describe careers in accounting, business research, chemical engineering, chemistry, communications, electrical engineering, information systems, materials management, mechanical engineering, polymers and materials science, and sales and marketing.

To find out more, write or phone:

Dow Chemical Co.
Employee Development Center
Dow Chemical USA
Midland, MI 48674
Phone: (517)636-1000

▶ Environmental Careers Organization

Provides information on: *Environmental Protection, Environmental Careers*

Participants of the Organization are upper-level undergraduate, graduate, and doctoral students, or recent graduates seeking professional experience relevant to careers in environmental fields. Their purpose is to foster professional development and the resolution of priority environmental issues in the public and private sectors, and facilitate exchange of information on environmental issues. Projects are in conservation services, public policy and community development, and technical services. Individual subject areas include administrative/legal assistance, communications, community development, education, energy, environmental assessments, hazardous substances, historic preservation, land use, natural resource management, pollution control, public/occupational health, recreation, transportation, and wildlife.

Information for free:

Annual Report.

Information for a fee:

Becoming an Environmental Professional. 1991. $15.95.

Complete Guide to Environmental Careers. 1990. $17.45

To find out more, write or phone:
Environmental Careers Organization
68 Harrison Ave., 5th Fl.
Boston, MA 02111
Phone: (617)426-4375

▶ Gannett Co., Inc.

Provides information on: *Women and Minorities: Job Opportunities in the Media, Publishing Careers*

Gannett Co., Inc. is an international news and information company. Gannett's newspaper group publishes 87 daily newspapers including *USA Today*. In addition to publishing, Gannett owns several other operations including television and radio stations, and an outdoor advertising company. Gannett employs 37,000 people; nearly 40 percent of Gannett employees are women. Numerous and varied career opportunities are highlighted in several Gannett publications. For newspaper and newsroom opportunities contact: Mary Kay Blake, Director/News Staff Recruiting. For other employment opportunities contact: Jose Berrios, Director/Personnel and EEO Programs.

Information for free:

Gannett Facts and Faces. 1987. 29 pages. Booklet describing Gannett's varied operations, growth potential, and hiring practices. Also profiles a number of employees and their backgrounds.

Gannett Co., Inc.: The Opportunity Company for Minorities. 8 pages. Booklet profiling successful minority employees. Lists names and locations of Gannett operations.

Gannett Co., Inc.: The Opportunity Company for Women. 8 pages. Booklet profiling successful women employees. Lists names and locations of Gannett operations.

To find out more, write or phone:
Gannett Co., Inc.
Mary Kay Blake, College Recruiter
1100 Wilson Blvd.
Arlington, VA 22234
Phone: (703)284-6000

▶ The Gap, Inc.

Provides information on: *Business and Finance Careers*

The Gap is one of the leading clothing retailers in the U.S. The company sells its own brand of clothes for adults and kids under four labels including Gap, GapKids, babyGap, and Banana Republic. The Gap operates more than 1,200 stores, some of which are located in Europe and Canada.

Information for free:

Gap. 1990. Provides company overview, description of management career opportunities, and regional office contacts.

To find out more, write or phone:

The Gap, Inc.
One Harrison
San Francisco, CA 94105
Phone: (415)952-4400

▶ General Electric Co.

Provides information on: *Computer Careers*

General Electric is well known for manufacturing refrigerators, washing machines, and other home appliances. GE operates its own training center for employees called Appliance Park University (APU). The University offers courses related to industrial mechanics, electronics, materials/processes, blueprint reading, and computer operation.

Information for free:

1992 APU Degree Catalog. 28 pages. Lists degrees offered and course requirements.

APU Responding to Change. 1992. 24 pages. Catalog. Lists course offerings in basic education and certificate programs as well as admission information.

To find out more, write or phone:

General Electric Co.
Donna Hill, College Recruiter
Appliance Park
Louisville, KY 40225
Phone: (502)452-4311

▶ General Mills, Inc.

Provides information on: *Science Careers, Engineering Careers, Marketing and Sales Careers, Computer Careers, Human Resources Careers*

General Mills is widely recognized as a leading maker of consumer food products. The corporation's hundreds of brand names appear on breakfast cereals, flour, baking mixes, snacks, and desserts. In addition, General Mills also owns two restaurant chains: Red Lobster and The Olive Garden. Career opportunities at General Mills exist

in a variety of areas including food science, manufacturing, engineering, research and development, sales, distribution, marketing, quality control, programming, and human resources.

Information for free:

Challenges in Technology and Operations. 20 pages. Booklet. Presents company overview and describes careers in Technology and Operations through employee profiles.

Winning with the Company of Champions. 28 pages. Presents company overview and employee profiles.

To find out more, write or phone:

General Mills, Inc.
Bill Dittmore, Recruitment and College Relations
PO Box 1113
Minneapolis, MN 55440
Phone: (612)540-2311

▶ General Motors Corp.

Provides information on: *Engineering Careers, Science Careers, Business and Finance Careers*

General Motors is one of the world's leading automotive manufacturers. Buick, Cadillac, Oldsmobile, Saturn, Chevrolet, and Pontiac vehicles are all made by General Motors. The corporation is headquartered in Detroit, Michigan and employs 700,000 people around the globe. In addition to manufacturing cars, employees also work at GM subsidiaries such as GMAC Financial Services, Electronic Data Systems Corporation (EDS), and Hughes Aircraft Company, which is a leader in defense electronics and commercial communication satellites.

Information for free:

Change the Way the World Moves. 20 pages. Booklet. Describes the many divisions within General Motors and the possibilities for employment. Related fact sheets list division locations, employee benefits, and necessary background for careers in engineering, science, business, and law.

To find out more, write or phone:

General Motors Corp.
James Sturtz
General Motors Building
3044 West Grand Blvd.
Detroit, MI 48202
Phone: (313)556-5000 or *Fax:* (313)556-5108

▶ Goodyear Tire & Rubber Co.

Provides information on: *Engineering Careers, Marketing and Sales Careers, Business and Finance Careers, Computer Careers*

Goodyear produces tire and rubber products. The company also specializes in chemical and plastic products as well as hundreds of consumer items. In addition to its U.S. plants, Goodyear has operations in 25 foreign countries. More than 111,000 people are employed by Goodyear in all aspects of production, manufacturing, distribution, and sales.

Information for free:

Opportunities for the '90s. Series of brochures highlighting specific career areas. Areas covered include engineering, sales, business/administrative, accounting and finance, computer science, and management information systems.

To find out more, write or phone:

Goodyear Tire & Rubber Co.
Corporate College Relations
1144 E. Market St.
Akron, OH 44316
Phone: (216)796-2121

▶ Hallmark Cards, Inc.

Provides information on: *Business and Finance Careers, Marketing and Sales Careers, Engineering Careers, Human Resources Careers*

Hallmark is best known for its greeting cards. The company also specializes in party and gift items, and home decorations. Hallmark employs about 21,000 full-time people and 12,000 part-time people worldwide. About 700 employees make up the creative staff. Other positions at Hallmark are related to business (services, marketing, research), distribution, engineering, sales, graphic arts, human resources, management information systems, finance, purchasing, and manufacturing.

Information for free:

Fact sheets profiling company history and areas of employment.

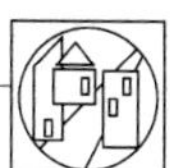

To find out more, write or phone:

Hallmark Cards, Inc.
Becky Yoxall
College Relations Department
PO Box 419580
Kansas City, MO 64141-6580
Phone: (816)274-5111 or *Fax:* (816)274-8513

▶ H&R Block

Provides information on: *Business and Finance Careers, Computer Careers, Marketing and Sales Careers*

H&R Block is the nation's largest tax preparation service and the largest seasonal white-collar employer, according to the company. Before being hired, prospective employees attend a company-sponsored income tax course. About 40,000 people work for H&R Block during tax time each year. H&R Block has 9,000 franchise offices located in 16 countries.

Information for free:

Career Opportunities with H&R Block. Information packet presenting company history and overview. Also lists employment positions in accounting, administrative services, office services, graphics, information systems, internal auditing, legal services, marketing, software support, and supply.

Field Automated Systems Support. Career Opportunities. Information packet describing job opportunities related to computers.

To find out more, write or phone:

H&R Block
Cindy Hall, Recruiting Specialist
4410 Main St.
Kansas City, MO 64111
Phone: (816)932-8395

▶ Hewlett-Packard Co.

Provides information on: *Engineering Careers, Computer Careers, Business and Finance Careers, Marketing and Sales Careers*

Hewlett-Packard is an international manufacturer of computing and electronic measuring equipment. The company's 10,000 products range from calculators and computer systems to electronic medical equipment. Hewlett-Packard, one of the 50 largest industrial corporations in America, has operations in more than 100 U.S. cities,

Europe, Canada, Latin America, and the Asia Pacific region. Hewlett-Packard employs 93,000 people in areas such as engineering, programming, finance, sales, and personnel.

Information for free:

Student Work Experience. Fact sheet. Outlines work options for college students and provides contact information.

Why Choose a Career in Personnel at Hewlett-Packard? 1989. Brochure. Highlights career opportunities in personnel.

Why Choose a Financial Career at Hewlett-Packard? 1989. Brochure. Highlights career opportunities in finance.

Why Choose Hewlett-Packard? 1988. 32 pages. Booklet providing overview of company, career opportunities, benefits, and interviewing tips.

To find out more, write or phone:

Hewlett-Packard Co.
Roger Milovina, Campus Coordinator
PO Box 10301
Palo Alto, CA 94303-0890
Phone: (415)857-2347

▶ Humana Inc.

Provides information on: *Healthcare Careers, Computer Careers*

Humana is one of the nation's largest health care organizations. The corporation manages more than 80 hospitals in 20 states, England, and Switzerland. Humana also provides health benefit plans for more than one million people. About 70,000 people are employed by Humana in a variety of career areas.

Information for free:

This is Humana. 1991. 8 pages. Booklet. Provides company overview and benefits of employment. Also available are company fact sheets and brochures on specific areas of employment, such as nursing and data processing.

To find out more, write or phone:

Humana Inc.
Doug Howell
Human Resources
500 West Main St.
PO Box 1438
Louisville, KY 40201-1438
Phone: (502)580-3416

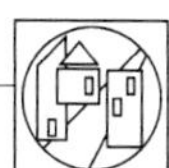

▶ James River Corp.

Provides information on: *Engineering Careers, Business and Finance Careers, Marketing and Sales Careers, Human Resources Careers*

James River Corporation is one of the world's leading manufacturers of paper. Some of the company's products include paper towels, tissues, napkins, paper plates and cups, and packaging for a number of popular products. More than 34,000 people are employed by James River Corporation in North America, and an additional 5,000 work in European subsidiaries. Many employees work in engineering, research and development, manufacturing, finance, sales and marketing, human resources, and management.

Information for free:

Career Challenges. 23 pages. Booklet. Provides overview of company, description of Associate Program for college graduates, career areas and qualifications.

To find out more, write or phone:

James River Corp.
Barbara Lanier, College Recruiting
Human Resource Planning and Development
PO Box 2218
Richmond, VA 23217
Phone: (804)644-5411 or *Fax:* (804)649-4428

▶ Kelly Services

Provides information on: *Employment, Business and Finance Careers, Marketing and Sales Careers*

Kelly Services provides temporary employees to assist businesses in a variety of areas. Employees may be hired for office work, marketing, light industrial, or technical work. Kelly Services gives temporary assignments to 550,000 employees annually. Depending on the nature of the assignment, Kelly may provide specific training. The company has more than 950 branch offices in the U.S. and several other countries, serving more than 180,000 customers.

Information for free:

Several fact sheets providing overview of company.

To find out more, write or phone:
Kelly Services
Denise Ridenour, Public Relations
Public Relations Department
999 West Big Beaver Rd.
Troy, MI 48084
Phone: (313)244-4305 or *Fax:* (313)244-4154

▶ Marriott Corp.

Provides information on: *Travel and Hospitality Careers*

The Marriott Corporation is a leading international lodging and hospitality company. Marriott operates more than 655 hotels and is one of the largest employers in the U.S. Marriott Corporation was founded in 1927 and today includes hotels, resorts, management services, restaurants, gift shops, and retirement communities. Career opportunities exist in all areas of the hospitality business.

Information for free:

Create Your Own Opportunity! Explore The Marriott Family of Businesses. Brochure. Provides career and contact information for a number of Marriott operations.

Hotel/Motel Careers. Lists career areas in the hospitality industry, training courses, and state lodging associations.

To find out more, write or phone:
Marriott Corp.
Doug Price, VP National Employment Marketing
Marriott Dr.
Washington, DC 20058
Phone: (301)380-1203

▶ Matsushita Electric Corp. of America

Provides information on: *Engineering Careers, Computer Careers, Science Careers*

Matsushita Electric Corporation of America operates 150 electronics manufacturing, sales and service facilities in the U.S., Canada, Mexico, and Puerto Rico. Matsushita manufactures such products as televisions, VCRs, telephones, flashlights, factory automation equipment, and computer keyboards. The corporation's brand names include Panasonic, Technics, and Quasar. Matsushita employs 11,000 people in North America, including many engineers, software experts, technical specialists, and scientists.

Information for free:

Matsushita Electric Corporation of America. 1991. 20 pages. Booklet providing overview of company and products, programs offered, and listing of subsidiary and affiliate company addresses.

To find out more, write or phone:

Matsushita Electric Corp. of America
Pam Borst
One Panasonic Way 3C-5
Secaucus, NJ 07094
Phone: (201)348-7000

▶ McKinsey & Co., Inc.

Provides information on: *Business and Finance Careers*

McKinsey & Company, Inc. is an international management consulting firm. Businesses hire McKinsey & Company to collect and analyze data, and make recommendations concerning the overall operation of their business. The company helps resolve internal management problems and respond to external conditions. McKinsey & Company employs 2,600 consultants and business analysts worldwide, all of whom are university graduates. Other employees at the company work in research, administration, or support positions.

Information for free:

The Firm and its Work. 1992. Fact sheets describing the company, employees, and recruiting policy.

To find out more, write or phone:

McKinsey & Co., Inc.
Tina Ege
55 E. 52nd St.
New York, NY 10022
Phone: (212)446-7000 or *Fax:* (212)446-8575

▶ National Association of Career Development Consultants

Provides information on: *Counseling, Careers*

The Association is made up of firms offering career counseling and outplacement services to business executives. It works to establish and advocate compliance to industry ethics, provides professional training and certification, helps prepare legislation relating to the industry, and seeks to increase public acceptance of outplacement programs.

Information for free:
Booklet on the Association's background, purpose, and standards.
Also available is a list of the Association's accredited firms and registered professionals.

To find out more, write or phone:
National Association of Career Development Consultants
1730 N. Lynn St., Ste. 502
Arlington, VA 22209
Phone: (703)525-1191 or *Fax:* (202)833-3014

▶ National Career Development Association (NCDA)

Provides information on: *Counseling, Careers*

NCDA is made up of professionals and others interested in career development or counseling in various work environments provide support to counselors, guidance personnel, and other professionals working in schools, colleges, military services, correctional institutions, business, community and government agencies, and in private practice. Services include publications, support for state and local activities, human equity programs, and continuing education and training for these professionals. The Association also acts as a link to business, labor, and industry.

Information for a fee:
Career Development Quarterly. $24/year. Journal.

To find out more, write or phone:
National Career Development Association
c/o American Association for Counseling and Development
5999 Stevenson Ave.
Alexandria, VA 22304
Toll-free: 1-800-545-AACD or *Phone:* (703)823-9800 or *Fax:* (703)823-0252

▶ J.C. Penney Co., Inc.

Provides information on: *Business and Finance Careers, Computer Careers*

J.C. Penney Company, Inc. operates nearly 1,400 department stores in the United States. Primary sale items are women's, men's, and children's apparel, cosmetics, jewelry, and home furnishings. The company also owns the Thrift Drug chain and several other retailing operations. J.C. Penney employs 196,000 people in a variety of areas such as management, information systems, business systems, accounting, auditing, and catalog production.

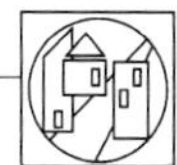

Information for free:

Background on the J.C. Penney Company, Inc. Fact sheet providing history of the company.

Benefits Highlights. Brochure. Outlines company benefits.

Looking at the Future.Yours. 16 pages. Booklet highlighting career opportunities.

Store Management. Brochure. Describes management responsibilities and provides regional contact information.

Store Management Internships. Brochure. Describes internship opportunities and provides regional contact information.

To find out more, write or phone:

J.C. Penney Co., Inc.
Meredith Thompson, College Recruiter
PO Box 659000
Dallas, TX 75265-9000
Phone: (214)591-1000 or *Fax:* (214)591-1315

▶ Rockwell International Corp.

Provides information on: *Engineering Careers, Computer Careers*

Rockwell International employs more than 100,000 people worldwide in four business areas: electronics, aerospace, automotive, and graphic systems. Rockwell produces such products as navigation systems, tactical weapons and sensors, telecommunications equipment, rocket propulsion systems, printing presses, and automotive drivetrain components.

Information for free:

Working Together. 1991. 16 pages. Provides overview of company divisions and products, and describes employee, student, and community programs.

To find out more, write or phone:

Rockwell International Corp.
Chris Castro
World Headquarters
2201 Seal Beach Blvd.
PO Box 4250
Seal Beach, CA 90740-8250
Phone: (310)797-3311

▶ Shell Oil Co.

Provides information on: *Engineering Careers, Science Careers, Computer Careers, Marketing and Sales Careers*

Shell is an oil, gas, and chemical company employing more than 30,000 people. Most of the company's operations are conducted in the U.S. These operations include gas exploration, offshore drilling, refining, and marketing. Shell also specializes in chemical manufacturing and coal production.

Information for free:

Working with Shell. 32 pages. Booklet. Provides company overview and product listing. Lists employment positions and related degree preference. Describes job responsibilities of engineers, scientists, chemists, geophysicists, geologists, programmers, sales representatives, and other business-related positions.

Other brochures include:

Computing in Shell;
Exploration Geophysics Careers with Shell Oil Company;
Mechanical Engineering in Shell Companies;
The Polymer Professions at Shell;
Professional Financial and Accounting Opportunities;
Shell Development Company.

To find out more, write or phone:

Shell Oil Co.
Human Resources
One Shell Plaza
PO Box 2463
Houston, TX 77252
Phone: (713)241-6161

▶ Snap-on Tools Corp.

Provides information on: *Marketing and Sales Careers, Business and Finance Careers, Engineering Careers, Computer Careers, Human Resources Careers*

Snap-on Tools Corporation manufactures more than 13,000 hand tools and related products. Tools such as screwdrivers, sockets, wrenches, and drills are commonly sold to automotive mechanics. In 1991, more than 5,000 independent dealers sold Snap-on Tools in several countries. Career opportunities at Snap-on Tools exist in marketing, finance, engineering, manufacturing, data processing, human resources, and other areas.

Information for free:
Your Quality Connection. Brochure. Provides overview of company and lists areas of employment.

To find out more, write or phone:
Snap-on Tools Corp.
Tammy Valeri, Public Relations
2801 80th St.
Kenosha, WI 53141-1410
Phone: (414)656-5200 or *Fax:* (414)656-5123

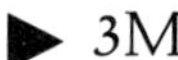

3M

Provides information on: *Science Careers, Marketing and Sales Careers*

3M (Minnesota Mining and Manufacturing Company) makes 60,000 products ranging from sandpaper and Post-it notes, to computer diskettes and medical equipment. In the U.S., 3M is divided into three business units: the Information and Imaging Technologies sector, Industrial and Consumer sector, and Life Sciences sector. 3M employs more than 89,000 people worldwide. Founded in 1902, the company has been featured on the covers of several business and research magazines. Many career opportunities at 3M are related to research, manufacturing, and marketing.

Information for free:
Getting to Know Us. 16 pages. Brochure. Highlights 3M's operations and products. Also available are several company fact sheets.

To find out more, write or phone:
3M
3M Center
St. Paul, MN 55144-1000
Phone: (612)733-1110

▶ U.S. Department of the Interior National Park Service

Provides information on: *Science Careers, Environmental Careers, National Parks*

The National Park Service manages 360 national parks, monuments, historic sites, and recreation areas. The preservation of these natural and cultural resources requires the help of permanent, seasonal, and volunteer workers. A wide range of jobs are available within the National Park Service such as park ranger, park police officer, general maintenance worker, administrative assistant, biological scientist, museum staff worker, and information specialist. Some positions may be applied for directly to the National Park Service, while others require applicants to be placed on an eligibility list. Applicants must be U.S. citizens and generally be at least 18 years old. For federal job information, applicants can write, visit, or call the nearest Federal Job Information Center found in the telephone directory under U.S. Government, or call the National Park Service personnel office at (202)208-4648.

Information for free:

Careers. 20 pages. Describes career opportunities, qualifications, and application procedures for National Park Service jobs. Includes a state listing of Federal Job Information/Testing Offices, and regional offices.

The National Parks: Index 1991. 112 pages. State listing and description of national parks, monuments, and related areas. Includes, maps, statistics, and regional contact information.

Also available are brochures on seasonal and volunteer employment opportunities.

To find out more, write or phone:

U.S. Department of the Interior
National Park Service
Personnel Office
PO Box 37127
Washington, DC 20013-7127
Phone: (202)208-4648

▶ Washington Post Company

Provides information on: *Publishing Careers*

The Washington Post Company is best known for publishing *The Washington Post* daily newspaper in Washington, D.C. The newspaper earned national recognition in the early 1970s for breaking the Watergate story. The Washington Post Company also publishes *Newsweek* magazine and owns several television stations.

Information for free:

Interesting Facts about The Washington Post. Brochure. Provides history and general information about the newspaper.

Job Hunter's Guide. 1991. Fact sheets offering tips on job hunting, resume writing, and interviewing.

The Making of The Washington Post. Describes processes involved with newspaper production.

What's Your Story? Brochure. Explains how to get news into the newspaper.

To find out more, write or phone:

Washington Post Company
Linda Erdos
1150 15th St., NW
Washington, DC 20071
Phone: (202)334-6600

To Contact People . . .

These books identify individual experts or organizations that can direct you to one.

▶ *The Address Book: How to Reach Anyone Who Is Anyone*

This book can be used to contact more than 3,500 prominent persons including political leaders, business executives, athletes, actors and actresses, artists, musicians, and writers. The book lists name and address. Names are listed alphabetically.
Biennial. Perigee Books.

▶ *Business and Finance Career Directory*

This directory is one of five titles that comprise the Career Advisor Series: Advertising Career Directory, Book Publishing Career Directory, Business and Finance Career Directory, Marketing and Sales Career Directory, and Travel and Hospitality Career Directory. Each directory lists companies and other sources of information and contains essays written by top executives in these fields.
Biennial. Gale Research Inc.

▶ *Canadian Who's Who*

This book lists about 12,000 notable Canadians in Canada and abroad based on position or achievement. Entries include name, address, personal and career data.
Annual. University of Toronto Press.

▶ *Career Employment Opportunities Directory*

This directory describes about 1,250 companies that employ college graduates. Separate editions are available for students studying liberal arts and social sciences, business administration, engineering and computer sciences, and science. The book provides company name and general description, career opportunities, job locations,

special programs, and contact address. Companies are arranged in alphabetical order.
Biennial. Ready Reference Press.

▶ *Career Information Center*

This 12-volume series provides information on occupations requiring levels of education from high school diploma through postdoctoral work. Each volume includes a section listing accredited institutions offering training from vocational through graduate levels. Institutions offering only bachelor's and graduate level work are not included. A second section lists the names and addresses of trade associations and professional organizations. For institutions, the book lists name, address, and programs and degrees offered.
1989. Glencoe Publishing Company.

▶ *Career Opportunities for Minority College Graduates*

The publication lists over 900 companies, organizations, and schools representing 24 occupational fields and five continuing educational alternatives. Entries include name, address, and personnel contact name or department; phone numbers are listed in many entries. Arranged by occupation, then geographically.
Paoli Publishing, Inc.

▶ *Career & Vocational Counseling Directory*

Locate career and vocational counseling offices with this book. It provides name, address, phone, name of owner or manager, and number of employees. Entries are arranged in geographical order.
Annual. American Business Directories, Inc.

▶ *Chronicle Career Index*

Use this book to locate over 500 government agencies, nonprofit organizations, trade associations, and other groups that offer occupational and education guidance materials. Entries include source name, address, materials offered, brief description, and price. Listings are alphabetical.
Annual. Chronicle Guidance Publications, Inc.

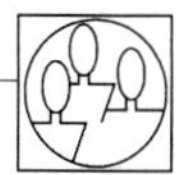

▶ *College Placement Council National Directory: Who's Who in Career Planning, Placement, and Recruitment*

Use this directory to contact some 2,400 college and university offices concerned with helping graduates find jobs. The book also lists about 2,300 companies with staff assigned to recruiting and hiring college graduates. For colleges, the book provides name, address, contact information, interview dates for undergraduates and graduates, months of graduation, dates of various career days or fairs, whether alumni placement is handled, and student enrollment (including minority data). For employers, the book lists company name, contact information, nature of business, and number of employees. Colleges are arranged in geographical order; employers are arranged alphabetically.

Annual. College Placement Council.

▶ *Directory of Labour Organizations in Canada*

This directory lists over 600 unions, congresses, and other labor organizations in Canada. Entries are arranged by organization type.

1992. Canadian Government Publishing Centre, Bureau of Labor Information.

▶ *Directory of Special Programs for Minority Group Members: Career Information Services Employment Skills Banks, Financial Aid Sources*

This book covers about 2,000 private and governmental agencies offering financial aid, employment assistance, and career guidance programs for minorities. Entries include organization or agency name, address, phone, contact name, type of organization, purpose, and description of services and activities in the equal employment opportunity employment area. Arranged alphabetically.

1990. Garrett Park Press.

▶ *Directory of State Industrial, Economic and Commerce Department and Purchasing Agencies*

The directory covers state industrial and economic development departments, commerce departments, housing finance agencies, purchasing agencies, and securities agencies. Entries are arranged geographically.

1992. B. Klein Publications.

▶ *Directory of U.S. Labor Organizations*

The directory contains more than 200 national unions and professional and state employees associations engaged in labor representation. It also includes historical and statistical data on the labor movement and unions. Entries are arranged alphabetically for all AFL-CIO affiliated and major independent unions; separate section lists AFL-CIO headquarters and central bodies.
1992. BNA Books.

▶ *Focus on Careers*

This publication lists hotlines and print and nonprint resources for teens investigating career options. It also examines career choices and plans and includes definitions and statistics.
1991. ABC-CLIO.

▶ *Hoover's Handbook of American Business*

The handbook lists approximately 500 companies that represent all major industries, as well as lists of competitors in each industry.
1992. Reference Press, Inc.

▶ *International Careers*

This book lists United States corporations, government and private nonprofit organizations that place employees abroad, and large foreign-based companies. It covers how to prepare for and pursue an international position.
Bob Adams, Inc.

▶ *International Who's Who*

This book covers 20,000 prominent persons worldwide. Entries include name, nationality, personal and career information, honors, awards, writings, address, and phone. Names are arranged alphabetically.
Annual. Europa Publications Ltd.

▶ *Job Bank Guide to Employment Services*

The guide covers more than 4,000 employment agencies, temporary help services, executive search firms, and career counseling centers. It is arranged by geographic location, then specialization.
Bob Adams, Inc.

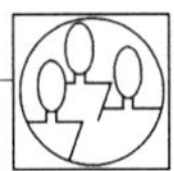

▶ *Liberal Arts Jobs: Where They Are and How to Get Them*

More than 300 job opportunities available to liberal arts majors are listed. Included are company name, address, phone, necessary qualifications and skills, job title and function, and entry-level positions. A list of the top 15 fields for liberal arts majors and job-hunting strategies are featured.
1989. Peterson's Guides, Inc.

▶ *Professional Careers Sourcebook*

This book identifies some 7,700 career planning resources, including publishers of related periodicals, career guides, test guides, educational directories, and reference guides and handbooks; professional associations; standards/certification agencies; sponsors of programs, scholarships, grants, fellowships, and awards; and other sources of career planning information.
Biennial. Gale Research Inc.

▶ *Summer Employment Directory of the United States*

Use this source to find some 15,000 camps, resorts, amusement parks, hotels, businesses, national parks, conference and training centers, ranches, and restaurants offering about 90,000 temporary summer jobs; listings are paid. Entries include name and address, length of employment, pay rate, fringe benefits, duties, qualifications, and application deadline and procedure. The book is arranged geographically, then by type of employer.
Annual. Peterson's Guides, Inc.

▶ *Top Professions: The 100 Most Popular, Dynamic, and Profitable Careers in America*

This publication describes the top careers from arts and media to engineering sciences, including average starting salary range, forecast for demand for professionals in the field, and highlights of entry-level positions. It can be used to find professional associations in the 100 fields described.
1989. Peterson's Guides, Inc.

▶ *Vocational Careers Sourcebook*

This book covers some 135 vocational careers with listings of career planning assistance organizations, publishers of related periodicals, career guides, and test guides, industry associations, standards and certification agencies, sponsors of pro-

grams, scholarships, grants, and other financial aid programs, and more.
Biennial. Gale Research Inc.

▶ *Who's Who in America*

This book contains information on 79,000 people, primarily in the U.S., considered to be of current national interest because of achievement or position. Entries include name, address, personal data, career data, memberships, special achievements, and publications. Names are listed alphabetically; a separate volume indexes people by profession and location.
Biennial. Updated quarterly. Marquis Who's Who.

▶ *Who's Who of American Women*

This book contains information on more than 30,000 high-profile women in all fields. Entries include name, address, personal, educational, and career data, professional association membership, special achievements, awards, and writings. Names are arranged alphabetically.
Biennial. Marquis Who's Who.

▶ *Who's Who in Finance and Industry*

This directory lists over 23,500 individuals involved in the business community. Entries are arranged alphabetically.
1991. Marquis Who's Who.

▶ *Who's Who in the World*

This directory covers more than 31,000 people of current international interest because of their achievement or position. Entries include name, address, biographical data, civic activities, awards, writings, and other information. Names are arranged alphabetically.
Biennial. Marquis Who's Who.

▶ *A Working Woman's Guide to Her Job Rights*

This publication includes a list of state and federal agencies in charge of enforcing the rights of working women. Entries include agency name and address.
1992. U.S. Department of Labor.

5
Social Issues

▶ Chapter 5 covers these topics:

Animal Rights
Consumer Affairs
Homelessness
Hunger
Literacy
Poverty

▶ Related topics appear in chapters on:

Education; Family Connections and Concerns; Government and Public Affairs; Health and Personal Concerns; Science and Environment

▶ Ideas for research topics:

The Animal Rights Movement
Case Studies in the Power of Consumer Protest
Combatting Homelessness—Not Just a Housing Issue
The Conditions of Food Animals on Factory Farms
The Controversy over Genetically Altered Foods
Factors Influencing Consumer Decision-Making
Food Salvage Projects
The High School Graduate Who Can't Read—Fact or Fiction?
Homelessness and Mental Illness
Homelessness and Veterans of War
How to Make an Effective Complaint about a Product or Service
The Importance of Food Labels
International Literacy Campaigns
The Linkss between Poverty and Crime
Literacy Programs in the Workplace
NIMBY (Not in My Backyard) vs. Efforts to Help the Homeless
The Practice of Consumer Law
Private vs. Public Efforts to Help the Poor—A Historical Overview
Ralph Nader and the Birth of Consumerism
Shelters and Soup Kitchens: Keeping the Homeless Alive
Starting Early for Lifelong Literacy
The Temporary Emergency Food Assistance Program

▶ Ideas for research topics (continued):

Truth in Advertising—Who Should Judge?
UNICEF Efforts to End Hunger
The United Nations' Response to Hunger and Homelessness Due to Disasters and War
The Use of Animals in Laboratory Experiments
Vegetarianism
Volunteerism in Hunger Programs
What Do Energy-Efficiency Ratings Tell Us?
Who are the Poor in the U.S.?
Why Some People Can't Afford to Work
"Work Fare"—Is It Making a Difference?

To Contact Organizations . . .

▶ American Affordable Housing Institute

Provides information on: *Homelessness, Low-Income Housing*

The Institute conducts studies designed to find new solutions to housing affordability and availability problems in local, state, and national settings. It emphasizes preventing homelessness, revitalizing urban neighborhoods, increasing the affordability and supply of housing for first-time homebuyers, expanding capital for investment in low- and moderate-income housing, meeting the housing needs of America's senior citizens, and assisting the development of housing policy at the state and local levels.

Information for free:
American Affordable Housing Institute. Brochure.

To find out more, write or phone:

American Affordable Housing Institute
Rutgers University
PO Box 118
New Brunswick, NJ 08903
Phone: (908)932-6812 or *Fax:* (908)932-7974

▶ American Anti-Vivisection Society

Advocates abolition of vivisection, the practice of cutting or operating on living animals for physiological or pathological investigation. The Society opposes all types of experiments on living animals, including poisoning, burning, freezing, electric shocks, food and drink deprivation, and psychological torture.

Information for a fee:

Animal Liberation. 1990. $8.95. Covers the issues of animal suffering and exploitation.
Animal Factories. 1990. $12.95. Facts, figures, and photos concerning the farms that produce animals for food.
"Alcoholic" Rats (and other Alcohol Research Using Animals). 1989. $1. Monograph.
Keyguide to Information Sources in Animal Rights. 1989. $24.95. An overview of animal rights literature and resources.
Psychology Experiments on Animals: A Critique of Animal Models of Human Psychopathology. 1982. $1. Monograph.
The Rights of Nature. 1989. $12.95. Explores the relationship between humans and nature, including non-human animals.

The Struggle for Animal Rights. 1987. $7.95. A view of what animal activists must do in order to succeed.

Also offers a variety of fliers and brochures for $1 or under.

To find out more, write or phone:

American Anti-Vivisection Society
Noble Plaza, Ste. 204
801 Old York Rd.
Jenkintown, PA 19046
Phone: (215)887-0816 or *Fax:* (215)887-2088

▶ American Consumers Association

Provides information on: *Consumer Affairs, Product Safety*

The Association provides information on consumer goods and services, including product quality, cost, safety, and effectiveness. The exchange of information beneficial to the health and welfare of the American consumer is a primary goal.

Information for free:
Pamphlets are available by written request.

To find out more, write or phone:

American Consumers Association
332 S. Michigan Ave., Ste. 824
Chicago, IL 60604
Phone: (312)922-5250 or *Fax:* (312)922-2688

▶ Animal Welfare Information Center (AWIC)

Provides information on: *Animal Rights*

The Animal Welfare Information Center is for those interested in obtaining information or publications covering many aspects of animal welfare, including methods for the humane care, use, and handling of warm-blooded animals in research, testing, and education. It covers such subjects as regulations of the 1986 Animal Welfare Act; care, handling, and management of animals used in research; teaching and exhibition; training guides and manuals for animal care personnel; and ethical issues.

Information for free:
Bibliographies:
Animal Welfare Legislation and Regulation;
Ethical and Moral Issues Relating to Animals;
Transport and Handling of Livestock;

Welfare of Experimental Animals.
Reference Briefs:
Animal Euthanasia;
Exercise for Dogs.
Fact Sheets:
AWIC Users Tips;
Information Resources for Students and Teachers;
Resources for Information on Alternatives and Animal Welfare.
Titles listed are a representative sample of the sources offered; contact AWIC for more information on additional publications. When placing an order, please send a self-addressed stamped envelope to AWIC.

To find out more, write or phone:
Animal Welfare Information Center
U.S. Dept. of Agriculture
National Agricultural Library, Rm. 205
10301 Baltimore Blvd.
Beltsville, MD 20705
Phone: (301)504-6212 or *Fax:* (301)504-5472

▶ Animal Welfare Institute (AWI)

Provides information on: *Animals, Animal Rights, Birds, Whales, Endangered Species*

The Animal Welfare Institute promotes the humane treatment of animals. The Institute's specific goals include the development and use of non-animal testing methods, prevention of painful animal experiments by high schoool students, reform of cruel methods of wild animal trapping, banning the importation and sale of wild-caught birds, preservation of species from extinction, and reform of cruel treatment of food animals.

Information for free:
The African Elephant. Fact sheet exposing Zimbabwe's false claims on their elephant populations.
Alternatives that Don't Harm or Destroy Animals. 1 page.
Attitudes Towards Animals. 3 pages.
Mistreatment of Laboratory Animals Endangers Biomedical Research.
Save the Whales and the Dolphins. Flier describing threats to the survival of whales and dolphins with suggestions of ways to help.

Information for a fee:

Animal Welfare Institute Quarterly. $15. Reports on treatment of animals in laboratories, commercial trade, and factory farms.

Animals and Their Legal Rights. 1990. 441 pages. $8.

Endangered Species Handbook. 1986. 244 pages. $10.

Facts About Furs. 1980. 257 pages. $10. Offers information on the way furs are obtained throughout the world.

Flight to Extinction, The Wild-Caught Bird Trade. 1992. 27 pages. $5.

Physical and Mental Suffering of Experimental Animals. 1979. 195 pages. $5.

The Trade in Live Wildlife. 1987. 36 pages. $5.

Whales vs. Whalers: A Continuing Commentary. $5. A series of articles on efforts to prevent the extinction of whales.

To find out more, write or phone:

Animal Welfare Institute
Christine Stevens, Pres.
PO Box 3650, Georgetown Sta.
Washington, DC 20007
Phone: (202)337-2332 or *Fax:* (202)338-9478

▶ Bread for the World

Provides information on: *Hunger, Poverty*

A religious lobbying group, Bread for the World focuses on U.S. policy matters that vitally affect hungry people. The organization maintains Bread for the World Institute on Hunger and Development, which offers research and education on policies related to hunger and development. It concentrates on issues such as financial assistance to poor countries; military spending; agriculture; Third World debt; trade; and domestic poverty, hunger, and unemployment.

Information for free:

Bread for the World Intern Program. Brochure.
Bread for the World Newsletter.

Information for a fee:

Maintaining Local Groups. $.25. Brochure.
Organizing a Local Group. $.25. Brochure.

To find out more, write or phone:

Bread for the World
802 Rhode Island Ave., NE
Washington, DC 20018
Toll-free: 1-800-822-7323 or *Phone:* (202)269-0200 or *Fax:* (202)529-8546

▶ Barbara Bush Foundation for Family Literacy

Provides information on: *Literacy*

The Foundation works to establish literacy as a family value and to break the intergenerational cycle of illiteracy in American families. It supports programs that bring parents and children together to develop mutual reading and literacy skills, and encourages a home environment that fosters the child's educational development. The Foundation encourages recognition of volunteers, educators, students, and effective literacy programs. It also provides support training for volunteers and teachers and offers assistance to those interested in establishing family literacy efforts.

Information for free:
Family Reading Tips. Many other brochures are also available.

Information for a fee:
First Teachers: A Family Literacy Handbook for Parents, Policy Makers, and Literacy Providers. $4.

To find out more, write or phone:
Barbara Bush Foundation for Family Literacy
1002 Wisconsin Ave., NW
Washington, DC 20007
Phone: (202)338-2006 or *Fax:* (202)337-6754

▶ Center for Alternatives to Animal Testing

Provides information on: *Animal Rights, Product Safety*

The Center for Alternatives to Animal Testing works for the development of scientifically acceptable alternatives (methods that minimize animal distress, reduce animal usage, or replace whole-animal tests) for use in product safety testing. The Center distributes "scientifically correct" information on alternatives, their uses, advantages, and disadvantages.

Information for free:
The Johns Hopkins Center for Alternatives to Animal Testing. Quarterly. Newsletter covering international alternative test developments.
Also offers article reprints on such subjects as alternatives to animal use in research, testing, and education, including toxicity projects.

To find out more, write or phone:

Center for Alternatives to Animal Testing
Joan Poling
Johns Hopkins University
615 N. Wolfe St.
Baltimore, MD 21205
Phone: (410)955-3343 or *Fax:* (410)955-0258

▶ Center for Consumer Research

Provides information on: *Consumer Affairs*

The Center is a place where scholars from a number of disciplines work together to study the factors influencing consumer decision-making and behavior. Research results are published in professional journals.

To find out more, write or phone:

Center for Consumer Research
University of Florida
342 Matherly Hall
Gainesville, FL 32611
Phone: (904)392-0161

▶ Citizens to End Animal Suffering and Exploitation (CEASE)

Provides information on: *Animal Rights*

CEASE is a group working to raise public awareness of animal rights through advertising, legislation, protest, and education.

Information for free:

Animal Rights. Pamphlet.

Information for a fee:

CEASE Newsline. Bimonthly. $20. Membership activities newsletter; includes legislative updates.

To find out more, write or phone:

Citizens to End Animal Suffering and Exploitation
Doreene Close, Exec. Dir.
PO Box 44-456
Somerville, MA 02144
Phone: (617)628-9030 or *Fax:* (617)628-9034

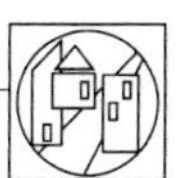

▶ Coalition to Protect Animals in Entertainment (CPAE)

Provides information on: *Animal Rights*

The Coalition is a network of organizations interested in protecting animals in the entertainment industry. CPAE provides follow-up investigation and action on reported animal abuse cases. The Coalition also fosters elimination of the profiting aspect of animal cruelty in movies, TV, commercials, circuses, zoos, rodeos, and all areas of entertainment.

Information for free:
Alerts. Periodic newsletter.

To find out more, write or phone:
Coalition to Protect Animals in Entertainment
Nancy Burnet, Exec.Dir.
PO Box 2448
Riverside, CA 92516
Phone: (714)682-7872

▶ Community for Creative Non-Violence (CCNV)

Provides information on: *Homelessness, Poverty*

CCNV works to combat homelessness and poverty in the U.S. It serves as a nonpolitical group working to influence federal legislation impacting the homeless.

Information for free:
Pamphlets.

Information for a fee:
Housing and Homeless: A Teaching Guide. $3. Book.

To find out more, write or phone:
Community for Creative Non-Violence
425 2nd St., NW
Washington, DC 20001
Phone: (202)393-1909 or *Fax:* (202)783-3254

▶ Consumers Union (CU)

Provides information on: *Consumer Affairs, Product Safety, Nutrition, Travel and Recreation, Smoking, Substance Abuse, Family Planning, Global Warming, Fitness, Alcoholism*

Consumers Union provides consumers with information and advice on products, services, health, and personal finance. It tests, evaluates, and rates the performance, convenience, safety, and economy of operation of a wide range of products, from foods and cleaning supplies to appliances and automobiles. It reports on questionable business practices, unsafe product design, inadequate labeling, and health quackery. CU publishes a newspaper column and a magazine, is involved in radio and television programming, and distributes video cassettes. Its books can be found in many bookstores and libraries. CU reports are also transmitted direct to consumers through personal computers and telecommunications devices.

Information for free:
A 4-page listing of buying guides and books on cars, children's concerns, consumer issues, food and nutrition, health and fitness, home design and maintenance, law, personal finance, and travel (priced at $3.95 and up).

Information for a fee:
Consumer Reports. Monthly magazine. $20/year.
Contraceptive Handbook. 1992. $18.95.
Facts about Smoking. 1991. $18.85. Also publishes similar books on alcohol and drug use.
Fight Global Warming: 29 Things You Can Do. 1991. $6.95.
How and Why: A Kid's Book about the Body. 1988. $9.95.
Straight Talk about Weight Control. 1990. $15.95.
Treating Acne. 1992. $16.95.
Used Car Buying Guide. 1992. $8.95.
What's Wrong with My Car? 1990. $16.95.

To find out more, write or phone:
Consumers Union
101 Truman Ave.
Yonkers, NY 10703
Toll-free: 1-800-272-0722 or *Phone:* (914)378-2000

▶ Contact Center Inc.

Provides information on: *Literacy, Criminal Justice, Voluntarism*

Contact Center specializes in human service and criminal justice. Originally begun as a referral service on jobs and housing for convicted felons, its focus has extended to almost every area of human need. Divisions of Contact Center focus on literacy services, human services, and volunteer services, referring inquirers to various local agencies and programs.

Information for free:

Enclose a self-addressed, stamped envelope. Additional postage necessary for publications larger than four pages.

International Literacy Information. 1 page. A list of organizations working with literacy internationally.

Key State Literacy Contacts. 2 pages.

Literacy Questions and Answers: General Facts. 1 page.

State and Local Literacy Hotlines. 5 pages.

Contact Center also distributes information on GED produced by the American Council on Education, information on workforce literacy produced by the Business Council for Effective Literacy, information on libraries and literacy produced by the American Library Association, and literacy statistics compiled by Michigan Literacy, Inc.

To find out more, write or phone:

Contact Center Inc.
PO Box 81826
Lincoln, NE 68501-1826
Toll-free: 1-800-228-8813 or *Phone:* (402)464-0602 or *Fax:* (402)464-5931

▶ Coors Brewing Co.

Provides information on: *Literacy*

In 1990, Coors Brewing Co., a major beer brewery, launched a five-year, $40 million program committed to reaching 500,000 adults with literacy services. The program, Coors "Literacy. Pass It On." addresses all levels of the national illiteracy problem: raising awareness, recruiting volunteers, supporting a hotline, and generating funds. The toll-free hotline (800-626-4601) helps direct non-readers and volunteer tutors to programs in their local areas. The hotline database contains information on 18,000 literacy programs and approximately 60,000 human services programs throughout the U.S. and its territories.

Information for free:

Information packet of fact sheets on the Coors "Literacy. Pass It On." program, detailing corporate involvement and participating personalities.

To find out more, write or phone:

Coors Brewing Co.
Mary Burch, Manager, Corporate Communications
Golden, CO 80401
Toll-free: 1-800-525-3786 or *Phone:* (303)277-6165

▶ Council of Better Business Bureaus (CBBB)

Provides information on: *Consumer Affairs, AIDS, Substance Abuse*

The Council is supported by 240,000 businesses and professional firms in all fields and 200 Better Business Bureaus operating in the United States, Canada, and Israel. Its purposes are to provide information to consumers before they purchase products and services to help them to be better buyers. The CBBB settles consumer complaints through arbitration and other means. It works to serve as a spokesperson for business in the consumer field, establish voluntary self-regulation of national advertising, and strengthen consumer education programs. CBBB sponsors Auto Line, a national mediation and arbitration service between automobile owners with complaints and participating automobile companies.

Information for a fee:
The CBBB offers "Tips On" booklets for $1 each on such subjects as AIDS treatment, cable TV, car repair, child care, employment services, funerals, medical services, quackery and teenagers, substance abuse, and video systems.
Several books are also offered:

The Better Business Bureau A to Z Buying Guide. $9.95. Gives buying information on over 100 products and services.

How to Protect Your Business. $4.95. Gives information on "schemes" against businesses. Also includes a directory of organizations and agencies that provide assistance and information.

Investor Alert! How to Protect Your Money. $9.95. Counsels consumers on the warning signs of investment fraud.

To find out more, write or phone:
Council of Better Business Bureaus
4200 Wilson Blvd., Ste. 800
Arlington, VA 22203
Phone: (703)276-0100 or *Fax:* (703)525-8277

▶ End Hunger Network

Provides information on: *Hunger, Media*

The Network's purposes are to involve the media and entertainment industry in efforts to end hunger, educate the public on hunger issues, create resources and support for hunger organizations, and to spark individual and community action. The Network brings together agencies, businesses, educators, service groups, and government to produce media events, programs, and audiovisual materials.

Information for free:
Annual Report.

To find out more, write or phone:

End Hunger Network
222 N. Beverly Dr.
Beverly Hills, CA 90210
Phone: (310)273-3179 or *Fax:* (818)906-0157

▶ Families for the Homeless

Provides information on: *Homelessness, Mental Health*

The organization is made up of individuals interested in educating the public about homelessness in America. Along with the National Mental Health Association, the group supports Homelessness in America, a traveling exhibit of photos and a video.

To find out more, write or phone:

Families for the Homeless
c/o John Ambrose
National Mental Health Association
1021 Prince St.
Alexandria, VA 22314
Phone: (703)684-7722

▶ Alan Shawn Feinstein World Hunger Program

Provides information on: *Hunger, Africa, Southeast Asia, Poverty*

The Program works to end world hunger, particularly in Africa and South Asia. Projects focus on causes of hunger, agricultural sustainability, role of local organizations, hunger measurement, rights to food, hunger prevention policy, and biotechnology studies. The Program conducts a Hunger Research Exchange, which links approximately 70 groups studying hunger in more than 22 countries.

Information for free:
Anthropological Perspectives on Diet. 1984. Reprint.
Beyond Hunger in Africa: Breaking the Spell of Monoculture. 1988. Reprint.
Ending Hunger in the Global Century. 1987. 12 pages. Occasional paper.
Famine Today: Hope for Tomorrow. 1985. 20 pages. Occasional paper.
Hunger in History: Food Shortage, Poverty, and Deprivation. 1990. Special report.
The Hunger Report. Annual.
Overcoming Hunger in the 1990s. 1990. Special report.
Poor People and Threatened Environments: Global Overviews, Country Comparisons, and Local Studies. 1991. Research report.
Wealth and Poverty in Rural India. 1988. Reprint.
A publication list and general information fact sheet are also available.

To find out more, write or phone:
Alan Shawn Feinstein World Hunger Program
Brown University
130 Hope St.
Box 1831
Providence, RI 02912
Phone: (401)863-2700 or *Fax:* (401)863-2192

▶ Freedom From Hunger Foundation (FFH)

Provides information on: *Hunger, Healthcare, Nutrition*

The Foundation assists communities, organizations, and institutions in Africa, Asia, Central America, South America, and the U.S. to eliminate the causes of chronic hunger through leadership development and self-help projects. FFH provides educational programs in health care and nutrition, conducts fundraising activities, and provides financial resources to promote income generation and increase food production. It maintains a resource center including a library of books, documents, and periodicals on nutrition, agriculture, health, community development, and income-generating activities.

Information for free:

Annual Report.

Freedom from Hunger: A Historical Perspective. Pamphlet on the organization's history and purposes.

Freedom from Hunger Foundation Newsbriefs. Quarterly. Newsletter reporting on the Foundation's progress and international development.

Freedom from Hunger Foundation Position Paper. 1990. 4 pages. A report on combating chronic hunger.

To find out more, write or phone:

Freedom From Hunger Foundation
1644 DaVinci Ct.
PO Box 2000
Davis, CA 95617
Phone: (916)758-6200 or *Fax:* (916)758-6251

▶ Fund for Animals

Provides information on: *Animal Rights*

The Fund for Animals works to protect wildlife and fight cruelty to animals, both domestic and wild, by means of legal action, direct activism, public education, and lobbying. It publicizes and influences public opinion on environmental and animal issues through books, press releases, articles, meetings, and special events.

Information for free:

Fund for Animals. Biennial. Newsletter.

To find out more, write or phone:

Fund for Animals
200 W. 57th St.
New York, NY 10019
Phone: (212)246-2096 or *Fax:* (212)246-2633

▶ Homelessness Information Exchange (HIE)

Provides information on: *Homelessness*

The Exchange provides information and research results on homelessness policies and programs to local service providers and government agencies. The organization compiles statistics and has databases on research, programs, and worldwide contacts and experts to assist agencies in preparing facilities and programs for the homeless.

Information for a fee:

City Initiatives: Comprehensive Planning to Address Homelessness. $10. Presents a framework for addressing both the service needs of the homeless and the structural problems which contribute to homelessness.

Family and Child Homelessness. $10. Summarizes the extent, causes and effects of homelessness among families and children.

General Information. $10. Explains the causes of homelessness, population characteristics, misconceptions, federal responses, policy issues, and relevant research.

Helping the Homeless in Your Community $10. Reviews ways to educate, volunteer, and advocate for the homeless in a community.

Homewords. Quarterly. $10/year. Highlights model projects, public and private funding strategies, relevant research, and technical advisors.

Transitional Housing. $10. Offers an introduction to the concepts of transitional housing and its role as an intermediate step to independent living.

To find out more, write or phone:

Homelessness Information Exchange
1830 Connecticut Ave. NW, 4th Fl.
Washington, DC 20009
Phone: (202)462-7551 or *Fax:* (202)234-9864

▶ The Hunger Project (THP)

Provides information on: *Hunger, International Development*

The Hunger Project is an educational organization working to eliminate world hunger by the year 2000. THP informs the public about worldwide hunger and starvation and encourages involvement in helping to solve the problem.

Information for free:

Global Newsletter. Provides an update on activities and accomplishments of The Hunger Project.

Information for a fee:

African Farmer: The Key to Africa's Future. 56 pages. $4. Magazine designed to elevate the status of the African food farmer.

Ending Hunger: An Idea Whose Time Has Come. 1985. $19.95. A reference book providing an overview of hunger, and the issues involved in solving it.

The Hunger Project Papers. $2. A series of papers on hunger and development issues intended for opinion- and policy-makers.

To find out more, write or phone:
The Hunger Project
1 Madison Ave., 8A
New York, NY 10010
Phone: (212)532-4255

▶ Institute for Research on Poverty

Provides information on: *Social Welfare, Poverty, Employment, Native Americans, Teenage Pregnancy*

The Institute studies the nature, causes, and cures of poverty in the U.S. This involves researching related topics such as economics, sociology, political science, social work, law, social science, psychology, and education. The Institute examines the causes of poverty and inequality, including income, education, minority status, women and children at risk, and health issues. It also examines efforts against poverty such as welfare, child support, employment programs, social security, and disability transfers.

Information for free:
Focus. 4/year. Newsletter. Contains short essays on selected pieces of research.
Insights. Periodic bulletin. Contains brief summaries on research findings.
A publications booklet is also available listing reprints, discussion papers, articles, and books.

Information for a fee:
American Indian Household Structure and Income. 1988. 10 pages. $2. Reprint.
Breaking the Chains: From Teenage Girls to Welfare Mothers, or, Can Social Policy Increase Options? 48 pages. $3.50. Discussion paper.
How Welfare Really Works. 1987. 12 pages. $2. Reprint.
Knowledge is Better Than Money: The Effect of the Food Stamp Program on Nutrient Intake. 74 pages. $3.50. Discussion paper.
Poverty in the U.S.: Why is it so Persistent? 1988. 46 pages. $2. Reprint.
Teen Parents and Child Support: Eligibility, Participation, and Payment. 1988. 20 pages. $2. Reprint.

To find out more, write or phone:
Institute for Research on Poverty
University of Wisconsin—Madison
Social Science Bldg., Rm. 3412
Madison, WI 53706
Phone: (608)262-6358 or *Fax:* (608)262-4747

▶ Interfaith Hunger Appeal (IHA)

Provides information on: *Hunger, Nutrition, Healthcare, Vocational Education, Literacy*

A cooperative hunger awareness and development education program, the Interfaith Hunger Appeal promotes public awareness of the causes and effects of world hunger and encourages public involvement in the development of policies to end world hunger. IHA works to fund overseas development programs in agricultural education, health care, nutrition, and vocational and literacy training. It conducts a national media campaign to alert Americans to the world food crisis.

Information for free:
1989-90 Hunger Report. 47 pages.
Hunger TeachNet. Quarterly. Newsletter for college faculty.
Institute Report. 41 pages.
Interfaith Hunger Appeal Annual Report. Pamphlet.

To find out more, write or phone:
Interfaith Hunger Appeal
475 Riverside Dr., Ste. 635
New York, NY 10115
Phone: (212)870-2035 or *Fax:* (212)870-2040

▶ Laubach Literacy International (LLI)

Provides information on: *Literacy*

The organization seeks to reduce adult illiteracy worldwide by motivating and supporting the teaching of illiterate adults and older youths to a level of listening, speaking, reading, writing, and basic math skills enabling them to solve their daily problems. LLI develops materials, trains volunteer literacy workers, recruits volunteers, and fosters increased public awareness of the problem of illiteracy. It also operates New Readers Press (NRP), a division that publishes educational materials for adults with limited reading skills and resources for teachers and tutors in the U.S. It maintains a library on adult literacy, adult basic education, and volunteer tutoring.

Information for a fee:
Basic Skills for the Workplace. $25. A guide to developing basic skills training in the workplace.
The Childbearing Year. $7.50. This book helps mothers-to-be learn about good prenatal care.
The Constitution Made Easier. $4.95. The Constitution is presented to students in a clear, simplified manner in this book.

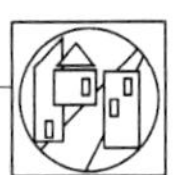

Government Today. $13.50. While building reading comprehension and critical-thinking skills, this book looks at local, state, and federal government, and their effects on the minority and majority groups of the nation.

Help Yourself: How to Take Advantage of Your Learning Styles. $7.95. A reference guide for students who want to maximize their learning strengths.

Literacy for Social Change. $11.50. Describes a successful model of literacy education that combines learning and community action.

Making the Most of News For You. $3.50. Guide that suggests ways to increase awareness of world events.

Our United States. $9.90. Provides a look at the history, geography, natural resources, and industries in the U.S.

Say the Word. $9. A guide to improving word recognition skills.

When a Baby is New. $2.75. Addresses important aspects of caring for a newborn.

Also offers many textbooks for math, writing, social studies, science, literature, and reading courses.

To find out more, write or phone:

Laubach Literacy International
1320 Jamesville Ave.
Box 131
Syracuse, NY 13210
Phone: (315)422-9121 or *Fax:* (315)422-6369

▶ Literacy Research Center

Provides information on: *Literacy*

The Center conducts research on literacy and literacy-related community services and consulting activities. Projects include cross-cultural studies of literacy retention in developing nations, adult literacy, computers in reading and writing instruction, workplace literacy, adults' persistence in literacy programs, quality of literacy programs, cross and multicultural issues in literacy access, family and intergenerational studies, development and use of technology, and adult development of reading, writing, and numeracy. The Center distributes information on literacy issues.

Information for free:

NCAL Connections. Quarterly newsletter.

To find out more, write or phone:
Literacy Research Center
University of Pennsylvania
Graduate School of Education
3700 Walnut St., Rm. A-36
Philadelphia, PA 19104
Phone: (215)898-1925 or *Fax:* (215)898-9804

▶ National Alliance to End Homelessness

Provides information on: *Homelessness, Low-Income Housing, Social Welfare*

The Alliance works to solve the problem of homelessness and prevent its continued growth. The organization works closely with the public, private, and nonprofit sectors to start programs to help homeless people. It supports policies and programs that reduce homelessness, engages in research to analyze the nature of homelessness and the elements of successful program solutions, and conducts educational programs.

Information for a fee:
And Miles to Go. $15. Deals with children and homelessness.
Homelessness: The Impact on Child Welfare in the 90's. $6.95. Report addressing the problems of housing families with young children.
Preventing Homelessness. $25. Examines seven state and local homelessness prevention programs operating in the United States.
Recycling Homes for Homeless People: A Guide to Federal Property Disposition Programs. $5. Looks at federal programs that make repossessed properties available to nonprofit groups for the homeless.
Shelterforce. Bimonthly. $3/single copy; $18/year. Covers the "affordable housing community."
What You Can Do to Help the Homeless. $3.95.

To find out more, write or phone:
National Alliance to End Homelessness
1518 K St. NW, Ste. 206
Washington, DC 20005
Phone: (202)638-1526 or *Fax:* (202)638-4664

▶ National Anti-Vivisection Society (NAVS)

Provides information on: *Animal Rights*

The Society provides information on alternatives and ways to oppose the use of animals in medical research, toxicity testing, and classroom teaching. In addition to its

publications program, NAVS sponsors programs to develop alternative research methods and to repeal state laws that allow animal shelter and pound animals to be used for laboratory experiments.

Information for free:

Alternatives to Animal Research and Testing. 8 pages. A look at alternatives to the use of nonhuman animals.

Animal Shelter? or Halfway House to Horror? 3 pages. Facts about pound seizure for animal experimentation.

The Campaign for Life. Overview of the arguments against the exploitation of nonhuman animals in science.

Some of Us Don't See Eye to Eye. 3 pages. Facts on the Draize Eye and Skin Irritancy Test.

Information for a fee:

Alcoholic Rats and Other Research Using Animals. 127 pages. $3.95.

All That Dwell Therein: Essays on Animal Rights and Environmental Ethics. 249 pages. $18.95.

Animal Rights and Human Morality. 182 pages. $13.95.

Animals and Christianity: A Book of Readings. 210 pages. $14.95.

The Case for Animal Rights. 425 pages. $9.95.

Christianity and the Rights of Animals. 197 pages. $12.95.

In Defense of Animals. 224 pages. $6.95.

Of Mice, Models, and Men. 323 pages. $19.95.

Science, Animals and Evolution. 221 pages. $5.95.

To find out more, write or phone:

National Anti-Vivisection Society
53 W. Jackson Blvd., Ste. 1552
Chicago, IL 60604-3795
Phone: (312)427-6065 or *Fax:* (312)427-6524

▶ National Association for Biomedical Research (NABR)

Provides information on: *Animal Rights*

The Association is a nonprofit organization committed to the responsible use and humane care of laboratory animals. The membership advocates using only as many animals as necessary and minimizing pain or distress animals may experience. The membership also monitors and attempts to influence legislation and regulations on behalf of members who are dependent on animals for biomedical research and testing.

Information for free:

1991 Highlights.

NABR Alert. Identifies opportunities for NABR members to participate in the legislative and regulatory process.

NABR Annual Report. A review of events and trends affecting the laboratory animal issue.

NABR Update. 30/year. Newsletter.

To find out more, write or phone:

National Association for Biomedical Research
818 Connecticut Ave., NW, Ste. 303
Washington, DC 20006
Phone: (202)857-0540 or *Fax:* (202)659-1902

▶ National Center for Children in Poverty (NCCP)

Provides information on: *Poverty, Education, Social Welfare, Single Parents, Hunger, Healthcare*

NCCP goals are to strengthen programs and policies for children and their families who live in poverty in the United States. The Center provides information in the areas of maternal land child health, family support, and early childhood care, and education.

Information for free:

News and Issues. Quarterly. 8 pages. Newsletter.

Information for a fee:

Alive and Well? A Research and Policy Review of Health Programs for Poor Young Children. 132 pages. $11.95. Outlines the extent of health problems among children in poverty, the causes of these problems, the history of U.S. governmental health care programs, and suggestions on possible public approaches to provide improved health and safety for poor children.

Changing Needs for a Changing Future: The Need for Educational Leadership. 20 pages. $2. This text, based on a speech, calls for systemic changes in our educational system in order to educate at-risk children.

Five Million Children: A Statistical Profile of Our Poorest Young Citizens. 96 pages. $12.95.

Young Children in Poverty: An Annotated Bibliography of Books and Reports. Annual. 20 pages. $3. Initiates a series of annual Center bibliographies and supplements that categorize and describe up-to-date reports and monographs in many areas related to children in poverty, minorities, single mothers, the uninsured, social policies, welfare reform, early childhood care and education, family support, maternal and child health, and hunger and food distribution.

To find out more, write or phone:

National Center for Children in Poverty
Columbia University
154 Haven Ave.
New York, NY 10032
Phone: (212)927-8793 or *Fax:* (212)927-9162

▶ National Clearinghouse on Literacy Education (NCLE)

Provides information on: *Literacy, Bilingual/Multilingual Education*

The Clearinghouse provides information, materials, and technical assistance on literacy education for adults and out-of-school youth with limited English-language skills. It is concerned with native language literacy, English as a second language (ESL), bilingual education, family literacy, vocational literacy, workforce literacy, workplace literacy, and tutor training.

Information for free:

ERIC Digests. 2 pages. Titles include:
Listening to Students' Voices: Materials Written By and For Adult LEP Literacy Learners;
Using Newspapers in Adult ESL Literacy Programs;
Using Closed Captioning TV for Literacy Development.
Minibibs. 2 pages. Mini-bibliographies of selected documents in ERIC. Titles include:
Approaches to Teaching Literacy to LEP Adults;
Curriculum Guides for Adult Literacy;
Family/Intergenerational Literacy;
The Role of Volunteer Tutors in Adult Literacy Programs;
Workplace Literacy.
Resource Guides. $2. Guides to current print and technical assistance resources. Titles include:
Family English Literacy;
Correctional Literacy Education;
A Dialogue Journal Bibliography.
Writing Our Lives: Reflections on Dialogue Journal Writing with Adults Learning English. $14.95. Describes the use of dialogue journals by adults learning English;
Directory of Literacy Programs. 1991. 250 pages. $15. A guide to local literacy providers for limited-English-proficient adults and out-of-school youth. Includes state and national contacts as well.

To find out more, write or phone:

National Clearinghouse on Literacy Education
The Center for Applied Linguistics
1118 22nd St., NW
Washington, DC 20037
Phone: (202)429-9292 or *Fax:* (202)429-9766

▶ National Coalition for the Homeless (NCH)

Provides information on: *Homelessness, Poverty, Substance Abuse*

The National Coalition for the Homeless is a private, nonprofit organization that serves as a clearinghouse for information on homelessness issues. In addition to its publications program, NCH is involved in lobbying, public education, litigation, coalition-building, national resource networking, community service, and homeless empowerment.

Information for free:

Safety Network. Monthly. Newsletter that contains information about states' legal and legislative efforts to serve the poor and homeless and about federal actions related to poverty and homelessness.

Homelessness in America: A Summary. 1990. An overview of the causes and consequences of homelessness, demographics of the homeless population, and suggestions on how to get involved in helping to end homelessness.

State Homeless Persons' Assistance Act Summary. 1989.

Information for a fee:

Addiction on the Streets: Homelessness and Substance Abuse in America. 1992. 46 pages. $5. Report discussing the relationship between homelessness and substance abuse.

American Nightmare: A Decade of Homelessness in the United States. 1989. $5.

Broken Lives: Denial of Education to Homeless Children. 1987. $3.

Closing Door: Economic Causes of Homelessness. 1990. 23 pages. $5. Examines economic factors contributing to increasing homelessness in the United States.

Heroes Today, Homeless Tomorrow?: Homelessness Among Veterans in the United States. 1991. 32 pages. $5. Examines the high incidence of homelessness among veterans.

The International Right to Shelter. 1989. $3.

Mourning in America: Health Problems, Mortality and Homelessness. 1991. 34 pages. $5. Report documenting the deaths of hundreds of homeless persons in 1991.

Over the Edge: Homeless Families and the Welfare System. 1988. $3.

Rural Homelessness in America: Appalachia and the South. 1987. $1.

To find out more, write or phone:
National Coalition for the Homeless
1621 Connecticut Ave., No. 400
Washington, DC 20009
Phone: (202)265-2371 or *Fax:* (202)265-2615

▶ National Consumer Law Center

Provides information on: *Consumer Affairs*

The National Consumer Law Center is a specialized resource in consumer and energy law funded by federal, state, and foundation grants. The Center defines recurring patterns in the problems of low-income consumers and develops a series of alternative solutions using legislation, lawyer training, and development of new service delivery systems. It conducts analyses of weatherization and energy assistance programs for low-income homeowners, renters, and state and federal agencies.

To find out more, write or phone:
National Consumer Law Center
11 Beacon St.
Boston, MA 02108
Phone: (617)523-8010 or *Fax:* (617)523-7398

▶ National Consumers League (NCL)

Provides information on: *Consumer Affairs, Product Safety, Victims*

The League encourages citizen participation in governmental and industry decision-making. NCL conducts research, and represents citizens' interests on such consumer and worker issues as insurance, credit, health, privacy, minimum wage, communications, labor standards, telemarketing fraud, air safety, and product safety and standards. It also coordinates the Alliance Against Fraud in Telemarketing, and the Child Labor Coalition.

Information for free:
Guide to Warning Labels on Nonprescription Medications. Brochure. Gives information on five common warning labels.
Swindlers are Calling. Brochure that offers tips on recognizing a crook and ways to avoid becoming a victim.
A general information fact sheet and publication list are also available.

Information for a fee:
DIAL 900: What Does it Mean? $1. Brochure. Explains what 900 numbers are and how to recognize deceptive promotions.

The Earth's Future is in Your Grocery Cart. $1. Brochure. Helps consumers make "environmentally friendly" product choices.

Food and Drug Interactions. $1. Brochure that discusses the effects of medication as related to a person's diet.

Here Today.Gone Tomorrow. $1. Brochure. Explains renters insurance.

NCL Bulletin. Bimonthly. Included in $20 membership fee. Newsletter. Provides current information on consumer issues.

Oops! New Drivers Guide to Automobile Insurance. $1. Brochure that answers questions about automobile insurance.

Pap Test: Assuring Your Good Health. $1. Brochure. Explains what a Pap test is and who is at risk for cervical cancer.

Questions to Ask: Take Charge of Your Health. $1. Brochure. Offers suggested questions consumers should ask regarding health care, and offers tips on choosing the right professionals.

To find out more, write or phone:

National Consumers League
815 15th St. NW, Ste. 928
Washington, DC 20005
Phone: (202)639-8140

▶ National Injury Information Clearinghouse (NIIC)

Provides information on: *Consumer Affairs, Product Safety*

NIIC is a national data collection system that investigates, studies, and offers injury data and information relating to the causes and prevention of death, injury, and illness associated with consumer products. NIIC maintains a file of consumer complaints and reported incidents received through letters or telephone calls citing injuries or potential injury situations, and newspaper accounts of product-related accidents.

Information for free:

Analysis of Choking Related Hazards Associated with Children's Products. 1989.

Electric Shock Accidents Involving Hand-Held Electric Hair Dryers. 1985.

Estimates of Residential Swimming Pool Deaths and Injuries. 1990.

Fire Hazards Involving Children Playing with Cigarette Lighters. 1987.

Fireworks Injuries. 1981.

Power Lawn Mower Injuries. 1990.

Additional reports are available on fire and burn hazards, electrical hazards, dangers associated with children's recreational products or activities, poisonings, and mechanical products hazards.

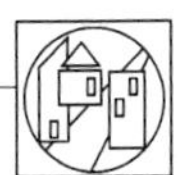

To find out more, write or phone:
National Injury Information Clearinghouse
5401 Westbard Ave., Rm. 625
Washington, DC 20207
Toll-free: 1-800-638-2772 or *Phone:* (301)504-0424 or *Fax:* (301)504-0124

▶ National Resource Center on Homelessness and Mental Illness

Provides information on: *Homelessness, Mental Health*

The Center serves as a resource for information and technical assistance on the housing and service needs of the mentally ill homeless. It maintains a library, compiles statistics, and has a bibliographic database search service.

Information for free:
Access. Bimonthly. Newsletter featuring articles on service delivery, housing, research and program evaluation, staff training, and federal, state, and local initiatives.
Also publishes free information packets.

To find out more, write or phone:
National Resource Center on Homelessness and Mental Illness
Policy Research Associates
262 Delaware Ave.
Delmar, NY 12054
Toll-free: 1-800-444-7415 or *Phone:* (518)439-7415 or *Fax:* (518)439-7612

▶ National Student Campaign Against Hunger and Homelessness (NSCAHH)

Provides information on: *Homelessness, Hunger, Africa, Southeast Asia, Mental Health*

This is an organization of colleges and high schools organized to educate students on and promote student interest in world and domestic hunger and homelessness. The Campaign involves site visits, phone consultations, and manuals to assist students in developing and running programs to combat poverty. The Campaign sponsors international development projects in Africa, Asia, and Latin America, promotes educational and community outreach programs, and provides professional on-site training.

Information for free:

The Hunger Cleanup Manual. Single copy is free. A step-by-step manual on how to lead a hunger cleanup.

Information for a fee:

Fall Organizing Guide. 65 pages. $6.25. A manual on national fall programs incorporating tips on organizing a sleep-out and a candidate's forum to fact sheets on hunger and homelessness.

Food Salvage. $6.25. A guide to beginning a food salvage program on your campus.

Going Places. $6.25. Lists internships, travel, and career opportunities in the field of hunger, housing, homelessness, and grassroots development.

Hunger and Homelessness Action: A Resource Book for Colleges and Universities. $20. A guide for recruitment, media promotion, and fundraising.

Setting a New Course: Expanding Collegiate Curriculum to Incorporate the Study of Hunger and Homelessness. $6.25. A guide to help colleges or universities expand their curricula to include courses on domestic and international hunger and homelessness issues.

Students Making a Difference. Monthly. $15. Newsletter of the NSCAHH.

Also publishes sets of fact sheets that cover various aspects of hunger and homelessness, including hunger in Ethiopia, federal food assistance programs, and homelessness and the mentally ill. $2/packet.

To find out more, write or phone:

National Student Campaign Against Hunger and Homelessness
29 Temple Pl.
Boston, MA 02111
Phone: (617)292-4823 or *Fax:* (617)292-8057

▶ National Volunteer Clearinghouse for the Homeless

Provides information on: *Homelessness, Voluntarism*

The National Volunteer Clearinghouse for the Homeless is a Washington, D.C.-based center working to provide for the homeless who live in the city, as well as inform the public on the plight of the homeless in America. The Clearinghouse also matches volunteers with local service providers who need assistance. Providers list the services they offer, hours of operation, volunteer needs, etc. Volunteers can write or phone the Clearinghouse to obtain detailed information about local opportunities.

Information for a fee:

DC Directory of Volunteer Opportunity for Youths. Annual. $25.

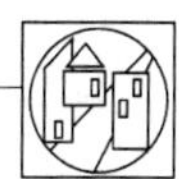

Wish List. Annual. $10.

The Clearinghouse also distributes pamphlets and brochures about the Clearinghouse and volunteer opportunities.

To find out more, write or phone:

National Volunteer Clearinghouse for the Homeless
1313 New York Ave., NW, Ste. 303
Washington, DC 20005
Phone: (202)638-2664

▶ People for the Ethical Treatment of Animals (PETA)

Provides information on: *Animal Rights, Vegetarianism*

PETA is an educational and activist group that opposes all forms of animal exploitation. The group seeks to educate the public against negative, uncaring attitudes toward animals through documentary films, slides, and pictures of current conditions in slaughterhouses and experimentation laboratories. The organization conducts rallies and demonstrations to focus attention on what the group sees as the three major institutionalized cruelty issues: the exploitation and abuse of animals in experimentation, the manufacturing of fur apparel, and slaughtering for human consumption.

Information for free:

Aspin Hill Memorial Park. Leaflet that tells the history of PETA's animal sanctuary.

Literature Available From PETA. A guide to available pamphlets and fliers.

Information for a fee:

The PETA Guide to Becoming an Activist. 70 pages. $5. A guide to basic animal rights activism, from working with the media, to designing leaflets, and organizing meetings and demonstrations.

The PETA Guide to Compassionate Living. 32 pages. $2. Provides information on cruelty-free living, and the benefits of a vegan diet.

PETA Factsheets. $7. Examines aspects of animal rights, from spaying and neutering companion animals to animals used in cancer research.

To find out more, write or phone:

People for the Ethical Treatment of Animals
Box 42516
Washington, DC 20015
Phone: (301)770-7444 or *Fax:* (301)770-8969

▶ Primate Supply Information Clearinghouse (PSIC)

Provides information on: *Animal Rights*

The Clearinghouse provides communication between research institutions concerning the exchange of non-human primates or their tissues. PSIC promotes the sharing of animals to decrease the need to import animals for research purposes, ultimately decreasing the number of animals needed. The Clearinghouse also helps municipal zoos in locating and placing primates.

Information for a fee:
Offers hundreds of bibliographies each for $6.50, on primate behavior, ecology, and conservation; physical aspects, such as the nervous system; and on colony management, including:
Primate Welfare, Well-Being and Enrichment Studies and Legislation.

To find out more, write or phone:
Primate Supply Information Clearinghouse
University of Washington
Regional Primate Research Center, SJ-50
Seattle, WA 98195
Phone: (206)543-5178 or *Fax:* (206)685-0305

▶ Public Citizen

Provides information on: *Consumer Affairs, Product Safety*

Public Citizen is an organization that was formed by Ralph Nader to support the work of citizen advocates. Areas of focus include consumer rights in the marketplace, safe products, a healthful environment and workplace, clean and safe energy sources, corporate and government accountability, group buying to enhance marketplace clients, and citizen empowerment. Methods for change used by the group include lobbying, litigation, monitoring government agencies, research, and public education.

Information for free:
With purchase of any other publication,
Medical Records: Getting Yours. Guide explaining the importance of access to personal medical information. Regular price, $5.

Information for a fee:
All the Vice-President's Men. 36 pages. $10. Report exposing the operation of Dan Quayle's Council on Competitiveness, which "can secretly review regulations and pressure agencies to change them."

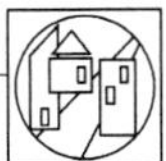

The Big Boys: Power and Position in American Business. 576 pages. $11. Portraits of America's top business leaders.

Consumer Packet on Silicone Gel Breast Implants. 74 pages. $6. Answers questions about breast implants.

Mammography Screening and Ranking of 11 Washington DC Area Facilities. 41 pages. $7. Provides information on the effectiveness, benefits, and risks of mammograms.

Representing Yourself. 270 pages. $13. Guide on how to solve everyday legal problems without a lawyer, including how to contest traffic violations and how to write your own will.

Women's Health Alert. 324 pages. $10. Provides facts and opinions on health practices, drugs, and products that affect women, including breast implants, birth control, and weight loss products.

Worst Pills Best Pills. 500 pages. $10. Lists 104 drugs that can cause harm and possibly death.

To find out more, write or phone:

Public Citizen
2000 P St., NW
Washington, DC 20036
Phone: (202)833-3000

▶ Results

Provides information on: *Hunger*

Results conducts grassroots citizen lobbying focused on ending world hunger. The group works to emphasize the importance of individual effort and monetary donations. It sponsors a monthly study session to determine lobbying goals for use in letter-writing campaigns intended to make government representatives aware of viable U.S. contributions toward ending world hunger. They also conduct a monthly conference call among members, hunger experts, leaders of international organizations, and members of Congress.

Information for a fee:

Entry Point. Quarterly. $25/year. Price includes membership.

To find out more, write or phone:

Results
236 Massachusetts Ave. NE, Ste. 300
Washington, DC 20002
Phone: (202)543-9340 or *Fax:* (202)546-3228

▶ Scientists Center for Animal Welfare (SCAW)

Provides information on: *Animal Rights*

SCAW is a group of scientists and others that support research on animals. It provides a forum for the discussion of public policy and the scientist's responsibilities regarding standards of animal care and use. The Center develops educational resource material on Institutional Animal Care Use Committees, animal pain, and national guidelines on humane procedures in animal research.

Information for a fee:
Annotated Bibliography on Laboratory Animal Welfare. 1991. $15.
Guidelines for the Well-being of Rodents in Research. $25.
Science and Animals: Addressing Contemporary Issues. $25.

To find out more, write or phone:
Scientists Center for Animal Welfare
4805 St. Elmo Ave.
Bethesda, MD 20814
Phone: (301)654-6390 or *Fax:* (301)907-3993

▶ Student Action Corps for Animals (SACA)

Provides information on: *Animal Rights, Student and Teacher Rights, Vegetarianism*

The Student Action Corps seeks to encourage youth participation in the animal rights movement and to enhance awareness of animal rights issues. The group serves as a national network and clearinghouse, and as an advocacy and counseling group on the issue of student rights and empowerment. It provides information on animal rights issues and writes overviews of issues for students and teachers. A Stop Dissection Campaign throughout the U.S. is coordinated, and student questions about dissection-refusal and vegetarianism are answered.

Information for a fee:
101 Non-Animal Biology Lab Methods. $2.
SACA News. 1-3/year. $7. Newsletter for high school and college students covering animal rights. Includes resource listings.
Their Eyes Don't Lie. $3.75. A fold-out poster set.
Also publishes brochures and leaflets, which are available for a donation.

To find out more, write or phone:

Student Action Corps for Animals
Rosa Feldman, Co-Founder
PO Box 15588
Washington, DC 20003
Phone: (202)543-8983 or *Fax:* (202)265-5459

▶ World Hunger Year (WHY)

Provides information on: *Hunger, Poverty*

WHY provides information to the general public, the media, and policy-makers on the extent and causes of hunger in the U.S. and abroad. It develops programs and policies to combat hunger and supports local organizations that promote food self-reliance and jobs.

Information for free:
RAI Update. Monthly.

Information for a fee:
Why. Magazine. Quarterly. $18. Covers the topic of world hunger and poverty.

To find out more, write or phone:

World Hunger Year
261 W. 35th St., Rm. 1402
New York, NY 10001
Phone: (212)629-8850 or *Fax:* (212)465-9274

To Contact People . . .

These books identify individual experts or organizations that can direct you to one.

▶ *The Address Book: How to Reach Anyone Who Is Anyone*

This book can be used to contact more than 3,500 prominent persons including political leaders, business executives, athletes, actors and actresses, artists, musicians, and writers. The book lists name and address. Names are listed alphabetically.
Biennial. Perigee Books.

▶ *Alternative America*

The publication covers some 12,000 groups concerned with alternative lifestyles, social change, consumerism, appropriate technology, cooperative living and ventures, including associations, publishers, and nonprofit and cooperative undertakings. The entries include the group's name, address, and keywords indicating major concerns. They are arranged geographically.
Annual. Resources.

▶ *American Association for Laboratory Animal Science—Membership Directory*

The directory covers 4,500 persons and institutions professionally concerned with the production, use, care, and study of laboratory animals. Entries include name, address, phone, and degree, and are arranged geographically.
Annual. American Association for Laboratory Animal Science.

▶ *American Homeless*

This book lists leading organizations and agencies dealing with homelessness in America. Entries include names and biographical sketches of prominent activists, advocates, and legislators; and location of print and nonprint information on homelessness.
ABC-CLIO.

▶ *Canadian Who's Who*

This book lists about 12,000 notable Canadians in Canada and abroad based on position or achievement. Entries include name, address, personal and career data.
Annual. University of Toronto Press.

▶ *Community of the Book: A Directory of Selected Organizations and Programs*

This book can be used to identify about 100 organizations that administer literacy projects, and promote books, reading, and the study of books. Entries include organization name, address, phone, year founded, purpose, sources of funding, description of activities, and publications. Information is arranged alphabetically by organization title.
1989. Publications Office, Library of Congress.

▶ *Consumer Sourcebook*

Use this book to contact approximately 8,000 federal, state, and city agencies that provide aid and information to the consumer. Coverage includes consumer finance, health, safety, environmental concerns, corporate responsibility, product safety and reliability, as well as nongovernmental associations, centers, and institutes active in consumer issues. For agencies and organizations, the book lists name, address, phone, fax, hotlines, description of purpose and services, publications, and name of contact for most entries. For companies, the book lists company name, address, and phone for customer relations. Information is arranged by subject, then by type of organization.
Biennial. Gale Research Inc.

▶ *Consumer's Resource Handbook*

Use this handbook to contact more than 2,700 corporate consumer contacts, automobile manufacturers, corporate contacts, Better Business Bureau offices, industry third-party dispute resolution programs, trade associations, state and local consumer protection offices, and other federal and state agencies that handle consumer complaints. Generally each entry contains company or agency name, name and title of contact, address, phone, including toll-free numbers and numbers for telecommunication devices for the deaf. Information is classified by type of agency.
Biennial. U.S. Office of Consumer Affairs.

▶ *Directory of Certified Product Safety Managers*

The directory covers about 400 members certified as competent in the field of product safety management. Entries include name and title; company name, address, and phone. They are arranged alphabetically.
Biennial. Board of Certified Product Safety Management.

▶ *Everybody's Money Consumer's Directory*

Use this directory to contact federal, state, and local government agencies; senators and representatives; radio and television broadcasters; manufacturers and suppliers of services; and others to whom to address complaints or inquiries. The book lists name, address, phone, and contact. Information is classified by type of organization.
Biennial. Credit Union National Association.

▶ *International Who's Who*

This book covers 20,000 prominent persons worldwide. Entries include name, nationality, personal and career information, honors, awards, writings, address, and

phone. Names are arranged alphabetically.
Annual. Europa Publications Ltd.

▶ *Laubach Literacy Action Directory*

Use this directory to contact more than 900 local literacy councils and associates. The book also lists some 2,500 certified volunteer trainers who teach the Laubach Method to tutors for older youth, adult English speakers, and speakers of other languages who want to improve their reading and basic skills. The book provides group name, chairman, address, and phone. For trainers, the book provides name, type of certification, and address. Entries are arranged geographically.
Annual. Laubach Literacy Action.

▶ *National Association of Social Workers Register of Clinical Social Workers*

The Register lists about 17,000 clinical social workers who applied for listing under established criteria, which include education, certification or state licensing, supervised and clinical experience, and advanced specialization credentials. Entries are arranged geographically.
Biennial. National Association of Social Workers.

▶ *Professional Workers in State Agricultural Experiment Stations and Other Cooperating State Institutions*

The directory covers academic and research personnel in all agricultural, forestry, aquacultural, home economics, and animal husbandry fields at experiment stations and academic institutions with agricultural programs. Entries include station or institution name, address, phone; names of personnel, their degrees and titles, and, in some cases, individual phone numbers; personnel are listed by major scientific or administrative areas. The arrangement of the book is geographical.
Annual. United States Government Printing Office.

▶ *Who's Who in America*

This book contains information on 79,000 people, primarily in the U.S., considered to be of current national interest because of achievement or position. Entries include name, address, personal data, career data, memberships, special achievements, and publications. Names are listed alphabetically; a separate volume indexes people by profession and location.
Biennial. Updated quarterly. Marquis Who's Who.

▶ *Who's Who of American Women*

This book contains information on more than 30,000 high-profile women in all fields. Entries include name, address, personal, educational, and career data, professional association membership, special achievements, awards, and writings. Names are arranged alphabetically.

Biennial. Marquis Who's Who.

▶ *Who's Who Among Human Services Professionals*

The publication covers nearly 20,000 human service professionals in such fields as counseling, social work, psychology, audiology, and speech pathology. Entries include name, address, education, work experience, and professional association memberships. The arrangement of the entries is alphabetical.

Biennial. National Reference Institute.

▶ *Who's Who in the World*

This directory covers more than 31,000 people of current international interest because of their achievement or position. Entries include name, address, biographical data, civic activities, awards, writings, and other information. Names are arranged alphabetically.

Biennial. Marquis Who's Who.

▶ *Research Centers Directory*

Coverage includes over 13,000 university-related and other nonprofit research organizations that carry on continuing research programs in all areas of study. This includes research institutes, laboratories, experiment stations, computing centers, research parks, technology transfer centers, and other facilities and activities in the U.S. and Canada. Entries include unit name, name of parent institution, address, phone, fax, principal fields of research, name of director, year founded, and related information. Information is classified by broad subjects, then alphabetical by unit name.

Annual. Gale Research Inc.

Health and Personal Concerns

▶ Chapter 6 covers these topics:

Abortion
AIDS
Alcoholism
Death and Dying
Eating Disorders
Fitness
Mental Health
Nutrition
Pregnancy and Birth Technology
Self-Help Groups
Sexuality
Smoking
Steroid Use and Effects
Substance Abuse
Suicide

▶ Related topics appear in chapters on:

Beliefs, Cults, and Sects; Family Connections and Concerns; Social Issues

▶ Ideas for research topics:

AIDS and the Homosexual Population
AIDS and Intravenous Drug Abuse
Alcohol and Drugs and College Campuses
Alcoholics Anonymous and the Twelve Steps to Recovery
Alternative Methods of Childbirth
Anorexia Nervosa
Arguments For and Against the Legalization of Marijuana
Babies Born Addicted
Both Sides of the Abortion Issue
Children of Alcoholics
Crack Cocaine
Depression as an Illness
Do Mandatory Urine Tests Violate Our Right to Privacy?
Drinking and Driving
Drug-Use Trends in America
Eating Disorders and Cocaine Abuse
Effective School Health Education Programs to Prevent the Spread of AIDS
The Effects of Smoking on the Fetus
The Euthanasia Controversy

▶ Ideas for research topics (continued):

The Fetal Alcohol Syndrome
The Glamorous Depiction of Smoking in the Media
HIV Transmission During Blood Transfusion
Homosexuality
Methods of Birth Control
Nicotine Dependence
Parental Notification Policies in U.S. Abortion Facilities
Philosophies Behind Natural Childbirth Methods
The Physical and Psychological Effects of Alcohol
Roe v. Wade: Reproduction Rights
The Role of Nutrition in Fighting Disease
Sex Education in Public Schools
Smoking and Teenagers
State and Federal Mental Health Programs
Steroids and Substance Abuse in Sports
Successful Drug and Alcohol Prevention Programs
Successful Self-Help Groups
Suicide: Effects on the Victim's Family
Transmission of the HIV Infection During Dental Procedures
What Are "Designer Drugs?"
What You Can Do to Prevent HIV and AIDS

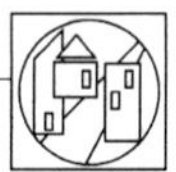

To Contact Organizations . . .

▶ Action on Smoking and Health (ASH)

Provides information on: *Smoking*

ASH works for effective national legal action to protect the rights of "the nonsmoking majority" against problems caused by smoking. ASH is concerned with reducing the negative effects of smoking; fighting unfair and deceptive cigarette advertising and promotion practices; making the tobacco industry pay for harm caused by smoking; and increasing exposure of antismoking messages. Founder John F. Banzhaf, III filed the complaint which resulted in the Federal Communications Commission ruling that broadcasters were required to provide "a significant amount of time" for antismoking messages. ASH supported the law that banned radio and television cigarette advertising effective January 2, 1971, has testified on behalf of strong warnings about health hazards being included on cigarette packages and in print advertising, and actively participated in the establishment of nonsmoking sections in public places.

Information for a fee:

ASH Smoking and Health Review. Bimonthly. $15/year. Newsletter covering medical, legal, regulatory, commercial, institutional, and humorous news related to smoking.

To find out more, write or phone:

Action on Smoking and Health
2013 H St., NW
Washington, DC 20006
Phone: (202)659-4310

▶ Adolescent Pregnancy Prevention Clearinghouse

Provides information on: *AIDS, Employment, Marriage, Education, Teenage Pregnancy, Dropouts, Alcoholism*

The Adolescent Pregnancy Prevention Clearinghouse handles requests for information and clarification on the connection between teenage pregnancy and broader life questions for youth. The Clearinghouse handles inquiries regarding teenage dropouts, pregnancy and pregnant students, and sex education. Research and referral services are accepted via telephone, facsimile, and mail.

Information for a fee:

Adolescent Pregnancy: What Schools Can Do. 1986. 16 pages. Exposes the link between poor basic academic skills and teen pregnancy and describes how schools can improve a teenager's ability and motivation to delay pregnancy.

Adolescent Pregnancy: Whose Problem Is It? 1986. 12 pages. $4.50.

The Adolescent and Young Adult Fact Book. 1991. 164 pages. $13.95. Details family income, health status, drug and alcohol abuse, and other statistics about Americans aged 10-24.

Lack of Health Insurance Makes a Difference. 1989. 16 pages. $4.50 Investigates the problem among adolescents and young adults of being uninsured. Includes a discussion of family income, family educational attainment, and other factors related to the insurance status of young Americans.

Latino Youths At a Crossroads. 1990. 32 pages. $4.75. Provides an overview of this diverse and fastest-growing segment of the youth population, much of it presented in charts and graphs. Focusing on the areas of education, employment, marriage, and childbearing, the report also provides recommendations to ensure that Latino adolescents achieve long-term economic security as adults.

Teenage Pregnancy: An Advocates Guide to the Numbers. 1988. 52 pages. $7.45.

Teens and AIDS: Opportunities for Prevention. 1988. 30 pages. $4.50.

What About the Boys? Teenage Pregnancy Prevention Strategies. 1988. 44 pages. $4.50 Examines adolescent male sexual attitudes and behavior, how they differ from those of females, and suggests reasons these differences exist. Focuses on pregnancy prevention and provides examples of specific programs for males.

To find out more, write or phone:

Adolescent Pregnancy Prevention Clearinghouse
Children's Defense Fund
122 C St., NW
Washington, DC 20001
Phone: (202)628-8787 or *Fax:* (202)783-7324

▶ AIDS Action Council (AAC)

Provides information on: *AIDS*

The Council serves as a representative in Washington, DC of local groups that offer information, education, and services concerning AIDS. AAC maintains the AIDS Action Foundation, lobbies Congress to increase AIDS research funding, and monitors federal medical research.

Information for a fee:

AIDS Action Update. Monthly. $15 minimum contribution.

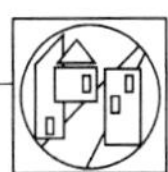

To find out more, write or phone:

AIDS Action Council
2033 M St. NW, Ste. 802
Washington, DC 20036
Phone: (202)986-1300 or *Fax:* (202)296-1292

▶ AIDS Resource Foundation for Children

Provides information on: *AIDS*

AIDS Resource Foundation for Children operates homes for children with HIV, AIDS, or AIDS-Related Complex (ARC) who are well enough to be released from the hospital but are in need of foster care placement or respite care. The Foundation provides support services to families coping with AIDS or related diseases, operates foster parent recruitment, training, and support programs, and collects and distributes toys and clothing. It also sponsors summer camp for families, and conducts HIV training workshops, community outreach programs, and agency networking.

Information for free:

Newsletter. 3/year.

To find out more, write or phone:

AIDS Resource Foundation for Children
St. Clare's Home for Children
182 Roseville Ave.
Newark, NJ 07107
Phone: (201)483-4250 or *Fax:* (201)483-1998

▶ Al-Anon Family Group Headquarters

Provides information on: *Self-Help Groups, Alcoholism*

Al-Anon is a free, self-help program that offers help for those whose lives have been or continue to be affected by the problem drinking of a family member or friend. The group operates Alateen for members 12-20 years of age whose lives have been adversely affected by someone else's drinking problem, usually a parent's.

Information for free:

Catalog: Al-Anon/Alateen CAL.
Catalog: Reading for Recovery.

Information for a fee:

Adult Children of Alcoholics: Newcomer's Packet. 9 pieces. $1.75. Pamphlets for those who have grown up with parental alcoholism.

Al-Anon's Twelve Steps and Twelve Traditions. 142 pages. $6.50. A collection of essays, personal reflections, and stories from Al-Anon members about the principles of the program.

Alateen—Hope for Children of Alcoholics. 115 pages. $5.50. Covers the history of Alateen, the steps, traditions, slogans, and personal stories of Alateen members.

Al-Anon Family Groups. 177 pages. $6.50. Explains the purpose of the group, how it works, and how it is held in unity.

Alcoholism, A Merry-Go-Round Named Denial. 18 pages. $.60. Pamphlet showing members the part they play in the disease.

Alcoholism, the Family Disease. 48 pages. $.60. Covers a variety of information and inspiration.

Did You Grow Up with a Problem Drinker? $.25. Twenty personal questions to help decide if one can benefit from Al-Anon.

If Your Parents Drink Too Much. 24 pages. $.40. A cartoon booklet containing stories of teenagers with parents who have drinking problems.

Living With Sobriety: Another Beginning. 48 pages. $2. Includes such topics as jealousy, facing dry drunks, slips, and reality.

What's "Drunk," Mama? 32 pages. $1.25. A book for younger children to understand alcoholism.

To find out more, write or phone:

Al-Anon Family Group Headquarters
Midtown Sta.
PO Box 862
New York, NY 10018-0862
Toll-free: 1-800-356-9996 or *Phone:* (212)302-7240 or *Fax:* (212)869-3757

▶ Alcohol Research Information Service (ARIS)

Provides information on: *Alcoholism*

ARIS collects and distributes information on the manufacture, sale, and use of alcohol and alcoholic products, especially as related to the health and well being of the people in the United States. Its research supports the conclusion that the use of alcoholic beverages has a net harmful effect. ARIS also studies other drugs and gambling addiction.

Information for a fee:

Almost All You Ever Wanted to Know about Alcohol.But Didn't Know Who to Ask! 32 pages. $.95. Provides facts and definitions concerning alcohol abuse and alcoholism.

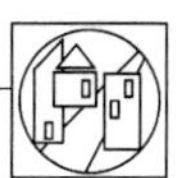

The Bottom Line on Alcohol in Society. Quarterly. 64 pages. $20/year. Deals with research, issues, events, and opinions relating to public policy in the field of alcohol problems, with special emphasis on prevention.

Is Someone Concerned About Your Drinking? 20 pages. $.50. Deals with reasons people give to prove they cannot be alcoholic.

A Little About Alcohol. 40 pages. $2.25. Gives facts and ideas about alcohol for children in the early grades.

A Little More About Alcohol. 68 pages. $2.75. Offers facts, information, and ideas about alcohol use, misuse, and abuse to students in the middle grades.

To find out more, write or phone:

Alcohol Research Information Service
1106 E. Oakland Ave.
Lansing, MI 48906
Phone: (517)485-9900 or *Fax:* (517)485-1928

▶ Alcoholics Anonymous World Services (AA)

Provides information on: *Self-Help Groups, Alcoholism*

The Association is made up of people recovering from alcoholism. AA maintains that members can solve their common problem and help others achieve sobriety through a 12-step program that includes sharing their experience, strength, and hope with each other.

Information for free:

A.A. at a Glance. A flyer containing facts on A.A.

Information on Alcoholics Anonymous.

A Message to Teenagers. Flyer.

Problems Other Than Alcohol.

Information for a fee:

A.A. and the Gay/Lesbian Alcoholic. $.40. Pamphlet covering experiences of sober gay and lesbian alcoholics.

A.A. Comes of Age. $5.10. Tells how A.A. got started, how the steps and traditions evolved, and how A.A. grew and spread overseas.

A.A. in Prison: Inmate to Inmate. 128 pages. $2.95. A collection of 32 stories sharing the experience of those who found A.A. while in prison.

Alcoholics Anonymous. $5. The basic text of A.A. describing the recovery program.

Do You Think You're Different? $.30. A pamphlet describing how A.A. can work for someone "different"—Black, Jewish, teenager, or senior citizen.

Living Sober. 88 pages. $2. A booklet demonstrating how A.A. members live and stay sober.

Too Young? $.25. Pamphlet for teenagers interested in the A.A. program.
Young People and A.A. $.30. Ten young A.A.'s tell how the program works for them.
Also offers other books, pamphlets (many are under $1), directories, special literature packages, filmstrips and slides, audiocassettes, and literature in over 20 languages and braille.

To find out more, write or phone:
Alcoholics Anonymous World Services
Grand Central Station
PO Box 459
New York, NY 10163
Phone: (212)870-3400 or *Fax:* (212)576-8497

▶ Alternatives to Abortion International/Women's Health and Education Foundation (AAI/WHEF)

Provides information on: *Abortion*

AAI/WHEF assists women with problem pregnancies and offers non-abortion counseling and practical services. AAI does not engage in legislative or judicial activities and/or lobbying, but develops programs to assist those contemplating abortion by offering emotional, medical, legal, and social support.

To find out more, write or phone:
Alternatives to Abortion International/Women's Health and Education Foundation
1213 1/2 S. James Rd.
Columbus, OH 43227-1801
Phone: (614)239-9433

▶ American Anorexia/Bulimia Association

Provides information on: *Eating Disorders*

The Association serves as an information source for anorectics, families of anorectics, psychiatric social workers, nurses, psychiatrists, physicians, and others interested in the problems of anorexia nervosa and bulimia. Anorexia nervosa is a serious illness of deliberate self-starvation with profound psychiatric and physical components. Bulimia is characterized by recurrent episodes of binge eating, followed by self-induced vomiting or purging by laxatives and diuretics.
The Association offers a newsletter on eating disorders and other informational publications.

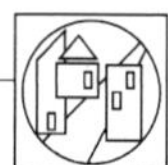

To find out more, write or phone:

American Anorexia/Bulimia Association
418 E. 76th St.
New York, NY 10021
Phone: (212)734-1114

▶ American Association of Suicidology

Provides information on: *Suicide*

The Association seeks to recognize and encourage suicidology, which is the study of suicide, suicide prevention, and related phenomena of self-destruction. The group advances education, offers information through programs and publications, and cooperates with other organizations in suicidology.

Information for free:

Survivor's Resource List. A listing of books, pamphlets, and other resources which may be of interest to survivors and those who help them.

Information for a fee:

Adolescent Suicide: Assessment and Intervention. 1991. $17.50. Gives advice on how to work with the suicidal adolescent.

My Son, My Son: A Guide to Healing After a Suicide in the Family. 1984. $10.95. Written to help survivors in their healing.

Stronger Than Death. 1992. $19.95. A psychiatrist and mother discusses her son's suicide.

Suicide in Later Life. 1992. $22.95. Covers issues surrounding elderly sucide.

Surviving Suicide. Quarterly. $20/year. Newsletter for and about survivors of suicide.

To find out more, write or phone:

American Association of Suicidology
2459 S. Ash
Denver, CO 80222
Phone: (303)692-0985 or *Fax:* (303)756-3299

▶ American Council on Alcohol Problems

Provides information on: *Alcoholism*

The American Council on Alcohol Problems seeks long-range solutions to the problems caused by alcohol. It uses research, educational, and legislative approaches for the prevention of alcoholism and other alcohol-related problems. The Council coordinates the work of state affiliates who carry on their programs under provisions of the 21st Amendment, putting alcohol control largely at the state level.

Information for free:
Donor Letter. Newsletter.

To find out more, write or phone:

American Council on Alcohol Problems
3426 Bridgeland Dr.
Bridgeton, MO 63044
Phone: (314)739-5944

▶ American Council for Drug Education (ACDE)

Provides information on: *Substance Abuse, Alcoholism, Smoking*

The Council's purpose is to educate the American public about the health hazards associated with tobacco, alcohol, marijuana, cocaine, crack, and other psychoactive drug use. It believes that an informed public is the nation's best defense against drug abuse. The Council gives special attention to the urgent educational needs of children, adolescents, and young adults, co-dependents and co-workers of drug abusers, pregnant women, disadvantaged minorities, and other high-risk groups.

Information for a fee:

Getting Tough on Gateway Drugs: A Guide for the Family. $8.95. Explores the dangers of "gateway" drugs (alcohol, tobacco, and marijuana) which often lead to further drug abuse. Written to help families prevent and solve drug problems.

The Purposes of Pleasure: A Reflection on Youth and Drugs. $6.25. Discusses how the search for pleasure motivates drug use and affects maturation, learning, and behavior.

Thinking About Drugs and Society: Responding to an Epidemic. $7.50. Traces the history of drug use and explores questions about the "right" to use drugs, the harm drugs cause, drug testing, and other issues.

Cocaine: A Second Look. $2.50. Pamphlet.

Cocaine: The Bottom Line. $2.50. Pamphlet.

Cocaine Today. $2.50. Pamphlet.

Drug Digest Library Pamphlet Series. $3.50/set or $.35 each. Includes such titles as Marijuana and Alcohol Combinations, Marijuana and Driving, and Alcohol and the Adolescent.

Drugs & Pregnancy: It's Not Worth the Risk. $3. Pamphlet.

Marijuana Today: A Compilation of Medical Findings for The Layman. $3. Pamphlet.

Marijuana: The National Impact on Education. $2.50. Pamphlet.

Marijuana and You: Myth and Fact. $.45. Pamphlet.

Seven Reasons Pamphlet Series. $1.40/set or 35 cents each. Aimed at 8 to 12 year olds and their parents. Includes such topics as alcohol, crack cocaine, steroids, and tobacco.

Treating the Marijuana-Dependent Person. $3. Pamphlet.

To find out more, write or phone:
American Council for Drug Education
204 Monroe St., Ste. 110
Rockville, MD 20850
Toll-free: 1-800-488-DRUG or *Phone:* (301)294-0600 or *Fax:* (301)294-0603

▶ American Fitness Association (AFA)

Provides information on: *Fitness*

Physicians, psychologists, exercise physiologists, and other health and fitness professionals, corporations, interested individuals are Association members. The group promotes interest, involvement, and education in health and fitness, and attempts to influence legislative action concerning health and fitness. It sponsors seminars, sports clinics, and competitions. The AFA endorses athletic events and sports-related tours.

To find out more, write or phone:
American Fitness Association
820 Hillside Dr.
Long Beach, CA 90815
Phone: (310)596-0977 or *Fax:* (213)596-0977

▶ American Puffer Alliance

Provides information on: *Smoking*

The Alliance is a group of associates and activists working to end "the current anti-smoking crusade and restore the rights and freedoms of smokers." The Alliance conducts research, offers organizing assistance, and maintains archives.

Information for free:
Demonstration flyers.

Information for a fee:
American Smokers Journal. Quarterly. $24/year.

To find out more, write or phone:
American Puffer Alliance
c/o Foster Gunnison, Jr.
1 Gold St., Ste. 22-ABC
Hartford, CT 06103
Phone: (203)547-1281

▶ American Self-Help Clearinghouse

Provides information on: *Self-Help Groups*

The Self-Help Clearinghouse provides information about national self-help groups. The Clearinghouse commonly responds to callers having one of a variety of disabilities, illnesses, or stressful life situations. Callers can be referred to an appropriate regional clearinghouse or to a volunteer-run support group. Other services include consultation on starting a self-help group.

Information for free:

Developing a Self-Help Support Network for Persons with a Rare Illness - Some Suggestions for Initial Outreach. 6 pages.

Ideas and Considerations for Starting a Self-Help Mutual Aid Group. 2 pages. Enclose a self-addressed, stamped envelope. Handout with overview for laypersons.

Self-Help Clearinghouses in U.S. and Canada. Enclose a self-addressed, stamped envelope. Single-page listing of state and province phone contacts.

Information for a fee:

Helping Ourselves - Helping Others: A Guide to Starting Mutual Aid Self-Help Groups for Depression and Manic Depression. 1989. 32 pages. $9.

Self-Help Groups for People Dealing with AIDS. 48 pages. 1987. $9. Booklet providing ideas for starting different types of AIDS groups including those for IV drug users, women, and Black and Hispanic communities.

The Self-Help Sourcebook: Finding and Forming Mutual Aid Self-Help Groups. 160 pages. Third edition, 1990. $9. Directory of more than 500 national support and self-help groups and state and local clearinghouses. Contains listings on health-related disabilities, including mental health groups and parenting/family groups.

Starting Self-Help Groups for Quitting Smoking and for Ex-Smokers. 13 pages. 1989. Includes stop-smoking resources and bibliography of pamphlets, books, and articles.

Youth Engaged in Self-Help: A Guide for Starting Youth Self-Help Groups. 30 pages. 1985. $5.

To find out more, write or phone:

American Self-Help Clearinghouse
St. Clares-Riverside Medical Ctr.
25 Pocono Rd.
Denville, NJ 07834-2995
Phone: (201)625-7101

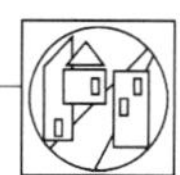

▶ Americans for a Sound AIDS Policy (ASAP)

Provides information on: *AIDS*

ASAP is an advisory board of doctors, public health professionals, legislators, and businessmen assisting in the formulation of a workable public policy on AIDS that will be understood and accepted by the public. The group encourages the public to react compassionately toward persons affected, infected, or ill with AIDS. ASAP promotes early diagnosis and reducing transmission of the epidemic through public health intervention strategies such as confidential and voluntary partner notification. It supports development of treatment, diagnostics, vaccines, and the eventual cure of the disease.

Information for a fee:
ASAP News. 6/year. 8 pages. $25.
Christians in the Age of AIDS. $10.
The Church's Response to the Challenge of AIDS/HIV: A Guideline for Education and Policy Development. 55 pages. $6.
Information packets, including the following are available for $5 each:
AIDS/HIV in the Workplace,
AIDS/HIV and Sexuality Education,
Data on Risks Related to Condom Use and AIDS/HIV Transmission,
General AIDS/HIV Information,
HIV and Teenagers.

To find out more, write or phone:
Americans for a Sound AIDS Policy
PO Box 17433
Washington, DC 20041
Phone: (703)471-7350 or *Fax:* (703)471-8409

▶ Anxiety Disorders Association of America (ADAA)

Provides information on: *Mental Health*

The Association's activities include providing information about anxiety disorders and how they affect people's lives, finding out more about the causes and treatment of anxiety disorders, and helping people with anxiety disorders find treatment and self-help methods.

Information for a fee:
An information packet is available for $3.
ADAA Reporter. $10/year. Newsletter.
Anxiety Disorders in Children. 8-page booklet. $.60.

Anxiety Disorders: Helping a Family Member. $.60.
Breaking the Panic Cycle. Gives practical steps for coping with panic and phobias.
Consumer's Guide to Treatment. $.60.
Help Yourself: A Guide to Organizing a Phobia Self-Help Group. $15. Guide on how self-help groups can organize and run successfully.
National Self-Help Network Group Directory. $7.
Phobias. 8 pages. $.60. Booklet.

To find out more, write or phone:

Anxiety Disorders Association of America
6000 Executive Blvd., No. 513
Rockville, MD 20852-3883
Phone: (301)231-9350 or *Fax:* (301)231-7392

▶ BACCHUS of the U.S.

Provides information on: *Alcoholism*

BACCHUS members promote alcohol awareness and include students, advisers, faculty, and staff of colleges and universities in the U.S. and Canada. Through positive peer pressure, the group promotes responsible decisions regarding the use of alcohol and discourages irresponsible or illegal use of alcohol. It encourages alternative social activities, such as coffee houses, talent shows, and fund runs. BACCHUS is the acronym for Boost Alcohol Consciousness Concerning the Health of University Students, and also the name of the Roman god of wine. Information for a fee:
Alcohol and Women. $.30. Offers an in-depth look at the issues women face in terms of alcohol use.
Are You at Risk?: The Personal Risk Evaluation Guide. $.30. Provides students a non-threatening opportunity to evaluate their drinking behavior.
Building Your BACCHUS Chapter. $1.50. Includes sample constitution and blank charter application.
Children of Alcoholics. $.30. Designed to help those students dealing with family issues and alcohol.
The Choice Is Yours. 1991. $.30. Raises issues such as personal decision-making, peer pressure, and the risks involved with drinking.
Guide to a Successful Party. $.30. Provides guidelines for hosting of events where alcohol may or may not be served.
Sex Under the Influence (for men) and (for women). 1991. $.30. In separate editions, addresses the topic of alcohol use and sex.
Tips on Sipping. $.30. Explores the concept of responsible decision making, the effects of alcohol, social event planning, and caring for intoxicated persons.

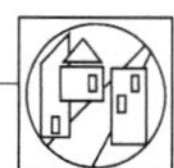

Why Do I Know It, and They Don't?: How to Help a Friend with a Drinking Problem. $.30.
Raises the issue of how to assist someone with a drinking problem.

To find out more, write or phone:
BACCHUS of the U.S.
National Headquarters
PO Box 100430
Denver, CO 80250-0430
Phone: (303)871-3068

▶ Barr-Harris Center for the Study of Separation and Loss During Childhood

Provides information on: *Death and Dying*

The Center conducts research on the immediate and long-term effects of parental separation and death upon the development of younger children. The organization offers consultation services, collects data on families, and develops educational programs. Research results are published in books and journals.

To find out more, write or phone:
Barr-Harris Center for the Study of Separation and Loss During Childhood
180 N. Michigan Ave.
Chicago, IL 60601
Phone: (312)726-6300

▶ Birthright, United States of America

Provides information on: *Abortion, Parenting*

The organization is made up of groups operating independently in the U.S. to help pregnant women find alternatives to abortion. All chapters are private and interdenominational, supported by contributions, and operated by volunteers. The group operates childbirth education classes and parenting programs.

Information for free:
The National Pulse. 6/year. Newsletter.

Information for a fee:
The Life Guardian. 6/year. $6.

To find out more, write or phone:
Birthright, United States of America
686 N. Broad St.
Woodbury, NJ 08096
Toll-free: 1-800-848-LOVE or *Phone:* (609)848-1819 or *Fax:* (609)848-2380

▶ Canadian Fitness and Lifestyle Research Institute

Provides information on: *Fitness, Sports*

The Institute's mission is to improve the wellbeing of Canadians through research and the distribution of information on physically active lifestyles. The organization is concerned with population fitness levels, recreation habits, and other lifestyle patterns of Canadians.

Information for free:
Annual Report.
List of Resources.

Information for a fee:
Active Living for Canadian Children and Youth: A Statistical Profile. 1992. $18. A report containing information related to physical activity patterns, behavior, and preferences of children and youth.
Canadian Youth and Physical Activity. 1983. $6. Report examining health practices and physical activity levels of Canadian youth.
Changing Times: Women and Physical Activity. 1984. $6. Describes fitness levels, activity patterns, and practices of girls and women in Canada.
Fitness and Aging. 1982. $4. Focuses on the fitness and activity levels of Canadians over the age of 55.
Highlights. 1983-1986. $2/each, $10/series. A series of 72 one-page summaries on Canadian fitness, covering such titles as
Health Practices of Children and Youth,
The Physically Active High School Graduate: An Endangered Species?
Do Young Women Start Smoking for Weight Control?
Body Mass Index: On the Fatness of Canadian Youth.
Also includes information on more than 10 different sports, including swimming, tennis, golf, skiing, hockey, curling, and skating.

To find out more, write or phone:
Canadian Fitness and Lifestyle Research Institute
313-1600 James Naismith Dr.
Gloucester, ON, Canada K1B 5N4
Phone: (613)748-5791 or *Fax:* (613)748-5792

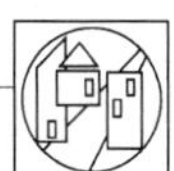

▶ Center for Alcohol Studies (CAS)

Provides information on: *Alcoholism, Child Abuse*

The Center for Alcohol Studies researches, studies, and treats alcoholism. It documents and offers information about alcohol and its effects on human behavior and functioning.

Information for a fee:

Alcohol Intoxication and Drug Use Among Teenagers. $1.25. Pamphlet.

Alcohol-Related Acts of Violence: Who Was Drinking and Where the Acts Occurred. $1. Pamphlet.

Alcoholism and Child Abuse: A Review. $2.75.

Drinking Among Teenagers: A Sociological Interpretation of Alcohol Use by High-School Students. 127 pages. $14.95. Reports on knowledge and attitudes of drinking by adolescents.

Drinking in America. 222 pages. $10.95. Traces the evolution of American drinking practices.

School-Aged Children of Alcoholics: Theory and Research. $2. Pamphlet comparing school-aged children of alcoholic and nonalcoholic parents.

What is Alcohol? And Why do People Drink? $2.50. Pamphlet introducing what alcohol is, and how it affects the body and behavior.

What Shall we Teach the Young About Drinking? $2.50. Pamphlet that describes methods for classroom teaching about alcohol use.

To find out more, write or phone:

Center for Alcohol Studies
Rutgers, State University of New Jersey
Busch Campus
Smithers Hall
Piscataway, NJ 08854
Phone: (908)932-2190

▶ Center for Death Education and Research

Provides information on: *Death and Dying*

The Center sponsors research on grief and bereavement, as well as studies of attitudes and responses to death and dying. It collects and offers relevant materials, provides speakers to concerned groups, and conducts workshops.

Information for free:

Center for Death Education and Research booklet describing the Center's activities. Includes a list of available publications.

Understanding the Experience of Grief. Pamphlet.

Information for a fee:
Anticipatory Grief, Stress, and the Surrogate Griever. 1981. 8 pages. $2.
Childhood Bereavement and Later Behavior Disorder Hypothesis. 1975. $2.
The Sociology of Death. 1977. $2.

To find out more, write or phone:
Center for Death Education and Research
University of Minnesota
1167 Social Science Bldg.
Minneapolis, MN 55455
Phone: (612)624-1895

▶ Center for Reproductive Law and Policy

Provides information on: *Abortion, Reproductive Rights*

The Center for Reproductive Law and Policy is a politically active research organization dedicated to preserving the reproductive freedom of women. The Center takes a look at federal legislation and regulations regarding women's reproductive rights, abortion, and sexual abstinence programs. It also sponsors public education programs.

Information for free:
Reproductive Freedom News. Biweekly. Newsletter. Provides updates on legislative issues affecting reproductive freedom, and includes news from other parts of the world.

To find out more, write or phone:
Center for Reproductive Law and Policy
120 Wall St.
New York, NY 10005
Phone: (212)514-5534

▶ Center for Science in the Public Interest

Provides information on: *Nutrition*

The Center for Science in the Public Interest is an organization of scientists, nutrition educators, journalists, and lawyers concerned with the effects of science and technology on society. The Center produces educational materials and attempts to influence policy decisions with regard to American health and diet. Past work has centered primarily on food safety and nutrition problems at the national level,

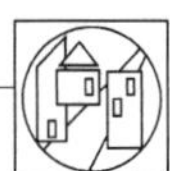

including legal actions to ban unsafe and poorly tested food additives. The Center also campaigns for better food labeling and action against deceptive food advertising, especially advertising directed at children.

Information for a fee:

Fast-Food Guide. 1991. $7.95. Includes complete nutritional breakdowns of virtually all food items offered by over one dozen leading chains.

Nutrition Action Health Letter. 10/year. $20/year. Promotes public education concerning food and nutrition, the food industry, and relevant government regulations and legislation, diet, importance of attitude and lifestyle, additives and preservatives, the organic versus chemical farming controversy, and the implications of agribusiness.

Safe Food: Eating Wisely in a Risky World. 1991. $9.95. Offers practical tips and suggestions on how to reduce exposure to unsafe ingredients, additives, and pollutants.

To find out more, write or phone:

Center for Science in the Public Interest
1875 Connecticut Ave. NW, No. 300
Washington, DC 20009-5728
Phone: (202)332-9110 or *Fax:* (202)265-4954

▶ Childbirth Education Foundation (CEF)

Provides information on: *Pregnancy and Birth Technology*

The Foundation is made up of physicians, nurses, childbirth educators, childbirth reform activists, concerned parents, and individuals dedicated to providing alternatives for a more meaningful childbirth experience, and to promoting reform in childbirth issues and in the treatment of the newborn. CEF promotes home births, birthing centers, certified nurse-midwife pregnancy management and delivery, family togetherness and infant bonding, "nonviolent birth" for mother and child, and breastfeeding. It distributes literature to libraries, parents, maternal care providers, and educators regarding childbirth, trends in childbirth, safe alternatives, and the treatment of newborns and infants. The group compiles statistics and conducts extensive research related to childbirth, newborn, and infant care and maintains a library.

Information for free:

CEF Newsletter. Periodic.

Information for a fee:

Membership Directory. Periodic. Price included in $15 membership dues.

To find out more, write or phone:
Childbirth Education Foundation
James E. Peron, Founder & Exec.Dir.
PO Box 5
Richboro, PA 18954
Phone: (215)357-2792

▶ Children of Alcoholics Foundation

Provides information on: *Self-Help Groups, Alcoholism*

The Foundation educates the public about children of alcoholics and alcohol abusers and stimulates interest in seeking solutions to their problems. The organization promotes research, educational and informational programs, and public discussion on alcoholism, alcohol abuse, and its effects on children. It provides research results and encourages the government to assist children of alcoholics and provide solutions to their problems.

Information for free:
Children of Alcoholics Foundation Catalogue of Materials. Includes order form.

Information for a fee:
Children of Alcoholics. 1982. 50 pages. $5.
Children of Alcoholics: A Review of the Literature. 1985. 70 pages. $10.
Children of Alcoholics in the Medical System: Hidden Problems, Hidden Costs. 1990. 30 pages. $5.
Children of Alcoholics on the Job. 1989. 26 pages. $5.
Parental Consent: Helping Children of Addicted Parents Get Help. 1991. 22 pages. $5.
Report of the Conference on Prevention Research. 1985. 15 pages. $5.
Report on the Conference on Research Needs and Opportunities for Children of Alcoholics. 1984. 21 pages. $2.50.

To find out more, write or phone:
Children of Alcoholics Foundation
Migs Woodside, Pres.
Grand Central Sta.
PO Box 4185
New York, NY 10163-4185
Toll-free: 1-800-359-COAF or *Phone:* (212)754-0656 or *Fax:* (212)754-0664

▶ Choice for Dying

Provides information on: *Death and Dying*

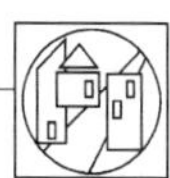

Choice for Dying educates the public and health professionals on the legal, ethical, and psychological implications of terminal care decision making. They distribute the "Living Will" (document that lets people express in writing their wishes regarding care during terminal illness) and a document on the medical power of attorney, which allows individuals to appoint someone else to make medical decisions for them if they become incapacitated. Choice for Dying also sponsors workshops and education programs, and maintains a library of books, legal cases, and audiovisual materials on death and dying.

Information for a fee:

About Advance Medical Directives. 15 pages. $1.50. An introduction to living wills and health care agent appointments.

The Complete Guide to Living Wills. $7.95. Step by step guide through the preparation of advance directives. Also includes strategies for dealing with the health care system.

Map of State Legislation. $1. Shows state-by-state status of legislation for living will declarations.

Options at the End of Life: A Study Guide on Active Euthanasia. $15. Examines merits and dangers of legitimizing active euthanasia.

The following pamphlets priced at $1.50 each are also offered:

Medical Treatments and Your Living Will;

The Right to Die: Questions and Answers;

Stopping Unwanted Medical Treatment: Questions to Ask, People Who Can Help;

What You Should Know About Medical Durable Powers of Attorney, Proxy Appointments and Health Care Agents;

What You Should Know About Nutrition and Hydration by Tube.

To find out more, write or phone:

Choice for Dying
250 W. 57th St.
New York, NY 10107
Phone: (212)366-5540 or *Fax:* (212)765-8441

▶ Cocaine Anonymous World Services (CA)

Provides information on: *Self-Help Groups, Substance Abuse*

The group is made up of men and women who share their experience, strength, and hope that they may solve their common problem and help others to recover from addiction and remain free from cocaine and all other mind-altering drugs. Applies the Alcoholics Anonymous World Services' 12-step approach to persons addicted to cocaine.

Information for a fee:
Each brochure is available for 15 cents plus shipping and handling costs:
To the Newcomer.
The First 30 Days.
Tools of Recovery.
Choosing your Sponsor.
A Higher Power.
26 Tips for Staying Clean.
Self Test for Cocaine Addict.
And All Other Mind Altering Substances.
Suggestions for Relapse Prevention and Recovery.
What Is C.A.?

To find out more, write or phone:
Cocaine Anonymous World Services
3740 Overland Ave., Ste.-G
Los Angeles, CA 90034
Toll-free: 1-800-347-8998 or *Phone:* (310)559-5833

▶ Community Nutrition Institute

Provides information on: *Senior Citizens, Hunger, Nutrition, Education*

The Institute specializes in food and nutrition issues which include hunger, food quality and safety, nutrition research, food programs, education, and food labeling and marketing.

Information for a fee:
Creative Recreation and Socialization for Senior Citizen Centers. $15.
How to Develop a Home Delivered Meals Program. $20.
Organizing Volunteers. $5.
Also available: set of three food service management brochures, including purchasing, quality control, and menu planning. $12.
Nutrition service providers guides, including program management, site management, accounting and financial management, and training. $10-$15. Include a $5 postage and handling fee.

To find out more, write or phone:
Community Nutrition Institute
2001 S St. NW, Ste. 530
Washington, DC 20009
Phone: (202)462-4700

▶ The Compassionate Friends (TCF)

Provides information on: *Parenting, Death and Dying, Self-Help Groups, Suicide*

This nondenominational, informal, self-help organization is open to families who have experienced the death of a child. Its purposes are to promote and aid parents in the positive resolution of grief, and to foster the physical and emotional health of bereaved parents and siblings. Chapters offer support and understanding by providing "telephone friends" who may be called, identifying sharing groups that meet monthly, and offering information concerning the grieving process.

Information for a fee:

After Suicide. $8.95. A guide for those struggling with the aftermath of suicide, including explaining events to children, and dealing with feelings of guilt, anger, and shame.

Empty Arms—Coping After Miscarriage, Stillbirth, and Infant Death. $6.50. A book of shared feelings of newly bereaved parents.

Helping Children Cope With Grief. $15.95. Describes necessary skills for working with grieving children.

150 Facts About Grieving Children. $5. Book covering the grief of children and how parents can help.

Sibling Grief. 12 pages. $1.25. A booklet for parents to help the child whose brother or sister has died.

TCF National Newsletter. Quarterly. $10. Focuses on grief-related issues, including poetry, book reviews, and program information.

TCF Sibling Newsletter. Quarterly. $5. Covers issues relating to sibling grief.

When Will I Stop Hurting? Dealing with a Recent Death. $3.95. A booklet that offers insights into the grief process and suggestions for coping.

TCF offers a wide range of pamphlets for $.15 each covering such issues as a child's death; caring for surviving children; suggestions for clergy, teachers, and school counselors; and helping a grieving co-worker.

To find out more, write or phone:

The Compassionate Friends
PO Box 3696
Oak Brook, IL 60522-3696
Phone: (708)990-0010 or *Fax:* (708)990-0246

▶ Data Archive on Adolescent Pregnancy and Pregnancy Prevention

Provides information on: *Sexuality, Family Planning, Teenage Pregnancy, Pregnancy and Birth Technology*

The Archive is a computer-readable file containing information from more than 110 major studies of teen sex behavior. The Archive holds data dealing with adolescent family life, sexuality, contraception, pregnancy, childbearing, parenting, and family planning. The Archive provides information, training, seminars, workshops, technical assistance, and online search services, primarily to researchers and practitioners.

Information for free:
A general information brochure, and catalog of products are available.

Information for a fee:
Just the Facts. $15. Illustrated book that will help parents, older teens, and others make decisions regarding sexuality, contraception, pregnancy, and parenthood.
Letters to Dr. Know. $15. Book containing letters from teenagers regarding various aspects of sexual behavior.
What's Your Teen-Sex Knowledge Quotient? $15. Written in a quiz-book format to help teens answer important questions about teenage sexuality.

To find out more, write or phone:
Data Archive on Adolescent Pregnancy and Pregnancy Prevention
Sociometrics Corporation
170 State St., Ste. 260
Los Altos, CA 94022-2812
Phone: (415)949-3282

▶ Debtors Anonymous (DA)

Provides information on: *Self-Help Groups*

DA is a fellowship of men and women who share their experience, strength, and hope with each other that they may solve their commom problem of compulsive debting. It has adapted the Twelve Steps of Alcoholics Anonymous World Services for compulsive debtors. It establishes and coordinates self-help support groups for people seeking to live prosperously without incurring unsecured debt.

Information for a fee:
Ways and Means. Quarterly. $8/year. Newsletter.

To find out more, write or phone:
Debtors Anonymous
Diana D., Contact
PO Box 400
New York, NY 10163
Phone: (212)642-8220

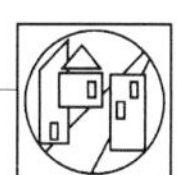

▶ Drug Policy Foundation

Provides information on: *Substance Abuse, AIDS*

The Foundation promotes alternative methods such as legalization, decriminalization, and medicalization of currently illegal substances including marijuana and heroin, to curb drug abuse while protecting the rights of the individual. The group believes that legal drugs, clean needles, and effective drug treatment would vastly improve the health of addicts, slow the spread of AIDS, and decrease crime. The Foundation assists in legislation to change federal drug possession laws. They support vigorous police action against drug traffickers, but strongly oppose the use of urine tests in employment.

Information for free:

The Drug Policy Collection. Catalog listing the various publications and videos available through the Foundation.

The Drug Policy Foundation Bibliography of Drug Related Literature.

Information for a fee:

Drug Prohibition and the Conscience of Nations. 1990. 250 pages. $9.95. An anthology of current writings on the drug dilemma that examines the drug related theories of politicians and intellectuals.

Friedman and Szasz on Liberty and Drugs. 1992. 150 pages. $12.95. Focuses on the relationship between the philosophy of liberty and drug prohibition.

The Great Issues of Drug Policy. 1990. 325 pages. $19.95. A collection of articles written by drug experts offers in-depth analyses of a variety of issues relating to the current drug problem.

National Drug Reform Strategy. 1992. 32 pages. $5. Criticizes the Bush drug war and presents the Foundation's 1992 agenda for refocusing anti-drug efforts on treatment and education, and alternatives to strict prohibition.

New Frontiers in Drug Policy. 1991. 428 pages. $24.95. A collection of articles written by researchers, workers, and activists in the movement to reform drug laws and policies.

To find out more, write or phone:

Drug Policy Foundation
4801 Massachusetts Ave. NW, Ste. 400
Washington, DC 20016-2087
Phone: (202)895-1634 or *Fax:* (202)537-3007

▶ Drugs and Crime Data Center and Clearinghouse

Provides information on: *Substance Abuse*

This service offers data about illegal drugs, drug law violations, drug-related crime, drug-using offenders in the criminal justice system, and the impact of drugs on criminal justice administration. The Clearinghouse distributes information summaries and selected bibliographies on specific drugs-and-crime topics and provides statistics and bibliographic citations by mail or telephone.

Information for free:

Catalog of Selected Federal Publications on Illegal Drug and Alcohol Abuse.
Crack Cocaine.
Drugs and Crime Data Center and Clearinghouse Brochure.
Drugs and Crime Facts.
Drug Use and Crime.
Drug Use Trends.
Gangs, Drugs, and Violence.
Juveniles and Drugs.
Minorities, Drugs, and Crime.
State Drug Resources: 1992 National Directory. 130 pages. A guide to state agencies that address drug abuse concerns, as well as federal agencies to be used as information contacts.
Women, Drugs, and Crime.

To find out more, write or phone:

Drugs and Crime Data Center and Clearinghouse
1600 Research Blvd.
Rockville, MD 20850
Toll-free: 1-800-666-3332

▶ Emotions Anonymous (EA)

Provides information on: *Self-Help Groups, Mental Health*

Emotions Anonymous is a fellowship of men and women united to help themselves and others recover from emotional illness. To address emotional problems, EA adapts the Twelve Steps of Alcoholics Anonymous World Services. The group also offers literature and information, provides telephone referrals to local chapters, and conducts children's services.

Information for a fee:

Carrying the E/A Message. Monthly. $.95/single issue, $7/year. Newsletter containing articles, personal stories, and EA activities.
Emotions Anonymous. 251 pages. $5.50 soft cover. Covers the tools and principles of the program and of the Twelve Steps.

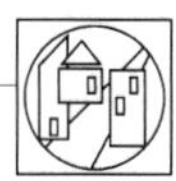

The Enormity of Emotional Illness. $.75. Pamphlet discussing the effects of emotional illness and the "hope" EA can offer.

Group Starter Packet. $10. Contains all group pamphlets, recovery pamphlets, issues of EA's Message magazine, and more.

Introduction to Children's EA. $.15. A general information sheet explaining how EA can work for children ages 5 through 12.

Introduction to Loners EA. $.25. A pamphlet for those unable to attend meetings.

Introduction to Youth EA. $.15. A pamphlet explaining the YEA program for teenagers.

You Are Not Alone—The EA Pamphlet. $.35. Contains the Twelve Steps, slogans, traditions, concepts, and prayers of EA.

To find out more, write or phone:

Emotions Anonymous
PO Box 4245
St. Paul, MN 55104
Phone: (612)647-9712 or *Fax:* (612)647-1593

▶ Family Life Information Exchange

Provides information on: *Adoption, Family Planning, Pregnancy and Birth Technology, Teenage Pregnancy, Sexually Transmitted Diseases*

The Exchange collects and distributes information on family planning, adoption, and adolescent pregnancy. It also refers Information Exchange users to other information centers on topics beyond its scope.

Information for free:

Family and Adolescent Pregnancy.
Many Teens are Saying "NO".
PHS Guidelines for Counseling and Testing to Prevent HIV and AIDS.
Sexually Transmitted Diseases Treatment Guidelines.
Teenage Pregnancy and Fertility in the U.S.
Trends in Adolescent Pregnancy and Childbearing.
Your Contraceptive Choices: For Now, For Later.

Also available are informed consent forms for sterilization, and a professional guidebook on adoption.

To find out more, write or phone:

Family Life Information Exchange
PO Box 37299
Washington, DC 20013-7299
Phone: (301)585-6636

▶ Fitness Research Center

Provides information on: *Fitness*

The Center examines the relationships between lifestyle behaviors, quality of life, organizational productivity, and health care costs. It maintains a search service for reviews and a library on topics relevant to wellness programs.

Information for a fee:
Healthline. Monthly. $15/year. Newsletter.

To find out more, write or phone:
Fitness Research Center
University of Michigan
401 Washtenaw Ave., Rm. 103
Ann Arbor, MI 48109-2214
Phone: (313)763-2462 or *Fax:* (313)763-2206

▶ Food and Nutrition Information Center (FNIC)

Provides information on: *Nutrition, Diseases, Eating Disorders*

The FNIC is one of several information centers at the National Agricultural Library. Its collection of materials deals with topics such as the relationship between diet and disease, nutrient composition, food science and technology, food service management, food safety and sanitation, U.S. food and nutrition programs, and nutrition education. The Center will answer specific food and nutrition questions.

Information for free:
The FNIC has developed catalogs, bibliographies, and reading lists called Nutri-Topics. Single copies of titles in the Nutri-Topics series are available for free, including:
Adolescent Pregnancy and Nutrition;
Anorexia Nervosa and Bulimia;
Nutrition and the Handicapped;
Nutrition, Learning and Behavior;
Sensible Nutrition;
Sports Nutrition;
Vegetarian Nutrition;
Weight Control.
Also available:
Dietary Guidelines for Americans. 1990. 27 pages. Brochure. Outlines a healthy diet.
Food & Information Center. 1988. Brochure. Provides general information about the Center including type of users, services provided, and topics covered.

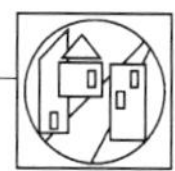

To find out more, write or phone:
Food and Nutrition Information Center
United States Dept. Agriculture
National Agricultural Library
10301 Baltimore Blvd., Rm. 304
Beltsville, MD 20705-2351
Phone: (301)504-5719 or *Fax:* (301)504-5472

▶ Gay Men's Health Crisis

Provides information on: *AIDS*

The group is a social service agency for the clinical treatment of AIDS. It provides support and therapy groups for AIDS patients and their families, and offers Patient Recreation Services. The agency sends volunteer crisis counselors to work with AIDS patients, and sponsors a buddy system in which helpers visit clients at home and assist with household tasks. The organization also provides legal and financial services, sponsors lectures and AIDS prevention programs, and maintains a library.

To find out more, write or phone:
Gay Men's Health Crisis
129 W. 20th St.
New York, NY 10011
Phone: (212)807-6664 or *Fax:* (212)337-3556

▶ Georgia Institute of Human Nutrition

Provides information on: *Nutrition, Diseases*

The Institute investigates the role of nutrition in the development of diseases. It looks at regional programs in prevention and treatment of nutrition-related disorders in relation to the cardiovascular system, hypertension, neoplasia, mothers and infants, obesity and metabolism, alcoholism, and nutritional deficiencies. The Institutes' research results are published in journals.

To find out more, write or phone:
Georgia Institute of Human Nutrition
Medical College of Georgia
Augusta, GA 30912
Phone: (706)721-4861 or *Fax:* (706)721-4400

▶ Group Against Smokers' Pollution (GASP)

Provides information on: *Smoking*

Nonsmokers who are adversely affected by tobacco smoke unite in this association to promote the rights of nonsmokers, educate the public about the problems of second-hand smoke, and regulate smoking in places where nonsmokers are exposed. The group supports the establishment and enforcement of laws and other public policy measures that reduce environmental tobacco smoke; provides information and referral services; and distributes educational literature, buttons, posters, and bumper stickers.

Information for free:
A list of nonsmokers' publications and reprints.

Information for a fee:

Cutting Tobacco's Toll. 1978. 40 pages. Recommended for high school students and adults. Covers worldwide smoking trends and public policy developments, including the role of nonsmokers' rights movement.

Fact Brochure on Second-Hand Smoke. $.25.

Involuntary Smoking—Risks for Nonsmokers. 1987. 27 pages. $1. Gives scientific evidence and public perceptions on second-hand smoke that provide a foundation for the nonsmokers' rights movement.

Nonsmokers' Liberation Guide. 10 pages. $1.

Smoking in the Workplace. 1988. 15 pages. $1. Covers safety, productivity, effects on nonsmokers, and other factors relating to smoking in the workplace.

Smoking Policy: Questions and Answers. 1989. 20 pages. $3 each. Ten fact sheets designed to guide employers and other policy-makers in making good policy decisions about smoking. Covers such topics as the health effects of smoking, smoking cessation programs, ventilation, and smoking and the female work force.

Stop Blowing Smoke in My Face. 1972. 70 pages. $3. A landmark publication of the nonsmokers' rights movement. Includes such topics as smoking in the classroom, in the home, and in the car.

To find out more, write or phone:

Group Against Smokers' Pollution
Willard K. Morris, Sec.
PO Box 632
College Park, MD 20741-0632
Phone: (301)459-4791

▶ The Health Learning Center

Provides information on: *Parenting, Pregnancy and Birth Technology*

The Health Learning Center is a resource for information, books, and other materials on multiple-birth pregnancy and parenting.

Information for free:
Lifetime of Health. Quarterly. Magazine.

To find out more, write or phone:
The Health Learning Center
Northwestern Memorial Hospital
Prentice Women's Hospital and Maternity Center
Superior St. & Fairbanks Ct.
Chicago, IL 60611
Phone: (312)908-2000

▶ Heartbeat

Provides information on: *Suicide*

Persons who have lost a loved one due to suicide provide an atmosphere for grieving participants to receive support, understanding, direction, and encouragement from those who have successfully resolved their grief. Heartbeat offers a "postvention" education program aimed at preventing the suicide of survivors.

Information for a fee:
Forming Heartbeat Chapters. $10. Manual.

To find out more, write or phone:
Heartbeat
LaRita Archibald, Founder
2015 Devon St.
Colorado Springs, CO 80909
Phone: (719)596-2575

▶ Hemlock Society (HS)

Provides information on: *Death and Dying, Suicide*

HS is a society of individuals supporting the option of active voluntary euthanasia for the advanced terminally ill and the seriously incurably ill. The Hemlock Society promotes a climate of public opinion tolerant of the terminally ill individual's right to end his or her own life in a planned manner, and works to improve existing laws on assisted suicide. The group believes that the final decision to terminate one's life should be one's own; it does not encourage suicide for any reason other than terminal illness.

Information for a fee:

Dealing Creatively With Death. 186 pages. $12. Manual of death education covering such issues as death ceremonies, the right to die, and cremation.

Death With Dignity. 109 pages. $6. Book about a new law permitting physician aid in dying.

Euthanasia and Religion: A Survey of the Attitudes of the World Religions to the Right to Die. 156 pages. $10.

Final Exit: The Practicalities of Self-Deliverance and Assisted Suicide for the Dying. 196 pages. $16.95.

Hemlock Quarterly. Included in $25 membership fee. Newsletter covering right to choose to die issues.

Is This the Day? 112 pages. $8.

Last Wish. 236 pages. $9. A controversial true story of "a mother's dark victory and a daughter's love."

Let Me Die Before I Wake: How Dying People End Their Suffering. 176 pages. $10.

The Right to Die: Understanding Euthanasia. 372 pages. $10.

To find out more, write or phone:

Hemlock Society
PO Box 11830
Eugene, OR 97440-3900
Phone: (503)342-5748 or *Fax:* (503)345-2751

▶ Hogg Foundation for Mental Health

Provides information on: *Mental Health, Suicide, Homelessness, Domestic Violence, Marriage, Senior Citizens*

The Foundation is devoted to the study of mental health. It gathers information on community programs and studies on teacher burnout, adolescent suicide, homelessness, children at risk, care of the mentally ill, and aging.

Information for free:

The Camping Connection. Describes the coalition of organizations that provide children with special needs and their families with a weekend getaway.

The Children Who Could Not Come Out to Play. Boys and girls who have "lived behind closed doors because of their 'differentness'" is the subject of this booklet.

Coping with Parental Guilt. About parents with retarded or emotionally or physically impaired children.

Hogg Foundation Annual Report.

The Hogg Foundation: Programs and Policies for Grants. Leaflet answering questions about program activities.

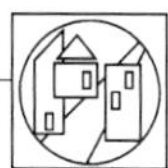

Publications List 1992. Booklet listing many sources of information, their prices, and how to order them.

Relatedness: Pearls on a String of Life. Relays the message that self-worth and a sense of belonging are higher when aging persons interact with others.

Sex-Rated Comments. Deals with sex education in the family.

What is Mental Health?

Information for a fee:

Adolescents and Suicide: Restoring the Kin Network. 1988. 24 pages. $.75. Describes how to provide appropriate support or a "Kinship Support System" in order to prevent reoccurrence of suicidal behavior.

Aging Parents and Dilemmas of their Children. 1981. 26 pages. $.60. Discusses the range of emotions that affect families of the elderly.

The Challenge for Mental Health: Minorities and Their World Views. 1984. 36 pages. $.60. Addresses ethnic factors in mental health services.

Children, Choices, and Change. 1988. 120 pages. $3. A fact book containing information on problem areas affecting childhood in Texas, including abuse, health care, education, poverty, and more.

Current Issues in Mental Health Law. 1989. 32 pages. $.50. Pamphlet giving simple explanations of contemporary mental health law.

Family Violence: The Well-Kept Secret. 1979. 36 pages. $.50 Addresses the high incidence of violence in families and the steps one community took to provide assistance.

Mental Health of Immigrants and Refugees. 1990. 348 pages. $9. Addresses "the mental health challenge of new residents from throughout the world."

Mental Health in Nursing Homes. 1975. 16 pages. Examines ways in which nursing home employees and volunteers can enrich the lives of elderly residents.

Understanding the Homeless: From Research to Action. 1988. 36 pages. $.70. Report on how some homeless came to be where they are, barriers to improvement, and their own opinions of their condition and living standards.

What Makes Dual Career Marriages Tick? 1987. 20 pages. $.50.

To find out more, write or phone:

Hogg Foundation for Mental Health
University of Texas
Austin, TX 78713-7998
Phone: (512)471-5041 or *Fax:* (512)471-9608

▶ Human Life Center

Provides information on: *Marriage, Sexuality, Family Planning, Abortion*

The Human Life Center is an independent, nonprofit organization that covers the areas of marriage and family, sexuality, family planning, abortion, infanticide, euthanasia, and related subjects. The Center publishes research results, and promotes and assists other organizations that deal with human life concerns.

To find out more, write or phone:
Human Life Center
University of Steubenville
Steubenville, OH 43952
Phone: (614)282-9953

▶ Institute for Advancement Study of Human Sexuality

Provides information on: *Sexuality*

The Institute centers on studies of erotology and human sexual behavior and attitudes. Research results are published in books, papers, and dissertations. The Institute maintains an extensive library.

To find out more, write or phone:
Institute for Advancement Study of Human Sexuality
Exodus Trust
1523 Franklin St.
San Francisco, CA 94109
Phone: (415)928-1133

▶ Institute of Nutrition

Provides information on: *Nutrition*

The Institute concentrates on nutrition-related projects and nutrition/health assessment, including studies on nitrates and nitrites, lactose intolerance, and caffeine. Research results are published in professional journals and workshop proceedings. The organization advises state and federal government offices and agencies on nutrition programs and policies and collects, analyses, and manages nutritional data.

To find out more, write or phone:
Institute of Nutrition
University of North Carolina
311 Pittsboro St., CB 7410
Chapel Hill, NC 27599-7410
Phone: (919)966-1094 or *Fax:* (919)966-6762

▶ International Association of Parents and Professionals for Safe Alternatives in Childbirth (NAPSAC)

Provides information on: *Pregnancy and Birth Technology, Parenting, Teenage Pregnancy*

NAPSAC is an association of parents, midwives, physicians, nurses, health officials, social workers, and childbirth educators dedicated to establishing medically-safe, family-centered childbirth programs. The group promotes education concerning the principles of natural childbirth, encourages communication and cooperation among parents, medical professionals, and childbirth educators, assists in the establishment of maternity and childbearing centers, and provides education to parents and parents-to-be.

Information for free:
Publication lists and NAPSAC International brochure.

Information for a fee:
Birth Over Thirty. $7.95. Addresses birth and labor, breastfeeding, cesarean prevention, natural childbirth, and nutrition issues.
Circumcision Decision. $.30. Pamphlet.
Directory of Alternative Birth/Consumer Guide. $6.95. Contains information on birth centers, midwifery, home birth, natural childbirth, and underwater birth.
Emergency Medical Treatment for Children. $7.95.
Feed Your Kids Right. $4.95. Covers nutrition for children and during pregnancy.
Heart and Hands (Guide to Midwifery). $17.95. Addresses such issues affecting midwives and mothers as birth and labor, breastfeeding, home birth, mother's postpartum care, newborn care and behavior, and prenatal and postpartum exercises.
Husband-Coached Childbirth. $18.95. Covers the father's participation in the Bradley method of childbirth.
Mom and Dad and I are Having a Baby. $7.95. A children's book taking a Christian viewpoint of birth and labor, breastfeeding, natural childbirth, and parenting.
NAPSAC News. Quarterly. Subscription included in $20 membership dues. Newsletter covering association news, book reviews, and calendar of events.
Teenager's Guide to Childbirth. $.30. Pamphlet covering birth, labor, and prenatal care.

To find out more, write or phone:
International Association of Parents and Professionals for Safe Alternatives in Childbirth
Rte. 1, Box 646
Marble Hill, MO 63764
Phone: (314)238-2010

▶ International Childbirth Education Association (ICEA)

Provides information on: *Pregnancy and Birth Technology, Reproductive Rights, Teenage Pregnancy, Parenting*

The Association's main purpose is to further the educational, physical, and emotional preparation of expectant parents for childbearing and breastfeeding. The group works to increase public awareness on current issues related to childbearing. It cooperates with physicians, nurses, physical therapists, hospitals and others interested in furthering parental participation and minimal medical intervention in uncomplicated labors. It also promotes the development of safe, low-cost alternatives in childbirth that recognize the rights and responsibilities of those involved. ICEA publishes literature pertaining to family-centered maternity care.

Information for free:

Bookmarks. 5/year. Contains news and reviews of new books and other ICEA materials.

Information for a fee:

Baby Lore: Ceremonies, Myths and Traditions to Celebrate a Baby's Birth. 1991. 161 pages. $22.95. A collection of birth traditions and customs from cultures around the world.

Every Moment, Every Memory of the First Nine Months. 1991. 175 pages. $20. Information about the changes taking place for mother and baby for each month of pregnancy.

The Illustrated Book of Pregnancy and Childbirth. 1991. 121 pages. $19.95. Answers questions about reproduction and childbirth.

Teen Parenting: Discipline from Birth to Three. 1991. 182 pages. $9.95. Provides discipline strategies for the adolescent parent.

ICEA also has available a number of brochures and pamphlets on topics such as breastfeeding, cesarean sections, childbirth techniques, and parenting. Also offers audio and videocassettes.

To find out more, write or phone:

International Childbirth Education Association
PO Box 20048
Minneapolis, MN 55420
Phone: (612)854-8660

▶ International Council for Health, Physical Education and Recreation (ICHPER)

Provides information on: *Fitness*

ICHPER is a group of government and professional organizations concerned with programs, policies, and the educational aspects of health, physical education, sports, and recreation. The Council serves as a clearinghouse for exchange of information and ideas and represents members' interests in the field. The Council also compiles statistics and conducts study and research in cooperation with national groups and governmental organizations.

Information for a fee:

National Policies and Practices Concerning the Role of Physical Education and Sports in Education of Youth. $5.

Planning Inexpensive Facilities and Equipment for Physical Education, Sports and Recreation Programs. $5.

To find out more, write or phone:

International Council for Health, Physical Education and Recreation
1900 Association Dr.
Reston, VA 22091
Phone: (703)476-3486 or *Fax:* (703)476-9527

▶ International Institute for the Study of Death (IISD)

Provides information on: *Death and Dying, Suicide*

The Institute is an investigative group of scholars and scientists interested in issues raised by death and dying. IISD brings together academics in religion, nursing, medicine, philosophy, psychology, and parapsychology to discuss death and dying, including the dying process, euthanasia, suicide, bereavement, and the possible afterlife. The group hopes to develop new methods of thinking and investigation in the subjects of death and dying.

Information for a fee:

ESP and Personality Patterns. $12.50. Looks at the famous sheep-goat experiments considered among the strongest evidence of ESP.

The Mighty Stranger: An Example of Interaction Between the Transcendental and the Psychical. $4. Research paper.

Reincarnation: Fact or Fable? $15.95. Leading authorities from Europe, India, Japan, the Commonwealth of Independent States, and the U.S. offer views about reincarnation.

Religion and Parapsychology. $22.75. Discussion of the relationship between religion and parapsychology.

Review of Six Books on Death and Dying. $2.

Tests for Communication with the Dead. $4. Research paper.

Three Views of Death and Their Implications for Life. $4. Research paper.

What Survives? Contemporary Explorations of Life After Death. $12.95. Examines questions about life after death.

To find out more, write or phone:
International Institute for the Study of Death
PO Box 8565
Pembroke Pines, FL 33084
Phone: (305)936-1408

▶ "Just Say No" International

Provides information on: *Substance Abuse, Alcoholism*

"Just Say No" International is the parent group of 11,000 local "Just Say No" clubs with a combined total of over 330,000 members aged 5-14 in the United States. The organization conducts educational programs on the dangers of tobacco, alcohol, and illegal substance abuse. It awards grants for drug prevention programs and conducts leadership training seminars. It also sponsors "Just Say No" Awareness Week to help create a climate in schools and communities that discourages drug use.

Information for free:
Just Say No Newsletter. 3/year. Contains prevention news and research results.
Just Say Notes. Quarterly. Newsletter featuring club updates, list of activities, and calendar of events.
Also offers brochures, stickers, and other promotional materials.

To find out more, write or phone:
"Just Say No" International
2101 Webster St., Ste. 1300
Oakland, CA 94612
Toll-free: 1-800-258-2766 or *Phone:* (510)451-6666

▶ Kinsey Institute for Research in Sex, Gender, and Reproduction, Inc.

Provides information on: *Sexuality, Sexually Transmitted Diseases, Marriage, Homosexuality*

The Institute studies the effects of prenatal exposure to drugs and hormones, American human sexual behavior, sexual orientation as it relates to sexually transmitted diseases, and sexual identity roles and attitudes, including studies of sexual and psychosexual development, gender, and reproduction. The Kinsey

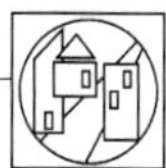

Institute publishes an internationally syndicated newspaper column and operates an information service that responds to telephone and written requests.

Information for free:
Lists of books and bibliographies.

Information for a fee:
The Enjoyment of Love in Marriage. 1969. $1.
The Kinsey Institute New Report on Sex. 1990. 560 pages. $22.95. Answers frequently asked questions about many aspects of sex and reproduction, such as male and female anatomy, puberty and sexual development, bisexuality and homosexuality, and sexually transmitted diseases.
Sexual Signatures: On Being a Man or a Woman. 1975. $8.95.
Where do Babies Come From and How to Keep Them There. 1978. $8.50.
Also offers many bibliographies, including:
Alcohol and Sex Behavior. 1981. $6.50.
Masturbation. 1987. $18.50.
Obesity and Sex Behavior. 1980. $1.
Orgasmic Dysfunctions. 1982. $15.50.
Premature Ejaculation. 1987. $6.50.
Sex Counseling. 1979. $23.
Sex Fantasies. 1986. $10.50.

To find out more, write or phone:
Kinsey Institute for Research in Sex, Gender, and Reproduction, Inc.
Morrison Hall, 3rd Fl.
Bloomington, IN 47405
Phone: (812)855-7686

▶ Levi Strauss & Co.

Provides information on: *AIDS, Counseling*

Levi Strauss & Co. is one of the world's largest apparel manufacturers with nearly 31,000 employees at production, distribution, and sales facilities located worldwide. Levi Strauss & Co. has launched many AIDS/HIV initiatives including employee education sessions, counseling and referral services, and contributions to public education, patient care, and AIDS agencies. The company is involved in hosting an AIDS in the Workplace Conference, helping organize AIDS agencies in its plant communities, raising food, clothing, and funds for people with AIDS, and volunteering for AIDS organizations.

Information for free:
Levi Strauss & Co. HIV/AIDS Program Package. Details the company's activities in the area of AIDS and explains their corporate philosophy with regard to the disease.

To find out more, write or phone:
Levi Strauss & Co.
Mary Gross, Manager, Corporate Communications
Levi's Plaza
1155 Battery St.
San Francisco, CA 94111
Phone: (415)544-7220 or *Fax:* (415)544-1693

▶ Licensed Beverage Information Council

Provides information on: *Alcoholism, Drunk Driving*

The Council is made up of national trade associations concerned with all aspects of alcoholic beverages. Its purpose is to plan and conduct multimedia public education programs on the health effects of drinking during pregnancy, alcoholism as an identifiable and treatable illness, teenage drinking, and drunk driving. The Council can provide information on abusive drinking to high school and college students, and pregnant women. It actively promotes alcohol intervention and treatment for pregnant alcoholic women and offers information based on current scientific research.

Information for free:
Brochures.

To find out more, write or phone:
Licensed Beverage Information Council
1225 I St. NW, Ste. 500
Washington, DC 20005
Phone: (202)682-4776 or *Fax:* (202)682-4707

▶ Narcotic Educational Foundation of America

Provides information on: *Substance Abuse*

The Foundation provides education about narcotics and other drugs in order to warn youth and adults about the dangers of drug abuse. It has produced films and maintains a film library. The Foundation operates a library and reading room, and conducts research.

Information for free:
Offers student reference sheets that outline the dangers associated with the use of various substances, such as:
Drugs and the Automotive Age;
Get the Answers—An Open Letter to Youth;
Glue Sniffing;
Some Things You Should Know About Prescription Drugs.

To find out more, write or phone:
Narcotic Educational Foundation of America
5055 Sunset Blvd.
Los Angeles, CA 90027
Phone: (213)663-5171

▶ Narcotics Anonymous (NA)

Provides information on: *Self-Help Groups, Substance Abuse*

NA is an organization of recovering addicts throughout the world who offer help to others seeking recovery. Members meet regularly to support each other in their recovery using the 12-step program adapted from Alcoholics Anonymous World Services. NA also publishes books and audiotapes.

Information for free:
Newsline. 3-4/year.

Information for a fee:
NA Way Magazine: The International Journal of the Fellowship of Narcotics Anonymous. Monthly. $15/year. Features experiences of members during their recoveries.
Information pamphlets are also available.

To find out more, write or phone:
Narcotics Anonymous
PO Box 9999
Van Nuys, CA 91409
Phone: (818)780-3951 or *Fax:* (818)785-0923

▶ National Abortion Federation (NAF)

Provides information on: *Abortion, Reproductive Rights*

NAF is a national professional forum for abortion service providers and others committed to making safe, legal abortions accessible to all women. The Federation unites abortion service providers into a professional community dedicated to health care, upgrades abortion services by providing standards and guidelines, serves as a clearinghouse of information on the variety and quality of services offered, and keeps abreast of educational, legislative, and public policy developments in reproductive health care. NAF maintains a library on abortion, contraception, sexuality, sociology, and health and medical subjects.

Information for free:
Publications list.

Information for a fee:

Empowering Clinics: A User's Guide to Victim Impact Statutes. 1992. 34 pages. $7. Summary of state statutes against anti-choice protesters.

Having an Abortion? Your Guide to Good Care. 1990. 15 pages. $.75. A consumer guidebook that answers common abortion questions and provides a step-by-step explanation of what to expect when seeking abortion services.

Hospitals Have Essential Role in Abortion Services. 1989. $4.75. A paper for lobbying/education to prevent restrictions on hospital abortions.

Parental Involvement Laws: A Guide for Abortion Providers. 1991. 32 pages. $5.

Truth About Abortion Fact Sheet Series. 1985-1990. $2 each. Includes such topics as teenage women, abortion and the law, public support for abortion, and economics of abortion.

Who Will Provide Abortions? Ensuring the Availability of Qualified Practitioners. 1991. 27 pages. $5. Summarizes the reasons for physicians' declining participation in abortion care.

To find out more, write or phone:

National Abortion Federation
1436 U St. NW, Ste. 103
Washington, DC 20009
Toll-free: 1-800-772-9100 or *Phone:* (202)667-5881 or *Fax:* (202)667-5890

▶ National Abortion Rights Action League

Provides information on: *Abortion*

The group's purpose is to develop and promote pro-choice attitudes in order to maintain the right to legal abortion for all women. The League initiates and coordinates political action, briefs members of Congress, testifies at hearings on abortion and related issues, organizes state affiliates to boost awareness, and supports pro-choice candidates for elected office.

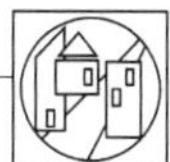

To find out more, write or phone:

National Abortion Rights Action League
1101 14th St. NW, 5th Fl.
Washington, DC 20005
Phone: (202)408-4600 or *Fax:* (202)408-4698

▶ National AIDS Information Clearinghouse (NAIC)

Provides information on: *AIDS*

The National AIDS Information Clearinghouse was established to provide accurate and current information on AIDS programs, materials, and services. Its purposes are to: identify and respond to the information needs of those involved in HIV-prevention programs; distribute publications; provide technical assistance and an information and communications network among organizations involved in the fight against AIDS; and provide information about ongoing HIV and AIDS clinical trials. Staff specialists with broad knowledge of AIDS issues are available to answer questions, make referrals, and locate publications pertaining to HIV infection and AIDS. NAIC's Publications Distribution Service is a direct source of free government-approved HIV and AIDS educational materials; more than 80 titles are available.

Information for free:

AIDS and You. Pamphlet explaining what HIV is, how it is transmitted, how to prevent infection, and what to do if you think you have AIDS.

AIDS Prevention Guide. Presents the facts about AIDS and offers answers to common questions.

Caring for Someone with AIDS. Offers guidelines for home care for people with AIDS.

Condoms and Sexually Transmitted Diseases.Especially AIDS. 14-page brochure answers frequently asked questions about condoms.

HIV Infection and AIDS: Are You at Risk? Gives information on the relationship between infection with HIV and AIDS, and offers information on voluntary HIV testing and early intervention.

How You Won't Get AIDS. Pamphlet explaining how you can and cannot get AIDS.

Voluntary HIV Counseling and Testing: Facts, Issues, and Answers. Brochure for those whose behavior makes them more vulnerable to HIV infection and AIDS.

Understanding AIDS. Explains the facts about AIDS in a question-answer format.

Women, Sex, and AIDS. Provides information about HIV and women, including pregnancy and HIV, HIV testing, and how to talk to a partner about AIDS.

To find out more, write or phone:

National AIDS Information Clearinghouse
Centers for Disease Control
PO Box 6003
Rockville, MD 20850
Phone: 800-458-5231 or *Fax:* (301)738-6616

▶ National Alliance for the Mentally Ill (NAMI)

Provides information on: *Mental Health, Substance Abuse, Homelessness, Suicide*

The Alliance is made up of self-help/advocacy groups concerned with the severe and chronic mentally ill. The organization provides emotional support and practical guidance to families, and educates and informs the public about mental illness. NAMI promotes research in the neurosciences and clinical sciences. The national office offers information and resource materials and maintains contact with legislative agencies and other mental health organizations.

Information for a fee:

Children and Adolescents with Mental Illness. 1988. 221 pages. $12.30. Helps with such issues as choosing therapists and hospitals, future planning, and educational and legal rights of children.

Coping with Mental Illness in the Family: A Family Guide. 1991. 68 pages. $4.50. Handbook giving information on mental illness and coping strategies for families.

Dual Diagnosis: Counseling the Mentally Ill Substance Abuser. 1990. 191 pages. $16.10. About simultaneous treatment of mental illness and substance abuse.

Hidden Victims. 1988. 194 pages. $16.10. Practical knowledge about siblings, spouses, parents, and adult children of the mentally ill.

The Hyperactive Child, Adolescent, and Adult. 1987. 172 pages. $6.60. Discusses Attention Deficit Disorder and medical and psychological treatment.

Overcoming Depression. 1987. 319 pages. $9.45. Describes the disease and offers practical information on its diagnosis, research, and treatment.

Schizophrenia: Straight Talk for Families and Friends. 1986. 264 pages. $3.75. Deals with the treatment and services in realistic terms.

A Street is Not a Home: Solving America's Homeless Dilemma. 1990. 356 pages. $12.90. A guidebook for dealing with homelessness in general and of mentally ill persons.

Suicide: Why? 1989. 100 pages. $12.30. Book that takes the view that suicide is usually caused by brain disorders.

Also offers fact sheets for $2, brochures for $.50 each, and handbooks for $1 and $2 about such topics as health insurance, pensions, religious outreach, and different illnesses and treatments.

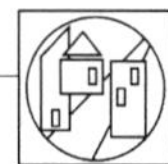

To find out more, write or phone:
National Alliance for the Mentally Ill
2101 Wilson Blvd., Ste. 302
Arlington, VA 22201
Phone: (703)524-7600 or *Fax:* (703)524-9094

▶ National Anorexic Aid Society (NAAS)

Provides information on: *Eating Disorders*

The Society is made up of persons suffering from anorexia nervosa, bulimia, and related eating disorders; families of victims; and educators, doctors, and mental health professionals. It works with medical and mental health professionals to call attention to anorexia nervosa and bulimia so that problems can be discussed and causes and treatments explored. The Society also provides parents, educators, family physicians, and clergy with information that will aid in the early recognition, diagnosis, and treatment of eating disorders.

Information for a fee:
Eating Disorders Information Packet. $5.
NAAS Newsletter. Quarterly. Price included in $12 membership dues. Includes book reviews.

To find out more, write or phone:
National Anorexic Aid Society
1925 E. Dublin-Granville Rd.
Columbus, OH 43229
Phone: (614)436-1112

▶ National Association of Anorexia Nervosa and Associated Disorders (ANAD)

Provides information on: *Eating Disorders*

Anorexics and bulimics, their families, health professionals, and others interested in the problems of anorexia nervosa and bulimia form the association. Chapters in 45 states, Canada, South Africa, Italy, Saudi Arabia, Colombia, and Germany seek a better understanding of anorexia nervosa and associated eating disorders, as well as methods of prevention and cures. The Association works to educate the public and health professionals on illnesses relating to eating disorders and encourages and promotes research on the cause of eating disorders, methods of prevention, types of treatment and their effectiveness, and basic facts about victims. The group compiles and provides information about eating disorders. It also fights against the production, marketing, and distribution of dangerous diet aids and the use of misleading advertisements.

To find out more, write or phone:

National Association of Anorexia Nervosa and Associated Disorders
Vivian Meehan, Exec.Dir.
Box 7
Highland Park, IL 60035
Phone: (708)831-3438 or *Fax:* (708)433-4632

▶ National Association of NonSmokers (NANS)

Provides information on: *Smoking*

The Association promotes laws concerning nonsmoking and the rights of nonsmokers. It educates young people on the relationship between smoking and health, and maintains a toll-free hotline to answer members' questions about specific nonsmokers' rights.

Information for free:
Brochure describing NANS and the dangerous effects of tobacco smoke.

Information for a fee:
Newsletter. Quarterly. Price included in $10 membership dues.

To find out more, write or phone:

National Association of NonSmokers
8701 Georgia Ave., Ste. 200
Silver Spring, MD 20910
Toll-free: 1-800-USA-NANS or *Phone:* (202)667-6653 or *Fax:* (301)650-9004

▶ National Center for Education in Maternal and Child Health (NCEMCH)

Provides information on: *Nutrition, Healthcare, AIDS, Pregnancy and Birth Technology*

NCEMCH is a national resource which provides information and educational services, as well as technical assistance to organizations, agencies, and individuals with maternal and child health interests. The Center links maternal and child health professionals, practitioners, administrators, educators, and the public to sources of information and services, and supports their efforts to improve the health care of mothers, children, and families. Subject areas covered by the Center include maternal

health, infant health, child health, adolescent health, children with special health care needs, and maternal and child health services and programs.

Information for free:

Adolescent Health: Catalog of Products. 1990. 153 pages.
Adolescent Pregnancy-Resource Guide. 1990. 18 pages.
Caring for Our Future: The Content of Prenatal Care. 1989. 126 pages.
Children with HIV/AIDS: A Sourcebook for Caring. 1990. 86 pages.
Children with Special Health Care Needs-Resource Guide. 1990. 18 pages.
Health of America's Youth. 1990. 37 pages.
Infant Care. 1989. 120 pages.
Prenatal Care-Resource Guide. 1990. 14 pages.
Preterm and Low Birthweight Infants-Resource Guide. 1990. 6 pages.

To find out more, write or phone:

National Center for Education in Maternal and Child Health
38th & R Sts., NW
Washington, DC 20057
Phone: (202)625-8400 or *Fax:* (202)625-8404

▶ National Clearinghouse for Alcohol and Drug Information

Provides information on: *Alcoholism, Substance Abuse, Steroid Use and Effects*

The Clearinghouse serves as a national resource for up-to-date print and audiovisual materials about alcohol and other drugs. The Clearinghouse was established by the The Office of Substance Abuse Prevention to lead the federal government's efforts toward the prevention and intervention of alcohol and other drug abuse among the nation's citizens, with special emphasis on youth and families living in high-risk environments. The Clearinghouse offers free, personalized database searches, and distributes grant announcements and application kits. Information on alcohol and other drugs and on the prevention, intervention, and treatment of substance abuse is available in a variety of formats, including fact sheets, posters, brochures, pamphlets, resource lists, directories, kits, and books.

Information for free:

Anabolic Androgenic Steroids and Substance Abuse in Sport. 1989. 16 pages. Information packet. Describes the side effects of steroid use.

Cocaine/Crack: The Big Lie. 1991. 9 pages. Booklet that describes effects of cocaine and provides profiles of former addicts.

Drug Abuse and Drug Abuse Research. 1991. 281 pages. Triennial report to Congress on drug research progress.

NIDA Capsules. Information packet containing short chapters on AIDS, cocaine abuse, heroin, marijuana, drug abuse treatment, drug abuse and pregnancy, and related topics.

NIDA Research Report Series. Booklets. Each issue provides brief but detailed research findings on a single health issue.

OSAP's Clearinghouse Publications Catalog. 1992. 65 pages. Lists resources available from the Office of Substance Abuse Prevention.

Schools Without Drugs: The Challenge. Bimonthly booklet issued during the school year. Provides information, news articles, and columns on drug issues as related to students.

The Use of Steroids in Sports Can Be Dangerous. Fact sheets that provide information on the risk of steroid use.

What You Can Do About Drug Use in America. 28 pages. Booklet that describes various drugs, the stages of use, and contact information for groups involved in treatment.

Information for a fee:

Prevention Pipeline. Bimonthly. $20. Offers current information on drug use prevention.

To find out more, write or phone:

National Clearinghouse for Alcohol and Drug Information
PO Box 2345
Rockville, MD 20852
Toll-free: 1-800-SAY-NO-TO or *Phone:* (301)468-2600

▶ National Institute of Mental Health Information Resources and Inquiries Branch

Provides information on: *Mental Health, AIDS, Suicide, Fitness, Eating Disorders, Divorce*

The National Institute of Mental Health's Information Resources and Inquiries Branch collects and distributes information on a variety of topics related to mental health. Among the topics of concern to the Institute are Alzheimer's Disease, AIDS, attitudes toward mental illness, child and family, depression, general mental health, minority and special populations, schizophrenia, suicide, and treatment issues. The Information Resources and Inquires Branch accepts telephone inquiries on any aspect of mental health, provides referrals, and makes available nearly 100 publications, many at no charge for single copies.

Information for free:

Let's Talk About Depression. 1991. 2 pages. Pamphlet targeted to Black teenagers and young adults.

Plain Talk About Adolescence. 1985. 2 pages.

Plain Talk About Physical Fitness and Mental Health. 1984. 3 pages.

Useful Information On.Anorexia Nervosa & Bulimia. 1987. 15 pages. Reviews two eating disorders, gives background information, and lists ways to help a person affected by an eating disorder.

What To Do When a Friend is Depressed: Guide for Students. 1988. 8 pages. Brochure offering information on depression and ways to help a depressed person.

When Parents Divorce. 1981. 22 pages.

When Someone Close has AIDS: Acquired Immunodeficiency Syndrome. 1989. 15 pages.

Information for a fee:

You Are Not Alone: Facts About Mental Health and Mental Illness. $1. Booklet describing how to recognize the need for help due to mental illness.

To find out more, write or phone:

National Institute of Mental Health
Information Resources and Inquiries Branch
Parklawn Bldg., Rm. 15C-05
5600 Fishers Ln.
Rockville, MD 20857
Phone: (301)443-4513

▶ National Library of Medicine (NLM)

Provides information on: *AIDS, Nutrition, Fitness, Healthcare*

The National Library of Medicine is a government clearinghouse that collects materials in all major areas of the health sciences and to a lesser degree in such areas as chemistry, physics, botany, and zoology. Its collection is available for use by health professionals, students, and others interested in health science. MEDLARS (Medical Literature Analysis and Retrieval System) is the computerized system of databases offered by NLM. A person may search the computer files either to produce a list of publications (bibliographic citations) about a specific question or to retrieve factual information.

Information for a fee:

NLM makes available hundreds of publications including bibliographies.

AIDS Bibliography. $7.50. Listing of references to current articles on AIDS. Each issue consists of about 60 pages of references to journal articles and books dealing with AIDS.

Current Bibliographies in Medicine. $3.25. Approximately 14 bibliographies per year are issued on a variety of biomedical topics. Mail orders to: Superintendent of

Documents, PO Box 371954, Pittsburgh, PA 15250-7954 or phone (202) 783-3238.

To find out more, write or phone:
National Library of Medicine
8600 Rockville Pike
Bethesda, MD 20894
Toll-free: 1-800-638-8480 or *Phone:* (301)402-1076 or *Fax:* (301)496-0822

▶ National Mental Health Association (NMHA)

Provides information on: *Mental Health*

The Association is a consumer advocacy organization devoted to fighting mental illnesses and promoting mental health. NMHA advocates funding for research to discover new and better ways to treat and prevent mental illness, supports a community mental health center program, engages in visitations to hospitals, nursing homes, board and care homes, and centers to assess adequacy of care, and works with mental hospitals, government agencies, and private organizations for the rehabilitation of recovered patients. It serves as central national source for educational materials on mental illness and mental health; conducts public education on mental illnesses and the need for public action through newspapers, magazines, radio, and television.

Information for free:
FOCUS: NMHA's Official Newsletter. Annual. Includes Association news, calendar of events, and research news.
Prevention Update. Annual newsletter.

Information for a fee:
Adolescent Suicide. $.25.
Coping With a Child's Stuttering Problem. $.15.
Helping a Child to Cope With Separation and Divorce. $.15.
Nervous Mannerisms and What's Behind Them. $.15.
Legislative Alert: Children's Mental Health. $20. Annual newsletter.
A Teenager's Guide to Surviving Stress. $.35.
Teens and Self-Esteem: Feeling Good About Yourself. $1.
The Warning Signs of Mental Illness. $.50.
Women's Changing Roles: Finding a Balance for Mental Health. $.40.
Also publishes many federal program summaries, policy resources, training and education resources, and posters for under $20.

To find out more, write or phone:

National Mental Health Association
1021 Prince St.
Alexandria, VA 22314-2971
Toll-free: 1-800-969-NMHA or *Phone:* (703)684-7722 or *Fax:* (703)684-5968

▶ National Parents Resource Institute for Drug Education (PRIDE)

Provides information on: *Substance Abuse, Steroid Use and Effects, Smoking, Alcoholism*

PRIDE operates in the U.S. and in nine other countries to prevent drug and alcohol use by adolescents. It believes the strongest defense against adolescent drug use is the parental instinct to protect the young. The Institute makes available information on drugs such as alcohol, marijuana, cigarettes and tobacco, morphine, methadone, cocaine, crack, opium, heroin, codeine, and barbituates and issues such as damage to lung and bronchial tissue from marijuana use, adolescent health and social consequences of alcohol use, and parental methods of determining a child's drug usage.

Information for free:

Pride—Catalog of Products and Services. 11 pages. A catalog that contains books, brochures, videos, workshops, and other products and services on drug prevention and education.

Information for a fee:

800-Cocaine. 98 pages. $3.95. Discusses cocaine and its physical, psychological, and emotional effects on children.

Anabolic Steroids: A New Drug Dilemma. $3.50. Provides facts about the muscle-building drug which can lead to physical or psychological dependence.

Cocaine: The Great White Plague. 362 pages. $14.95. Looks at the debate over cocaine, presenting the ideas of influential thinkers of the past 100 years.

The Facts About Drugs and Alcohol. 132 pages. $3.95. Provides facts about various drugs, and discusses such topics as adolescent drug and alcohol use, how to recognize an overdose, and how to find the right treatment program.

How to Say No and Keep Your Friends. 99 pages. $7.95. Offers young people a step-by-step method to deal with peer pressure.

Keep Off the Grass. 362 pages. $9.95. Presents the latest scientific and medical evidence of the damaging effects of marijuana use.

What Teens Need to Know About Drinking, Drugs, and Sex. $4.50. Examines what can happen when a teenager mixes alcohol, drugs, and sexual activity.

When to Say Yes! and Make More Friends. 107 pages. $7.95. This motivational book teaches young people how to create more friendships and join groups involved in constructive activities.

To find out more, write or phone:

National Parents Resource Institute for Drug Education
The Hurt Bldg., Ste. 210
50 Hurt Plaza
Atlanta, GA 30303-9709
Phone: (404)577-4500 or *Fax:* (404)688-6937

▶ National Resource Center on Women and AIDS

Provides information on: *AIDS, Rape, Sexual Harassment and Discrimination, Domestic Violence*

The Center provides information on issues involving women and AIDS, focusing on AIDS among women of color and low-income women. It develops policy options and provides assistance to other organizations working with women and/or AIDS.

Information for free:

Center for Women Policy Studies Publications Catalog.

Information for a fee:

Campus Gang Rape: Party Games? 1985. $5. Examines campus gang rape, fraternity parties, alcohol, drugs, and pornography.

In Case of Sexual Harassment.A Guide for Women Students. 1986. $4. Gives examples of harassment, lists actions that women can take, describes legal options, and lists resources.

Federal Laws and Regulations Prohibiting Sex Discriminations in Educational Institutions. 1990. $5. A wall chart describing and comparing coverage of federal laws against sex discrimination in education.

"Friends" Raping Friends: Could it Happen to You? 1987. $4. A guide offering advice on all aspects of acquaintance rape.

The Guide to Resources on Women and AIDS. 1991. $25. Includes a directory of AIDS programs serving women, case studies of women and AIDS, and essays on current issues.

Legal Help for Battered Women. 1989. $5. Offers information about law and legal remedies for women confronting domestic violence.

Looking for More than a Few Good Women in Traditionally Male Fields. 1987. $5. Looks at the problems women face, and includes recommendations to enable institutions to attract and keep women in male-dominated fields.

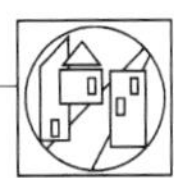

More than Survival: Higher Education for Low Income Women. 1991. $15. Describes two studies on low income women who attended college in Massachusetts.
The SAT Gender Gap: Identifying the Causes. 1989. $20. A report identifying biases in the SAT that account for women's lower scores.
Women, Pregnancy and Substance Abuse. 1991. $15. Discusses the legal, social, and medical aspects of substance abuse among women.

To find out more, write or phone:
National Resource Center on Women and AIDS
Center for Women Policy Studies
2000 P St. NW, Ste. 508
Washington, DC 20036
Phone: (202)872-1770

▶ National Self-Help Clearinghouse (NSHC)

Provides information on: *Self-Help Groups*

NSHC provides access to self-help groups and increases the awareness of the importance of mutual support. The organization encourages and conducts training activities, carries out research and makes referrals to self-help groups and clearinghouses.

Information for a fee:
How to Organize a Self-Help Group. $6.
New Dimensions in Self-Help. $5.
Organizing a Self-Help Clearinghouse. $5.
Self-Help Reporter. Quarterly. $10.
A list of local clearinghouses throughout the United States. $1. Enclose a self-aaddressed, stamped envelope.

To find out more, write or phone:
National Self-Help Clearinghouse
25 W. 43rd St., Rm. 620
New York, NY 10036
Phone: (212)642-2944

▶ National Wellness Association (NWA)

Provides information on: *Nutrition, Fitness, Smoking*

NWA is the nonprofit link to national and international wellness information, resources, and programs and services. Subject areas include nutrition and exercise, body fat, pregnancy and aerobics, heart disease, stress management, shopping for healthier foods, and other wellness skills. The NWA provides consultation services on a variety of topics including: design and implementation of new programs, or the expansion and enrichment of existing programs; and behavior change and risk-reduction programs such as nutrition, weight control, stress management, cholesterol reduction, physical fitness, and stopping smoking.

Information for free:

Wellness Resources for Health Care and Wellness Professionals. Catalog of publications, videos, and other resources.

Information for a fee:

Healthylife for Seniors. $7.45. Presents an introduction to the wellness workshop, and an introduction to the wellness promotion topics that are of the greatest concern to senior citizens, retirees, and pre-retirees.

High Level Wellness. $9.95. Serves as an introduction to the concept of wellness. Topics include the wellness ethic, the five dimensions of wellness, and a wellness resource guide.

Kicking Your Stress Habits: A Do-It-Yourself Guide for Coping with Stress. $10. Offers an approach to understanding and coping with stress.

To find out more, write or phone:

National Wellness Association
1319 Fremont St., South Hall
Stevens Point, WI 54481
Phone: (715)346-2172 or *Fax:* (715)346-3733

▶ Nutrition Education Association (NEA)

Provides information on: *Nutrition*

NEA educates the public on the importance of good nutrition as a means of acquiring and maintaining good health. Communication among medical investigators, researchers, and practitioners concerned with nutrition is promoted, and a 12-lesson home study course in the new nutrition (which emphasizes the importance of nutrition in the prevention and cure of disease) is offered.

Information for a fee:

Crackdown on Cancer with Good Nutrition. $11.

Home Study Course in the New Nutrition. $15.95. Covers such topics as weight control, arthritis, allergies, heart disease, stress and depression, and children's problems and behavior and nutrition.

Switchover!: The Anti-Cancer Cooking Plan for Today's Parents and Their Children. 160 pages. $10.95.

To find out more, write or phone:
Nutrition Education Association
PO Box 20301
3647 Glen Haven
Houston, TX 77225
Phone: (713)665-2946

▶ O-Anon General Service Office (OGSO)

Provides information on: *Self-Help Groups, Eating Disorders*

OGSO's purposes are to offer comfort, hope, and friendship to families and friends of compulsive overeaters, help them grow spiritually by working with the Twelve Steps, patterned after Alcoholics Anonymous World Services, and give understanding and encouragement to the compulsive overeater.

Information for a fee:
O-Anon Newsletter. 3/year. Included in $5 annual membership dues.

To find out more, write or phone:
O-Anon General Service Office
PO Box 4305
San Pedro, CA 90731
Phone: (310)547-1570

▶ Obsessive-Compulsive Anonymous (OCA)

Provides information on: *Mental Health, Self-Help Groups*

OCA is an association of people who have obsessive-compulsive disorders. These disorders are characterized by recurrent unpleasant thoughts and/or repetitive, irrational mannerisms that the person feels compelled to perform. OCA follows the Twelve-Step method originated by Alcoholics Anonymous World Services to assist members in their recovery.

Information for a fee:
Obssessive Compulsive Anonymous. $15.

To find out more, write or phone:
Obsessive-Compulsive Anonymous
PO Box 215
New Hyde Park, NY 11040
Phone: (516)741-4901 or *Fax:* (212)768-4679

▶ Overeaters Anonymous (OA)

Provides information on: *Self-Help Groups, Eating Disorders*

Men and women who meet to share their experiences, strength, and hope in order to arrest the disease of compulsive overeating are members of OA. The OA program follows the Twelve Steps and Twelve Traditions of Alcoholics Anonymous World Services.

Information for free:

Overeaters Anonymous Catalog. Complete selection of conference-approved literature and related materials.

Information for a fee:

For Today. 374 pages. $5.95. Offers inspiring readings for each day of the year.

Lifeline. Monthly. $10/year. International journal of recovery, featuring stories and letters from OA members.

Lifeline Sampler. 448 pages. $7. A selection of stories and letters chosen from the journal.

Overeaters Anonymous. 218 pages. $5.95. Presents personal stories of recovering OA members, and views of the program by non-OA professionals.

Also published are a number of posters, pamphlets, videos and brochures. Some brochures include:

A Program of Recovery. 15 cents. A brief summary of OA's twelve-step program.

To the Teen. $.30. Personal recovery stories by teenage OA members. Includes a questionnaire to help teens determine if they are compulsive overeaters.

Treatment and Beyond. $.40. Explains OA's recovery program.

To find out more, write or phone:

Overeaters Anonymous
Jorge N. Sever, Exec.Dir.
PO Box 92870
Los Angeles, CA 90009
Phone: (310)618-8835 or *Fax:* (310)618-8836

▶ Parents Anonymous

Provides information on: *Self-Help Groups, Child Abuse, Parenting*

Parents Anonymous works for the prevention and treatment of child abuse. It believes that parents should not be labeled, but rather that all parents will experience problems at some time in their parenting careers, and all are deserving of help. The group operates educational programs.

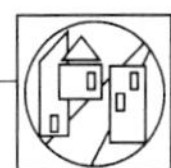

To find out more, write or phone:

Parents Anonymous
Curtis Richardson, Pres.
520 S. Lafayette, Ste. 316
Los Angeles, CA 90057
Toll-free: 1-800-421-0353 or *Phone:* (213)388-6685 or *Fax:* (213)388-6896

▶ Partnership for a Drug Free America (DFA)

Provides information on: *Substance Abuse*

The Partnership is a coalition of individuals and organizations representing the advertising, production, and communications industries that seeks to utilize creative skills to change social attitudes toward illegal drugs. DFA believes that drug abuse is a major crisis affecting American families and work environments. It works to reverse what the group views as current public acceptance and complacency toward illegal drugs. The group creates anti-drug advertisements and conducts research to assess attitudinal changes toward illegal drugs, monitor usage trends, and evaluate the effectiveness of these advertisements.

Information for free:

Network News. Bimonthly.
Partnership for a Drug Free America Newsletter. Quarterly.

To find out more, write or phone:

Partnership for a Drug Free America
405 Lexington
New York, NY 10174
Phone: (212)922-1560

▶ President's Council on Physical Fitness and Sports

Provides information on: *Fitness*

The President's Council on Physical Fitness and Sports produces informational materials on exercise, school physical education programs, sports, and physical fitness for youth, adults, and the elderly. The Council also sponsors the Presidential Physical Fitness Awards Program, which recognizes students who achieve standards on five fitness tests.

Information for free:

The Council produces a number of brochures and pamphlets including:
Building a Healthier Company,
Exercise for a Lifetime: A Game Plan to Improve Your Physical Fitness,

Fitness Fundamentals: Guidelines for Personal Exercise Programs,
The Physically Underdeveloped Child,
Walking for Exercise and Pleasure.

To find out more, write or phone:
President's Council on Physical Fitness and Sports
450 5th St., NW, Ste. 7103
Washington, DC 20001
Phone: (202)272-3430

▶ Rational Recovery Systems (RRS)

Provides information on: *Substance Abuse, Self-Help Groups, Eating Disorders, Alcoholism*

The organization assists in recovery from substance abuse and other addictive behavior, and conducts self-help groups teaching people how to become emotionally independent from alcohol, chemicals, or food. They promote the belief that the individual has the power to overcome addiction, rather than relying on spiritualism. RRS uses the psychological techniques of rational emotive therapy to help people learn to reject irrational thoughts and beliefs that impede recovery.

Information for a fee:
Fatness: The Small Book. $14.95.
The Small Book: A Revolutionary Alternative For Overcoming Alcohol and Drug Dependency. $18.
Also publishes various flyers and promotional material.

To find out more, write or phone:
Rational Recovery Systems
PO Box 800
Lotus, CA 95651
Phone: (916)621-4374 or *Fax:* (916)621-2667

▶ Ray of Hope

Provides information on: *Self-Help Groups, Suicide*

Ray of Hope is a self-help organization offering support for coping with suicide, loss, and grief. The group organizes suicide survivor support groups, offers training courses and consultation, and provides research on bereavement recovery.

Information for a fee:
After Suicide: A Ray of Hope. $16.95 plus $3 shipping and handling.

After Suicide: A Unique Grief Process. $3.95 plus $1.50 shipping and handling.

To find out more, write or phone:

Ray of Hope
PO Box 2323
Iowa City, IA 52244
Phone: (319)337-9890

▶ Research and Training Center on Family Support and Children's Mental Health

Provides information on: *Mental Health*

The Center studies methods to improve services to families with children having serious mental, emotional, or behavioral disorders. Areas of interest of the group include family support strategies, services to minority families, professional school curricula, and interorganizational collaboration. It conducts studies on parent organizations, family/professional collaboration, family coping strategies and the use of community resources, culturally appropriate service models, family involvement in the development and evaluation of community based services, and family empowerment.

Information for free:
A listing of available publications.

Information for a fee:

Annotated Bibliography: Parents of Emotionally Handicapped Children: Needs, Resources, and Relationships with Professionals. $7.50. Covers relationships between professionals and parents, parent self-help support and advocacy groups, and parents' problems and guidelines.

Brothers and Sisters of Children with Disabilities: An Annotated Bibliography. $5. Addresses the effects of children with disabilities on their brothers and sisters.

Changing Roles, Changing Relationships: Parent-Professional Collaboration on Behalf of Children with Emotional Disabilities. $4.50.

Choices for Treatment: Methods, Models, and Programs of Intervention for Children with Emotional Disabilities and Their Families. $6.50. A bibliography listing literature written since 1980 on the range of therapeutic interventions used with young people with emotional disabilities.

Gathering and Sharing: An Exploration Study of Service Delivery to Emotionally Handicapped Indian Children. $4.50. Covers current services, successes, programs, and innovations from Idaho, Oregon, and Washington.

Respite Care: A Key Ingredient of Family Support. 1989. $5.50. Conference proceedings, including speeches and presentations on such topics as starting respite programs, and financing services.

Taking Charge: A Handbook for Parents Whose Children Have Emotional Handicaps. $7. Handbook addressing such issues as parents' feelings about themselves and their children, legal issues, and childhood depression.

To find out more, write or phone:

Research and Training Center on Family Support and Children's Mental Health
Portland State University
PO Box 751
Portland, OR 97207-0751
Phone: (503)725-4040 or *Fax:* (503)725-4882

▶ Schizophrenics Anonymous (SA)

Provides information on: *Self-Help Groups, Mental Health*

SA is a self-help organization sponsored by the American Schizophrenia Association. Groups are made up of people diagnosed with schizophrenia who meet to share experiences, strengths, and hopes in an effort to help each other cope with common problems and recover from the disease. The rehabilitation program follows the 12 principles of Alcoholics Anonymous World Services.

Information for a fee:

Newsletter. Biannual. $15.
Also distributes guidelines for establishing SA groups.

To find out more, write or phone:

Schizophrenics Anonymous
Elizabeth A. Plante, Dir.
1209 California Rd.
Eastchester, NY 10709
Phone: (914)337-2252

▶ Sex Addicts Anonymous (SAA)

Provides information on: *Self-Help Groups, Sexuality*

SAA's purpose is to provide a support group for sex addicts. The group has adapted the 12-step program of Alcoholics Anonymous World Services in dealing with abnormal sexual behavior. Sex addicts are described as people who compulsively repeat sexual behavior that is damaging to their lives.

Information for a fee:

The Plain Brown Wrapper. Monthly. $6. Newsletter.
SAA Directory. Annual. $4 plus $3 shipping and handling.
Also publishes brochures and pamphlets.

To find out more, write or phone:

Sex Addicts Anonymous
PO Box 3038
Minneapolis, MN 55403
Phone: (612)339-0217

▶ Sex Information and Education Council of the U.S. (SIECUS)

Provides information on: *Sexuality, AIDS*

The Council develops, collects, and distributes information and promotes comprehensive education about sexuality. SIECUS affirms that sexuality is a natural and healthy part of living and supports the right of individuals to make responsible sexual choices.

Information for free:

Include a self-addressed, stamped business-size envelope for free publications.
Children, Adolescents and HIV/AIDS Education. 1991.
Condom Availability Programs. 1992. 4 pages. A fact sheet about HIV, young people, and the importance of the use of condoms. Includes a summary of condom availability programs in place or being developed.
Current Resources for HIV/AIDS Education. 1992.
The National Coalition to Support Sexuality Education. 1992. 2 pages. Fact sheet on NCSSE, which consists of more than 50 national nonprofit organizations that promote the health, education, and social concerns of today's youth.
Performance Standards and Checklist: For the Evaluation and Development of School HIV/AIDS Education Curricula for Adolescents. 1989. 9 pages. Presents procedures for use by decision makers who are producing or assessing curricula. Includes a 6-page checklist for evaluating HIV/AIDS education curricula.

Information for a fee:

Guidelines for Sexuality Education, Kindergarten Through Twelfth Grade. 1991. 52 pages. $5. Represents a consensus about what should be taught in a comprehensive sexuality education program.
Healthy Adolescent Sexual Development. 1990. 42 pages. $15. Presents the opinions of 23 experts in the field about healthy adolescent sexual development.
Oh No! What Do I Do Now? Messages about Sexuality: How to Give Yours to Your Child. 1983. 24 pages. $2. Helps parents of preschool children analyze their feelings,

formulate responses, and become more comfortable in discussions about sexuality with their children.

Winning the Battle: Developing Support for Sexuality and HIV/AIDS Education. 1991. 64 pages. $18. Offers guidelines on how to develop and maintain community support for sexuality and HIV/AIDS education programs.

Reports and bibliographies on sexuality topics are also available.

To find out more, write or phone:

Sex Information and Education Council of the U.S.
130 W. 42nd St., Ste. 2500
New York, NY 10036
Phone: (212)819-9770

▶ Society for Assisted Reproductive Technology

Provides information on: *Pregnancy and Birth Technology*

The Society works to extend knowledge of human in vitro fertilization techniques, conducts educational programs, and gathers and distributes information.

To find out more, write or phone:

Society for Assisted Reproductive Technology
c/o American Fertility Society
2140 11th Ave. S., Ste. 200
Birmingham, AL 35205
Phone: (205)933-8494

▶ Society for the Scientific Study of Male Psychology and Physiology

Provides information on: *Sexuality, Rape, Suicide*

The Society concentrates on the study of male psychology and physiology, including sex roles, rape, sexism, and women's history. It examines male and female differences relating to suicide, homicide, and other crimes, health, and development. The organization answers the public's questions on relevant topics.

To find out more, write or phone:

Society for the Scientific Study of Male Psychology and Physiology
321 Iuka
Montpelier, OH 43543
Phone: (419)485-3602

▶ Society for the Scientific Study of Sex

Provides information on: *Sexuality*

The Society conducts scientific meetings for presentation of research papers, organizes symposia, seminars, and workshops, and promotes educational programs dedicated to the advancement of knowledge about sexuality.

Information for a fee:

The Society Newsletter. Quarterly. $10/year. Contains information of interest to sexuality researchers.

Also publishes brochures and research material.

To find out more, write or phone:

Society for the Scientific Study of Sex
c/o Howard J. Ruppel, Jr.
PO Box 208
Mt. Vernon, IA 52314
Phone: (319)895-8407 or *Fax:* (319)895-6203

▶ Stop Teen-Age Addiction to Tobacco (STAT)

Provides information on: *Smoking*

The organization works to raise public awareness of the role of tobacco advertisements and promotions in influencing children to smoke. Working in cooperation with merchants to prevent children from purchasing cigarettes, STAT conducts programs in schools to encourage children not to start smoking and to quit if they have started. It conducts research and maintains a library.

Information for a fee:

STAT News. 2/year. Included in $25 membership dues.

Tobacco Free Youth Reporter. 2/year. Included in $25 membership dues.

To find out more, write or phone:

Stop Teen-Age Addiction to Tobacco
121 Lyman St., Ste. 210
Springfield, MA 01103
Phone: (413)732-7828 or *Fax:* (413)732-4219

▶ Survivors of Incest Anonymous (SIA)

Provides information on: *Self-Help Groups, Sexual Abuse, Incest*

SIA serves as a support group and self-help recovery program for any adult who was a victim of sexual abuse as a child. It follows a 12-step approach, modeled after Alcoholics Anonymous World Services, to assist members in their recovery.

Information for free:
Directory. Bimonthly. Enclose a self-addressed, stamped envelope.

Information for a fee:
SIA World Service Bulletin. Bimonthly. $12.50.
Also publishes brochures, introductory information packet for $5, and a full information packet for $23.50.

To find out more, write or phone:
Survivors of Incest Anonymous
Linda L. Davis, Public Info. Officer
PO Box 21817
Baltimore, MD 21222
Phone: (410)433-2365

▶ TARGET National Resource Center

Provides information on: *Substance Abuse, AIDS, Steroid Use and Effects, Smoking, Alcoholism*

The Center provides information on alcohol, marijuana, cocaine, steroids, amphetamines, barbiturates, AIDS, and tobacco, through brochures, posters, booklets, and articles.

Information for free:
Catalog of publications and other resources.

Information for a fee:
Crack. 24 pages. $1.50. Contains the basic facts about crack use and abuse.
Drugs and the Athlete.a Losing Combination. $1. Nine-page booklet published by the NCAA explains the latest and best information available on the problem of drugs in sports and society at large. Describes drugs and their effects and gives recommendations on how to handle drug-related problems.
Story of Steroids. $5. Material concerning steroids, written with the layman in mind.
Teaming for Prevention. $1. Encourages parents, students, their coaches, and activity leaders to join forces to prevent the abuse of tobacco, alcohol, and other drugs.
When You Look in the Mirror, What Do You See? 24 pages. $2.50. This pamphlet helps adolescents understand their self-image and how it affects the way others see them.

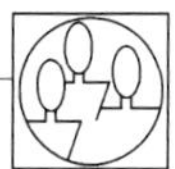

To find out more, write or phone:
TARGET National Resource Center
Susie Reinene, Coordinator
11724 NW Plaza Circle
PO Box 20626
Kansas City, MO 64195
Toll-free: 1-800-366-6667 or *Phone:* (816)464-5400 or *Fax:* (816)464-5571

▶ Transnational Family Research Institute

Provides information on: *Abortion*

The Institute develops research on couple communication, fertility regulation, and choice behavior. It seeks to increase understanding of psychosocial, demographic, epidemiological, and public health aspects of fertility-regulating behavior and of the abortion/contraception relationship. The group also encourages studies on the effects of changes in sex roles and prevention of unwanted pregnancy.

Information for a fee:
Abortion Research Notes. $25. Enclose a self-addressed, stamped envelope.

To find out more, write or phone:
Transnational Family Research Institute
8307 Whitman Dr.
Bethesda, MD 20817
Phone: (301)469-6313 or *Fax:* (301)469-0461

▶ Youth Suicide National Center

Provides information on: *Suicide*

The Center coordinates and supports efforts to reduce youth suicide. It develops and offers educational materials, provides educational programs and services, reviews current youth suicide prevention programs, and establishes model programs.

To find out more, write or phone:
Youth Suicide National Center
445 Virginia Ave.
San Mateo, CA 94402
Phone: (415)342-5755

To Contact People . . .

These books identify individual experts or organizations that can direct you to one.

▶ *The Address Book: How to Reach Anyone Who Is Anyone*

This book can be used to contact more than 3,500 prominent persons including political leaders, business executives, athletes, actors and actresses, artists, musicians, and writers. The book lists name and address. Names are listed alphabetically.
Biennial. Perigee Books.

▶ *American Academy of Psychiatrists in Alcoholism & Addiction—Membership Directory*

Coverage includes about 900 member psychiatrists, and psychiatric-medical students concerned with alcohol and drug abuse. Entries provide name, address, and phone. Names are arranged alphabetically.
Annual. American Academy of Psychiatrists in Alcoholism & Addictions.

▶ *American Association of Sex Educators, Counselors, and Therapists National Register*

The directory covers about 2,560 members of the American Association of Sex Educators, Counselors, and Therapists. Entries include name, address, phone, highest degree, and certification status. Arrangement is geographical.
Biennial. American Association of Sex Educators, Counselors, and Therapists.

▶ *American Medical Directory*

In a four volume set, coverage includes more than 633,000 physicians in the United States, and United States physicians in foreign countries. Entries include name, address, year licensed, medical school, type of practice, primary and secondary specialties, and board certifications. Arrangement of the book is geographical by city; federal service and U.S. physicians abroad are in a separate section. Volume 1 of the set is an alphabetical/geographical index.
Biennial. American Medical Association.

▶ *American Psychiatric Association—Biographical Directory*

Coverage includes 35,000 member psychiatrists. Entries provide name, address, phone, biographical information, professional titles and memberships, education,

hospital affiliations, and related career information. Names are listed alphabetically.
1989. American Psychiatric Association.

▶ *American Psycyhological Association—Directory*

Coverage includes over 70,000 members of the Association in the United States, Canada, and abroad. Entries provide name, address, phone, biographical data, major field, areas of specialization, highest degree, present position, and related career information. Names are arranged alphabetically.
Quadrennial. American Psychological Association.

▶ *American Society for Adolescent Psychiatry—Membership Directory*

Coverage includes 1,500 members of the Society. Entries provide name, office address, and phone. Names are arranged alphabetically.
Biennial. American Society for Adolescent Psychiatry.

▶ *Association of Halfway House Alcoholism Programs of North America Membership Directory*

Information on about 600 alcoholism programs is covered in this directory. Entries include name, address, phone, director's name, number of beds, target population, and substance abused. Arrangement of the book is geographical.
Biennial. Association of Halfway House Alcoholism Programs of North America.

▶ *Canadian Who's Who*

This book lists about 12,000 notable Canadians in Canada and abroad based on position or achievement. Entries include name, address, personal and career data.
Annual. University of Toronto Press.

▶ *Directory of Family Planning Grantees, Delegates, and Clinics*

The directory covers about 4,500 family planning clinics and recipients of grants funded by Title X of the Public Health Service Act through the Department of Health and Human Services. Entries include name and address, and are arranged geographically by DHHS region.
1991-1992. Family Life Information Exchange.

▶ *Directory of Medical Specialists*

Coverage includes more than 400,000 board-certified specialists in over 20 areas of medical practice from allergy to urology. Entries include name, office address, phone, biographical data, education, and career information. Names are classified by specialty, then geographical.
Biennial. Marquis Who's Who.

▶ *Directory of Suicide Prevention/Crisis Intervention Agencies in the United States*

The publication covers about 600 suicide prevention and crisis intervention centers. Entries include center name, sponsoring organization name (if different), address, phone, emergency phone number, and hours of service. Arrangement of the directory is geographical.
Annual. Response.

▶ *Directory of Survivors of Suicide Support Groups*

Use the directory to find information on 220 support groups in the U.S. and Canada for family, friends, and other survivors of people who commit suicide. Entries include name, address, phone, and are arranged geographically.
Annual. American Association of Suicidology.

▶ *Guide to the Nation's Hospices*

Coverage includes about 1,500 hospices, care centers, and other programs serving terminally ill people. Entries include name of hospice program, institution name, address, and phone, name and title of principal executive, service area, and scope of services. Information is arranged geographically.
Annual. National Hospice Organization.

▶ *How to Find Information about AIDS*

The publication covers approximately 600 organizations, counseling, educational, and referral services, treatment facilities, local and state health departments, federal and private sources of research and grant funding, and hotlines. Entries include organization, agency, or hotline name, address, phone, and brief description.
1991. The Haworth Press, Inc.

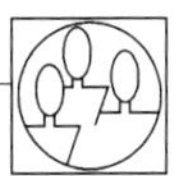

▶ *International Academy of Nutrition and Preventive Medicine Membership Directory*

The directory covers 500 persons having doctoral degrees in one of the health care professions (medicine, osteopathy, dentistry, etc.). Entries include name, office address, degree, and areas of occupational specialization. Arrangement of the publication is geographical.

Annual. International Academy of Nutrition and Preventive Medicine.

▶ *International Who's Who*

This book covers 20,000 prominent persons worldwide. Entries include name, nationality, personal and career information, honors, awards, writings, address, and phone. Names are arranged alphabetically.

Annual. Europa Publications Ltd.

▶ *Local AIDS Services: The National Directory*

Use this directory to locate nearly 2,500 organizations that provide AIDS-related services and information. This includes counseling, financial and legal services, health care, local health departments, community-based organizations, housing assistance, state AIDS coordinators, social security regional AIDS coordinators, NIAID (National Institute of Allergy and Infectious Diseases) AIDS Treatment and Evaluation Units, and AIDS information hotlines. Entries provides organization, agency, or facility name, address, phone, and description of services. Information is arranged geographically.

Biennial. U.S. Conference of Mayors.

▶ *National Directory of Drug Abuse and Alcoholism Treatment and Prevention Programs*

Coverage includes 11,000 federal, state, local, and privately funded agencies administering or providing drug abuse and alcoholism treatment and prevention services. Entries provide name of agency, address, phone, and whether the agency's purpose is treatment or prevention of drug, alcohol, or drug/alcohol abuse. Information is arranged geographically.

Annual. U.S. National Institute on Drug Abuse.

▶ *National Home Care and Hospice Directory*

Use this directory to locate approximately 14,000 home care and hospice providers in the U.S. and Puerto Rico. Entries include agency name, address, phone, director's name, product/service provided, and payment sources. Information is arranged in geographic order by state and town.
Annual. National Association of Home Care.

▶ *Self-Help Sourcebook*

Over 700 national and selected self-help groups for addictions, disabilities, illnesses, parenting, and other stress-causing problems are covered in this publication. Entries include group name, address, phone, purpose, number of chapters, and name and title of contact. The book is classified by subject.
Biennial. American Self-Help Clearinghouse.

▶ *T.A.P.P. Sources: A National Directory of Teenage Pregnancy Prevention*

Use this directory to locate about 600 teenage pregnancy prevention programs. Entries include program name, address, phone, names and titles of key personnel, number of employees, geographical area served, financial data, and description of services. Information is arranged in geographical order.
1989. Women's Action Alliance.

▶ *Who's Who in America*

This book contains information on 79,000 people, primarily in the U.S., considered to be of current national interest because of achievement or position. Entries include name, address, personal data, career data, memberships, special achievements, and publications. Names are listed alphabetically; a separate volume indexes people by profession and location.
Biennial. Updated quarterly. Marquis Who's Who.

▶ *Who's Who of American Women*

This book contains information on more than 30,000 high-profile women in all fields. Entries include name, address, personal, educational, and career data, professional association membership, special achievements, awards, and writings. Names are arranged alphabetically.
Biennial. Marquis Who's Who.

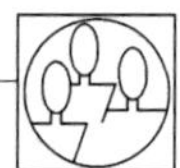

▶ *Who's Who in the World*

This directory covers more than 31,000 people of current international interest because of their achievement or position. Entries include name, address, biographical data, civic activities, awards, writings, and other information. Names are arranged alphabetically.

Biennial. Marquis Who's Who.

7

Science and Environment

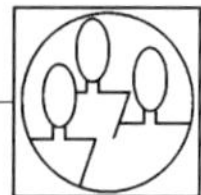

▶ Chapter 7 covers these topics:

Acid Rain
Animals
Birds
Cats
Dinosaurs
Dogs
Earthquakes
Electric Cars
Endangered Species
Floods
Future Technology
Hazardous Waste
Horses
Hurricanes
Inventors and Inventions
National Parks
Natural Disasters
Nuclear Energy
Ozone Depletion
Pollution
Rain Forest Preservation
Recycling
Science
Ultralight Flight
Volcanos
Weather
Whales

▶ Related topics appear in chapters on:

Social Issues

▶ Ideas for research topics:

The Accumulation of Toxic Chemicals in the Great Lakes
Achievements of the Oil and Hazardous Material Emergency Response Industry
Alternatives to Tropical Deforestation
Approaches to Reducing Acid Rain
Beach Cleanup Activities
Biological Diversity
Building Engineering for Storm Damage Reduction
The Changing National Park System
The Chernobyl Nuclear Accident
The China Syndrome
Conservation and Protection of the Oceans and Marine Mammals
Ecotourism and its Role in Third World Development
The Effects of Natural Disasters on People and Property
Efforts to Protect America's Wetlands
Electric Cars

▶ Ideas for research topics (continued):

The Endangered Species Act
Endangered Species of the World
Environmental Consequences of War
Environmental Engineering
The Greenhouse Effect
The Hazards of Pesticides
Laws and Regulations Regarding Pollution
Military Reductions of Nuclear Weapons
Natural Gas and Oil Exploration
Nuclear Waste Storage
Office Recycling Programs
Oil Spill Cleanup Efforts
Preparing For Natural Disasters
The Problem of Plastics in the Oceans
Recycling in the Schools
Resource Depletion and Rural Poverty
Sanctuaries for Endangered Animals
Solar Power
Source Separation Recycling
State and Federal Government Pollution Regulations
Strategies for Reducing Municipal Solid Waste
Strategies to Control Carbon Emissions
Successful Community Recycling Programs
Theories on Why Dinosaurs Died Out
Three Mile Island Nuclear Accident
Trash and Hazardous Waste Incinerator Emissions
Ultralight Flight
Weather Predictability
What Dinosaur Fossils Can Tell Us

To Contact Organizations . . .

▶ Acid Rain Foundation

Provides information on: *Acid Rain, Air Pollution, Global Warming*

The Foundation develops and raises public awareness of the problems associated with acid rain, air pollutants, and global climate change. The term acid rain is used to describe precipitation such as rain, snow, sleet, hail, and fog that acts as an acid in nature because its pH is less than 5.0 to 5.6, the natural range of pH values of water. The Foundation works to support research and encourage long-range planning and informed decision-making to help bring about the resolution of acid deposition and air pollutants issues.

Information for a fee:

Acidification Today and Tomorrow. 231 pages. $15.95.

Bibliography-Acid Rain and

Bibliography-Air Pollutants/Forests. $8.95 each. Listing of scientific papers, symposia, books, conference proceedings, and pamphlets.

Recognizing Pollution Damage in Forest Trees, 1984. 16 pages. $8.00. Special color issue of the German Forestry Journal. Contains colored photographs. German reprint, plus English translation.

Information packets on acid rain, air pollution, and global climate change are distributed for $9.95 each. The packets contain brochures, booklets, legislation, and articles published by scientists, industry, government and public interest groups, and others.

To find out more, write or phone:

Acid Rain Foundation
1410 Varsity Dr.
Raleigh, NC 27606-2010
Phone: (919)828-9443 or *Fax:* (919)515-3593

▶ Affiliated Inventors Foundation

Provides information on: *Inventors and Inventions*

The Foundation offers encouragement and assistance to independent inventors, and supplies inventors with sufficient information on each phase of their invention. Also provided are low-cost or free patent attorney and consultant services.

Information for a fee:

Inventors' Digest. Bimonthly. $20. Magazine.

To find out more, write or phone:
Affiliated Inventors Foundation
2132 E. Bijou St.
Colorado Springs, CO 80909-5950
Toll-free: 1-800-525-5885 or *Phone:* (719)635-1234

▶ Air Resources Information Clearinghouse (ARIC)

Provides information on: *Acid Rain, Air Pollution, Ozone Depletion, Global Warming*

The Clearinghouse is a nonprofit organization that gathers, organizes, and distributes information on air resource issues such as acid rain, ozone depletion, indoor air pollution, and the greenhouse effect and global climatic change. It supports the belief that by removing communication barriers, individuals, public officials, businesses, and organizations will be motivated to work toward solutions to environmental problems. ARIC provides bibliographic services, and online access to databases.

To find out more, write or phone:
Air Resources Information Clearinghouse
Center for Environmental Information, Inc.
46 Prince St.
Rochester, NY 14607-1016
Phone: (716)271-3550 or *Fax:* (716)271-0606

▶ Alliance for Acid Rain Control and Energy Policy

Provides information on: *Global Warming, Acid Rain, Ozone Depletion*

The Alliance lobbies for passage of cost-effective acid rain control legislation. It supports flexible approaches to reducing emissions responsible for acid rain, incentives for emissions reduction, and the burden of cost for emissions reduction being placed on governments or polluting states. The group makes use of the findings of the Center for Clean Air Policy to set specific emissions goals for states, industries, and utilities and suggest emissions-reducing tactics such as emissions trading among industries, use of clean coal by utilities, and more efficient use of energy by industrial and utility plants.

Information for a fee:
Acid Rain: Road to a Middleground Solution. 1987. $20. Report on specific pollution reduction goals.

An Efficient Approach to Reducing Acid Rain: The Environmental Benefits of Energy Conservation. 1989. $25. An analysis of two energy conservation programs on two major utility systems.

Healing the Environment, Part One: State Options for Addressing Global Warming. 1989. Report outlining steps states can take to address the problem.

Healing the Environment, Part Two: A Look at Coalbed Methane as a Cost-Effective Means of Addressing Global Climate Change. 1991. Study examining the economic feasibility of recovering coalbed methane.

Midwest Coal by Wire: Addressing Regional Acid Rain and Energy Problems . 1987. $20.

To find out more, write or phone:

Alliance for Acid Rain Control and Energy Policy
444 N. Capitol St., Ste. 526
Washington, DC 20001
Phone: (202)624-5475

▶ American Association of Inventors

Provides information on: *Inventors and Inventions*

Private inventors and other interested individuals are members of the Association. It provides assistance with the development of ideas, patent applications, marketing, and production. The group conducts problem solving, creativity, and critical thinking conferences for children.

Information for free:

Through the Keyring.
The Gatling Gun. Bimonthly. Free to members and students.

To find out more, write or phone:

American Association of Inventors
2853 State
Saginaw, MI 48602
Phone: (517)799-8208

▶ American Association of State Climatologists

Provides information on: *Weather*

The Association promotes applied climatology and climatological services in the U.S. Climatologists compile statistics, and maintain biographical archives.

Information for free:

State Climatologist. 4/year.

To find out more, write or phone:
American Association of State Climatologists
Dr. Ken E. Kunkel, Pres.
Midwest Region Climate Center
2204 Griffith Dr.
Champaign, IL 61820
Phone: (217)244-8226

▶ American Dog Owners Association

Provides information on: *Dogs*

The Association is a volunteer organization of dog owners that seeks to educate the public on the responsibilities of pet ownership. The group advocates stringent laws applying to vicious dogs and their owners.

Information for a fee:
Newsletter. Bimonthly. Included in $10 membership dues.

To find out more, write or phone:
American Dog Owners Association
1654 Columbia Tpke.
Castleton, NY 12033
Phone: (518)477-8469

▶ American Horse Council (AHC)

Provides information on: *Horses*

The Council is a national organization of individuals, groups, and companies interested in horses or the horse industry. AHC unites, informs, and represents America's horse community. AHC also promotes equitable taxation and legislation; maintains liaison with government agencies and advises members of current national developments affecting the horse industry.

Information for free:
Enclose a self-addressed, stamped envelope.
AHC Horse Industry Fact Sheet.
Animal Rights vs. Animal Welfare and the Horse Industry.
Educational Opportunities in the Horse Industry.

Information for a fee:
AHC Horse Industry Directory 1991-92. $15.
Basic Horse Safety Manual. $3.

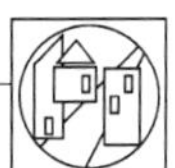

Racehorse Medication Rules: Drug Testing Programs: Penalty and Appeals Procedures. 1987. $25.
State Racehorse Medication Rules: Table Summaries. $15.
Summary of Medical Rules for Competition Horses. 1989. $5.

To find out more, write or phone:
American Horse Council
1700 K St. NW, No. 300
Washington, DC 20006
Phone: (202)296-4031 or *Fax:* (202)296-1970

▶ American Humane Association (AHA) Animal Protection Division

Provides information on: *Animals, Animal Rights, Dogs*

The Animal Protection Division of the American Humane Association is dedicated to preventing cruel, neglectful, or abusive treatment of animals. The Division produces and distributes training manuals, research reports, films, pamphlets, posters, guidelines, and magazines. The Division also conducts research and supports legislation protecting animals.

Information for free:
Advocate. Quarterly. Sample copy. $15/year regular subscription with membership. The magazine covers American Humane Association's animal protection activities, legislative updates, and information on pet care and health.

Information for a fee:
Dog Training Tips. $.60. A professional dog trainer covers the daily procedures that make up a basic dog obedience course.
Pet Overpopulation and the Benefits of Neutering Your Pet. $.60. Pamphlet. Describes how neutering can control pet overpopulation.
Product Testing. $.60. Brochure explains product testing done on animals.
Protecting Pets from Household Poisons. $.60. Instructs homeowners how to recognize various toxic hazards around the house and prevent the poisons from harming pets.

To find out more, write or phone:
American Humane Association
Animal Protection Division
63 Inverness Dr., E.
Englewood, CO 80112
Toll-free: 1-800-2-ASK-AHA or *Phone:* (303)792-9900 or *Fax:* (303)792-5333

▶ American Meteorological Society (AMS)

Provides information on: *Science, Weather, Tornadoes, Hurricanes, Floods*

Society membership includes professional meteorologists, oceanographers, hydrologists, interested students and others working to develop and distribute information on atmospheric, oceanic, and related hydrologic sciences. The Society's activities include scholarship programs, career information, certification of consulting meteorologists, and a seal of approval program to recognize competence in radio and television weathercasting. The AMS issues statements of policy to assist public understanding on weather modification, forecasting, tornadoes, hurricanes, flash floods, meteorological satellites, and other subjects.

Information for free:

American Meteorological Society. Pamphlet describing AMS objectives, activities, and publications.

Publications of the American Meteorological Society.

Information for a fee:

The 1938 Hurricane. 1988. $22.95.

The American Weather Book. 1989. $20.

The Atmosphere Chart. $22.95.

Early American Tornadoes (1586-1870). 1970. $20.

Early American Winters (1604-1820). 1966. $20.

Early American Winters (1821-1870). 1967. $20.

A Field Guide to the Atmosphere. $17.95, paperback.

The Global Climate Chart. $22.95.

The History of Meteorology (to 1800). 1983. $25.

Journal of Climate. Monthly. $17.50/year for students.

Monthly Weather Review. $25/year for students.

The Weather Factor. 1989. $20.

To find out more, write or phone:

American Meteorological Society
45 Beacon St.
Boston, MA 02108-3693
Phone: (617)227-2425 or *Fax:* (617)742-8718

▶ American Museum of Natural History

Provides information on: *Science*

The Museum concentrates on the research activities and fields of natural sciences, including anthropology, astronomy, entomolgy, mineral sciences, ornithology, and

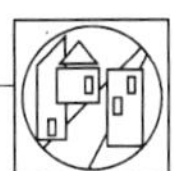

paleontology. It conducts field explorations worldwide, and maintains a library, and a special collection for research purposes.

To find out more, write or phone:

American Museum of Natural History
Central Park W. & 79th St.
New York, NY 10024
Phone: (212)769-5000

▶ American Pet Society

Provides information on: *Animals*

The Society promotes responsible pet ownership, sponsors charitable and educational programs, and offers children's services.

Information for free:

Pet News. 3-4/year. Published in cooperation with Western World Pet Supply Association.

To find out more, write or phone:

American Pet Society
406 S. 1st Ave.
Arcadia, CA 91006
Phone: (818)447-2222 or *Fax:* (818)447-8350

▶ American Society for the Prevention of Cruelty to Animals (ASPCA)

Provides information on: *Animal Rights, Animals*

The Society seeks to provide effective means for the prevention of cruelty to animals, enforce all laws for the protection of animals, and promote appreciation for and humane treatment of animals. It works to maintain shelters for lost, stray, or unwanted animals, and to operate a veterinary hospital and a major low-cost spay/neuter clinic. ASPCA conducts educational programs and distributes animal-related information. It campaigns for legislation to improve animal welfare. The Society maintains a library resource center of books, periodicals, films, and animal-related information.

Information for free:

ASPCA Guidelines for Student Experiments Involving Animals.
ASPCA Origin, Purpose, Principles, and Beliefs. Brochure.

ASPCA Report. 3/year. Magazine on animal welfare issues. It includes articles on animal farming, genetic engineering of animals for food, animal experimentation, and ASPCA efforts to control and eliminate cruelty toward animals.
ASPCA Update.
Humane Education: Learning to Care. Brochure.
Taking Animals Out of Research: Problems.Solutions. 5-page article.

To find out more, write or phone:
American Society for the Prevention of Cruelty to Animals
441 E. 92nd St.
New York, NY 10128
Toll-free: 1-800-395-ASPC or *Phone:* (212)876-7700 or *Fax:* (212)348-3031

▶ American Telephone & Telegraph Co. (AT&T)

Provides information on: *Ozone Depletion*

American Telephone and Telegraph Company (AT&T) specializes in telecommunications and service. Most of AT&T's revenue comes from long-distance service. AT&T is also involved in an environmental and safety program. Goals of the program include phasing out ozone-depleting chlorofluorocarbons (CFCs) from its manufacturing operations, eliminating total toxic air emissions, decreasing manufacturing process waste through reduction and recycling, and improving safety. The company also maintains a 24-hour emergency environmental and safety hotline.

Information for free:
Brochure reporting on the company's environmental and safety activities.

To find out more, write or phone:
American Telephone & Telegraph Co.
Jill Christensen, Manager, Environment & Safety
131 Morristown Rd.
Basking Ridge, NJ 07920
Phone: (908)204-8265 or *Fax:* (908)204-8549

▶ Association of State and Interstate Water Pollution Control Administrators (ASIWPCA)

Provides information on: *Environmental Protection, Water Pollution*

The Association promotes coordination among state agency programs and those of the Environmental Protection Agency, Congress, and other federal agencies responsible for prevention, abatement, and control of water pollution.

Information for free:

ASIWPCA Subscriber Brochure and Information.

Information for a fee:

America's Clean Water—The States' Evaluation of Progress—1972-1982. $10.

ASIWPCA Annual Report 1991-92. $4.

Toxicity Elimination and Management—State Progress: ASIWPCA Conference Proceedings 1987. $10.

To find out more, write or phone:

Association of State and Interstate Water Pollution Control Administrators
Ms. Robbi J. Savage, Exec.Dir.
750 1st St., NE, Ste. 910
Washington, DC 20002
Phone: (202)898-0905 or *Fax:* (202)898-0929

▶ Big Island Rainforest Action Group

Provides information on: *Rain Forest Preservation, Environmental Protection*

The Group is dedicated to preserving the rainforests of the Hawaiian Islands and is particularly interested in stopping geothermal development in the Wao Kele O Puna forest on the Island of Hawaii. Activities have included testimony at public hearings, letter-writing campaigns, demonstrations, and political action.

Information for free:

Big Island Rainforest Action Group. Brochure. Explains the risks of geothermal development in Hawaii.

Hawaii: Paradise Lost? Describes the destruction of Hawaiian rainforests.

Numerous fact sheets providing details on geothermal development in Hawaii are also available.

To find out more, write or phone:

Big Island Rainforest Action Group
PO Box 341
Kurtistown, HI 96760
Phone: (808)966-7622

▶ Center for Earthquake Studies

Provides information on: *Natural Disasters, Earthquakes*

The Center studies the possibility of earthquakes, focusing on the New Madrid Fault system which runs through southeast Missouri, southern Illinois, and parts of

Arkansas, Tennessee, and Kentucky. The Center promotes earthquake preparedness and safe building practices, especially in schools.

Information for free:

Earthquake Guide. Pamphlet describing earthquakes, natural and man made hazards resulting from earthquakes, the Richter Magnitude and Modified Mercalli Intensity measurement scales, and more.

Information for a fee:

Specialized literature packages are available, for a $2 postage and handling fee, that cover planning and preparation for different businesses and for families and children.

Effects of Earthquakes in the Central U.S. 1990. 44 pages. $5.95. Covers earthquakes in the midwest with a list of earthquakes on the New Madrid fault from 1800 to 1990.

Field Trip Guide to Representative Earthquake Features in the New Madrid Seismic Zone. 62 pages. $10. Book describing features such as sand boils and crevasses in the region struck by the 1811-12 earthquake.

The New Madrid Earthquakes. 176 pages. $12.95. Describes the effects of the 1811-12 earthquake.

To find out more, write or phone:

Center for Earthquake Studies
Southeast Missouri State University
1 Univ. Plaza
Cape Girardeau, MO 63701-4799
Phone: (314)651-2019

▶ The Center for Marine Conservation (CMC)

Provides information on: *Marine Pollution, Endangered Species, Whales*

The Center for Marine Conservation is dedicated to the conservation and protection of the oceans and their habitats, especially marine mammals such as whales and sea turtles. It promotes public awareness and education, encourages and conducts science and policy research, and seeks to ensure that human activities will not lead to the extinction of these species. CMC activities have included beach cleanups and the establishment of a sanctuary for critically endangered humpback whales in the Caribbean. It sponsors scientific research, and conducts an international public information campaign.

Information for free:

Coastal Connection. Biannual. Newsletter updating beach cleanup activities around the country.

Sanctuary Currents. Quarterly. An 8-page newsletter concerning marine sanctuaries.

Information for a fee:

1991 International Coastal Cleanup Results. 1992. $10. A detailed report on findings of beach cleanups in the U.S. and other countries.

Citizen's Guide to Plastic in the Ocean: More Than a Litter Problem. $2. A citizen's handbook on the problem of plastic marine debris.

Cleaning North America's Beaches. $10. Detailed reports on beach cleanups held in 1988, 1989, and 1990. Specify report by year.

Environmental Quality in the Gulf of Mexico: A Citizen's Guide. $5.95. Discusses issues surrounding the future of the Gulf of Mexico, including offshore oil drilling and increased coastal population.

Federal Conservation and Management of Marine Fisheries in the United States. $19.95. A review of federal fisheries history, legislation, and management.

Shipping Safety and America's Coasts. $12. A follow-up report to the Exxon Valdez study examining commercial ship traffic and shipping accidents in U.S. waters.

Also distributes fact sheets, posters, slide shows, and videotapes.

To find out more, write or phone:

The Center for Marine Conservation
1725 DeSales St., NW
Washington, DC 20036
Phone: (202)429-5609 or *Fax:* (202)872-0619

▶ Center for Planning and Research, Inc.

Provides information on: *Natural Disasters, Earthquakes, Volcanos, Floods*

The Center's main research interests include disaster preparedness for earthquakes, floods, chemical spills, and volcanic eruptions. Research results are published in government reports.

To find out more, write or phone:

Center for Planning and Research, Inc.
450 San Antonio Rd.
Palo Alto, CA 94306-4641
Phone: (415)858-0252

▶ Citizens for a Better Environment (CBE)

Provides information on: *Pollution, Environmental Protection, Hazardous Waste, Water Pollution*

CBE works to reduce exposure to toxic substances in air, water, and land. A trained staff of scientists, researchers, and policy analysts evaluate specific problems, testify at legislative and regulatory hearings, and file suits in state and federal courts. CBE provides technical assistance to local residents and community-based organizations, including minority and low-income urban dwellers, and it publishes research reports and fact sheets.

Environmental Review. Quarterly. $25/year. Journal on the public health effects of pollution and measures aimed at reducing pollution from toxic substances; includes updates of the organization's activities and research reports.

To find out more, write or phone:

Citizens for a Better Environment
407 S. Dearborn, Ste. 1775
Chicago, IL 60605
Phone: (312)939-1530 or *Fax:* (312)939-2536

▶ Citizens for a Sound Economy Foundation (CSEF)

Provides information on: *Pollution*

CSEF was founded to improve public understanding of economic issues. It sponsors two environmental grassroots public policy organizations that advocate market- and science-based solutions to environmental problems. CSEF also distributes studies on economic issues and sponsors a public interest legal group.

Information for free:

Annual Report.
CSE Reports. Quarterly newsletter.
On Alert. Bimonthly newsletter.

Information for a fee:

Wasting America's Money, Part 2. $5. Book.

To find out more, write or phone:

Citizens for a Sound Economy Foundation
470 L'Enfant Plaza, E., SW, Ste. 7112
Washington, DC 20024
Phone: (202)488-8200 or *Fax:* (202)488-8282

▶ Clean Sites, Inc. (CSI)

Provides information on: *Hazardous Waste, Pollution*

CSI is an organization made up of representatives of environmental organizations and industries formed to identify parties responsible for abandoned hazardous waste sites, and to determine who will be financially responsible for the cleanup. CSI provides

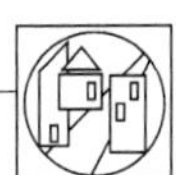

financial management services to collect, invest, and disburse responsible parties' funds for cleanup.

Information for a fee:

Hazardous Waste Sites and the Rural Poor: A Preliminary Assessment. 1990. $10.

Main Street Meets Superfund: Local Government Involvement at Hazardous Waste Sites. 1992. $20.

What Works? Alternative Strategies for Superfund Cleanups. 1991. $15. Only written requests accepted.

To find out more, write or phone:

Clean Sites, Inc.
1199 N. Fairfax St., Ste. 400
Alexandria, VA 22314
Phone: (703)683-8522 or *Fax:* (703)548-8733

▶ Clean Water Action (CWA)

Provides information on: *Environmental Protection, Pollution, Water Pollution, Hazardous Waste*

CWA is a national citizen action organization established to work for strong pollution controls and safe drinking water. CWA is active in toxic protection for communities and workplaces, preservation of the nation's wetlands, and promotion of alternative treatment technologies that recycle wastes. CWA was influential in the 1986 Superfund for Toxic Cleanup.

Information for a fee:

Clean Water Action News. Quarterly. $25/year. Newsletter reporting on efforts to preserve clean and safe water, control toxic chemicals, and protect the nation's natural resources; includes legislative news and reports of local, state, and regional environmental campaigns.

To find out more, write or phone:

Clean Water Action
c/o David Zwick
1320 18th St., NW
Washington, DC 20003
Phone: (202)457-1286

▶ Concern

Provides information on: *Pollution, Environmental Protection, Ozone Depletion*

Concern provides environmental information to individuals and groups and encourages them to take action in their communities. The organization develops and distributes community action guides that explain environmental issues and list resources. Concern responds to requests from the public on topics such as global warming and energy use, sustainable agriculture, air and water pollution, and solid waste.

Information for a fee:
The following guides are available for $4 each plus postage and handling:
Drinking Water: A Community Action Guide;
Farmland: A Community Issue;
Global Warming and Energy Choices;
Groundwater: A Community Action Guide;
Household Waste: Issues and Opportunities;
Pesticides;
Waste: Choices for Communities.

To find out more, write or phone:
Concern
1794 Columbia Rd., NW
Washington, DC 20009
Phone: (202)328-8160

▶ Concerned Pet Owners' Association (CPOA)

Provides information on: *Animals, Consumer Affairs*

This association of pet owners, manufacturers of pet-related products, consumer groups, veterinarians, and kennel owners works for informed consumer choice in selecting pet-related products and services. CPOA serves as a watchdog organization for pet-related product manufacturers and conflicts of interest in the business practices of veterinarians. The group maintains a small library.

To find out more, write or phone:
Concerned Pet Owners' Association
RD 1, Box 393
Port Matilda, PA 16870
Phone: (814)692-8484 or *Fax:* (814)231-1258

▶ Congressional Clearinghouse on the Future

Provides information on: *Future Technology, Environmental Protection, Civil Rights and Liberties*

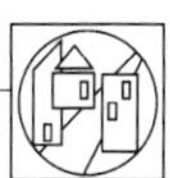

The goals of the Clearinghouse are to educate members of Congress and staff about emerging demographic, technological, and economic trends. It works to translate futures research findings into political action, and incorporate foresight into the policymaking process. Issues studied include challenges of the information age, the aging of America, policy impacts of biotechnology, global environmental issues, new civil rights issues, and public opinion and polling research. Reports issued by the Clearinghouse are available to the public.

To find out more, write or phone:

Congressional Clearinghouse on the Future
H2-555 House Annex 2
Washington, DC 20515
Phone: (202)226-3434

▶ Conservation International

Provides information on: *Environmental Protection, Rain Forest Preservation, Endangered Species*

The mission of Conservation International is to conserve ecosystems and biological diversity and the ecological processes that support life on earth. CI activities include education and conservation training. The group is working on conservation programs in more than 20 countries in Africa, Asia, Latin America, and North America.

Information for free:

Conserving the World's Biological Diversity. 1990.
The Debt-for-Nature Exchange: A Tool for International Conservation. 1991.
Earth Trips: Nature Travel on a Fragile Planet. 1991.
Ecotourism: The Uneasy Alliance. 1989.
Orion Magazine. Quarterly.
The Rain Forest Imperative: A Ten Year Strategy to Conserve Earth's Most Threatened Ecosystems. 1990.
Tropicus. Quarterly newsletter.

To find out more, write or phone:

Conservation International
1015 18th St., NW, Ste. 1000
Washington, DC 20036
Phone: (202)429-5660 or *Fax:* (202)887-5188

▶ Digit Fund

Provides information on: *Endangered Species, Environmental Protection, Rain Forest Preservation*

The Digit Fund is dedicated to studying and protecting the endangered mountain gorillas of central Africa. The group promotes preservation and conservation of the gorillas' rain forest habitat. It makes available curriculum for elementary and middle schools.

Information for a fee:

Digit Newsletter. Quarterly. $10 for students. Newsletter including current research programs, status of gorillas, and fundraising projects.

To find out more, write or phone:

Digit Fund
45 Inverness Dr., E.
Englewood, CO 80112
Toll-free: 1-800-851-0203 or *Phone:* (303)790-2349 or *Fax:* (303)790-4066

▶ Dinosaur Society

Provides information on: *Dinosaurs*

The Society promotes research and education in the study of dinosaurs. It asserts that dinosaurs are misrepresented by merchandisers, and assists in accurately revising products portraying dinosaurs to reflect current scientific knowledge. The society conducts charitable and educational programs, offers children's services, and holds lectures.

Information for a fee:

Dino Times. Monthly. Available with $19.95 annual membership. Children's magazine.

Dinosaur Report. Quarterly. Available with $25 associate membership.

To find out more, write or phone:

Dinosaur Society
PO Box 2098
New Bedford, MA 02741
Phone: (508)996-3946 or *Fax:* (508)997-2469

▶ Earthquake Education Center

Provides information on: *Natural Disasters, Earthquakes*

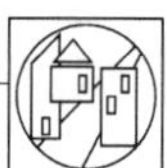

The Earthquake Education Center is involved in seismic studies, including seismic activity in lower South Carolina and daily seismic activity data reports to the United States Geological Survey. It distributes earthquake safety material to the general public.

Information for free:

Focus On. Quarterly newsletter.

To find out more, write or phone:

Earthquake Education Center
Charleston Southern University
9200 University Blvd.
PO Box 10087
Charleston, SC 29411-0087
Phone: (803)863-7531 or *Fax:* (803)863-8074

▶ Earthquake Engineering Research Center (EERC)

Provides information on: *Natural Disasters, Earthquakes*

The research center works to prevent loss of life and property damage resulting from future earthquakes, placing major emphasis on predicting intensities and potential damage. EERC maintains the National Information Service for Earthquake Engineering, which collects, organizes, and distributes information on earthquake engineering and structural dynamics. Research results are published in project reports, technical papers, and conference proceedings. The group has a library collection of books on earthquake engineering, seismology, geology, and disaster planning. The reference librarian will answer the public's questions on relevant topics.

Information for free:

EERC News. Semiannual newsletter.

Information for a fee:

EERC Reports. 15-20/year. $15-20 each.

Loma Prieta. Semiannual. $5. Catalog containing abstracts and citations pertaining to the 1989 earthquake.

To find out more, write or phone:

Earthquake Engineering Research Center
University of California, Berkeley
1301 S. 46th St.
Richmond, CA 94804-4698
Phone: (510)231-9554 or *Fax:* (510)231-9471

▶ Earthquake Engineering Research Institute (EERI)

Provides information on: *Natural Disasters, Earthquakes*

The Institute's membership includes researchers, professionals, government officials, and others working toward a solution to national earthquake engineering problems. The Institute conducts field investigations detailing the effects of destructive earthquakes, sponsors information exchange forums, and provides educational seminars.

Information for free:

Earthquake Engineering Research Institute. A brochure describing the Institute and its programs.

Information for a fee:

Anticipated Tokai Earthquake: Japanese Prediction and Preparedness Activities. 1984. 89 pages. $15.

Armenia Earthquake Reconnaissance Report. 1989. $15. The findings of the U.S. team on the Armenia earthquake of December 7, 1988. Conclusions focus on specific lessons to be learned from the building collapse that caused catastrophic loss of life.

Reducing Earthquake Hazards: Lessons Learned From Earthquakes. 1986. 208 pages. $15.

Urban Earthquake Hazards: Second Japan-U.S. Workshop Proceedings. 1988. 358 pages. $20. Speeches, papers, and abstracts are included.

To find out more, write or phone:

Earthquake Engineering Research Institute
499 14th St., Ste. 320
Oakland, CA 94612-1902
Phone: (510)451-0905 or *Fax:* (510)451-5411

▶ Earthwatch

Provides information on: *Science*

Earthwatch encourages individuals who have an interest in science and the humanities to become working members of research teams led by highly qualified scientists. Projects include field work in most disciplines of the sciences, such as archaeology, earth, marine and life sciences, and zoology, and in the humanities.

Information for a fee:

Earthwatch. Bimonthly. $25. Magazine covering current issues and a list of expeditions which members may join.

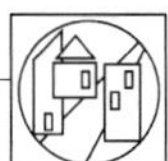

To find out more, write or phone:

Earthwatch
680 Mt. Auburn St.
Box 403
Watertown, MA 02272
Phone: (617)926-8200 or *Fax:* (617)926-8532

▶ Electric Auto Association (EAA)

Provides information on: *Future Technology, Electric Cars*

The EAA encourages the continued development of electric motors for automobiles and sponsors public exhibitions of electric vehicles. It conducts research and maintains a library on technical subjects pertaining to electric vehicles.

To find out more, write or phone:

Electric Auto Association
1249 Lane St.
Belmont, CA 94002
Phone: (415)591-6698

▶ Electric Power Research Institute

Provides information on: *Environmental Protection, Future Technology, Nuclear Energy*

The Electric Power Research Institute works to expand capabilities in electric power generation, delivery, and use. The Institute plans and manages research and development on behalf of the U.S. electric utility industry and the public. Research includes studies in generation and storage, nuclear power, electrical systems, energy analysis, and customer systems. The Institute's research department can be consulted on environmental issues from an industry perspective; it answers questions for a fee.

Information for a fee:

Research results are published in technical reports.
EPRI Guide to Communications Reports. Annual. $20.
EPRI Guide to Computer Programs. Annual. $20.
EPRI Guide to Technical Reports. Annual. $20.

To find out more, write or phone:

Electric Power Research Institute
3412 Hillview Ave.
PO Box 10412
Palo Alto, CA 94303
Phone: (415)855-2000 or *Fax:* (415)855-2954

▶ Endangered Species Coalition

Provides information on: *Endangered Species*

ESC is a coalition of conservation groups working to extend the Endangered Species Act and to ensure its effective implementation. Its objectives are to provide protection for all endangered and threatened animals and plants, to develop an efficient means of listing endangered or threatened species, and encourage international cooperation in the conservation of endangered and threatened species. The Coalition conducts educational, grassroots, and direct lobbying activities, and organizes meetings, letter-writing, and telephone campaigns.

Information for free:
Fact sheets on endangered species.

Information for a fee:
Endangered Species Act: A Commitment Worth Keeping. $5. Booklet.

To find out more, write or phone:

Endangered Species Coalition
1050 Thomas Jefferson St., NW, 7th Fl.
Washington, DC 20007
Phone: (202)333-7481

▶ Environmental Action Coalition

Provides information on: *Pollution, Environmental Protection, Recycling*

The Environmental Action Coalition educates the public about the nature and scope of major environmental problems. It maintains a resource center to help concerned citizens develop positive solutions to these problems, and motivates the public to become involved in solutions. The coalition conducts research, drafts legislative proposals, assists in implementing recycling programs, operates a water supply and conservation service, and maintains an environmental education program. The coalition's environmental library is open to the public by appointment.

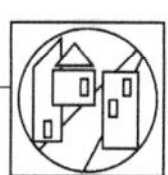

Information for free:

Environmental Action Coalition. Brochure. Explains organization's history and purpose, and includes membership information.

Also available are fact sheets listing slide shows, curriculum guides, and publications.

Information for a fee:

Cycle. Quarterly. Newsletter. $20 membership fee. Contains news on recycling and other environmental topics.

Plastics: America's Packaging Dilemma. 1990. $12.50.

Source Separation Recycling in New York City Apartment Buildings. 1991. $15.

To find out more, write or phone:

Environmental Action Coalition
625 Broadway
New York, NY 10012
Phone: (212)677-1601 or *Fax:* (212)941-8728

▶ Environmental Action Foundation (EAF)

Provides information on: *Hazardous Waste, Pollution, Acid Rain, Recycling, Environmental Protection*

EAF is a national group founded by the organizers of the first Earth Day to promote environmental protection through research, public education, organizing assistance, and legal action. Their work is currently focused in four major areas: toxics, energy, solid waste, and energy conservation.

Information for free:

Environmental Action Publications. Lists available publications. Includes a fact sheet on conserving methods available to individuals.

Information for a fee:

Acid Rain and Electricity Conservation. 1987. $20. Documents how electricity conservation can reduce toxic emissions and the cost of acid rain clean-up programs, thereby saving consumers and utilities millions of dollars.

Environmental Action Magazine. Quarterly. 36 pages. $25/year. Magazine covering environmental issues worldwide. Includes news, exposes, resource guides, human interest features, and citizen action alerts.

Fact Packets on Energy Issues. $4 per title. Covers global warming, the effects of electric and magnetic fields from transmission lines, state least-cost electricity planning, and making your home energy efficient.

Fact Packets on Pesticides. $4.

Fact Packets on Solid Waste. $5 per title. Covers bottle bills, composting, incineration, and small town and rural recycling. The following solid waste titles are $10 each: styrofoam, source reduction, degradable plastics, and disposable diapers.

Making Polluters Pay: A Citizen's Guide to Legal Actions and Organizing. 1986. 170 pages. $15. A workbook to help citizens gather information, work with lawyers, and hold companies responsible for the pollution they create.

Positive Steps Toward Waste Reduction. 1989. $5. Focuses on disposable diapers.

Wastelines. $10. Quarterly newsletter for activists. Covers news and analysis of waste reduction and recycling nationwide. Includes state legislative updates.

Wrapped in Plastics. 1988. 164 pages. $10. A comprehensive report on the environmental impact of plastics packaging. Topics include: the history and growth of plastics packaging; the "front-end" pollution of plastics production; recycling; degradable plastics; and source reduction legislation.

To find out more, write or phone:

Environmental Action Foundation
6930 Carroll Ave., Ste. 600
Takoma Park, MD 20912
Phone: (301)891-1100 or *Fax:* (301)891-2218

▶ Environmental Defense Fund (EDF)

Provides information on: *Environmental Protection, Pollution, Ozone Depletion, Rain Forest Preservation, Hazardous Waste, Acid Rain, Recycling, Water Pollution, Marine Pollution*

EDF links science, economics, and law to create solutions to current environmental problems. The organization works to stop ozone depletion, save tropical rainforests, clean up toxic waste, protect wetlands, control global warming, stop acid rain, increase recycling, protect antarctica, preserve water supplies, and protect wildlife and habitats. EDF initiates legal action, conducts environmental public service and education campaigns, and promotes research.

Information for free:

Recycle. It's The Everyday Way To Save The World. 1991. Pamphlet. Covers disposal facts, how to recycle, reduction tips, community and workplace recycling, and sources of additional information.

A general EDF fact sheet and publications list are also available.

Information for a fee:

Degradable Plastics: The Wrong Answer to the Right Question. 1989. 9 pages. $3. Lists products to avoid and names and addresses of companies who make them, as well as alternative products.

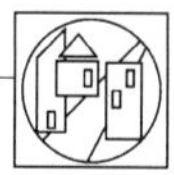

EDF Letter. Available with $10 student membership fee. Newsletter containing information on current environmental issues.

Fight Global Warming: 29 Things You Can Do. $7. Citizen's guide that explains the consequences of the greenhouse effect and what action must be taken.

On Thin Ice. 1988. $10. Discusses the disruption of the Antarctic ecosystem.

Polluted Coastal Waters: The Role of Acid Rain. 1988. $20. Links nitrates present in acid rain to harmful effects on the Chesapeake Bay and other coastal marine areas.

Radon: The Citizens' Guide. 1987. $2. Includes basic information for homeowners on the risks of radon.

Wait-and-See or Do-No-Harm? How to Protect Marine Ecosystems While Uncertainty Exists. 1991. $5.

Watching Birds: An Introduction to Ornithology. 1990. $12.95. Designed for the casual bird watcher.

To find out more, write or phone:

Environmental Defense Fund
257 Park Ave. S.
New York, NY 10010
Phone: (212)505-2100 or *Fax:* (212)505-2375

▶ Environmental Hazards Management Institute

Provides information on: *Hazardous Waste, Recycling*

The Institute focuses on international hazardous waste management. It sponsors Hazmat, a series of conferences on hazardous waste, open to the industry, regulatory personnel, and citizens. The Institute also produces and sells the Household Hazardous Waste Wheel, Educational Bookcovers, Kidswheel on Hazardous Household Products, and the Water Sense Wheel, interactive tools to educate workers, community leaders, and homeowners on issues of household hazardous waste and home water quality. It maintains a library on hazardous waste and toxicology, recycling, and waste minimization.

Information for free:

Newsletters are published quarterly.

To find out more, write or phone:

Environmental Hazards Management Institute
10 Newmarket Rd.
PO Box 932
Durham, NH 03824
Phone: (603)868-1496 or *Fax:* (603)868-1547

▶ Greenpeace U.S.A.

Provides information on: *Pollution, Environmental Protection, Endangered Species, Rain Forest Preservation, Hazardous Waste, Recycling, Ozone Depletion*

Greenpeace U.S.A. initiates active measures to aid endangered species, and monitors conditions of environmental concern including the greenhouse effect and toxic waste dumping.

Information for free:
Offers single copies of factsheets. Titles include;
Alaska's Arctic for Sale,
Energy (Alternative Sources),
Nuclear Campaign Overview,
Pesticides,
Plastics: An Environmental Menace, and
Tropical Rainforests.

Information for a fee:
A Citizen's Toxic Waste Audit Manual. 1990. 71 pages. $5. Helps citizens uncover and identify the pollution produced by local facilities.
Global Warming: The Greenpeace Report. 554 pages. $14.95. Explains the scientific data and the threat of global warming.
The Greenpeace Guide to Paper. 1990. 56 pages. $3. Examines the process of paper production and outlines its impact on the environment.
The Greenpeace Story. 160 pages. $14.95. Gives a history of the Greenpeace movement.
Market Development: The Key to Successful Recycling. 1989. 14 pages. $5. A study of the development of new markets to handle the abundance of materials collected for recycling.
Playing With Fire. 1991. 63 pages. $10. A report on hazardous waste incineration addressing the theory and practice of incineration.

To find out more, write or phone:
Greenpeace U.S.A.
1436 U St. NW
Washington, DC 20009
Phone: (202)462-1177 or *Fax:* (202)462-4507

▶ Household Hazardous Waste Project

Provides information on: *Hazardous Waste, Environmental Protection, Acid Rain*

The Project develops and promotes education and action concerning the identification, safe use, storage, and disposal of household hazardous wastes such as transmission fluid, paint, and batteries. They cooperate with other groups addressing issues such as health, waste disposal, water and air protection, fire safety, recycling, and poison prevention.

Information for a fee:

Guide to Hazardous Products Around the Home. 178 pages. $9.95. Explains product ingredients, health and safety issues, disposal, recycling outlets, safer product alternatives and more.

The Project also publishes the following Guide Sheets that answer questions about household hazardous products and provide guidelines for safe use, storage, and disposal:

Household Hazardous Products: Consumer Information. 25 cents.
Material Safety Data Sheets: Identifying Product Hazards. 50 cents.
Safe Use, Storage and Disposal of Paint. 25 cents.
Safe Use, Storage and Disposal of Pesticides. 25 cents.
Selecting Household Safety Equipment. 75 cents.

To find out more, write or phone:

Household Hazardous Waste Project
1031 E. Battlefield, Ste. 214
Springfield, MO 65807
Phone: (417)889-5000 or *Fax:* (417)889-5012

▶ Humane Society of the United States (HSUS)

Provides information on: *Animals, Animal Rights, Cats, Dogs, Endangered Species*

The Humane Society promotes public education to foster respect, understanding, and compassion for all creatures. Programs include reducing the overbreeding of cats and dogs and promoting responsible pet care; eliminating cruelty in hunting and trapping; exposing and eliminating painful uses of animals in research and testing; eliminating the abuse of animals in movies, television shows, circuses, and competitive events; correcting inhumane conditions for animals in zoos, menageries, pet shops, puppy mills, and kennels; stopping cruelty in the raising, handling, and transporting of animals used for food; addressing critical environmental issues in terms of their impact on animals and humans; and protecting endangered wildlife and marine mammals.

Information for free:

Sample copies of select periodicals are available.

Information for a fee:

Animal Activist Alert. Quarterly. Price included in $10 membership fee. Newsletter covering animal legislation.

HSUS News. Quarterly. Price included in $10 membership fee. Magazine covering HSUS activities.

Shelter Sense. 10/year. $8. Newsletter for those employed in or concerned with community animal control.

Also publishes a wide variety of pamphlets costing from $.10 to $5.00. For a publication list and/or an order form, contact HSUS. Examples include:

Animals. It's Their World Too!

Animal Rights

Caring for Your Dog

Controlling Fleas at Home

Fur Coats: Where Do They Come From?

National Wildlife Refuges: A Cruel Hoax

The Tangled Web of Animal Abuse: The Links between Cruelty to Animals and Human Violence.

To find out more, write or phone:

Humane Society of the United States
2100 L St., NW
Washington, DC 20037
Phone: (202)452-1100 or *Fax:* (202)778-6132

▶ INFOTERRA

Provides information on: *Environmental Protection, Pollution, Acid Rain, Hazardous Waste*

INFOTERRA is a clearinghouse of environmental information that handles more than 15,000 queries a year on every aspect of the human and physical environment, ranging from the control of lead pollution or acid rain to the best means of processing ink from banana plants or the safe disposal of industrial waste. Answers are usually provided free of charge. If a commercial database is used, or costly online searches are made, the user will be charged at cost.

Information for free:

INFOTERRA/USA Directory of Environmental Sources. 468 pages.

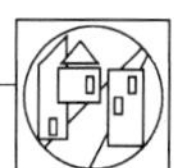

To find out more, write or phone:

INFOTERRA
EPA-Infoterra
Mailstop PM 211A
401 M St., SW
Washington, DC 20460
Phone: (202)260-5917 or *Fax:* (202)260-3923

▶ Institute for Disaster Research

Provides information on: *Natural Disasters, Hurricanes, Tornadoes*

The Institute studies the effects of natural disasters on people and property, including design of structures to resist extreme winds such as those created by tornadoes and hurricanes.

Information for a fee:
Coping with Hurricane Hazards. 1983. 8 pages. $1.20.
Effects of Wind on Buildings. 1983. 21 pages. $3.15.
Hurricanes and Houses: Hazards and Solutions. 1981. $2.50.
Hurricanes, Tornadoes, and Extreme Winds. 1979. 10 pages. $1.50.
Mobile Homes in Windstorms. 1977. 30 pages. $4.50.
Protection of Property and Occupants in Windstorms. 1977. 34 pages. $5.10.
Window Glass Failures in Windstorms. 1976. 8 pages. $1.20.

To find out more, write or phone:

Institute for Disaster Research
Texas Tech University
PO Box 41023
Lubbock, TX 79409-3476
Phone: (806)742-3476 or *Fax:* (806)742-3488

▶ Invent America! (IA)

Provides information on: *Inventors and Inventions*

Invent America! is an organization created to encourage American inventiveness and productivity. IA seeks to enhance public awareness of American inventions, both past and present. To do this, IA is locating and collecting patent models of the 19th century, most of which were sold at public auction by the U.S. Patent Office in 1925; IA plans to donate these models to the Smithsonian Institution. (Patent models are working replicas of original inventions.) The group also sponsors Invent America

Program, an educational competition for elementary school students and bestows awards and grants to the winning students, teachers, and schools.

Information for free:

Invent America! Creative Resource Guide. Annual.

Newsletter. Quarterly. Only written requests accepted. Include $2.95 for postage.

To find out more, write or phone:

Invent America!
510 King St., Ste. 420
Alexandria, VA 22314
Phone: (703)684-1836

▶ Inventors Workshop International Education Foundation

Provides information on: *Inventors and Inventions*

The Foundation provides instruction, assistance, and guidance to inventors in areas including: patent protection; patent searches for inventions; offering inventions for sale; getting inventions and products designed, produced, and manufactured; and choosing experts when required. The group organizes seminars and programs on invention promotion and conducts research.

Information for a fee:

Extraordinary Origins of Everyday Things. 463 pages. $10.95. Describes how and why hundreds of everyday items, customs, and expressions came to be. Gives stories of over 500 "phenomena", including how the zipper was invented.

Future Stuff. 237 pages. $8.95. Contains information on over 250 inventions that may or may not make it into the future. Includes new gadgets, food items, forms of transportation, and more.

The Home-Based Entrepreneur. 160 pages. $14.95. Presents information about working at home, including a start-up plan, and the legal and administrative responsibilities of a home-business owner.

How to Design Better Products for Less Money. 87 pages. $7.00. Gives insight into the practical applications in mechanical engineering for inventors.

How to Sell Your Own Invention. 128 pages. $10.00. Explains such things as how an invention can be sold prior to patenting, or how an inventor can have the patents and much of the work that went into developing it paid for by a client.

Invent a Toy and Get Rich. 117 pages. $21.95. Explains how to begin inventing by means of creative exercises. Also describes the process of developing, protecting, and selling ideas that work.

Inventors Guidebook: A Step by Step Guide to Success. 165 pages. $10.95. Explains the steps and stages of action required to bring an idea from conception to market readiness.

To find out more, write or phone:
Inventors Workshop International Education Foundation
3201 Corte Malpaso, Ste. 304-A
Camarillo, CA 93012
Phone: (805)484-9786 or *Fax:* (805)388-3097

▶ S.C. Johnson & Son, Inc.

Provides information on: *Ozone Depletion*

S.C. Johnson & Son is one of the largest private consumer-products companies in the U.S. The company manufactures insect control products, cleaning products, and personal care products. Raid insecticide and Off! insect repellent are two of the more popular products. Since the 1950s, the company has been involved in the development of many aerosol packaged products. Johnson & Son was the first company to remove dangerous chlorofluorocarbons (CFCs) from its aerosols, reducing harm to the ozone layer. Other environmental initiatives include a decrease in the amount of waste generated during the manufacturing process, and greater availability of recyclable packaging for its products.

Information for free:
Information packet outlining the company's environmental policy, environmental accomplishments, and facts about aerosols and the environment.

To find out more, write or phone:
S.C. Johnson & Son, Inc.
1525 Howe St.
Racine, WI 53403-5011
Phone: (414)631-2000 or *Fax:* (414)631-2133

▶ Keep America Beautiful

Provides information on: *Recycling, Environmental Protection*

Keep America Beautiful is a public service organization dedicated to improving waste handling practices by encouraging cooperation among government, business, and the public. The group sponsors the Keep America Beautiful System, a comprehensive community-wide approach to improved waste handling. The organization presents awards, and offers educational materials, promotional items, videos, and publications.

Information for free:

Single copies only are offered without charge.

Focus Fact Sheets. Fact sheets devoted to a variety of environmental issues.

Office Paper Recycling Tips. Fact sheet.

Overview: Solid Waste Disposal Alternatives. 26 pages. Covers source reduction and waste management.

Preserving Our National Heritage. 15 pages.

Tips for Preventing Litter in Your Community.

Information for a fee:

Recycling Realities: Facts, Myths & Choices. 16 pages. Booklet. $.65 each. Discusses capabilities and limitations of recycling.

Waste in the Workplace. $4.50. A step-by-step approach to reducing and recycling for small businesses.

To find out more, write or phone:

Keep America Beautiful
Mill River Plaza
9 W. Broad St.
Stamford, CT 06902
Phone: (203)323-8987

▶ Lawrence Hall of Science

Provides information on: *Science*

The Lawrence Hall of Science is a research center dedicated to increasing the public's awareness and understanding of science. The organization offers participatory exhibits as well as programs in biology, chemistry, computers, physics, and astronomy. It also serves as a center for teacher education, research, and curriculum development.

Information for a fee:

The LHS Quarterly. Available with $25 membership fee. The magazine covers topics of interest to the general public. Also lists exhibits, class schedule, and activities for kids.

To find out more, write or phone:

Lawrence Hall of Science
University of California
Berkeley, CA 94720
Phone: (510)642-4193 or *Fax:* (510)642-1055

▶ Manomet Bird Observatory (MBO)

Provides information on: *Birds, Environmental Protection, Rain Forest Preservation*

The Observatory conducts population studies of migrant land birds, shorebirds, terns, seabirds, herons, and the osprey. Other studies include tropical forest trees, marine mammals, and conservation problems. Census records of seabirds, shorebirds, and marine mammals are held.

Information for free:
MBO Newsletter. Quarterly.

To find out more, write or phone:
Manomet Bird Observatory
PO Box 1770
Manomet, MA 02345
Phone: (508)224-6521 or *Fax:* (508)224-9220

▶ National Air Toxics Information Clearinghouse (NATICH)

Provides information on: *Global Warming, Ozone Depletion, Acid Rain*

The Clearinghouse collects and distributes air toxics information submitted by state and local air agencies. NATICH also distributes information on the development of air toxics control programs. It stores information on air toxics in the NATICH database, which is accessible to the public. The Clearinghouse responds to requests for specific information.

Information for free:
Have an Air Toxics Question? Pamphlet that describes Clearinghouse services. Additional pamphlets and newsletters are available.

Information for a fee:
Reports of information in the NATICH database. Database access costs range from $10-$15/hour.

To find out more, write or phone:
National Air Toxics Information Clearinghouse
(MD-13)
Research Triangle Park, NC 27711
Phone: (919)541-0850

▶ National Animal Control Association (NACA)

Provides information on: *Animals*

NACA is made up of animal control agencies, humane societies, public health and safety agencies, corporations, and individuals that work to educate and train personnel in the animal care and control professions. The Association seeks to teach the public responsible pet ownership. It provides training guides for animal control officers, makes available audiovisual materials, and conducts research.

Information for a fee:
NACA News. Bimonthly. $15/year.
National Animal Control Association Training Guide. $22.95.

To find out more, write or phone:
National Animal Control Association
PO Box 1600
Indianola, WA 98342
Phone: 800-828-6474 or *Fax:* (206)297-2705

▶ National Audubon Society

Provides information on: *Endangered Species, Environmental Protection*

The National Audubon Society works to conserve native plants and animals and their habitats; to protect life from pollution, radiation, and toxic substances; to further the wise use of land and water; and to seek solutions for global problems involving the interaction of population, resources, and the environment. Through its public education program, the Society responds to inquiries about environmental and wildlife issues.

Information for free:
An activist packet, a high school teacher packet, and a recycling packet are available.

Information for a fee:
Audubon. Bimonthly. $20. Magazine.

To find out more, write or phone:
National Audubon Society
950 3rd Ave.
New York, NY 10022
Phone: (212)546-9100

▶ National Center for Earthquake Engineering Research

Provides information on: *Natural Disasters, Earthquakes*

The Center directs and coordinates research efforts among participating institutions in earthquake hazard studies and earthquake engineering. Its major objectives are to

enhance engineering to reduce loss of life and property by severe earthquakes. Studies by the Center include ground motion, and investigations of buildings, dams, and pipelines. It also examines issues such as postdisaster response and recovery. The group maintains an information service including a bibliographic database.

Information for free:

Technical Report Price List. Describes reports, lists prices, and tells buyers where to purchase them.

Information for a fee:

Earthquake Education Materials for Grades K-12. 1991. $15.
Earthquake Simulation Tests of a Low-Rise Metal Structure. 1988. $10.
Issues in Earthquake Education. 1992. $15.
On the Relation Between Local and Global Damage Indices. 1989. $15.
A Procedure for the Seismic Evaluation of Buildings in the Central and Eastern United States. 1992. $20.

To find out more, write or phone:

National Center for Earthquake Engineering Research
State University of New York-Buffalo
109 Red Jacket Quadrangle
Buffalo, NY 14261
Phone: (716)645-3391 or *Fax:* (716)636-3399

▶ National Congress of Inventors Organizations

Provides information on: *Inventors and Inventions*

The Congress coordinates information relating to inventor education and programs such as wanted and available inventions and organizations offering development and marketing assistance. It conducts educational programs, and maintains a library of books relating to invention, innovation, marketing, and idea development and protection.

Information for a fee:

America's Inventor. Quarterly. $1.25/issue.
Convert Ideas to Inventions. $5. Booklet.
Ethical Rules. $5. Booklet.
How to Get Ideas. $5. Booklet.
Inventing for Fun and Profit. $5. Booklet.
Marketing Your Invention. $19.95. Book.
New Concept Can Be Yours. $5. Booklet.

To find out more, write or phone:

National Congress of Inventors Organizations
PO Box 6158
Rheem Valley, CA 94570
Phone: (801)753-4700 or *Fax:* (510)376-7762

▶ National Dog Registry (NDR)

Provides information on: *Dogs*

The Registry works to stop the trafficking of stolen pets and to improve the means of identifying lost, strayed, injured, or dead animals. NDR encourages dog owners to have a permanent identification number tatooed on the pet's hind leg, and to register the animal with law enforcement agencies and humane societies.

Information for a fee:

Rescue Magazine. Periodic. $25/year. Lists NDR activities, pet health articles, and pet product reviews.

To find out more, write or phone:

National Dog Registry
Box 116
Woodstock, NY 12498
Toll-free: 1-800-NDR-DOGS or *Phone:* (914)679-2355 or *Fax:* (914)679-4538

▶ National Hurricane Center

Provides information on: *Natural Disasters, Hurricanes, Weather, Floods*

A part of the National Weather Service, the Hurricane Center provides operational forecast guidance and conducts research of tropical cyclones, coastal floods, and satellite and aircraft technology to be used for weather forecasting.

Information for free:

Charts are available of sea surface temperatures, and other data.

To find out more, write or phone:

National Hurricane Center
1320 S. Dixie Hwy.
Coral Gables, FL 33146
Phone: (305)666-4707

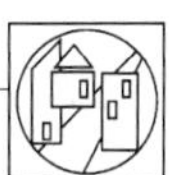

▶ National Meteorological Center (NMC)

Provides information on: *Weather*

The NMC is part of the National Weather Service. In addition to weather forecasting, the Center conducts research in the areas of numerical weather prediction, and applied climate research.

To find out more, write or phone:
National Meteorological Center
World Weather Bldg., Rm. 101
5200 Auth Rd.
Camp Springs, MD 20746
Phone: (301)763-8016

▶ National Museum of Natural History

Provides information on: *Animals, Science, Environmental Protection, Dinosaurs*

The Museum maintains natural science specimens and artifacts in the areas of anthropology, botany, entomology, invertebrate zoology, mineral sciences, paleobiology, and vertebrate zoology. Activities include field observations such as an investigation of the Caribbean coral reef ecosystems, and biological diversity in tropical Latin America.

Information for free:
History of Science. 1992. 36 pages. Publications catalog.

Information for a fee:
Orders require $2.25 postage and handling for first book, $1 for each additional book.
Birds to Watch. 1988. 208 pages. $19.95. Contains information on threatened birds of the world.
The Ecology and Biology of Mammal-Like Reptiles. 1987. 336 pages. $21.50. A collection of 21 essays.
Environment in Peril. 1991. 248 pages. $17.50. Topics include ozone depletion, global warming, thinning forests, extinction of species, toxic chemicals, overpopulation, and other issues.
Evolution and the Fossil Record. 1990. 288 pages. $19.95.
Perceptions of Animals in American Culture. 1989. 151 pages. $11.95.
Sharks in Question. 1989. 192 pages. $15.95. Provides answers to commonly asked questions about sharks.
Smithsonian Chart of Animal Evolution. 1991. $12. Full color chart showing the supposed relationships between animal groups.

To find out more, write or phone:
National Museum of Natural History
Tenth St. and Constitution Ave., NW
Washington, DC 20560
Phone: (202)357-2066 or *Fax:* (202)357-4779

▶ National Nuclear Data Center (NNDC)

Provides information on: *Nuclear Energy*

NNDC provides nuclear physics information services, including bibliographic scanning, data compilation, and critical appraisal of available information.

Information for free:
NNDC Newsletter. Quarterly.
Products and Services Manual. 1992. Lists available products, including databases and publications, and services.

To find out more, write or phone:
National Nuclear Data Center
Brookhaven National Laboratory
Bldg. 197D
Upton, NY 11973
Phone: (516)282-2902 or *Fax:* (516)282-2806

▶ National Park Foundation

Provides information on: *National Parks*

The Foundation was chartered by the U.S. Congress to provide private sector assistance and support to the National Park Service. It works to increase public awareness, appreciation, and understanding of the national parks and their services. Educational and outreach programs are part of the Foundation's activities.

Information for a fee:
Complete Guide to America's National Parks. Biennial. $12.95. Directory providing visitor information on more than 350 national park areas, as well as complete weather information on each area.

To find out more, write or phone:
National Park Foundation
1101 17th St. NW, Ste. 1102
Washington, DC 20036
Phone: (202)785-4500 or *Fax:* (202)785-3539

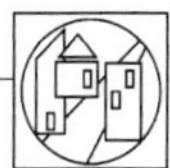

▶ National Parks and Conservation Association (NPCA)

Provides information on: *National Parks, Environmental Protection*

The National Parks and Conservation Association is a private educational and scientific organization interested in the preservation, promotion, and improvement of national parks and equivalent reserves. It also maintains a library.

Information for a fee:
National Parks. Bimonthly.
NPC Alerts. Periodic.
Parkwatcher. Bimonthly.
The above publications are included in the $25 membership dues.

To find out more, write or phone:

National Parks and Conservation Association
1015 31st St., NW
Washington, DC 20007
Toll-free: 1-800-628-7275 or *Phone:* (202)944-8530 or *Fax:* (202)944-8535

▶ National Recycling Coalition

Provides information on: *Recycling*

Coalition members include individuals and environmental, labor, and business organizations united to encourage the recovery, reuse, and conservation of materials and energy, and to make the benefits of recycling more widely known. The Coalition works to help change national policies on energy, waste management, taxes, and transportation that block recycling efforts. It believes consumers should be informed that recycled products are not inferior to products made with virgin materials, and encourages manufacturers to invest in the equipment required to make recycled products, and to make more of such products available at reasonable prices.

Information for free:

National Recycling Coalition Guide to Buying Products. A fact sheet detailing programs to ensure markets for recycled products.

Recycled Paper Facts and Figures. Answers such questions as "What products are made from recycled paper?" and "How is Paper Recycled?" Includes a recipe for making recycled paper.

To find out more, write or phone:
National Recycling Coalition
1101 30th St., NW
Washington, DC 20007
Phone: (202)625-6406 or *Fax:* (202)625-6409

▶ National Science Foundation (NSF)

Provides information on: *Science*

NSF is an independent agency concerned primarily with the support of basic and applied research and education in the sciences and engineering. NSF funds scientific research in mathematical, physical, biological, computer, engineering, social and other sciences, including unclassified research activities in matters relating to national security and international cooperation.

Information for free:
About the National Science Foundation. Flyer.
Alliances for Minority Participation. Fact sheet on Black colleges and universities.
Looking Up. An astronomical sciences newsletter containing news of current activities.
Loss of Biological Diversity: A Global Crisis Requiring International Solutions.
Research Assistantships for Minority High School Students.
Science—The Endless Frontier.
Young Scholars Program. Program announcement.

Information for a fee:
Antarctic Journal of the United States. Quarterly. $13/year. Reports on U.S. activities in Antarctica, and trends in the U.S. Antarctic Research Program.

To find out more, write or phone:
National Science Foundation
1800 G St. NW, Rm. 520
Washington, DC 20550
Phone: (202)357-9498

▶ National Severe Storms Forecast Center

Provides information on: *Weather, Tornadoes*

The Center provides weather forecast guidance and conducts a research and development program. It also conducts applied research to develop and use forecasting techniques of severe thunderstorms and tornadoes.

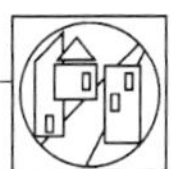

To find out more, write or phone:

National Severe Storms Forecast Center
601 E. 12th St.
Kansas City, MO 64106
Phone: (816)374-5922

▶ National Toxics Campaign (NTC)

Provides information on: *Environmental Protection, Pollution, Hazardous Waste, Water Pollution, Ozone Depletion*

The National Toxics Campaign's purposes are to obtain support for stronger laws against chemical contamination, monitor government enforcement practices, and to provide legislative advocacy.

Information for a fee:

America's Water Crisis? Fact? Or Fiction? $1. A brochure about America's water pollution problem.

Beyond the Rush to Burn: Alternative to Hazardous Waste Incineration. 1992. 35 pages. $12. Report presenting alternative and safer hazardous waste treatment.

A Consumer's Guide to Protecting the Ozone. 8 pages. $1.50. An overview of the ozone depletion problem, and how consumers can help save the ozone layer.

A Consumer's Guide to Protecting Your Drinking Water. 24 pages. $4. Discusses the different kinds of water filters and bottled water on the market.

Destroying Our Nation's Defenses: A Citizen Indictment of EPA. 45 pages. $12. Report on the ways that the Environmental Protection Agency has put up roadblocks to citizens fighting against toxics and other toxic threats.

Fighting Military's Toxics: A Citizen's Organizing Manual. 1991. $6. How to use "right-to-know" laws to identify toxic chemicals used and disposed of at military facilities.

No Free Launch: The Toxic Impact of America's Programs. 1990. 12 pages. $5. Reports on the environmental impact on the earth and the ozone layer of launching space shuttles.

Operation Ozone Shield: The Pentagon's War on the Stratosphere. 25 pages. $10. Exposes the military as the nation's largest ozone destroyer.

Shadow of the Land: A Special Report on Pesticides. 89 pages. $12. Study documenting the economic and environmental burden of pesticides.

Toxic Times. 3/year. $15. Newsletter covering National Toxics Fund concerns and activities.

To find out more, write or phone:

National Toxics Campaign
1168 Commonwealth Ave.
Boston, MA 02134
Phone: (617)232-0327 or *Fax:* (617)232-3945

▶ National Weather Service (NWS)

Provides information on: *Weather, Tornadoes, Hurricanes, Floods*

The National Weather Service monitors the weather for life-threatening dangers such as hurricanes, tornadoes, winter storms, and floods. It provides forecasts for pilots, boaters, water resource managers, utility, industrial, and recreational interests, farmers, and foresters.

To find out more, write or phone:

National Weather Service
1325 E. West Hwy.
Silver Spring, MD 20910
Phone: (301)443-8330

▶ Natural Hazards Research and Applications Information Center

Provides information on: *Natural Disasters, Earthquakes, Hurricanes, Tornadoes, Floods, Volcanos, Weather*

The Center is a national clearinghouse of research information on the economic loss, human suffering, and social disruption caused by earthquakes, floods, hurricanes, and other natural disasters. The Center works to improve communications among research workers, individuals, organizations, and agencies concerned with public action relating to natural hazards. It provides a quick response program to send researchers to the site of disasters soon after their occurrence.

Information for free:

Computer Information Retrieval Services Containing Natural Hazards Literature. 1976. 7 pages. Bibliography.

Natural Hazards Observer. Bimonthly newsletter covering new research and findings.

Information for a fee:

A Selected Annotated Bibliography of Recent Hazards Publications. Annual. $9.

The Environment and Behavior Monograph Series presents research findings on social response to extreme environmental events. $10 for current titles.

The Natural Hazards Research Working Paper Series offers research on people's adjustment to natural hazards. Titles available for $4.50 each include:

Disaster Recovery after Hurricane Hugo in South Carolina. 1991. 105 pages.

Five Views of the Flood Action Plan for Bangladesh. 1992. 37 pages.

Quick Response Research Reports include the following titles:

Community Preparation and Response to the Exxon Oil Spill in Kodiak, Alaska. 1990. 26 pages. $2.75.

Psychological Effects of Disaster on Children and Their Families: Hurricane Hugo and the Loma Prieta Earthquake. 1990. 38 pages. $3.75.

The Center publishes topical bibliographies and other reports.

To find out more, write or phone:

Natural Hazards Research and Applications Information Center
University of Colorado-Boulder
Institute of Behavioral Sciences #6
Campus Box 982
Boulder, CO 80309-0482
Phone: (303)492-6818 or *Fax:* (303)492-6924

▶ Natural Resources Defense Council (NRDC)

Provides information on: *Pollution, Environmental Protection, Hazardous Waste, Air Pollution, Water Pollution, Nuclear Energy, Ozone Depletion, Rain Forest Preservation*

The organization is dedicated to the wise management of natural resources through research, public education, and the development of public policies. NRDC concerns include land use, coastal protection, air and water pollution, nuclear safety and energy production, toxic substances, and protection of wilderness and wildlife.

Information for a fee:

The Amazing L.A. Environment Book. 1991. 147 pages. $8.95.

Cooling the Greenhouse: Vital First Steps to Combat Global Warming. 1989. 72 pages. $6.

Defending the Earth. $7.

An Environmental Agenda for Clean Water: Prevent, Protect, and Enforce. 1991. 10 pages. $1.

Farming in the Greenhouse: What Global Warming Means for American Agriculture. 1989. 34 pages. $7.50.

For Our Kid's Sake: How to Protect Your Child Against Pesticides in Food. 1989. 90 pages. $7.95.

NRDC Earth Action Guides. 8 pages. $1 each. Includes the guides "What You Can Do," "Saving the Ozone Layer," and "Reducing, Recycling, and Rethinking."

Pesticide Alert: A Guide to Pesticides in Fruits and Vegetables. 1987. 180 pages. $8.50.

Phasing Out Nuclear Weapons: A Report to the President and Congress from the Belmont Conference on Nuclear Test Ban Policy. 1989. 81 pages. $6.
The Rainforest Book: How You Can Save the World's Rainforests. 1990. 122 pages. $5.95.

To find out more, write or phone:
Natural Resources Defense Council
40 W. 20th St.
New York, NY 10011
Phone: (212)727-4412 or *Fax:* (212)727-1773

▶ The Nature Conservancy

Provides information on: *Environmental Protection, Rain Forest Preservation, Endangered Species*

The Nature Conservancy is an international organization that preserves plants, animals, and natural communities that represent the diversity of life on earth, by protecting the lands and water they need to survive. The Conservancy relies on a network of data centers that continually collect, verify, and distribute information on the occurences and status of rare species and ecosystems. It operates many protection programs, including Adopt-an-Acre which raises funds from individuals to save rainforests by assisting local organizations and people in their protection efforts.

Information for a fee:
The Nature Conservancy. Bimonthly. $25. Magazine.

To find out more, write or phone:
The Nature Conservancy
1815 N. Lynn St.
Arlington, VA 22209
Phone: (703)841-5300

▶ New York State Center for Hazardous Waste Management

Provides information on: *Hazardous Waste*

The Center conducts research in hazardous waste management. It focuses on developing technology and methods for destroying hazardous waste, treating hazardous waste so it can be safely disposed, reducing hazardous waste, and cleaning up inactive hazardous waste disposal sites. The Center acts as a clearinghouse for technical information by issuing reports and press releases and by acquiring and distributing information.

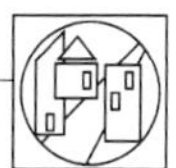

Information for free:

Research and Development Projects, Summary Descriptions.

Waste Management Research Report. 3/year. Each issue focuses on a major area of waste management.

Information for a fee:

Impediments to the Implementation of Alternative Technologies. 1990. $2.

Research and Development in Hazardous Waste Management. 1990. $15. A survey of U.S. centers and institutes.

Technical project summary reports are available for $5 each.

To find out more, write or phone:

New York State Center for Hazardous Waste Management
State Univ. of New York at Buffalo
Jarvis Hall 207
Buffalo, NY 14260
Phone: (716)645-3446

▶ North American Wildlife Foundation

Provides information on: *Animals, Wildlife Management*

The Foundation works to ensure the continuity of effective and practical research of management practices and techniques in order to benefit wildlife and other natural resources. It maintains a library of natural science subjects and wildlife restoration and management.

Information for a fee:

Canvasback of Minnedosa. $5. Handbook.

Managing Your Duck Marsh. $5. Handbook.

To find out more, write or phone:

North American Wildlife Foundation
102 Wilmot Rd., Ste. 410
Deerfield, IL 60015
Phone: (708)940-7776

▶ Nuclear Information and Resource Service (NIRS)

Provides information on: *Nuclear Energy*

NIRS is a national clearinghouse and networking center for people concerned about nuclear power issues. It is dedicated to a sound, non-nuclear energy policy, and serves safe energy and environmental activists with information, resources, and organizational assistance.

Information for a fee:

Alternative Energy Packet. $5. Includes reports, articles, and technical documents on recent developments in renewable and other enery sources.

BRC ("Below Regulatory Concern" Radioactive Waste) Packet. $8. Includes alerts, articles, policies, and NIRS comments on industry and government efforts to deregulate radioactive waste from nuclear power.

Chernobyl Packet. $5. Articles and newsclips relating to the Chernobyl nuclear accident. Includes recent information about the evacuations, the secrecy surrounding the incident, and the health and environmental impact.

Citizens Radiation Monitoring Packet. $10. Information on how to set up a citizen's radiation monitoring network around any nuclear facility.

Global Warming Packet. $5. Includes articles, reports, and other information on global warming, and the greenhouse effect.

"Low Level" Radioactive Waste Packet. $5. Material on commercial radioactive waste, including profiles of past and current dumps, NIRS factsheets, and recent alerts.

NIRS Energy Audit Manual. 1992. $24.95. A guide to conducting energy audits of campus, municipal, and other buildings.

NIRS Factsheets. $.10 each. Offers such titles as "Nuclear Accidents," "Emergency Planning," "Solar Energy," and "Renewable Energy."

The Nuclear Monitor. Biweekly. $20. Newsletter providing timely information on nuclear power, radioactive waste, and sustainable energy news and issues.

To find out more, write or phone:

Nuclear Information and Resource Service
1424 16th St., NW, Ste. 601
Washington, DC 20036
Phone: (202)328-0002 or *Fax:* (202)462-2183

▶ Pacific Basin Consortium for Hazardous Waste Research

Provides information on: *Hazardous Waste, Environmental Protection*

The Consortium addresses the issue of hazardous waste in the Pacific Basin, including waste reduction, treatment, and handling. It seeks to promote technology and information exchange and to develop a network of experts on hazardous waste. The group also maintains information on hazardous waste experts and organizations.

Information for free:

Agroforestry Practices in Vietnam. 1988. 33 pages.

Coastal Zone Activities and Sea Level Rise. 1988. 33 pages.

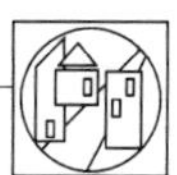

Community Organizations and Government Bureaucracies in Social Forestry. 1990. 51 pages.

East-West Center Program on Environment Newsletter. Quarterly newsletter.

Indigenous Systems of Common Property Forest Management in Nepal. 1989. 23 pages.

Information for a fee:

Environment, Natural Systems, and Development: An Economic Valuation Guide. 1983. 338 pages. $14.95.

The Real and Imagined Role of Culture in Development: Case Studies from Indonesia. 304 pages. $14.95.

Social Forestry in Asia: Factors That Influence Program Implementation. 361 pages. $7.50.

Socialist Economic Development and the Prospects for Economic Reform in Vietnam. 1991. 40 pages. $5.

South Asian Seas: A Review of the Oceanography, Resources, and Environment. 1991. 54 pages. $5.

Villagers, Forests, and Forestry: The Philosophy, Process, and Practice of Community Forestry in Nepal. 212 pages. $15.

To find out more, write or phone:

Pacific Basin Consortium for Hazardous Waste Research
East-West Center Program on Environment
1777 East-West Rd.
Honolulu, HI 96848
Phone: (808)944-7266 or *Fax:* (808)944-7298

▶ Pacific Whale Foundation

Provides information on: *Whales, Endangered Species*

The Pacific Whale Foundation is made up of scientists, conservationists, and volunteers united to prevent the extinction of marine mammals. The foundation's goal is to identify factors that harm the recovery of endangered marine mammals and work to get rid of or change those factors. The Foundation conducts research throughout the Pacific and provides conservation and educational programs involving whales, dolphins, porpoises, and other marine mammals. The group maintains a library of books and other publications on marine mammals and their habitat.

Information for a fee:

Fin and Fluke. Annual. Available with $20 annual membership.

Hawaii Humpback Whales. $15.

Soundings. Semiannual newsletter. Available with $20 annual membership.

To find out more, write or phone:

Pacific Whale Foundation
Kealia Beach Plaza, Ste. 25
101 N. Kihei Rd.
Kihei, HI 96753
Phone: (808)879-8811 or *Fax:* (808)879-2615

▶ Patent and Trademark Office

Provides information on: *Inventors and Inventions*

The Patent and Trademark Office administers the laws regarding patents for inventions. The Office examines applications for patents to determine eligibility, and grants patents when needed. The Office publishes issued patents, and records assignments of patents. It also registers trademarks.

Information for free:

Basic Facts About Patents. Provides a broad overview of the process of obtaining a U.S. patent.

Information for a fee:

General Information Concerning Patents. $2. Gives information concerning the application for and granting of patents.

To find out more, write or phone:

Patent and Trademark Office
U.S. Department of Commerce
Washington, DC 20231
Phone: (703)308-4455

▶ Pet Pride

Provides information on: *Cats*

Pet Pride is a national humane society for cats. It conducts a nonprofit shelter and clinic, and offers public education programs on proper cat care.

Information for free:

Purr-Ress. Quarterly.

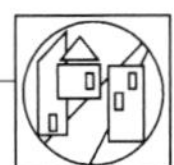

To find out more, write or phone:
Pet Pride
Ruth C. Argust, Pres.
PO Box 1055
Pacific Palisades, CA 90272
Phone: (310)836-5427

▶ Philip's Consumer Electronics Co.

Provides information on: *Future Technology, Electronic/Computer Games, Compact Disc-Interactive*

Philips Consumer Electronics Co. is a pioneer of compact disc-interactive (CD-I) players and discs. CD-I technology allows users to interact with the disc program, receiving responses based on user input.

Information for free:
Compact Disc Interactive Title Library. A catalog of CD-I programs offered by the company. It includes games, such as Backgammon and Connect Four; Music; programs for children; and special features, such as programs on the Smithsonian, Time-Life photography, and gambling at Caesers Palace.

To find out more, write or phone:
Philip's Consumer Electronics Co.
20720 S. Leapwood Ave., Ste. A
Carson, CA 90746
Toll-free: 1-800-845-7301

▶ Plastics Recycling Foundation

Provides information on: *Recycling*

The Foundation is composed of suppliers, manufacturers and users of plastics materials and products. They sponsor research in the recovery and reuse of plastics products (primarily plastic packaging material).

Information for free:
Annual Report.
Plastics Recycling—A Strategic Vision.
Plastics Recycling—From Vision to Reality.

To find out more, write or phone:
Plastics Recycling Foundation
Box 189
Kennett Square, PA 19348
Phone: (215)444-0659

▶ Point Reyes Bird Observatory

Provides information on: *Birds, Endangered Species*

The Observatory studies bird populations with emphasis on reproductive biology, ecology, communities, population monitoring, migratory patterns, environmental problems, endangered and threatened species, and the relationship of seabirds to the marine environment. It also conducts research on marine mammals and sharks.

Information for a fee:
Observer. Quarterly. $2.50/issue.
Also publishes research results in journals and its own monographs and books.

To find out more, write or phone:
Point Reyes Bird Observatory
4990 Shoreline Hwy.
Stinson Beach, CA 94970
Phone: (415)868-1221 or *Fax:* (415)868-1946

▶ Polaroid Corp.

Provides information on: *Recycling, Environmental Protection*

Polaroid Corp. designs, manufactures, and markets worldwide a variety of products, primarily instant cameras and photographic products. Polaroid is active in many areas of environmental concern including waste reduction, energy conservation, and recycling. The company's voluntary Green Lights program requires participants to install energy-efficient lighting in their facilities and to begin waste reduction and recycling programs. Company professionals often lend their expertise to community environmental groups as well.

Information for free:
Report on the Environment. Outlines Polaroid's policies and programs aimed at protecting the environment.

To find out more, write or phone:
Polaroid Corp.
549 Technology Sq.
Cambridge, MA 02139
Phone: (617)577-2000 or *Fax:* (617)577-5618

▶ Rainforest Action Network (RAN)

Provides information on: *Rain Forest Preservation, Environmental Protection*

The Network is concerned with preserving the world's rainforests. It focuses attention on issues including tropical timber, logging and importation, cattle ranching in rainforests, the activities of international development banks, and the rights of people who have historically lived in the rainforest. The Network organizes interested members of the public and sponsors letter writing campaigns, boycotts, and demonstrations; collaborates with other environmental, scientific, and grass roots groups; and aids communication among U.S. and international organizers.

Information for a fee:

Action Alert. Monthly. $25. Bulletin on issues requiring immediate public action. Includes addresses of influential individuals and organizations for members wishing to send letters of protest or support.

World Rainforest Report. Quarterly. $15. Contains progress reports of RAN programs, list of educational materials, and calendar of events. Also publishes fact sheets and distributes teacher's packet and booklet.

To find out more, write or phone:
Rainforest Action Network
450 Sansome St., Ste. 700
San Francisco, CA 94111
Toll-free: 1-800-989-RAIN or *Phone:* (415)398-4404 or *Fax:* (415)398-2732

▶ Rainforest Alliance (RA)

Provides information on: *Rain Forest Preservation, Environmental Protection*

The Rainforest Alliance is an international organization dedicated to the conservation of the world's tropical forests. Its primary mission is to develop and promote sound alternatives to tropical deforestation—opportunities for people to utilize tropical forests without destroying them. The Alliance also educates the public about tropical forests and conducts a media campaign to heighten awareness about the consequences of tropical deforestation.

Information for free:
The Allies in the Rainforest. A Catalog describing RA involvement and programs.
Plants That Give Life. Pamphlet.
Society for the Economic Bounty. Pamphlet.
There is Still Time.

Information for a fee:
The Canopy. Quarterly. $1. Newsletter.

To find out more, write or phone:
Rainforest Alliance
270 Lafayette St., Ste. 512
New York, NY 10012
Phone: (212)941-1900 or *Fax:* (212)941-4986

▶ Reynolds Metals Co.

Provides information on: *Recycling, Environmental Protection*

Reynolds Metals Co. is one of the world's largest fully-integrated aluminum producers. The company is involved in every step of aluminum production. Reynolds also manufactures plastic products, is involved in real estate development, and has interests in gold mining operations. Reynolds helped pioneer the field of consumer aluminum recycling. The company is also involved in various land reclamation and clean air projects.

Information for free:
A Commitment To Environmental Quality. Outlines Reynolds' environmental programs.
Also available are a number of brochures on aluminum recycling.

To find out more, write or phone:
Reynolds Metals Co.
6601 W. Broad St.
Richmond, VA 23230
Phone: (804)281-2000

▶ Society for the Preservation of Birds of Prey

Provides information on: *Birds, Endangered Species*

The Society believes in the strictest possible protection for birds of prey. It educates the public about the role of raptors in the ecosystem, opposes harvesting for falconry and the sale of the captive offspring, and certifies qualified health care facilities. The

Society maintains a collection of literature on raptor subjects, including a division of rare books and special collections.

Information for free:

By-Laws, Handbook for Members. 1984. Outlines Society procedures.

Falconry in America? Read What Some People Have to Say. 1980. Opposition to falconry by experts.

Harmony in Nature. A single-sheet flyer explaining a science lesson for grades 5-7.

List of Books, Papers, Articles on Birds of Prey Comprising a Library Collection. 1985. 24 pages. A list of resource material on a loan basis.

A People's History and the Birds of Prey. 1984. Traces the history of a nation's people and the influence of birds of prey.

The Plain Truth. 1988. Discusses the notion that birds of prey are beneficial.

To find out more, write or phone:

Society for the Preservation of Birds of Prey
J. Richard Hilton, Pres.
PO Box 66070
Los Angeles, CA 90066
Phone: (310)397-8216

▶ South Central Electric Vehicle Consortium (SCEVC)

Provides information on: *Future Technology, Electric Cars*

The Consortium conducts research on advanced electric vehicle technology.

To find out more, write or phone:

South Central Electric Vehicle Consortium
William Craven
238 Wisenbacker Engineering Research Center
College Station, TX 77843-3577
Phone: (409)845-8281 or *Fax:* (409)845-9287

▶ Southwest Parks and Monuments Association

Provides information on: *National Parks*

The Association is a nongovernmental organization founded by National Park Service personnel in the southwestern U.S. The group sponsors research projects on the history and natural history of National Park System areas in the Southwest. It offers literature on the interpretation of archaeology and natural history in national parks and monuments of the Southwest, including booklets for self-guiding trails, information on plants, animals, and birds of the area; and books on Indians, geology, archaeology, ruins, and history.

Information for a fee:

Aztec Ruins National Monument. 16 pages. $2.95. Describes the life of the prehistoric people who built this community.

California Parks Brochure. 50 cents. Brief description of 17 California parks, including 13 park service campgrounds.

Flowers of the Southwest Deserts. $9.95. Identifies plants of Southwestern plateaus.

The Great Encounter: Our National Parks Commemorating the Columbus Quincentennial. 16 pages. $2.95. Booklet documenting Spanish exploration and settlement in the United States.

Horned Lizards, Unique Reptiles of Western North America. 1981. 48 pages. $4.95. Contains evolution, development, and life cycles of lizards.

Poisonous Dwellers of the Desert. 48 pages. $2.50. Gives facts about dangerous insects, snakes, and other creatures.

Those Who Came Before: Southwestern Archeology in the National Park System. 184 pages. $12.95. Describes traditional cultural groups in the Southwest, and discusses national parks and monuments in the region.

The Complete Guide to America's National Parks. $12.95. Gives comprehensive information on the national park system and affiliated areas.

To find out more, write or phone:

Southwest Parks and Monuments Association
221 N. Court Ave.
Tucson, AZ 85701
Phone: (602)622-1999 or *Fax:* (602)623-9519

▶ Spill Control Association of America

Provides information on: *Hazardous Waste, Pollution*

The Association provides information on the oil and hazardous material emergency response and remediation industry's practices, trends, and achievements. It works with local, state, and federal government agencies responsible for laws and regulations regarding pollution caused by oil and hazardous materials, and cooperates in the development of industry programs and efforts so that pollutants are properly controlled and removed from land and water. The group collects and distributes educational and technical information and operates a library.

Information for free:

Spill Briefs. Quarterly. Newsletter covering current information, issues, and regulation regarding hazardous materials, oil spill cleanup, and the response industry.

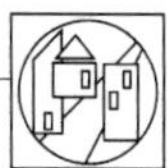

To find out more, write or phone:

Spill Control Association of America
400 Renaissance Center, Ste. 1900
Detroit, MI 48243
Phone: (313)567-0500 or *Fax:* (313)259-8943

▶ State and Territorial Air Pollution Program Administrators (STAPPA) Association of Local Air Pollution Control Officials (ALAPCO)

Provides information on: *Acid Rain, Air Pollution, Environmental Protection, Law*

STAPPA/ALAPCO is a national association of air quality officials in the states and territories and air pollution control officials in more than 165 major metropolitan areas. This group provides a means for members to encourage communication and cooperation among federal, state, and local regulatory agencies. The group promotes air pollution control activities, shares air quality related experiences, and discusses solutions to problems. The association focuses on issues such as acid rain and long-range transportation of air pollution, toxic air pollutants that pose acute or chronic health hazards, motor vehicle emissions, and indoor air pollution in homes and schools.

Information for free:

Comments of STAPPA/ALAPCO on the Administration's Clean Air Proposal. 1989.
Comments of STAPPA/ALAPCO on Conference Issues of the Clean Air Act. 1990.
Controlling Emissions of Nitrogen Oxides from Existing Utility Boilers under Title I of the Clean Air Act: Options and Recommendations. 1992.
Highlights of Global Warming Control and Stratospheric Ozone Protection Activities in Selected States. 1990.
Summary of the Clean Air Act Amendments of 1990. 1990.
Summary of Selected Innovative Ozone and Carbon Monoxide Control Strategies. 1989.
Summary of State Acid Rain Laws. 1986.

Information for a fee:

Air Permit and Emissions Fees. 1987. $15.
State and Local Agency Air Operating Permit Fee Systems Survey. 1992. $10.

To find out more, write or phone:

State and Territorial Air Pollution Program Administrators
Association of Local Air Pollution Control Officials
444 N. Capitol St. NW, Ste. 306
Washington, DC 20001
Phone: (202)624-7864 or *Fax:* (202)624-7863

▶ Student Conservation Association (SCA)

Provides information on: *National Parks, Environmental Protection, Environmental Careers*

The Association consists of individuals and groups working in cooperation with the National Park Service, the U.S. Forest Service, and other federal, state, local, and private agencies that manage public lands and natural resources. SCA offers educational programs for high school and college students and other adults to assist with the stewardship of national parks, forests, and other resource areas. High school participants build and repair structures and trails, and carry out ecological restoration work. College students and other adults assist professionals with wildlife research, wilderness management, environmental education, archaelogical surveys, and other tasks. SCA conducts educational and vocational programs providing job skill training, work experience, and exposure to career options in natural resource fields.

Information for free:

Annual Report.

Conservation Career Development Program. Brochure describing the CCDP program for students interested in conservation work.

SCA Fact Sheet.

Also publishes brochures on high school work groups and the resource assistant program.

To find out more, write or phone:

Student Conservation Association
Scott D. Izzo, Pres.
Box 550
Charlestown, NH 03603
Phone: (603)826-4301 or *Fax:* (603)826-7755

▶ 3M

Provides information on: *Pollution, Environmental Protection*

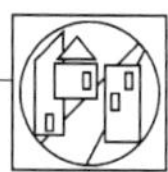

3M (Minnesota Mining and Manufacturing Company) is involved in the research, manufacture, and marketing of home and business products including pressure-sensitive tapes, photographic films, recording tapes, and insulating materials. 3M's environmental efforts focus on pollution prevention. The company's Pollution Prevention Pays (3P) program, introduced in 1975, seeks to eliminate pollution at the source. This is accomplished by reformulating products, modification of the manufacturing process, equipment redesign, and recycling and reuse of waste materials. An updated and expanded 3P program called 3P Plus focuses on long-term scientific research and stepped-up efforts to reduce sources of pollution in the manufacturing process.

Information for free:

Pollution Prevention Pays: Managing for a Better Environment. An information packet describing the 3P program.

To find out more, write or phone:

3M
Jo Ann N. Broom, 3P Program Coordinator
Environmental Engineering and Pollution Control Dept.
PO Box 33331
Bldg. 21-2W
St. Paul, MN 55133
Phone: (612)778-4791

▶ United Professional Horsemen's Association

Provides information on: *Horses*

The Association is made up of professional horse trainers involved in the show horse industry, and horse owners and breeders who work to educate the public about show horses and improve the industry. The Association sponsors a Challenge Cup Equitation Competition, Classics for Three-and Four-Year Olds, Horse Show Awards, Horse of the Year awards, and judges' seminars. It maintains a hall of fame.

To find out more, write or phone:

United Professional Horsemen's Association
Kentucky Horse Park
4059 Iron Works Pike
Lexington, KY 40511
Phone: (606)231-5070 or *Fax:* (606)254-2655

▶ U.S. Department of Energy Office of Conservation and Renewable Energy

Provides information on: *Future Technology*

The Office is responsible for both energy supply and demand technologies for utilities, industry, transportation, and buildings. Supply activities focus on increasing renewable energy resources, while demand programs encourage greater energy efficiency of all resources. Other activities deal with technology transfer, technical assistance, information distribution, and government assistance.

Information for free:

Conservation and Renewable Energy Technologies. Series of illustrated booklets that discuss renewable energy in relation to transportation, industry, buildings, utilities, and technical and financial assistance.

Tomorrow's Energy Today. Energy Efficiency and Renewable Energy. 1992. 15 pages. Booklet. Provides overview of the Office's programs and their goals.

To find out more, write or phone:

U.S. Department of Energy
Office of Conservation and Renewable Energy
1000 Independence Ave., SW
Washington, DC 20585
Toll-free: 1-800-523-2929 or *Phone:* (202)586-9220

▶ U.S. Department of the Interior National Park Service

Provides information on: *National Parks, Travel and Recreation*

The National Park Service is a group of 64 associations devoted to the preservation of the country's national parks.

Information for a fee:

Everglades Wildguide. 112 pages. $5.50. Describes and illustrates the natural interaction of the plant and animal communities in the Everglades of Florida.

Exploring the American West, 1803-1879. 128 pages. $6. Chronicles how the land between the Mississippi River and the Pacific Ocean was explored, surveyed, mapped, and settled.

Great Smoky Mountains National Park. 128 pages. $6. Describes the natural history of the Great Smokies.

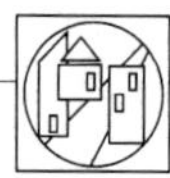

The Life of Isle Royale. 152 pages. $6. Provides the natural history of Isle Royale National Park, emphasizing the relationship of the plants and animals inhabiting this island in Lake Superior.

The National Parks: Camping Guide. 112 pages. $4. Lists more than 100 parks with camping facilities. Includes information on seasons, climatic data, access for disabled persons, and specifics for tent, RV, and backcountry campers.

The National Parks: Lesser-Known Areas. 48 pages. $1.50. Describes more than 170 parks that are little known to the traveling public.

The National Parks: Shaping the System. 128 pages. $4.75. Describes the growth of the National Park Service from its founding in 1916.

Washington DC. 176 pages. $5. A guide to about 110 monuments, memorials, museums, and other sites in and around Washington, DC.

To find out more, write or phone:

U.S. Department of the Interior
National Park Service
1849 C St., NW, Rm. 3104
Washington, DC 20240
Phone: (202)208-6985 or *Fax:* (202)208-7520

▶ U.S. Environmental Protection Agency Public Information Center

Provides information on: *Environmental Protection, Pollution, Acid Rain, Air Quality, Water Pollution, Hazardous Waste, Recycling*

The Public Information Center distributes nontechnical publications on a wide range of environmental topics, including acid rain, air quality, drinking water, gas mileage, indoor air, toxic substances, pesticides, radon, recycling, and wetlands. The center responds to requests from concerned citizens, federal, state, and local agencies, industry, teachers and educators, students, practitioners, researchers, librarians, policymakers, the media, business, community and environmental organizations, and the general public. PIC staff refers technical questions to the appropriate EPA Program Office, clearinghouse, docket, hotline, or other government agencies, provides on-site information services to visitors and EPA personnel, and provides online search service. The center distributes newsletters, brochures, fact sheets, a consumer guide, and educational materials.

Information for free:

America's Wetlands: Our Vital Link Between Land and Water. 1988. 8 pages. Booklet. Explains the value of wetlands, where they're located, and steps taken to protect them.

A Citizen's Guide to Pesticides. 1989.
Environmental Crisis in the Gulf: The U.S. Response.
Environmental Education Materials for Teachers and Young People. 1991.
Environmental Health Risk Education for Youth. 1991.
Glossary of Environmental Terms and Acronym List. 1989.
Is Your Drinking Water Safe? 1989.
The Next Environmental Policy: Preventing Pollution. 1991.
The President's Environmental Youth Awards. 1991.
Recycle. 1988.

Information for a fee:
EPA Journal. $10/year. Magazine. Covers a wide range of environmental topics.

To find out more, write or phone:
U.S. Environmental Protection Agency
Public Information Center
401 M St. SW
PM-211B
Washington, DC 20460
Phone: (202)260-2080 or *Fax:* (202)260-6257

▶ U.S. Geological Survey (USGS)

Provides information on: *Science, Natural Disasters, Earthquakes, Volcanos*

The Geological Survey is one of the federal government's earth science research and fact-finding agencies. Their objectives are to conduct research in geology, hydrology, mapping, and geography; analyze water, energy, and mineral resources; and publish reports and maps.

Information for free:
Guide to Obtaining USGS Information. Describes services provided by USGS information offices.
New Publications of the U.S. Geological Survey. A catalog of new publications released monthly.
Price and Availability List of U.S. Geological Survey Publications. Lists publication number and current price only.

Information for a fee:
Earthquakes and Volcanoes. Bimonthly bulletin. $6.50/year, $1.25/single copy.
Publications of the U.S. Geological Survey. 1991. $4.25.

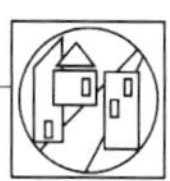

To find out more, write or phone:

U.S. Geological Survey
National Center
12201 Sunrise Valley Dr.
Reston, VA 22092
Phone: (703)648-6892

▶ U.S. Nuclear Regulatory Commission (NRC) Public Document Room (PDR)

Provides information on: *Nuclear Energy*

The Public Document Room processes and stores documents that the Nuclear Regulatory Commission generates or receives. The majority of PDR information pertains to licensing and regulation of nuclear facilities. PDR documents also cover information on NRC meetings, research, nuclear waste, export and import licenses, and other nuclear safety issues. PDR files are open for public use, with on-site reference assistance available. The reference staff responds to telephone, mail, and facsimile requests for information, assists patrons in formulating search strategies and in using the online catalog, and supplies printouts of search results to patrons at no charge. Written requests should be mailed to: U.S. Nuclear Regulatory Commission, Public Document Room, Washington, DC 20555.

Information for free:

Annual Report. 1991. 260 pages. Covers Nuclear Regulatory Commission activities and related events, and lists names and addresses of public document rooms located in each state.

Citizen's Guide to U.S. Nuclear Regulatory Commission Information. Updated periodically. Booklet. Describes the types of NRC information, the ways to obtain it, and services for particular audiences.

U.S. Nuclear Regulatory Commission Public Document Room File Classification System. Periodically updated. Contains detailed descriptions of the file classification system for documents available from the PDR.

Also provides regulatory guides, documents, and inspection reports for $.06 per page.

To find out more, write or phone:

U.S. Nuclear Regulatory Commission
Public Document Room
2120 L St., N.W.
Lower Level
Washington, DC 20037
Phone: (202)634-3273 or *Fax:* (202)634-3343

▶ United States Ultralight Association (USUA)

Provides information on: *Future Technology, Ultralight Flight*

The Association promotes the sport of ultralight aviation. Ultralights are very light, slow planes used for recreational flight. USUA represents members' interests on federal, state, and local levels, keeps members abreast of ultralight advancement, conducts educational programs, and sponsors competitions.

Information for free:
USUA Club List.
USUA Colibri/Observer Information.
USUA Instructor List. Please enclose a self-addressed stamped envelope.

Information for a fee:
Powered Ultralight Flying. $11.
Powered Ultralight Flying Training Course. $10.
Ultralight Aircraft Log. $6.
Ultralight Airmanship. $11.
Ultralight Flight. $14.
Ultralight Pilot Flight Log. $6.
Understanding the Sky: A Sport Pilot's Guide to Flying Conditions. $20.
USUA Guidelines for the Operation of Ultralight Vehicles at Existing Airports. $1.
USUA Instructor Flight Test Guide. $15.

To find out more, write or phone:
United States Ultralight Association
John Ballantyne, Pres.
PO Box 557
Mt. Airy, MD 21771
Phone: (301)898-5000 or *Fax:* (301)898-5846

▶ Virginia Polytechnic Institute and State University Center for the Study of Science in Society

Provides information on: *Science*

The Center conducts research on scientific change, history and philosophy of science and technology, key periods in the history of science, 20th century science and technology, and interaction of science, technology, and society. Research results are published in professional journals, books, and the Center's own publication series.

To find out more, write or phone:
Virginia Polytechnic Institute and State University
Center for the Study of Science in Society
Prof. Robert A. Paterson, Dir.
102 Price House
Blacksburg, VA 24061-0247
Phone: (703)231-7687 or *Fax:* (703)231-7013

▶ Weather Research Center

Provides information on: *Science, Weather, Hurricanes*

The Weather Research Center focuses on meteorology, oceanography, hurricanes, severe weather, and rainfall. Its research results are published in professional journals.

To find out more, write or phone:
Weather Research Center
3227 Audley
Houston, TX 77098
Phone: (713)529-3076

▶ Wild Horses of America Registry (WHAR)

Provides information on: *Horses*

WHAR is a group made of wild horse and burro registries organized to give recognition to America's wild horses removed from public lands. The group's goal is to establish a single program of management, protection, and control of wild horses and burros as called for under the Wild Horse and Burro Act of 1971. It seeks to educate the public on the traits of wild horses and their suitability for show, for trail and endurance riding, and for use as children's horses.

Information for free:
Wild Horse and Burro Diary. Quarterly. A complimentary issue is available.

To find out more, write or phone:
Wild Horses of America Registry
c/o Karen Sussman
6212 E. Sweetwater
Scottsdale, AZ 85254
Phone: (602)991-0273

▶ Wildlife Conservation Fund of America

Provides information on: *Animals, Wildlife Management*

WCFA was founded to protect the heritage of the American sportsman to hunt, fish, and trap; and to protect scientific wildlife management practices. The Fund is the legal defense, information, public education, and research arm of the Wildlife Education Fund of America. It provides legal research and facts about wildlife conservation and management, and maintains a national educational program concerning wildlife conservation.

Information for a fee:
Update. Quarterly. $15/year.

To find out more, write or phone:
Wildlife Conservation Fund of America
801 Kingsmill Pkwy.
Columbus, OH 43229-1137
Phone: (614)888-4868

▶ World Future Society

Provides information on: *Future Technology*

The World Future Society serves as a neutral clearinghouse for ideas about the future, including forecasts, trends, and scenarios. The Society operates the Futurist Bookstore, with over 300 futures-related titles.

To find out more, write or phone:
World Future Society
4916 St. Elmo Ave.
Bethesda, MD 20814
Phone: (301)656-8274 or *Fax:* (301)951-0394

▶ World Wildlife Fund & The Conservation Foundation

Provides information on: *National Parks, Endangered Species, Environmental Protection, Pollution, Ozone Depletion*

The World Wildlife Fund and The Conservation Foundation work to protect endangered wildlife, establish new protected areas, support scientific research, test new approaches for environmentally sound rural development, promote conservation education, and help shape government policy.

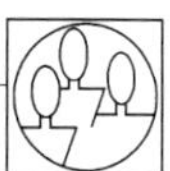

Information for a fee:

Conserving the World's Biological Diversity. 1990. 200 pages. $14.95. Addresses what biodiversity is, why it is important, and how it is threatened by current development and resource exploitation policies.

Environment and the Poor: Strategies for a Common Agenda. 1989. 232 pages. $15.95. Discusses the growing problem of resource depletion and rural poverty.

Getting at the Source: Strategies for Reducing Municipal Solid Waste. 1991. 160 pages. $15. A report presenting the findings of a committee designed to explore opportunities for waste reduction through changes in product design and use.

Great Lakes, Great Legacy? 1990. 345 pages. $20. Explores the destruction and accumulation of toxic chemicals in the Great Lakes basin.

National Parks for a New Generation: Visions, Realities, Prospects. 1985. 407 pages. $19.95. A report examining recent changes undergone by the National Park System, and its challenges ahead.

Ozone Diplomacy: New Directions in Safeguarding the Planet. 1991. 302 pages. $10.95. This publication evaluates the negotiating process of a 1987 international treaty mandating reductions in ozone-depleting chlorofluorocarbons and halons.

Power to Spare: The World Bank and Electricity Conservation. 1988. 67 pages. $12. Analyzes the potential for increased electrical efficiency in developing countries and the role of international lending agencies in financing higher electrical productivity.

WWF Atlas of the Environment. 1990. 192 pages. $19.95. The atlas explains the current environmental and conservation challenges, from population trends to climate protection. It includes more than 200 color maps and diagrams that highlight over 40 concerns and trends.

To find out more, write or phone:

World Wildlife Fund & The Conservation Foundation
1250 24th St., NW
Washington, DC 20037
Phone: (202)293-4800

To Contact People . . .

These books identify individual experts or organizations that can direct you to one.

▶ *The Address Book: How to Reach Anyone Who Is Anyone*

This book can be used to contact more than 3,500 prominent persons including political leaders, business executives, athletes, actors and actresses, artists, musicians,

and writers. The book lists name and address. Names are listed alphabetically.
Biennial. Perigee Books.

▶ *Agricultural and Veterinary Sciences International Who's Who*

Use this source to contact over 8,000 directors and senior staff of research establishments, academic establishments, and international advisory bodies in all areas of agricultural research including animal production, botany, fisheries, and zoology. Entries include name, address, phone, qualifications, biographical data, subjects of major interest, memberships, publications, scientific and research interest, and positions held during past 10 years. Entries are arranged alphabetically.
Triennial. Longman Group UK Ltd.

▶ *Air and Waste Management Association Government Agencies Directory*

Coverage includes United States and Canadian air pollution control and hazardous waste management agencies and personnel at federal, state or provincial, regional, and county levels, and the national sections of the International Joint Commission. Entries include agency name, address, phone, key staff members and their titles, divisions, branches, or offices, and phone numbers. Listings for state and local agencies include number of engineers, number of data analysts, number of public information specialists, and other supplemental personnel by function. Arrangement is by country then level of jurisdiction.
Annual. Air and Waste Management Association.

▶ *American Men and Women of Science*

Use this book to identify more than 125,000 U.S. and Canadian scientists active in the physical, biological, mathematical, computer science, and engineering fields. Entries include name, address, education, personal and career data, memberships, honors and awards, and research interest. Names are arranged alphabetically; indexed by scientific discipline.
Triennial. R.R. Bowker Co.

▶ *American Society of Zoologists—Membership List*

Use this source to locate about 4,000 college and university professors and graduate students in the field of zoology. Entries include name, institution, address, phone, fax, and divisional affiliation. Entries are arranged alphabetically.
Bimonthly. American Society of Zoologists.

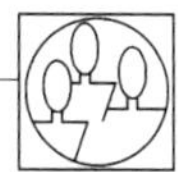

▶ *Aviation, Space, and Environmental Medicine Aerospace Medical Association Directory of Members Issue*

Use this directory to identify 4,200 medical and scientific personnel engaged in aviation, space research, and environmental medicine. The book lists name, address, type of membership, certifications, and specialties. Names are arranged in alphabetical order.
Annual. Aerospace Medical Association.

▶ *Biographical Dictionary of Scientists: Engineers and Inventors*

This book provides information on about 200 engineers and inventors. Entries include name, career, and educational data. Names are arranged in alphabetical order.
Peter Bedrick Books.

▶ *Canadian Who's Who*

This book lists about 12,000 notable Canadians in Canada and abroad based on position or achievement. Entries include name, address, personal and career data.
Annual. University of Toronto Press.

▶ *Cats Magazine—Directory of Cat Breeders Issue*

This issue provides contact information for more than 1,000 cat breeders in the U.S. and Canada. Entries include name of establishment, owner, address, phone, association memberships, breeds and colors in which interested, and other services available. Information is classified by breed, then geographical.
Annual. Cats Magazine, Inc.

▶ *Complete Guide to America's National Parks*

The guide covers approximately 60 areas administered by the National Park Service. Entries include park name, mailing address, driving directions, accessibility information, recreational activities, facilities, description of features and attractions in surrounding area, public transportation available, regional touring guides, and weather information. Arrangement of book is geographical.
Biennial. National Park Foundation.

▶ *Directory of Animal Care and Control Agencies*

Use this directory to locate more than 3,500 animal protection agencies. Canadian and some other foreign agencies are available as well as national and individual state

editions. Entries include agency name, address, and phone. Agencies are listed in geographical order.
Continuously updated. American Humane Association.

▶ *Directory of Paleontologists of the World*

This directory provides information on more than 7,000 paleontologists (scientists who use fossil remains, such as dinosaur bones, to study past geological periods). Entries include name, office address, year of birth, area of specialization or interest, and affiliation. Entries are arranged alphabetically.
1989. International Palaeontological Association.

▶ *Directory of State Waste Management Program Officials*

Use this source to locate approximately 60 state and territorial government agencies that regulate solid waste, recycling, hazardous waste, and Superfund activities. Entries include agency name, address, phone, and names and titles of key personnel. Entries are arranged geographically.
Annual. Association of State and Territorial Solid Waste Management Officials.

▶ *Energy Information Centers Directory*

This directory can be used to contact more than 90 energy information centers located at electric generating plants, research facilities, and other energy-related installations in the United States and Canada. The book lists name of center, address, phone, and type of center. Centers are arranged in geographical order.
1990. U.S. Council for Energy Awareness.

▶ *Environmental Address Book: How to Reach the Environment's Greatest Champions and Worst Offenders*

Coverage includes organizations concerned with the environment. The book also contains a section listing people and organizations whose actions affect the environment positively or negatively. A "Media and Celebrities" chapter lists notable people, newsletters, and television networks concerned with the environment. Entries include organization name and address. The book is arranged by subject.
1991. Perigee Books.

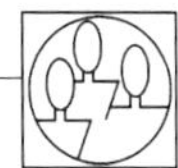

▶ *Guide to Experts in Forestry and Natural Resources*

Use this book to contact approximately 70 consulting scientists and researchers trained in forestry, biology, economics, plant pathology, entomology, and other fields pertaining to natural resource conservation. Entries include personal name, address, and phone. The book is arranged by field of expertise.

1992. Northeastern Forest Experiment Station, Forest Service, United States Department of Agriculture.

▶ *Hazardous Waste Practitioners Directory*

Use this directory to contact 120 engineering firms responsible for designing cleanup solutions for hazardous waste sites. Entries include company name, address, phone, office locations, corporate data, and firm activities. Names are arranged alphabetically.

Annual. Hazardous Waste Action Coalition.

▶ *Horse Industry Directory*

Use this source to contact organizations concerned with all aspects of the horse industry, including the transportation and selling of horses, trail upkeep, rodeos and racing, and services such as veterinary education and licensing. It also includes a list of state horse specialists and state veterinarians. Entries include organization name, address, phone, and names and titles of key personnel. Entries are classified by service.

Annual. American Horse Council.

▶ *International Who's Who*

This book covers 20,000 prominent persons worldwide. Entries include name, nationality, personal and career information, honors, awards, writings, address, and phone. Names are arranged alphabetically.

Annual. Europa Publications Ltd.

▶ *List of Water Pollution Control Administrators*

This book contains information on about 60 water pollution control administrators. Information includes name, title, agency, address, phone, and fax. State administrators are listed in geographic order; regional administrators are listed by name of interstate commission.

Annual. Association of State and Interstate Water Pollution Control Administrators.

▶ *National Weather Service Offices and Stations*

Use this book to contact offices and stations operated by or under the supervision of the National Weather Service. Offices in the United States, Mexico, the Caribbean, Central and South America, and Oceania are included. The book lists station and airport name, type of station, call letters, International Index Number, latitude, longitude, elevation; and number, type, and frequency of weather observations. The book is arranged geographically.

Annual. U.S. National Weather Service.

▶ *Nuclear Regulatory Commission: General Information, Addresses, Phone Numbers, and Personnel Listing*

This directory covers 15 offices of the United States Nuclear Regulatory Commission and approximately 120 nuclear power plants. Entries include building name, and address for NRC offices. For power plants, entries include site name, address, name and phone of backup project director, project director name, phone and licensing assistant, names and phone of resident inspectors and other key personel. Entry arrangement for offices is alphabetical, and for power plants entries are arranged geographically.

Annual. Nuclear Regulatory Commission.

▶ *Ornithological Societies of North America Membership Directory*

This directory can be used to locate 7,000 scientists who study birds and are members of the individual bird societies that make up the Ornithological Societies of North America. Entries include name, address, year of membership, class of membership, and year elected to class. Entries are arranged alphabetically.

Triennial. Wilson Ornithological Society.

▶ *Pure-Bred Dogs American Kennel Gazette List of Clubs Issues*

This publication provides contact information for about 4,000 show-giving and dog obedience clubs. A list of field trial clubs is also published. Entries include club name, name of contact, and address. Entries are arranged in geographic order.

Annual. American Kennel Club.

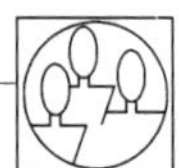

▶ *U.S. Environmental Protection Agency Advisory Committees Charters, Rosters and Accomplishments*

Coverage includes members of the federal advisory committees currently reporting to the Environmental Protection Agency. Entries for members include name and address; rosters also include date term expires. Arrangement of the book is by committee.
Annual. Management and Organization Division, U.S. Environmental Protection Agency.

▶ *Who Is Who in Service to the Earth*

Coverage includes 5,000 individuals, agencies, organizations, and others involved in projects affecting the earth. Entries for individuals include name, organization name, address, phone, fax, and projects. Project entries include name and description.
1991. VisionLink Education Foundation.

▶ *Who's Who in America*

This book contains information on 79,000 people, primarily in the U.S., considered to be of current national interest because of achievement or position. Entries include name, address, personal data, career data, memberships, special achievements, and publications. Names are listed alphabetically; a separate volume indexes people by profession and location.
Biennial. Updated quarterly. Marquis Who's Who.

▶ *Who's Who of American Women*

This book contains information on more than 30,000 high-profile women in all fields. Entries include name, address, personal, educational, and career data, professional association membership, special achievements, awards, and writings. Names are arranged alphabetically.
Biennial. Marquis Who's Who.

▶ *Who's Who in the Biobehavioral Sciences*

Use this book to identify approximately 1,400 professionals in the biobehavioral sciences, including such disciplines as behavioral medicine, psychophysiology, biopsychiatry, health psychology, and holistic medicine. Entries include name, address, credentials, current activities, association membership, and awards or honors. Names are listed in alphabetical order.
Triennial. Research Institute of Psychophysiology.

▶ *Who's Who in Energy Recovery from Waste*

This source covers over 675 individuals, government agencies, institutes and universities, associations, publishers of trade journals and books, public interest groups, manufacturers and distributors of equipment, investment bankers, counselors, and consultants involved in energy recovery from municipal wastes. Entries include organization name, address, phone, and contact name. The book is arranged by type of organization or activity.
1989. National Technical Information Service.

▶ *Who's Who in Environmental Engineering*

Coverage includes about 2,600 licensed professional environmental engineers who have been certified in one or more of seven specialities: air pollution control, general environmental engineering, industrial hygiene, hazardous waste management, radiation protection, solid waste management, and water supply and wastewater. Entries include name, affiliation, address, phone, area of specialization, and biographical data. Names are arranged alphabetically; indexes are arranged geographically and by area of specialization.
Annual. American Academy of Environmental Engineers.

▶ *Who's Who in Ozone*

The publication covers approximately 1,000 member individuals, corporations and medical societies in 35 countries interested in the science, technology, and applications of ozone, particularly in the treatment of drinking water, wastewater, air, and medicine; includes about 700 members in the United States. Listed is each member's name, address, phone, fax, and telex. Arranged geographically.
Annual. International Ozone Association.

▶ *Who's Who in Science and Engineering*

Coverage includes details on 21,000 prominent people in aerospace, microcircuitry, lasers, genetics, biotechnology, and all disciplines of science and engineering. Entries include published works, awards, notable findings, patents, and works in progress.
1992. Marquis Who's Who.

▶ *Who's Who in Technology*

This book contains information on 38,000 engineers, scientists, inventors, and researchers. Entries include name, title, affiliation, address, biographical data, patents, technical field of activity, area of expertise, and other information. Names are arranged

alphabetically.
1989. Gale Research, Inc.

▶ *Who's Who in the World*

This directory covers more than 31,000 people of current international interest because of their achievement or position. Entries include name, address, biographical data, civic activities, awards, writings, and other information. Names are arranged alphabetically.
Biennial. Marquis Who's Who.

▶ *World Directory of Nuclear Utility Management*

Use this source to locate personnel at nuclear utility and nuclear power plants in operation or under construction. Entries include company name, headquarters' addresses, names and titles of key personnel; plant addresses, names of managers and purchasing agents, plant size and type, date of commercial operation, and refuelling cycle. Entries are arranged geographically.
Annual. American Nuclear Society.

8

Education

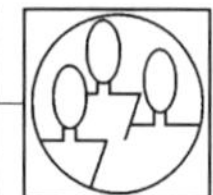

▶ Chapter 8 covers these topics:

College Testing and Entrance Requirements
Dropouts
Gifted and Talented Students
Higher Education
Learning Disabled Students and Learning Disabilities
Scholarships
Vocational Education

▶ Related topics appear in chapters on:

Social Issues; History and Heritage

▶ Ideas for research topics:

Alternative Education Settings for At-Risk Youth
A Comparison of Degree Requirements in State Universities and Private Colleges
Choosing the "Right" College or Training Program
A Comparison of High School Curricula in the U.S. and Japan
The Controversy over Standardized Tests
Coping with School Budget Cuts
Curriculum Differences in U.S. Catholic, Private, and Public School Systems
Differences between U.S. and Japanese Education
Integrating Academic and Vocational Studies
The Role of Vocational Education in Economic Development
Scholarship Programs for Needy Students
The Social Implications of Childhood Bullies
Successful Dropout Prevention Programs
Trends in College Tests Scores in the U.S. from 1970-1990
Uniforms and Dress Codes—Coming Back for New Reasons?
The Variety of Approaches to Gifted Education

▶ Ideas for research topics (continued):

Vocational Options for Students with Learning Disabilities

Vocational Preparation for Students with Limited English Proficiency

Vocational Preparation for Teen Parents

What Do Women's Colleges Offer Their Students?

What is a College Degree Worth?

Which Colleges Are Most Selective and How Do They Choose Students?

Would Education Vouchers Undermine Public Schools?

 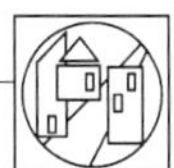

To Contact Organizations . . .

▶ ACCESS ERIC

Provides information on: *Education*

ACCESS ERIC provides reference and referral services for the Educational Resources Information Center (ERIC), a national education network and database for education literature. Topics include educational practices, educational research, and educational resources. ACCESS ERIC staff answers questions, refers callers to subject-specific information sources, offers online access to data found in a number of ERIC directories, and generally acts as a referral service between the ERIC system and its users.

Information for free:

All About ERIC. Booklet that describes ERIC, reference and referral services, searching the database, ordering ERIC documents, and ERIC directories and information products.

ERIC Users' Interchange. Biannual newsletter. Provides users with information on database searching, current ERIC developments, and publication ordering information.

A Pocket Guide to ERIC. Describes the computerized ERIC database, corresponding print publications, and how to use services that provide access to the educational information.

Information for a fee:

Catalog of ERIC Clearinghouse Publications. $8. Lists about 500 current education titles.

To find out more, write or phone:

ACCESS ERIC
Samuel Y. Fustukjian, Exec.Off.
1600 Research Blvd.
Rockville, MD 20850
Toll-free: 1-800-USE-ERIC or *Phone:* (301)251-5045 or *Fax:* (301)251-5212

▶ American Association for Gifted Children

Provides information on: *Gifted and Talented Students*

The Association works to help gifted children reach their potential and use their many talents to benefit others. It encourages understanding on the part of the public about the needs and problems of the gifted and talented through a program of cooperation with community and professional groups.

Information for free:

Insights. 2/year. A publication for students.

Tip Network Newsletter. 2/year. For members, parents, and others dealing with gifted children.

Information for a fee:

College Guide. Annual. $6.50.

Educational Opportunities Guide. Annual $15.00.

To find out more, write or phone:

American Association for Gifted Children
c/o Talent Identification Program
Duke University
1 W. Duke Bldg., Campus Dr.
Durham, NC 27708
Phone: (919)684-3847

▶ American Council on Education

Provides information on: *Higher Education, Sports, Colleges and Universities*

The Council serves as an advocate for adult education and operates a 5,000-volume library on higher education. It provides training, seminars, and workshops, and distributes information on current topics in education.

Information for a fee:

The College Tuition Spiral. 1990. 112 pages. $12.95. Discusses why college tuitions have been increasing at twice the rate of inflation.

The Rules of the Game: Ethics in College Sport. 1989. 224 pages. $19.95. A compilation of 14 chapters by athletic directors, college presidents, coaches, and journalists covering the history of intercollegiate athletics, to minimum academic standards for athletes to racial discrimination, and women in athletics.

Diploma Mills: Degrees of Fraud. 1988. 224 pages. $21.95. Presents the problem of illegitimate colleges and universities and their fraudulent claims.

To find out more, write or phone:

American Council on Education
Library and Information Service
One Dupont Circle, NW, Ste. 670
Washington, DC 20036
Phone: (202)939-9300 or *Fax:* (202)833-4760

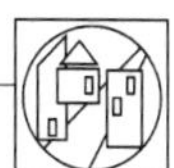

▶ Association for Gifted and Talented Students (AGTS)

Provides information on: *Gifted and Talented Students*

Association members include parents, educators, and other individuals interested in meeting the educational and social needs of gifted and talented students. AGTS members develop and implement extracurricular programs for the gifted and talented. Monitors legislation affecting gifted and talented children and the programs available to them.

Information for a fee:

Gifted-Talented Digest. Quarterly. $20/year. Includes articles of gifted and talented students for parents and teachers; contains student publications.

To find out more, write or phone:

Association for Gifted and Talented Students
Dr. Neil Kestner, Pres.
Northwestern State University
Natchitoches, LA 71497
Phone: (318)357-4572 or *Fax:* (318)357-4223

▶ Center for Academic Precocity

Provides information on: *Gifted and Talented Students*

The Center offers educational facilitation services to students, grades pre-kindergarten through grade 11, who measure high in mathematical or verbal reasoning skills. Research by the Center focuses on longitudinal studies, which follow participants through their academic careers and adulthood.

To find out more, write or phone:

Center for Academic Precocity
Arizona State University
College of Education
Tempe, AZ 85287-2711
Phone: (602)965-4757 or *Fax:* (602)965-9144

▶ Council for Exceptional Children

Provides information on: *Gifted and Talented Students, Learning Disabled Students and Learning Disabilities, Child Abuse, Dropouts, Suicide*

The Council for Exceptional Children is dedicated to improving the quality of education for all exceptional children, both disabled and gifted, and supporting the professionals that serve them. The Council sponsors the ERIC Clearinghouse on Handicapped and Gifted Children, a national, nonprofit clearinghouse for information on children who are mentally gifted, mentally disabled, visually or hearing impaired, physically disabled, learning disabled, and those who have speech or behavioral impairments.

Information for a fee:

Abuse and Neglect of Exceptional Children. 1991. 44 pages. $8.90. Examines the role of the educator in dealing with abused and neglected children.

Alcohol and Other Drugs: Use, Abuse, and Disabilities. 1991. 33 pages. $8.90. Shows evidence that some disabled adolescents are at greater risk for abuse of drugs and alcohol.

College Planning for Gifted Students. 1989. 150 pages. $19.50.

Depression and Suicide: Special Education Students at Risk. 1991. 45 pages. $8.90. Looks at the educator's role in detecting signs of depression and suicide in children.

Flyer File on Gifted Students. 1990. $24. A collection of 21 digests that answer questions about educating gifted and talented children.

Hidden Youth: Dropouts from Special Education. 1991. 37 pages. $8.90. Looks at the characteristics of schools and students that place students at risk for dropout.

Language Minority Students with Disabilities. 1991. 56 pages. $8.90. Examines ways to help.

Reducing Undesirable Behaviors. 1991. 33 pages. $8.90. Describes strategies to minimize undesirable behavior.

Special Health Care in the School. 1991. 56 pages. $8.90. Examines special health care needs of such students as those with traumatic brain injury, HIV, AIDS, and those that need ventilator assistance.

The Council provides custom computer searches, on specific topics, of the computerized Educational Resources Information Center (ERIC) and Exceptional Child Education Resources (ECER) databases. Prices vary depending on request. Also available are ERIC Minisearches, a printout of up to 10 citations with abstracts or up to 25 references without abstracts on a specific topic for $15.

To find out more, write or phone:

Council for Exceptional Children
Jeptha Greer, Dir.
Department of Information Services
1920 Association Dr.
Reston, VA 22091
Phone: (703)264-9474 or *Fax:* (703)264-9494

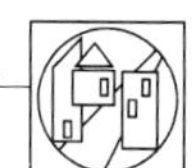

▶ Council for Exceptional Children Division on Career Development

Provides information on: *Learning Disabled Students and Learning Disabilities*

The Division promotes professional growth, research, legislation, and information gathering activities. It encourages interaction among persons and organizations involved in the career development of exceptional individuals.

Information for a fee:
Career Development for Exceptional Individuals. Biannual. $20. Journal.

To find out more, write or phone:

Council for Exceptional Children
Division on Career Development
Dr. Robert Ianacone, Pres.
1920 Association Dr.
Reston, VA 22091-1589
Phone: (703)620-3660 or *Fax:* (703)264-9494

▶ Council for Exceptional Children Division on Mental Retardation

Provides information on: *Learning Disabled Students and Learning Disabilities*

The goal of the Division is to advance education, general welfare, and research in the education of individuals with mental retardation. It promotes competency of teachers of students with mental retardation, public understanding, and legislation needed to accomplish goals.

Information for a fee:
M.R.eport. 3x/year. Included in $12 membership dues.

To find out more, write or phone:

Council for Exceptional Children
Division on Mental Retardation
c/o Dr. Dana M. Anderson
245 Cedar Springs Dr.
Athens, GA 30605
Phone: (404)546-6132 or *Fax:* (404)542-2321

▶ Educational Testing Service (ETS)

Provides information on: *Education, College Testing and Entrance Requirements, Financial Aid*

ETS is devoted to measurement and research, primarily in the field of education. Testing programs are used for school and college admission, student guidance and placement, awarding degree credit for independent or advanced learning, occupational and professional licensing and certification, and continuing education.

Information for free:

Borrowing for Education. Provides detailed information on federal student loan programs.

Common Sense on Preparing for an Admission Test. Addresses the concerns parents and students have about issues related to coaching for admission tests.

Educational Testing Service Publications Catalog. Lists hundreds of educational testing resources including free publications on certification examinations and specialized tests and programs.

Focus 25: Beyond High School: The Transition to Work. Reviews the problems that high school graduates or dropouts face in their transition from school to work.

HBCU-ETS Test-Taking Tip Sheet—General. Provides general test-taking hints and strategies.

Preparing for Tests. Describes admission tests, discusses test preparation, and offers specific tips for test takers.

Information for a fee:

Choice in Montclair, New Jersey. A Policy Information Paper, 1990. $5. Reviews a variety of public school choice programs.

Earning and Learning: The Academic Achievement of High-School Juniors with Jobs. 20 pages. $3. A comparison of working and nonworking high-school juniors' academic performance across five core subject areas.

From School to Work. A Policy Information Report, 1990. $3.50. Discusses student work during high school, skills acquired in the classroom and those needed in the workplace, and the weak linkages between school and the workplace.

To find out more, write or phone:

Educational Testing Service
Marilyn Halpern, Manager
Rosedale Rd.
Princeton, NJ 08541
Phone: (609)734-5686

▶ ERIC Clearinghouse on Adult, Career and Vocational Education (ERIC/ACVE)

Provides information on: *Vocational Education, Literacy, Careers*

ERIC/ACVE collects and distributes information in the following areas of adult and continuing, career, and vocational/technical education: basic literacy training, professional skill upgrading, career awareness, career decisionmaking, career development, career change, experience-based education, industrial arts, corrections education, employment and training programs, youth employment, work experience programs, education/business partnerships, entrepreneurship, adult retraining, rehabilitation for the handicapped, family/intergenerational literacy, dislocation of youth from elementary/secondary education, ethics in the workplace, workplace literacy, preparation for multiple careers, and career development as the fifth basic skill.

Information for free:
A complete listing of "No-Cost Resources" may be obtained from ERIC/AVE's User Services Department on request.
The ERIC File. Quarterly newsletter.
Job-Related Basic Skills. Resource list.
ERIC/ACVE General Information. Pamphlet.
Job Search Methods.
Helping At-Risk Youth Make the School-to-Work Transition.
Jobs in the Future.
Locating Job Information.

Information for a fee:
Retaining At-Risk Students: The Role of Career and Vocational Education. 1988. $6.00. Reviews causes of at-risk status and implications for the U.S. labor force.
Transition, Special Needs, and Vocational Education. 1986. $5.25. Vocational education's role in employment of special needs youth.
School To-Work Transition for At-Risk Youth. 1989. $8.75. Describes process needed for at-risk youth to secure employment and an adult life-style.

To find out more, write or phone:
ERIC Clearinghouse on Adult, Career and Vocational Education
Ohio State Univ.
1900 Kenny Rd.
Columbus, OH 43210-1090
Toll-free: 1-800-848-4815 or *Phone:* (614)292-4353 or *Fax:* (614)292-1260

▶ ERIC Clearinghouse on Higher Education

Provides information on: *Colleges and Universities, Financial Aid, Higher Education*

The Clearinghouse offers literature relating to college and university conditions, problems, programs, and students. Topics of concern to the Clearinghouse include curricular and instructional programs, institutional research, federal programs, professional education (medicine, law, etc.), professional continuing education, collegiate computer-assisted learning and management, graduate education, university extension programs, teaching-learning, legal issues and legislation, and business or industry educational programs leading to a degree.

Information for a fee:

"High Risk" Students in Higher Education: Future Trends. 105 pages. $17. Examines factors affecting minority, female, low-income, and handicapped bachelor's degree students.

Minority Access to Higher Education. 55 pages. $6.50. Looks at the current status of minority enrollment in higher education.

Peer Teaching: To Teach is to Learn Twice. 88 pages. Describes the practice and benefits of using students as teachers.

Raising Academic Standards: A Guide to Learning Improvement. 100 pages. $7.50. Reviews learning improvement programs for postsecondary students.

Renewing Civic Capacity: Preparing Students for Service and Citizenship. 133 pages. $15. Examines the responsibilities of citizenship, its relation to success in a democracy, and the way institutions can help.

The Student as Commuter: Developing a Comprehensive Institutional Response. 101 pages. $15. Points out the need for a response by institutions to the growing number of commuting students.

Student Financial Aid and Women: Equity Dilemma? 153 pages. $10.

Student Goals for College and Courses: A Missing Link in Assessing and Improving Academic Achievement. 119 pages. $15. Looks at the "frequently-overlooked educational goals of students with the expectations of institutions."

Student Retention Strategies. 67 pages. $6.50 Reviews issues of student retention and strategies to improve it.

Student Stress: Effects and Solutions. 115 pages $7.50. Explores stress experienced by students and methods of reducing it.

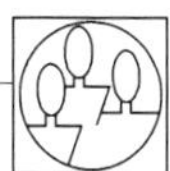

To find out more, write or phone:

ERIC Clearinghouse on Higher Education
George Washington Univ.
1 Dupont Circle, Ste. 630
Washington, DC 20036
Phone: (202)296-2597 or *Fax:* (202)296-8379

▶ ERIC Clearinghouse on Tests, Measurement and Evaluation (ERIC/TM)

Provides information on: *College Testing and Entrance Requirements*

ERIC/TM conducts research, evaluation, and analysis in the behavior and social sciences and is a leader in the plain English movement. ERIC/TM gathers articles, reports, and papers in the areas of testing and other measurement devices, research design, and methodology. It distributes information concerning tests, measurement, and evaluation. ERIC/TM accepts inquiries via telephone, mail, or fax, and provides referrals, computer searches, and search strategy development.

Information for free:

Offers a series of two-page information sheets on current measurement and evaluation topics. Titles include:

Alternatives to Standardize Tests. 1985.
Communicating Scholastic Success. 1989.
Constructing Classroom Achievement Tests. 1989.
Educational Measurement Productivity. 1990.
The GED Testing Program. 1989.
Preparing Students to Take Standardized Achievement Tests. 1989.
Talking to Your High School Students About Standardized Tests. 1989.
The ERIC Clearinghouse on Tests, Measurement, and Evaluation (ERIC/TME): A Growing Resource. 1991. Report.
The ERIC Clearinghouse on Tests, Measurement, and Evaluation Product Catalog. 1992.

Information for a fee:

Assessing Higher Order Thinking Skills. 1986. $7.50. Addresses the testing of higher order thinking skills as a major reform movement.
The Effects of Testing on Teaching and Curriculum in a Large Urban School District. 1984. $6. Describes improvements in instruction-using tests.
Intelligence, Intelligence Testing, and School Practices. 1980. $4.50. A report on intelligence testing as a school practice.
Issues in College Placement. 1990. $12.50. Discusses student placement in communications and mathematics.

Legal Issues in Testing. $3. Describes 10 legal cases and one law dealing with issues of test validity and use.

Measures for Adult Literacy Programs. $19.50. Provides evaluations of 63 assessment instruments.

The Statewide Assessment of Writing. 1985. $7.50. Looks at the current status of writing assessment in each state and includes a state-by-state listing of current writing assessment programs.

To find out more, write or phone:

ERIC Clearinghouse on Tests, Measurement and Evaluation
American Institute for Research
3333 K St., NW, Ste. 200
Washington, DC 20007
Phone: (202)342-5060

▶ Foundation for Exceptional Children (FEC)

Provides information on: *Gifted and Talented Students, Learning Disabled Students and Learning Disabilities*

Foundation members include institutions, agencies, educators, parents, and other persons concerned with the education and personal welfare of gifted or disabled children. FEC activities focus on the educational, vocational, social, and personal needs of the handicapped child and the neglected educational needs of the gifted. The Foundation also seeks funding from public memberships, foundations, and corporate and government grants.

Information for free:

Foundation for Exceptional Children-Focus. Periodic. Newsletter providing information on the foundation's programs, committees, financial support, and board of directors.

To find out more, write or phone:

Foundation for Exceptional Children
1920 Association Dr.
Reston, VA 22091
Phone: (703)620-1054

▶ Gifted Child Society (GCS)

Provides information on: *Gifted and Talented Students, Learning Disabled Students and Learning Disabilities*

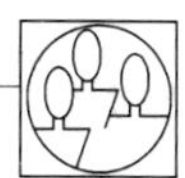

The Society provides educational enrichment and support for gifted children through national advocacy and the Saturday Workshop Program and Summer Super Stars, which offer more than 60 different classes. GCS trains educators to meet the special needs of gifted children, provides assistance to parents facing special challenges in raising gifted children, and seeks public recognition of their special needs. The Society maintains clinical services that offer testing, counseling, remediation, and treatment for underachieving, learning disabled, and other groups of gifted children.

Information for free:
How to Help Your Gifted Child.
Private Sector: New Answers to Old Budget Questions.
Saturday Workshop Activities Catalog. Semiannual.

To find out more, write or phone:

Gifted Child Society
190 Rock Rd.
Glen Rock, NJ 07452
Phone: (201)444-6530

▶ Higher Education Research Institute

Provides information on: *Higher Education, African Americans*

The Institute studies higher education institutions, federal and state policy assessment, minority access to higher education, student and faculty development, retention, and women, leadership, and values in higher education. Survey data is collected on 280,000 freshmen from 600 institutions each fall, and follow-up surveys are conducted after 2-4 years. Research results are published in books, monographs, and articles.

Information for a fee:

The American College Student 1991 Report. 1992. 214 pages. $15. Provides information on the college student experience two and four years after college entry. Covers such issues as student satisfaction and involvement, changing values, and career development.

The American College Teacher. 1990. 104 pages. $12. Provides a profile of teaching faculty at American colleges and universities, covering such issues as job satisfaction and stress.

The American Freshman: Twenty-Five Year Trends. 1991. 192 pages. $25. Provides trends data for entering freshman classes on academic skills, demographics, career plans, and attitudes and values.

The Black Undergraduate: Current Status and Trends in the Characteristics of Freshmen. 1990. 22 pages. $8. This study examines changes in black college freshmen in the past two decades, covering family background, financial aid, self-concept, and career choices.

The Courage and Vision to Experiment. 1991. pages. $10. Provides the results of a study of Hampshire College, an experimenting liberal arts school in Massachusetts.

Predicting College Student Retention. 1989. 110 pages. $8. A practical guide for those interested in predicting student retention.

To find out more, write or phone:

Higher Education Research Institute
University of California, Los Angeles
Graduate School of Education
Los Angeles, CA 90024
Phone: (310)825-1925

▶ Leta Hollingworth Center for the Study and Education of the Gifted

Provides information on: *Gifted and Talented Students*

The Center is involved in the development of curriculum for gifted children, studies on the cognitive styles of gifted children (especially as related to achievement in productive thinking and mathematics), and research on tests and methodology used in the identification of gifted children. The Center responds to inquiries regarding specific studies.

Information for free:

Resources for Parents and Teachers of Gifted Children. Biannual.

To find out more, write or phone:

Leta Hollingworth Center for the Study and Education of the Gifted
Columbia University
Teachers College
Box 170
New York, NY 10027
Phone: (212)678-3851

▶ Law School Admission Council/Law School Admission Services

Provides information on: *College Testing and Entrance Requirements, Law*

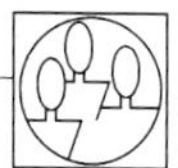

The Council constructs and administers the law school admission test (LSAT). It provides services to law schools in admissions process, and provides information to law school applicants.

Information for free:

LSAT Preparation Tools and Legal Education Books. A list of study-aid books. Includes prices and ordering information.

Information for a fee:

Financing Your Law School Education. $12. A guide to finding the best financial aid program. Includes tips on how to manage debt.

The Official Guide to U.S. Law Schools. $14. Lists 176 U.S. law schools including admission profiles, requirements, and tuition and financial aid facts.

The Official LSAT Prep Book. $15. Contains 100 of each LSAT question type.

Prep Tests. $6 each. Copies of real LSAT tests to use as practice.

Prep Workbooks. $10 each. Separate workbooks for practice on each section (Analytical Reasoning, Logical Reasoning, and Reading Comprehension) of the LSAT.

The Right Law School for You. $11. Contains information on how to apply to law school and how to make your application stand out.

To find out more, write or phone:

Law School Admission Council/Law School Admission Services
PO Box 40
Newtown, PA 18940
Phone: (215)968-1101

▶ Learning Disabilities Association of America (LDA)

Provides information on: *Learning Disabled Students and Learning Disabilities*

LDA's purpose is to define and find solutions for a broad range of learning problems. LDA works to advance the education and general well-being of students who have learning disabilities arising from perceptual, conceptual, or subtle coordinative problems, sometimes accompanied by behavior difficulties. The Association works directly with school systems in planning and implementing programs for early identification and diagnosis of learning disorders.

Information for a fee:

Adolescence and LD (A Time Between). $1.

Attention Deficit Disorder in Teenagers and Young Adults. 1988. $3.

Career Planner: A Guide for Students with Disabilities. 1981. $4.

Dyslexia. What You Can and Can't Do About It. $2.50.

Feeling Good About Yourself: Teens and Self-Esteem. 1988. $1.

From High School to College: Keys to Success for Students With Learning Disabilities. 1988. $19.

List of Colleges/Universities That Accept Students With LD. 1992. $4.

Living with a Learning Disability - A Handbook for High School and College Students. 1986. $3.

The School Survival Guide for Kids with LD - Ways to Make Learning Easier and More Fun. 1991. $11.95.

A Student's Guide to Good Grades. 1990. $14.

Unlocking Potential: College and Other Choices for Learning Disabled People. $12.95.

YES YOU CAN! A Booklet to Help Young People with LD Understand and Help Themselves. 1987. $3.50.

The LDA also publishes directories listing summer camps for LD students and colleges/universities that accept students with LD.

To find out more, write or phone:

Learning Disabilities Association of America
4156 Library Rd.
Pittsburgh, PA 15234
Phone: (412)341-1515 or *Fax:* (412)344-0224

▶ Migrant Dropout Reconnection Program

Provides information on: *Vocational Education, Migrant Workers, Dropouts*

The Program works to increase the number of migrant farmworker youth enrolled in alternative educational or vocational programs. It identifies migrant farmworker youth who have dropped out of the U.S. public education system and offers information on health, educational, financial aid, and career services to them.

Information for free:

Prime Time. 6/year. Newsletter.

To find out more, write or phone:

Migrant Dropout Reconnection Program
c/o Robert Lynch, Dir.
BOCES Geneseo Migrant Center
Holcomb Bldg., Rm. 210
Geneseo, NY 14454
Toll-free: 1-800-245-5681 or *Phone:* (716)245-5681

▶ National Association of Private, Nontraditional Schools and Colleges Clearinghouse and Information Center

Provides information on: *Higher Education, Colleges and Universities*

The Clearinghouse collects and distributes information about private, nontraditional education, including information on program diversity and accreditation status. The Clearinghouse maintains and distributes a listing of private, nontraditional schools.

Information for a fee:
Information and accreditaton brochures, $1 each.
Comparability of California's State Approved Schools and Regionally Accredited Schools. $1.
Comparisons of Traditional and Nontraditional Education. $1.50.
Criterion Compliance Check Sheets. $10.
Degree Programs of Member Institutions. $2.

To find out more, write or phone:
National Association of Private, Nontraditional Schools and Colleges
Clearinghouse and Information Center
182 Thompson Rd.
Grand Junction, CO 81503
Phone: (303)243-5441

▶ National Center for Learning Disabilities

Provides information on: *Learning Disabled Students and Learning Disabilities*

The Center promotes increased public awareness of learning disabilities, provides resources and referrals to volunteers, parents and professionals working with the learning disabled, and develops programs for the learning disabled. They also conduct seminars on topics including grantmaking, legislative advocacy, and employing the learning disabled.

Information for a fee:
Newsletter. 3/year. $3.
Their World. Annual. $10. Magazine.

To find out more, write or phone:
National Center for Learning Disabilities
99 Park Ave., 6th Fl.
New York, NY 10016
Phone: (212)687-7211

▶ National Center for Research in Vocational Education (NCRVE)

Provides information on: *Vocational Education*

NCRVE was established to conduct research and related activities designed to increase the access of all Americans to a high quality of work life. The Center examines and provides information on what students need to know, how best to help them learn it, and how best to use this knowledge in the work place.

Information for free:

The 1992 Agenda for the National Center for Research in Vocational Education. MDS-030.

Tip Sheet for Vocational Education Writers. Pamphlet.

Information for a fee:

CenterWork. Newsletter.

Changes in the Nature and Structure of Work: Implications for Skills and Skill Formation. $6.50. Paper is an analysis of how changes in the economy and workplace are affecting the skills required on the job and the institutional processes through which these skills are acquired.

The Directory of Human Resources to Better Serve Learners with Special Needs in Vocational Education. 50 cents. Contains names and addresses of contact persons in state and national agencies, associations, and organizations.

Exemplary Urban Career-Oriented Secondary School Programs. $13.00. Contains case studies on nine successful inner-city secondary programs in New York City, Chicago, and Los Angeles which have specialties related to specific industries.

Increasing Vocational Options for Students with Learning Handicaps. $5. Recommendations on specific ways vocational options for students with learning handicaps can be improved are based on an examination of 30 exemplary programs in six states.

New Limits to Growth: Economic Transformation and Occupational Education. $5.50. Paper analyzes the issue of employers being squeezed between their growing need for skilled employees and the shrinking supply of well-educated people entering the workforce.

Participation of Special Education Students in High School Vocational Education: The Influence of School Characteristics. $5. Study describing the features of schools that provide vocational training to large proportions of their special education students.

Resources to Facilitate the Transition of Learners with Special Needs from School-To-Work or Postsecondary Education. $6.

Separating the Wheat from the Chaff: The Role of Vocational Education in Economic Development. $4. Paper outlines different conceptions of economic development and indicates when vocational programs might have positive effects on employment, wages, and productivity.

To find out more, write or phone:

National Center for Research in Vocational Education
Univ. of California at Berkeley
1995 Univ. Ave., Ste. 375
Berkeley, CA 94704-1058
Toll-free: 1-800-762-4093 or *Phone:* (510)642-4004 or *Fax:* (510)642-2124

▶ National Center for Youth with Disabilities

Provides information on: *Learning Disabled Students and Learning Disabilities*

The Center works to improve the health and social functioning of young people with disabilities. The organization distributes information, provides technical assistance and consultation, and increases coordination of services between the health care system and others.

Information for free:

Connections. Quarterly. Newsletter. Contains current information, features, and statistics pertaining to youth with disabilities.

To find out more, write or phone:

National Center for Youth with Disabilities
University of Minnesota
Box 721-UMHC
Harvard St. at East River Rd.
Minneapolis, MN 55455
Toll-free: 1-800-333-6293 or *Phone:* (612)626-2825

▶ National Coalition Against Censorship

Provides information on: *Censorship, Freedom of Speech, Student and Teacher Rights*

The Coalition serves as a clearinghouse on book-banning litigation in public schools. Its members include religious, educational, professional, artistic, and labor and civil rights groups. The Coalition collects and distributes information about censorship efforts throughout the country, working with organizations, individuals, and the media. Other activities include conducting meetings for discussion and debate of First Amendment issues, sponsoring major conferences on freedom of expression, and providing a wide variety of educational materials and programming resources to professionals and the public.

Information for a fee:

Newsletter. Quarterly. $25/year.

To find out more, write or phone:

National Coalition Against Censorship
275 7th Ave., 20th Fl.
New York, NY 10001
Phone: (212)807-6222 or *Fax:* (212)807-6245

▶ National Dropout Prevention Center

Provides information on: *Dropouts*

The Center is dedicated to reducing the dropout rate in schools. It works to identify youth at risk, restructure the schooling process, increase access to education and employment, and heighten public consciousness. The Center acquires and organizes information related to dropout prevention through a collection of databases containing prevention program profiles, calendar of events, statistics, and related contacts.

Information for free:

The Focus Database. The Nation's Premier Resource in Dropout Prevention. Brochure. Overview of database of information related to working with students who may drop out of school.

Partnerships: The Keystone of Dropout Prevention. Brochure. Highlights the effectiveness of public/private partnerships in meeting the needs of youth at risk. Additional programs and strategies are outlined in other free brochures.

Information for a fee:

Alternative Education. 1991. Monograph. $8.50. Discusses alternative education settings.

Effective Strategies for Dropout Prevention. 1990. Monograph. $2.50. Analysis of dropout prevention programs.

How to Indentify At-Risk Students. 1989. Report. $2.50.

School—Community—Partnerships: Building Foundations for Dropout Prevention. 1990. Monograph. $8.50.

Self-Esteem: The Key to Student Success. 1990. Report. $2.50. Discusses raising self-esteem as a component of dropout prevention.

Service Learning: Meeting the Needs of Youth at Risk. 1992. Monograph. $8.00.

To find out more, write or phone:

National Dropout Prevention Center
205 Martin St.
Clemson, SC 29634
Toll-free: 1-800-443-6392 or *Phone:* (803)656-2599

▶ National Medical Fellowships (NMF)

Provides information on: *Financial Aid, Asian Americans, African Americans, Hispanic Americans, Native Americans*

NMF promotes education of minority students in medicine, conducts a financial assistance program for first- and second-year minority medical students who are U.S. citizens, and conducts workshops in financial planning and management for medical and premedical students, administrators, and parents.

Information for free:
Annual Report.
NMF Update. Annual.

Information for a fee:
Informed Decision Making. 1988. $10.

To find out more, write or phone:
National Medical Fellowships
Leon Johnson Jr., Pres.
254 W. 31st St., 7th Fl.
New York, NY 10001
Phone: (212)714-0933 or *Fax:* (212)239-9718

▶ National Organization on Legal Problems of Education (NOLPE)

Provides information on: *Law, Student and Teacher Rights*

NOLPE is an independent organization that gathers and distributes information about current issues in school law. NOLPE's purpose is to improve education by encouraging understanding of the legal framework of education and the rights of students, parents, school boards, and school employees.

Information for a fee:
Education Law Update. Price ranges from $14.95 to $19.95. A compilation of papers by national experts in school law.
Search and Seizure in the Public Schools. $9.95. A monograph containing information on students' rights and the Fourth Amendment, police and school officials involvement, drug testing, and state or local standards that affect court rulings.

To find out more, write or phone:

National Organization on Legal Problems of Education
Southwest Plaza Building, Ste. 233
3601 SW 29th
Topeka, KS 66614
Phone: (913)273-3550 or *Fax:* (913)273-0423

▶ National Registration Center for Study Abroad (NRCSA)

Provides information on: *Higher Education*

NRCSA serves as a clearinghouse for study abroad and maintains information on schools in 40 countries. The Center responds to inquiries from people of all ages who wish to study in a foreign country, often to learn the native language.

Information for free:

New Horizons. Newsletter. Contains listing of foreign schools and prices.
The Worldwide Classroom. International program directory describing schools, curriculum, fees, and dates.

To find out more, write or phone:

National Registration Center for Study Abroad
823 N. 2nd St.
PO Box 1393
Milwaukee, WI 53201
Phone: (414)278-0631 or *Fax:* (414)271-8884

▶ National Research Center on Student Learning

Provides information on: *Education*

The Center concentrates on educational research that supports efforts to improve reasoning and problem solving skills of all students.

Information for a fee:

Research results are published in books and journals of psychology, education, and other disciplines.
The Center maintains a series of reprints and technical reports.
Publications List. $4.

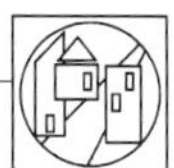

To find out more, write or phone:

National Research Center on Student Learning
University of Pittsburgh
3939 O'Hara St.
Pittsburgh, PA 15260
Phone: (412)624-7450 or *Fax:* (412)624-9149

▶ Southeastern Regional Office National Scholarship Service and Fund for Negro Students (SERO-NSSFN)

Provides information on: *African Americans, Scholarships*

The organization maintains a free college advisory and referral service for interested students and those enrolled in Talent Search and Upward Bound projects. It sponsors annual Student-College Interview Sessions and workshops for guidance and admissions counselors (dates and sites available upon request), and offers a database of student mailing lists for higher education institutions.

Information for free:
Brochures.

To find out more, write or phone:

Southeastern Regional Office National Scholarship Service and Fund for Negro Students
965 Martin Luther King, Jr. Dr., NW
Atlanta, GA 30314
Phone: (404)577-3990 or *Fax:* (404)577-4102

▶ Technical Assistance for Special Populations Program (TASPP)

Provides information on: *Vocational Education, Learning Disabled Students and Learning Disabilities*

TASPP is part of the National Center for Research in Vocational Education (Univ. of California at Berkeley). Located at the Univ. of Illinois, TASPP is designed to assist in the improvement of vocational education programs for special needs youth and adults. Its goals are to provide resource and referral services, to support networks of professionals serving the vocational education needs of special groups, and to provide technical assistance on selected topics or problems crucial to improving the quality of vocational education programs provided to special populations. The organization responds to requests for information regarding vocational programs for special populations. TASPP performs computerized information searches at no charge.

Information for free:

The 1990 Agenda for the National Center for Research in Vocational Education. Contains summaries of the 1990 research and service activities of the Center.

Human Resource Directory. Lists staff names, phone numbers, and areas of expertise.

TASPP Bulletin. 2/year. Newsletter covering issues related to vocational programs for special groups.

Tip Sheet for Vocational Education Writers. An introduction to the Center's agenda and selected research findings.

Information for a fee:

The Directory of Human Resources to Better Serve Learners with Special Needs in Vocational Education. $.50 Contains names and addresses of contact persons in state and national agencies and organizations.

Increasing Vocational Options for Students with Learning Handicaps. $5. Recommends ways vocational options for learning-disabled students can be improved.

Separating the Wheat from the Chaff: The Role of Vocational Education in Economic Development. $4. Outlines when vocational programs might have positive effects on employment, wages and productivity.

Students at Risk: Selected Resources for Vocational Preparation. $2.75. A resource guide containing publications, agencies, clearinghouses, and newsletters for those who serve at-risk students.

Students with Limited English Proficiency: Selected Resources for Vocational Preparation. $2.50. Lists publications, agencies, clearinghouses, and newsletters for limited-English proficient people.

Teen Parents: Selected Resources for Vocational Preparation. $2.25. Contains information and resources of interest to teen parents.

Vocational Preparation and General Education. $6.25. Paper about the collaboration of teaching in academic and vocational fields.

Vocational Teacher Education: A Context for the Future. $5. Discusses the effects of reforms in teacher education upon vocational teacher education.

Who Gets What and Why: Curriculum Decision-Making at Three Comprehensive High Schools. $5. Presents case studies of three high schools to learn how high school administrators, teachers, counselors, and students view the course offerings, student placement, and counseling processes at their schools.

To find out more, write or phone:

Technical Assistance for Special Populations Program
Carolyn Maddy-Bernstein, Exec.Off.
University of Illinois
National Center for Research in Vocational Education
345 Education Bldg.
1310 S. 6th
Champaign, IL 61820
Phone: (217)333-0807 or *Fax:* (217)333-5847

▶ United Negro College Fund (UNCF)

Provides information on: *African Americans, Higher Education*

UNCF is a fundraising agency for historically Black private colleges and universities and graduate and professional schools, all of which are private and fully accredited. The UNCF Department of Educational Services offers information on a broad range of educational and administrative programs.

Information for free:

Statistical Research Report. 91 pages. Covers the areas of enrollment, degrees, faculty and staff, student financial aid, and institutional finances.
UNCF Annual Report. 25 pages.

Information for a fee:

A Mind Is. 2-3/year. $3.50/single issue, $10/year. Magazine.
Also publishes government affairs, research, and statistical reports.

To find out more, write or phone:

United Negro College Fund
500 E. 62nd St.
New York, NY 10021
Phone: (212)326-1118

▶ United Student Aid Funds (USA FUNDS)

Provides information on: *Financial Aid*

This private, nonprofit corporation was organized to provide financial aid for students and their parents by guaranteeing low-cost loans. USA FUNDS operates in all 50 states, Puerto Rico, Pacific Trust Territories, and the Virgin Islands. Some 8,000 lenders and nearly 10,000 institutions of higher education participate in its programs, and loans are guaranteed through several different programs. Contributions from corporations and foundations help meet operating expenses, supplement reserves, and launch new programs.

Information for free:
Publishes an annual report and pamphlets.

To find out more, write or phone:
United Student Aid Funds
11100 USA Pkwy.
Fishers, IN 46038
Toll-free: 1-800-824-7044 or *Phone:* (317)849-6510

▶ University Evaluation and Examination Service

Provides information on: *College Testing and Entrance Requirements*

The Service duplicates, scores, and analyzes course examinations. It also assists faculty in developing and improving classroom tests, conducts institutional research projects, provides consulting services on questionnaire and survey design, and administers University tests for entering students.

To find out more, write or phone:
University Evaluation and Examination Service
University of Iowa
300 Jefferson Bldg.
129 E. Washington St.
Iowa City, IA 52242
Phone: (319)335-0356

▶ Vocational Industrial Clubs of America (VICA)

Provides information on: *Vocational Education*

VICA is made up of young people in state associations and local chapters of trade, industrial, technical and health occupations programs in high schools, area vocational schools, and junior and community colleges in the U.S., the Virgin Islands, Puerto Rico, and Canada. The organization promotes high standards of workmanship, scholarship, and trade ethics. The group develops students' leadership abilities and sense of civic responsibility, promotes industrial safety, and encourages cooperation of students, teachers, community leaders, labor, and business.

Information for a fee:
VICA Health Occupational Link. Biannual. Included in $5 student membership dues.

VICA Journal. Quarterly. $8/year. Tabloid for vocational students. Includes information on education and job and personal development skills. Lists VICA award winners.

VICA Professional: VP. 8/year. $1/single issue, or subscription included in $5 student membership dues. Also publishes curriculum material and brochures.

To find out more, write or phone:

Vocational Industrial Clubs of America
PO Box 3000
Leesburg, VA 22075
Toll-free: 1-800-321-VICA or *Phone:* (703)777-8810 or *Fax:* (703)777-8999

▶ Western Interstate Commission for Higher Education (WICHE)

Provides information on: *Higher Education*

The Commission is concerned with higher education and human resource issues, including mental health, high school graduate statistics, college tuition and fees in the western region, and minority enrollment and achievement. WICHE offers a student exchange program, educational telecommunications program, mental health program, operates a library of 3,500 volumes on higher education, and publishes research results.

Information for free:

1991 Annual Report. Highlights project activities, publications, grant awards, services, and membership during the previous fiscal year.

Enrollment Limits: A Response to Quality and Financial Concerns in Higher Education. 1991. A report examining policies and practices in states with limited enrollments.

Ethnic Minority Mental Health Workforce Projects/Publications. 1988. 32 pages. Provides abstracts of reports on ethnic minority issues.

Evolving Partnerships: Higher Education and the Rural West. 1990. Addresses the issue of higher education's role in the revitalization of the West.

Initiatives in Teacher Education Reform. 1990. Report looking at changes in teacher education programs.

Keeping the Promise: Access and Quality in a New Ecomonic Era. 1992. A discussion of how public colleges and universities can provide affordable and quality education.

Professional Student-Exchange Program: Academic Years 1992-1994. 1991. Schools and programs are listed, and application and eligibility procedures are explained.

State-University Efforts to Improve State Hospital Nursing: A Progress Report. 1988. Describes a plan of action for collaboration between nursing professionals and nursing educators.

Western Undergraduate Exchange Bulletin. 1992. Brochure describing opportunities available and listing schools and programs.

WICHE HRD Network. Quarterly. Newsletter focusing on mental health human resource development issues.

Information for a fee:

The Changing Role of Nurses in State Hospitals. 1987. $10. Discusses the impact of state hospital changes on nursing and nursing education in the West.

The Changing Role of the State Hospital. 1987. $10. Examines the state hospital's changing role in patient care.

A Crucial Agenda: Making Colleges and Universities Work Better for Minority Students. 1989. $10. Examines minority access and achievement.

Overcoming Failure: Program Models for Treatment of Severely Emotionally Disturbed Youth. 1982. $7.

The Road to College: Educational Progress by Race and Ethnicity. 1991. 112 pages $20. Studies the grade-by-grade progress of school children by racial or ethnic identification.

Setting the Agenda: Reform and Renewal in Undergraduate Education. 1989. $8.

Tuition and Fees in Public Higher Education in the West. Annual. $15. Lists tuition and fees for all public two-and four-year colleges and universities in 16 western states.

Also offers video and audio resources.

To find out more, write or phone:

Western Interstate Commission for Higher Education
PO Drawer P
Boulder, CO 80301-9752
Phone: (303)541-0200 or *Fax:* (303)497-2091

To Contact People . . .

These books identify individual experts or organizations that can direct you to one.

▶ *American Educational Research Association—Biographical Membership Directory*

The directory covers over 15,000 individuals involved in educational research and development. Entries are arranged alphabetically.

1991. American Educational Research Association.

▶ *Black Student's Guide to Scholarship*

Use this guide to contact providers of financial aid for Black students pursuing a college education. The book lists organization name, address, phone, name and title of contact, eligibility requirements, and description of award or grant. Information is arranged by category.
1991. Beckham House Publishers, Inc.

▶ *Canadian Who's Who*

This book lists about 12,000 notable Canadians in Canada and abroad based on position or achievement. Entries include name, address, personal and career data.
Annual. University of Toronto Press.

▶ *Council for Educational Development and Research—Directory*

The directory covers about 15 member educational research and development institutions; appendixes list key personnel of the Office of Educational Research and Improvement and the Department of Education. Organizations are arranged alphabetically; personnel are arranged by department or agency.
1991. Council for Educational Development and Research.

▶ *Directory of Facilities and Services for the Learning Disabled*

Use this book to contact some 500 facilities that help children and adults with diagnosed learning disabilities. The book also lists publishers and producers of books and other materials, organizations and agencies, special education clearinghouses, and educational software networks and distributors. For facilities, the book lists name, address, phone, name of director, number of staff, and information describing the facility. For other listings, the book provides name, address, and phone. Entries are arranged geographically.
Biennial. Academic Therapy Publications.

▶ *International Who's Who*

This book covers 20,000 prominent persons worldwide. Entries include name, nationality, personal and career information, honors, awards, writings, address, and phone. Names are arranged alphabetically.
Annual. Europa Publications Ltd.

▶ *Learning Disabilities: National Information and Advocacy Organizations*

The publication contains approximately 20 national information and advocacy organizations for learning-disabled youths and adults, their families, and professionals who serve them; approximately 55 publishers and distributors of books, periodicals, magazines, and other literature on the learning-disabled and those who serve them; and over 100 state-level agencies that administer public programs providing special education and rehabilitation for learning disabled persons. National organizations are arranged alphabetically; publishers and distributors are arranged alphabetically by author/editor name; and state organizations are arranged geographically.
1990. Library of Congress, National Library Service for the Blind and Physically Handicapped.

▶ *National Association of College Deans, Registrars and Admissions Officers Directory*

Use this book to contact some 325 deans, registrars, and admissions officers at nearly 90 predominantly Black schools. The book lists institution name, address, phone, names and titles of key personnel, enrollment, and whether a public or private institution. Names are arranged alphabetically.
Annual. National Association of College Deans, Registrars and Admissions Officers.

▶ *Scholarship Book: The Complete Guide to Private Scholarships, Grants, and Loans for Undergraduates*

The book includes information on 1,700 scholarships, fellowships, loans, and grants available to undergraduate students. The entries include program name, sponsoring organization name, address, phone, subject areas, number of scholarships and dollar amount, and application requirements. The guide is classified by subject.
Annual. Prentice Hall Press.

▶ *Scholarships, Fellowships, and Loans*

This book lists more than 3,000 scholarship funds. Entries include name of administering organization, address, description of program, qualifications necessary, selection criteria, available funds, fields for which scholarship is available, and application details. The book is arranged alphabetically by organization.
Biennial. Gale Research Inc.

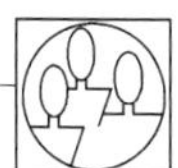

▶ *School Shop/Tech Directions—Directory of Federal and State Officials Issue*

The directory includes federal and state officials concerned with vocational, technical, industrial trade, and technology education in the United States and Canada. Entries are arranged by agency.

1992. Prakken Publications, Inc.

▶ *Who's Who in America*

This book contains information on 79,000 people, primarily in the U.S., considered to be of current national interest because of achievement or position. Entries include name, address, personal data, career data, memberships, special achievements, and publications. Names are listed alphabetically; a separate volume indexes people by profession and location.

Biennial. Updated quarterly. Marquis Who's Who.

▶ *Who's Who in American Education*

The publication covers approximately 20,000 leaders in the field of education. Entries are arranged alphabetically.

1992. National Reference Institute.

▶ *Who's Who of American Women*

This book contains information on more than 30,000 high-profile women in all fields. Entries include name, address, personal, educational, and career data, professional association membership, special achievements, awards, and writings. Names are arranged alphabetically.

Biennial. Marquis Who's Who.

▶ *Who's Who in the World*

This directory covers more than 31,000 people of current international interest because of their achievement or position. Entries include name, address, biographical data, civic activities, awards, writings, and other information. Names are arranged alphabetically.

Biennial. Marquis Who's Who.

9 Arts and Entertainment

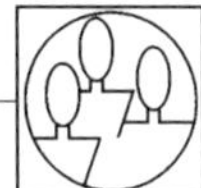

▶ Chapter 9 covers these topics:

Advertising
Cartoons
Celebrities
Effects of Television on Children
Film
Magazines
Media
Music
Performing Arts
Role-Playing Games
Sports
Television
Television Violence
Theater
Travel and Recreation
Women and Minorities: Depiction in the Media
Women and Minorities: Job Opportunities in the Media

▶ Related topics appear in chapters on:

Beliefs, Cults, and Sects; Government and Public Affairs; Social Issues

▶ Ideas for research topics:

For the Love of Oprah: The American Affair with Talk Shows
The American Obsession with Sports
Arguments For and Against the Colorization of Classic Films
The Changing Standards for Prime-Time Television
The Decline of the Theater in Modern Society
Depictions of Women and Minorities in the Media
The Effects of Mass Media on Primitive Cultures
Effects of Television Violence on Children
The Effects of the Videocassette Recorder on Movie Theater Ticket Sales
The Emergence of Prime-Time Black Family Sit-Coms
Glamorous Depictions of Smoking in Advertisements
The Importance of Media Coverage on Political Campaigns
The Importance of the Travel Industry to the Economy

▶ Ideas for research topics (continued):

The Influence of MTV on Fashion for Young People
The Influence of Music Lyrics on Teenagers
The Long-Term Effects of Little League Sports Participation
Media and Sports Figures: Have They Replaced Parents as Role Models?
Movie Ratings: Who Decides Who Can Watch What?
Obsessions with Stars: How Far Will Some Fans Go?
The Occurrence of Violent Acts in Children's Cartoons
Political Stances of Major American Newspapers
Pros and Cons of Government Regulation of Cable Television
The Strong Messages of Political Cartoons
Successful Sit-Coms throughout Television History
The Tabloids: Exposing the Private Lives of Public Figures
Television Cameras in the Courtrooms
Television Watching Trends in the U.S.
Tipper Gore and the Parents' Music Resource Center
The Use of Sports Figures in Advertising
Implications of Virtual Reality
What the Advent of High Definition Television Will Mean to the Industry

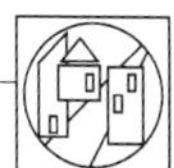

To Contact Organizations . . .

▶ A&E

Provides information on: *Television*

A&E, also known as the Arts and Entertainment Network, is a cable television network that is owned by Hearst, Capital Cities/ABC, Inc., and NBC, and provides comedy, drama, documentary, and performing arts programming. Letters about specific shows will be forwarded to their producers or staff.

To find out more, write or phone:

A&E
235 E. 45th St.
New York, NY 10017
Phone: (212)210-1328 or *Fax:* (212)949-7147

▶ ABC

Provides information on: *Television*

ABC, also known as the American Broadcasting Companies, Inc., is a major television network that provides news, sports, and entertainment programming. It is owned by Capitol Cities/ABC, Inc. Letters about specific shows will be forwarded to their producers or staff.

To find out more, write or phone:

ABC
77 W. 66th St.
New York, NY 10023-6298
Phone: (212)456-7777

▶ Academy of Family Films and Family Television

Provides information on: *Television, Film*

The Academy works to encourage and promote the arts and sciences of family entertainment. The Academy, made up of concerned individuals and groups, holds an annual awards ceremony to recognize television and film stars' contributions to family entertainment.

Information for free:
Newsletter. Quarterly.

To find out more, write or phone:
Academy of Family Films and Family Television
334 W. 54th St.
Los Angeles, CA 90037
Phone: (213)752-5811

▶ Academy of Motion Picture Arts and Sciences

Provides information on: *Film, Entertainers*

The Academy presents Oscar Awards for best picture, actress, actor, and many other categories; it also bestows student film awards. The Academy operates the National Film Information Service, providing historical and bibliographical information on the film industry and related topics. The Academy will not respond to fan mail or photo requests.

To find out more, write or phone:
Academy of Motion Picture Arts and Sciences
8949 Wilshire Blvd.
Beverly Hills, CA 90211
Phone: (310)247-3000 or *Fax:* (310)859-9619

▶ Academy of Television Arts and Sciences

Provides information on: *Television*

The Academy aims to advance the arts and sciences of television through services to the industry in education, preservation of television programs, and information and community relations. It works to foster creative leadership in the television industry. The organization presents the annual Primetime Emmy Awards, Los Angeles Area Emmy Awards, and Student Video Awards for outstanding achievement in the broadcasting industry. It sponsors the Television Academy Hall of Fame and maintains a library on television credits and historical material, the Television Academy Archives, and archives at UCLA of over 35,000 television programs. The group offers internships to students.

Information for a fee:
Emmy Magazine. Bimonthly. $23/year. General interest magazine of the television industry. Includes interviews, book reviews, and articles covering new technology and old shows.

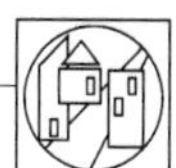

To find out more, write or phone:

Academy of Television Arts and Sciences
5220 Lankershim Blvd.
North Hollywood, CA 91601
Phone: (818)754-2800

▶ American Council for the Arts (ACA)

Provides information on: *Artists, Music, Performing Arts, Dance, Theater, Performing Arts Careers*

The Council was established to support and improve all the arts. It works to define and confront significant issues facing the field, including the needs of individual/originating artists, public and private support for the arts, arts education, cultural pluralism, and international cultural relations. ACA develops and distributes information for use by artists to improve their living conditions. It also works to provide information to arts administrators, arts patrons and policy makers, and others interested in the arts. The Council publishes trade and professional books and newsletters.

Information for a fee:

Arguing for Music/Arguing for Culture. 320 pages. 1990. $24.95. Discusses music in America today, the problems of new opera, performing and performers, and making culture possible.

How to Survive and Prosper as an Artist: A Complete Guide to Career Management. 1988. 194 pages. $9.95. Covers law, insurance, accounting, resumes, presentations, and public relations.

National Directory of Multi-Cultural Arts Organizations 1990. 190 pages. $15. Identifies nearly 1,200 organizations, listing names and addresses, the art form(s) and population group(s) served, and services offered.

Our Government and the Arts: A Perspective From the Inside. 1988. 554 pages $16.95.

The Status of Arts Education in American Public Schools. 1991. 270 pages. $15.95. A survey on music, visual arts, dance, and drama/theatre education in elementary and secondary schools.

Who's to Pay for the Arts? The International Search for Models of Support. 128 pages. 1989. $9.95. Examines the policies, structures, and financing of government arts support in a variety of Western nations.

Why We Need the Arts: 8 Quotable Speeches by Leaders in Education, Government, Business and the Arts. 80 pages. 1989. $9.95. Presented at the 1988 National Arts Convention.

To find out more, write or phone:
American Council for the Arts
1 E. 53rd St.
New York, NY 10022
Toll-free: 1-800-321-4510 or *Phone:* (212)223-2787 or *Fax:* (212)223-4415

▶ American Family Association (AFA)

Provides information on: *Effects of Television on Children, Pornography*

The American Family Association works for what it calls the biblical ethic of decency in American society, with a primary emphasis on television. The Association urges viewers to write letters to networks and sponsors, protesting shows that they find objectionable and encouraging the airing of alternative programs. AFA compiles statistics on broadcasts of scenes involving television sex, profanity, and alcohol use.

Information for free:
AFA Journal of the American Family Association. Monthly. Newsletter.

Information for a fee:
Anti-Christian Bias in America. $2. Reveals bias in government, media, and education.
The Case Against Pornography. $3. Book.
Christianity and Humanism: A Study in Contrasts. $2. An AFA study.
A Guide to What One Person Can Do About Pornography. $2. A guide to fighting pornography in your community.
The Man the Networks Love to Hate. $3. A history of AFA.
Pornography: A Report. $2. Looks at the effects of pornography.
Public School Sex Education: A Report. $2. A study on sex education programs and school-based health clinics.

To find out more, write or phone:
American Family Association
PO Drawer 2440
Tupelo, MS 38803
Phone: (601)844-5036

▶ American Film Institute (AFI)

Provides information on: *Film, Television, Cartoons, Radio and Television Careers, Film and Video Careers*

AFI is a nonprofit, nongovernmental corporation dedicated to preserving and developing the nation's artistic and cultural resources in film and video. The Institute's

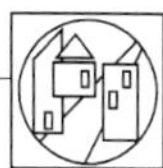

goals are to catalog and preserve America's film heritage, to promote the study of film as an art form, and to bring outstanding films to public attention.

Information for a fee:

The AFI Guide to College Courses in Film and Television. 1990. 286 pages. $19.95. Information from over 500 colleges and universities.

The Art of the Animated Image. 1987. 95 pages. $7.95. An introduction to animation.

Careers in Film and Television. 1991. 46 pages. $10.

Cinema Histories, Cinema Practices. 1984. 150 pages. $14.95. Essays and papers on film history.

Film and Television Grants and Scholarships. 1991. 56 pages. $10.

Film and Television Periodicals in English. 1990. 45 pages. $9. Lists over 160 periodicals.

Getting Started in Film. 1992. 398 pages. $16. Guide to film careers.

Storytelling in Animation: The Art of the Animated Image. 1988. 154 pages. $9.95. Articles and conversations with artists examine "the forgotten element, the story" in film.

To find out more, write or phone:

American Film Institute
John F. Kennedy Center for the Performing Arts
Washington, DC 20566
Phone: (202)828-4000

▶ American League of Professional Baseball Clubs

Provides information on: *Baseball*

The American League is composed of 13 teams in major United States cities, and one team in Canada. The League is comprised of two divisions, the East and the West, each with seven teams. The regular season consists of 162 games that are played from early April to early October. Each year the two division winners play a best-of-seven series for the American League pennant, with the winner advancing to the World Series to play the National League pennant winner. An All-Star Game held annually in July features the American League all-stars versus the National League all-stars.

Information for a fee:

American League Red Book. Annual. $10.95.

To find out more, write or phone:

American League of Professional Baseball Clubs
350 Park Ave.
New York, NY 10022
Phone: (212)339-7600 or *Fax:* (212)935-5069

▶ American Music Center

Provides information on: *Music, Musicians*

The Center encourages the creation, performance, and appreciation of contemporary American music. It maintains an information center and library of more than 33,000 contemporary American works, both published and unpublished, records and tapes, and biographical files on American composers.

Information for a fee:

Contemporary Music Ensembles. 1991. $12. Lists contact information on ensembles performing contemporary music.

Membership Directory. 1992. $12. Lists contact information of current members.

Music for Orchestra, Band, and Large Ensemble. 1982. $10. Catalog.

Opera and Music Theater Works. 1983. With current supplement. $6. Catalog.

Opera Companies and American Opera. 1990. $9. Information on companies interested in performing 20th century American opera and music theater works.

Opportunities for Composers. 1992. $12. A listing of ongoing grants competitions, and artist colonies for composers.

The Center offers an information packet for $12 that includes a composer, performer, or jazz insert.

To find out more, write or phone:

American Music Center
30 W. 26th St., Ste. 1001
New York, NY 10010-2011
Phone: (212)366-5260

▶ American Professional Soccer League

Provides information on: *Soccer*

The League is composed of two conferences, the American and the Western. Every year, the first and second place finishers from both the conferences qualify for the playoffs.

Information for free:

Weekly press releases.

Information for a fee:

Media Guide. Annual. $5.

To find out more, write or phone:
American Professional Soccer League
4330 Fair Lake Ct., Ste. 300B
Fairfax, VA 22033
Phone: (703)222-2403

▶ American Society of Newspaper Editors (ASNE)

Provides information on: *Literacy, Women and Minorities: Job Opportunities in the Media, Freedom of Information, Newspapers*

The Society is made up of directing editors who determine editorial and news policy on daily newspapers. It has committees concerned with such issues as journalism education, ethics, the First Amendment, freedom of information, international communication, literacy, minorities, and the future of newspapers.

Information for a fee:

ASNE Bulletin. 9/year. $20. A journalism review covering major press controversies, newspaper editing and writing, ethics, management, and minority recruitment. Includes legislative and ASNE news.

ASNE Proceedings. Annual. $25. Covers controversies concerning journalism education, ethics, and credibility.

Editors Exchange. 11/year. $24/3 years. Newsletter providing tips on news coverage, management hints, communicating with readers, editorial page updates, and minority affairs information.

To find out more, write or phone:
American Society of Newspaper Editors
PO Box 17004
Washington, DC 20041
Phone: (703)648-1144 or *Fax:* (703)620-4557

▶ Archives of Traditional Music

Provides information on: *Music*

The Archives of Traditional Music focuses on ethnomusicology, folklore, and linguistics, including studies of world music, oriental art music, some jazz, popular music, oral history, and oral narrative. It collects, preserves, and makes available phonorecordings of peoples from all parts of the world for ethnomusicological, anthropological, folkloristic, linguistic, and musicological research. Resources include a collection of 350,000 musical and narrative items, two audio laboratories, a video laboratory for dubbing archival materials, and a listening library of sound recordings of music and oral data, especially African, Afro-American, American Indian, and Latin American.

Information for a fee:
Resound. Quarterly. $20/year.

To find out more, write or phone:
Archives of Traditional Music
Indiana University
Morrison Hall
Bloomington, IN 47405
Phone: (812)855-4679 or *Fax:* (812)855-6673

▶ Association of American Editorial Cartoonists

Provides information on: *Cartoons*

Active and retired editorial cartoonists for newspapers, magazines, and syndicates are members of the Association. They promote and encourage the art of editorial cartooning nationally.

To find out more, write or phone:
Association of American Editorial Cartoonists
Sally Nicholson, Gen.Mgr.
4101 Lake Boone Tr., Ste. 201
Raleigh, NC 27607
Phone: (919)787-5181 or *Fax:* (919)787-4916

▶ Association of Performing Arts Presenters

Provides information on: *Performing Arts*

The Association consists of artists, businesses, and nonprofit arts organizations. The group works to improve the quality and extent of fine arts programming, promotes professional development of arts presenters, and fosters ethical and effective standards of business operations. It encourages diversity in the arts and freedom of artistic expression, and aids in the development of specific art forms.

Information for a fee:
21 Voices: The Art of Presenting the Performing Arts. 324 pages. $24. Gives an inside look at presenting organizations and the role of presenters in American culture.
An American Dialogue. 93 pages. $10. Report on the present status and the future of the presenting field.

Inside Arts Magazine. Quarterly. $24/year. Covers events and trends in the performing arts fields.

Presenting Performances. 208 pages. $17. Contains know-how information for the beginning presenter. Offers advice about organizational structure, financial planning, programming, and promotion.

Successful Fundraising. 302 pages. $20. A guide providing available resources, information on raising more money, getting fast results, and beating the competition.

To find out more, write or phone:

Association of Performing Arts Presenters
1112 16th St. NW, No. 400
Washington, DC 20036
Phone: (202)833-2787 or *Fax:* (202)833-1543

▶ The Athletics Congress of the USA (TAC/USA)

Provides information on: *Athletes, Track and Field*

TAC/USA is the national governing body for track and field, long distance running, and race walking in the United States. It arranges international competition for U.S. athletes, organizes national championship events, and provides clinics and training camps. TAC/USA also keeps official U.S. athletic records and maintains and enforces athletic rules. Its members include athletic clubs, high school and college/university athletic groups, athletic officials, statisticians, and fans. TAC/USA is affiliated with the International Amateur Athletic Federation (IAAF).

Information for a fee:

America's Best: A Compilation of U.S. Olympic and International Track and Field Stars, 1896-1987. Press guide. $10.

1992 American Athletics Annual. 13th edition. $10. Compilation of statistics.

1992-93 IAAF Handbook. $15. Includes history, committees, rules, statistics, and other data.

Youth Athletics Handbook. 1992. $5. Includes a schedule of competitions, youth records, and directory.

To find out more, write or phone:

The Athletics Congress of the USA
PO Box 120
Indianapolis, IN 46206-0120
Phone: (317)261-0500 or *Fax:* (317)261-0481

▶ Black Citizens for a Fair Media

Provides information on: *Women and Minorities: Depiction in the Media, Women and Minorities: Job Opportunities in the Media*

This community organization is concerned with employment practices in the television industry, images of Black people projected by television, and how those images affect viewers. The group works to improve programming, employment practices, and training of Blacks; and evaluates compliance with the Federal Communication Commission's equal opportunity rules for the electronic media.

To find out more, write or phone:

Black Citizens for a Fair Media
156-20 Riverside Dr., No. 13L
New York, NY 10032
Phone: (212)568-3168

▶ C-SPAN/C-SPAN II

Provides information on: *Television*

C-SPAN/C-SPAN II, also known as the Cable Satellite Public Affairs Network, provides coverage of U.S. Congress and public affairs events (C-SPAN, House of Representatives; C-SPAN II, Senate). Letters about specific shows will be forwarded to their producers or staff.

To find out more, write or phone:

C-SPAN/C-SPAN II
400 N. Capital St., NW, Ste. 650
Washington, DC 20001
Phone: (202)737-3220 or *Fax:* (202)737-3323

▶ Cartoon/Fantasy Organization (C/FO)

Provides information on: *Cartoons*

Organization members include enthusiasts of animated cartoons, especially Japanese fantasy-adventure cartoons. C/FO works to promote animated cartoons that are beyond the scope of traditional American animation and to spread information on them throughout the world. The group encourages preservation of character video games, books, comics, and toys in major comics specialty shops. C/FO translates and offers information in English on foreign cartoons, especially Japanese.

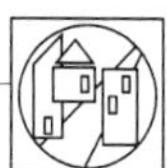

Information for a fee:

C/FO Monthly Bulletin. Price included in $12 membership dues. Newsletter.

To find out more, write or phone:

Cartoon/Fantasy Organization
11863 W. Jefferson Blvd.
Culver City, CA 90230
Phone: (310)827-3335

▶ CBS

Provides information on: *Television*

CBS, also known as the Columbia Broadcasting System, is a major television network and a subsidiary of CBS, Inc. that provides news, sports, and entertainment programming. Letters about specific shows will be forwarded to their producers or staff.

To find out more, write or phone:

CBS
51 W. 52nd St.
New York, NY 10019
Phone: (212)975-4321

▶ Center for Advanced Study in Theatre Arts

Provides information on: *Theater, Dance, Film*

The Center concentrates on the theatre arts, including studies of theatre, dance, and film as independent and interrelated arts. Current projects of the group focus on video interviews with theatre artists, publishing journals on American, Soviet, Western European, and East European theatre, drama, and film, and translations of foreign plays into English.

Information for a fee:

Journal of American Drama and Theatre. 3/year. $12/year. Covers American drama and theatre news and events.

Soviet and East European Performance. 3/year. $10/year. Covers drama, theatre, and film in the Commonwealth of Independent States (USSR) and Eastern Europe.

Western European Stages. 2/year. $10. Covers news and events of Western European theatre.

To find out more, write or phone:

Center for Advanced Study in Theatre Arts
City University of New York
33 W. 42nd St.
New York, NY 10036
Phone: (212)642-2225 or *Fax:* (212)642-2642

▶ Center for Media and Public Affairs

Provides information on: *Media, Elections, Television*

The Center's main purpose is to analyze the way news and entertainment media treat political and social issues. The Center also conducts surveys to determine the media's role in structuring the national and international agenda.

Information for free:
Publication brochure.

Information for a fee:

Balance and Diversity in PBS Documentaries. 1992. $10. Monograph.
Choice or Echo?: 1988 Election Coverage on National Public Radio. 1990. $10. Monograph.
Looking for J.R.: Media Coverage of the Oil Industry and the Energy Crisis. 1986. $10. Monograph.
Media Coverage of Global Warming 1985-1991. 1992. $10. Monograph.
Media Monitor. Monthly. Single issues $5 each. Newsletter. Provides scientific analysis of the media's coverage of current events or issues of interest. Back issues are also available covering such issues as abortion, Campaign '92, Desert Storm, health care, the war on drugs, and apartheid.
The New York News Media and the Central Park Rape. 1989. $10. Monograph.
Nuclear News: Expert Opinion and National Media Coverage of Nuclear Safety. 1986. $10. Monograph.
Racial and Ethnic Images on Talk Radio. 1990. $10. Monograph.
Television's Impact on Ethnic and Racial Images: A Study of Howard Beach Adolescents. 1988. $10. Monograph.
Watching America: What Television Tells Us About Our Lives. 1991. $24.95. Book.

To find out more, write or phone:

Center for Media and Public Affairs
2101 L St. NW, Ste. 405
Washington, DC 20037
Phone: (202)223-2942 or *Fax:* (202)872-4014

▶ Center for Research on the Influences of Television on Children (CRITC)

Provides information on: *Effects of Television on Children*

The Center studies the impact of television on children's cognitive and social behavior. It evaluates various forms, formats, and production features used to inform and educate children. CRITC conducts studies, experiments, and surveys of children on their processing of television, including attention, liking, comprehension, and home viewing in relation to the form and content of programs. Activities of the group include a three-year study of low-income urban children's patterns of time and media use, the effects of television on children's learning, and studies of visual imagery and its use in instructional television.

Information for free:

CRITC Publications and Recent Papers. 1992.

The Center offers copies of articles, papers, and chapters on the influences of television on children, including such titles as American Youth and Their Electronic Parents, Educating Children with Television, Subtle Sex-Role Cues in Children's Commercials, and The Effects of Television Form and Content on Boys' Attention and Social Behavior. The first five reprints requested are free, those over that amount are $2 each.

To find out more, write or phone:

Center for Research on the Influences of Television on Children
University of Kansas
Dept. of Human Development
Lawrence, KS 66045
Phone: (913)864-4646 or *Fax:* (913)864-5323

▶ Center for the Study of Sport in Society (CSSS)

Provides information on: *Sports*

The Center for the Study of Sport in Society is concerned with sport and social issues including sport history, sport sociology, sport journalism, sport and society, women and sports, the Olympics, sport business, race and sport, and sport in recent America. The Center sponsors a journalism award program and maintains computerized lists of sport sociologists and a sports journalism data retrieval system.

Information for a fee:

CSSS Digest. 3/year. $16. Price includes annual membership.

Journal of Sport and Social Issues. 3/year. $16. Price includes annual membership.

To find out more, write or phone:
Center for the Study of Sport in Society
Northeastern University
360 Huntington Ave.
Boston, MA 02115
Phone: (617)437-4025 or *Fax:* (617)437-5830

▶ Central Intercollegiate Athletic Association (CIAA)

Provides information on: *Sports, Colleges and Universities*

Colleges and universities holding regional accreditation and membership in the National Collegiate Athletic Association form the CIAA. It promotes the physical welfare of students, fosters athletic games, and recommends regulations to promote clean sports and maintain scholarship.

Information for free:
Statistics are available without cost.

Information for a fee:
Football Media Guide. Annual. $10.
Media guides, directories, and tournament programs are also published.

To find out more, write or phone:
Central Intercollegiate Athletic Association
PO Box 7349
Hampton, VA 23666
Phone: (804)865-0071 or *Fax:* (804)865-8436

▶ Centre for Youth and Media Studies

Provides information on: *Effects of Television on Children, Future Technology, Television*

The Centre concentrates on the study of youth and television in Canada, including studies on interactive television and videodiscs, and formative research for media production projects. It analyzes positive and negative impacts of visual and interactive technologies on cognitive, emotional, and social development. The Centre investigates existing and alternative television programming and designs and evaluates educational materials and activities that utilize media.

Information for a fee:
Analysis of the Adoption of a New Technology: The Videoway System. 1992. 22 pages. $25. A summary analysis.

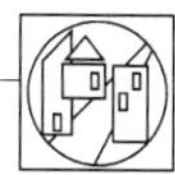

An Analysis of Children's Television Programming and Preferences in Canada 1991-1992. 133 pages. $25.

Children's Television. 1989. A pilot project in media education.

Children's Television. 1989. "The Formative Evaluation Research Model Applied to Children's Television."

Children's Television Viewing: A National Perspective 1988-1989. 9 pages. $1.

Research on Interactivity: Works in Progress. 1989. 11 pages. $3. Covers interactive television.

To find out more, write or phone:

Centre for Youth and Media Studies
University of Montreal
90 Vincent d'Indy
PO Box 6128, Branch A
Montreal, PQ, Canada H3C 3J7
Phone: (514)343-7739 or *Fax:* (514)343-2298

▶ CNN/Headline News

Provides information on: *Television*

CNN/Headline News, also known as the Cable News Network, is a cable television network and a subsidiary of the Turner Broadcasting System that provides news and information programming. Letters about specific shows will be forwarded to their producers or staff.

To find out more, write or phone:

CNN/Headline News
1 CNN Center
Atlanta, GA 30348-5366
Phone: (404)827-1503

▶ College Football Association

Provides information on: *Football, Colleges and Universities*

The Association consists of colleges and universities committed to a major college football program through scheduling strength, adequate playing facilities, and home game attendance. It aims to demonstrate that sponsorship of a quality intercollegiate football program is consistent with academic objectives by sustaining strict academic standards for student athletes, and to maintain high quality of college football for continuing public support.

Information for a fee:
Sidelines. Monthly. $10/year. Newsletter.

To find out more, write or phone:
College Football Association
6688 Gunpark Dr., Ste. 201
Boulder, CO 80301
Phone: (303)530-5566

▶ Dance Films Association

Provides information on: *Dance, Film*

The Association acts as intermediary between users, producers, and distributors of 16mm nontheatrical films and videotapes on all phases of dance.

Information for a fee:
Dance on Camera News. Bimonthly. Price included in $20 membership dues. Newsletter providing information on filmmakers and videotape producers in the dance field, film festivals, and new dance films available.
Dance Film and Video Guide. Book available with $20 membership fee and $5 shipping fee.

To find out more, write or phone:
Dance Films Association
Susan Braun, Exec.Dir.
1133 Broadway, Rm. 507
New York, NY 10010
Phone: (212)727-0764

▶ Dance Theater Workshop

Provides information on: *Performing Arts, Dance*

The Workshop is a group of choreographers, artistic directors, and performing arts companies seeking to create performance opportunities and to stimulate the development of new and wider public audiences for the individual artist. Activities include production and sponsorship of 75 artists and companies, preproduction counseling on publicity, promotion, and overall budget concerns, and assistance with specific dance and performance-related administrative questions. The Workshop acts as clearinghouse of dance information.

Information for free:
Poor Dancer's Almanac Newsletter. 2/year.

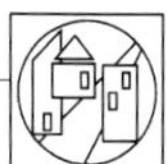

To find out more, write or phone:

Dance Theater Workshop
219 W. 19th St.
New York, NY 10011
Phone: (212)691-6500 or *Fax:* (212)633-1974

▶ The Disney Channel

Provides information on: *Television*

The Disney Channel is a cable television network that provides family entertainment programming. Letters about specific shows will be forwarded to their producers or staff.

To find out more, write or phone:

The Disney Channel
3800 W. Alameda Ave.
Burbank, CA 91505
Phone: (818)569-7500 or *Fax:* (818)566-1358

▶ ESPN

Provides information on: *Television, Sports*

ESPN, also known as the Entertainment and Sports Programming Network, is a cable television network and a subsidiary of Capital Cities/ABC Inc. that provides sports programming. Letters about specific shows will be forwarded to their producers or staff.

To find out more, write or phone:

ESPN
ESPN Plaza
Bristol, CT 06010
Phone: (203)585-2000

▶ European Travel Commission

Provides information on: *Travel and Recreation, Eastern Europe, Western Europe*

ETC represents European countries interested in promoting international goodwill and economic prosperity through tourism. The Commission also compiles statistics.

To find out more, write or phone:
European Travel Commission
630 5th Ave.
New York, NY 10111
Phone: (212)307-1200 or *Fax:* (212)307-1205

▶ Film Advisory Board (FAB)

Provides information on: *Film, Effects of Television on Children*

The Film Advisory Board previews and evaluates films in all media and promotes better family entertainment on television and in motion pictures and videocassettes. It advocates the use of symbols describing PG-rated film content, including L for language, S for sex, N for nudity, V for violence, and FR for frightening.

To find out more, write or phone:
Film Advisory Board
1727 1/2 N. Sycamore
Hollywood, CA 90028
Phone: (213)874-3644

▶ Fox Broadcasting Co.

Provides information on: *Television*

Fox Broadcasting Co. is a major television network and a subsidiary of Fox Inc. that provides entertainment programming. Letters about specific shows will be forwarded to their producers or staff.

To find out more, write or phone:
Fox Broadcasting Co.
10201 W. Pico Blvd.
Los Angeles, CA 90035
Phone: (213)203-3553

▶ Freedom to Advertise Coalition (FAC)

Provides information on: *Advertising, Freedom of Speech*

FAC is made up of advertising organizations united to protect the rights of advertisers to "truthfully and non-deceptively advertise all legal products." The Coalition works to protect the rights of commercial free speech as guaranteed by the Constitution and it opposes laws which would ban or restrict tobacco, alcohol, and other product advertising.

To find out more, write or phone:

Freedom to Advertise Coalition
John Fithian, Contact
c/o Patton, Boggs, and Blow
2550 M St. NW, Ste. 700
Washington, DC 20037
Phone: (202)457-6000 or *Fax:* (202)457-6315

▶ The Freedom Forum for Media Studies

Provides information on: *Media, Future Technology, Effects of Television on Children, Freedom of Information*

The Forum is primarily interested in mass communication and technological change. This includes mass media and the public trust, American institutions and the media, media freedom and accountability, impact of new communication technology on the communication industry and the public, the cost of libel, and politics and the media. The Center's Technology Studies Program examines how technology affects journalists and their work environments.

Information for free:

Caution! This Paper Has Not Been Fact Checked! A Study of Fact Checking in American Magazines. 1990. Working paper.
Communique. Monthly newsletter. Covers current media issues.
Do Victims Have Privacy Rights? 1986. Speech.
Eastern Europe and the Media: Some Views of Insiders. 1990. Special report.
The Freedom Forum Media Studies Center. Brochure.
The Media and Campaign '92—A Series of Special Election Reports. 1992.
Media Success in the Supreme Court. 1987. Working paper.
The Media at War: The Press and the Persian Gulf Conflict. 1991.
Television and Adolescent Sexuality. 1990. Reprint.
The center also issues a publications list, and numerous brochures, reports, working papers, speeches, conference papers, and article reprints.

Information for a fee:

Media Studies Journal. Quarterly. $20/year. Back issues are available for $5 each. Focuses on a different media topic each issue.

To find out more, write or phone:
The Freedom Forum for Media Studies
Columbia University
2950 Broadway
New York, NY 10027
Phone: (212)280-8392 or *Fax:* (212)280-5726

▶ HBO

Provides information on: *Television*

HBO, also known as Home Box Office, is a cable television network and a subsidiary of Time Warner, Inc. that provides movies, music, comedy, and sports programming. Letters about specific shows will be forwarded to their producers or staff.

To find out more, write or phone:
HBO
1100 Ave. of the Americas
New York, NY 10036
Phone: (212)512-1000

▶ Hockey Hall of Fame and Museum

Provides information on: *Ice Hockey, Athletes*

The Hockey Hall of Fame and Museum houses graphics, memorabilia, and trophies (including the Stanley Cup) that trace the history of hockey in Canada and internationally. Exhibits include The Early Days of Hockey, The Golden Age of Hockey, The Original Six, and Modern Day Professional Hockey. The Hall of Fame annually inducts distinguished players, executives, and officials.

To find out more, write or phone:
Hockey Hall of Fame and Museum
Exhibition Pl.
Toronto, ON, Canada M6K 3C3
Phone: (416)595-1345 or *Fax:* (416)971-5828

▶ Intercollegiate Soccer Association of America (ISAA)

Provides information on: *Soccer*

The ISAA is made up of universities, colleges, and junior colleges dedicated to promoting soccer at the college level. Each year, the Association names best offensive and defensive players, regional champions, and a men's and a women's academic all-

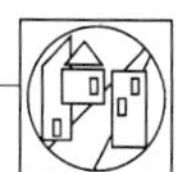

American team. The ISAA also conducts a weekly rating of the top 20 soccer teams in the nation and regional ratings in eight regions of the country.

Information for a fee:
ISAA Guide. Annual. $15.

To find out more, write or phone:
Intercollegiate Soccer Association of America
417 S. 14th St.
Quincy, IL 62301
Phone: (314)349-1967

▶ International Animated Film Society

Provides information on: *Cartoons, Film*

Society members include professional animators, fans, and students of animation. The group works to increase the understanding and quality of animation. The Society provides a search and rescue referral service to restore and repair damaged cells (individual celluloid frames), and it certifies the authenticity of artwork that may have been used in animated films. The Annual Animation Art Festival and presentation of the annual Annie Award for best animated film are other Society activities.

Information for a fee:
Annie Award Program. Annual. $10.
Inbetweener. Monthly. $15/year for full-time students.

To find out more, write or phone:
International Animated Film Society
PO Box 787
Burbank, CA 91503
Phone: (818)842-8330

▶ International Boxing Federation (IBF)

Provides information on: *Boxing*

The IBF is one of four major world boxing organizations that monitors the sport at the professional level and sanctions fights. It is comprised of professional boxers, managers, trainers, referees, and judges. The Federation develops uniformity and minimum safety standards for the sport and bestows awards. It operates a charitable program, conducts periodic training seminars, and compiles statistics.

To find out more, write or phone:
International Boxing Federation
134 Evergreen Pl., 9th Fl.
East Orange, NJ 07018
Phone: (201)414-0300

▶ International Gamers Association (IGA)

Provides information on: *Role-Playing Games*

The Association is made up of participants in strategy simulation games. Its purpose is to provide a tournament and record-keeping system for individuals interested in conflict simulation gaming. IGA sponsors face-to-face and play-by-mail competitions in sport, economic, political, and military simulations. The Association also conducts training in research, design, production, and marketing of strategy simulation games.

Information for a fee:
Wargamers Tabloid. Monthly. $20. Price includes yearly membership.

To find out more, write or phone:
International Gamers Association
c/o James H. Griset, Pres.
25302 Ave., 108
Terra Bella, CA 93270
Phone: (209)535-4604

▶ Ladies Pro Bowlers Tour (LPBT)

Provides information on: *Bowling*

The league is comprised of professional women bowlers. The LPBT conducts women's world-class championship professional bowling tournaments, presents performance awards, compiles annual and career competition statistics, and supplies photographic and other promotional services to the bowling industry.

To find out more, write or phone:
Ladies Pro Bowlers Tour
7171 Cherryvale Blvd.
Rockford, IL 61112
Phone: (815)332-5756

▶ Ladies Professional Golf Association (LPGA)

Provides information on: *Golf*

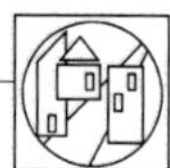

The LPGA is an organization established to promote an interest in and elevate the standards of women's professional golf. A major responsibility of the LPGA is to sponsor annual women's golf championships. The organization operates a hall of fame and also maintains statistics on tournaments, money winnings, and scoring.

Information for a fee:
LPGA Player Guide. Annual. $10.

To find out more, write or phone:
Ladies Professional Golf Association
2570 Vousia St., Ste. B
Daytona, FL 32114
Phone: (904)254-8800 or *Fax:* (713)980-4352

▶ Jerome Lawrence and Robert E. Lee Theatre Research Institute

Provides information on: *Theater*

The Institute focuses on theatrical activities in Western Europe from the 15th-19th centuries, especially festivals, theater architecture and machinery designs, costume designs, commedia dell'arte materials from the 19th and 20th centuries, American and English promptbooks, and general theater material from the 19th and 20th centuries. It provides primary materials to students and scholars for research and publication, including doctoral work. The Institute maintains special collections, including those on post-World War II American theater, archives of several regional American theatres, and special collections of artifacts from various theatrical sources in the Columbus, Ohio area.

Information for a fee:
Theatre Studies. Annual. $10.

To find out more, write or phone:
Jerome Lawrence and Robert E. Lee Theatre Research Institute
Ohio State University
1430 Lincoln Tower
1800 Cannon Dr.
Columbus, OH 43210-1230
Phone: (614)292-6614

▶ Magazine Publishers of America

Provides information on: *Magazines*

Magazine Publishers of America promotes magazines as an advertising medium, reports on federal legislation and postal rates and regulations, and provides information services. The organization conducts surveys on magazine finance, paper usage, and compensation. It also maintains an extensive library on all phases of magazine work, and publishes a newsletter.

To find out more, write or phone:

Magazine Publishers of America
575 Lexington Ave.
New York, NY 10022
Phone: (212)752-0055

▶ Major Indoor Lacrosse League (MILL)

Provides information on: *Lacrosse*

The Lacrosse League is composed of seven teams located in major cities in the eastern and midwestern states. The regular season lasts from late December to late March, with the MILL World Championship concluding the season in April. Each team within the League plays an eight-game schedule that includes four home and four away games.

Information for free:
An information packet including last year's World Championship Program, the League schedule, a history of lacrosse, demographics of fans, and information sheets on each team.

To find out more, write or phone:

Major Indoor Lacrosse League
9200 Ward Pkwy., Ste. 500
Kansas City, MO 64114
Phone: (816)926-0060 or *Fax:* (816)523-8641

▶ The Media Institute

Provides information on: *Freedom of Information, Media, Advertising, Television, Hispanic Americans, Freedom of Speech*

The Media Institute focuses on First Amendment issues, media analysis, communications policy-making, commercial speech, copyright law, new media technology, and developing media.

Information for a fee:
All books have a shipping and handling charge of at least $1.50.

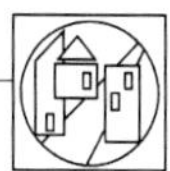

Advertising Rights: The Neglected Freedom—Toward a New Doctrine of Commercial Speech. 1991. 105 pages. $16.95. This book warns that commercial speech rights are being threatened by actions of Congress, state legislators, and regulators.

Beyond the Courtroom: Alternatives for Resolving Press Disputes. 1991. 166 pages. $12.95. A collection of essays on resolving disputes primarily of libel.

Cable Television and the First Amendment. 1986. 16 pages. $3. A paper arguing that cable should be awarded the same First Amendment rights as the unregulated newspaper industry.

Chemical Risks: Fears, Facts, and the Media. 1985. 72 pages. $12.95. This book examines print and broadcast coverage of three major chemical-related events.

Covering the Environmental Beat: An Overview for Radio and TV Journalists. 1991. 113 pages. $9.95. Covers why the issues are so publicized, how to understand the language of risk assessment, and more.

The Diversity Principle: Friend or Foe of the First Amendment. 1989. 75 pages. $10.95. Explores the issue of unwarranted restrictions on the First Amendment rights of media companies as speakers, and a resulting reduction of information reaching the individual.

Hispanic Media: Impact and Influence. 1990. 93 pages. $25. Takes a look at Spanish-language newspapers and radio and television stations in five major Hispanic markets in the U.S.

Reporting on Risk: Getting It Right in an Age of Risk. 1990. 77 pages. $8.95. Provides guidelines for journalists reporting on environmental and personal health risks.

Threats to Freedom of Information. 1985. 13 pages. $3. Traces the development of the Freedom of Information Act.

Wiring the Constitution: The New Media in an Information Age. 1987. 23 pages. $3. This monograph addresses current issues in communications technology.

To find out more, write or phone:

The Media Institute
Ruth A. Domboski, Dir. of Communications
1000 Potomac St. NW, Ste. 204
Washington, DC 20007
Phone: (202)298-7512 or *Fax:* (202)337-7092

▶ Media Research Center

Provides information on: *Media, Television*

The Center documents liberal political bias in news and entertainment media with special emphasis on television networks. It maintains a database containing summaries of all television network stories since 1987. The VHS videotape library contains all ABC, CBS, and NBC news shows from 1987 to the present, and also houses selected

PBS and CNN programs. The Center's research results are published in newsletters and books.

To find out more, write or phone:

Media Research Center
113 S. West St., 200
Alexandria, VA 22003
Phone: (703)683-9733 or *Fax:* (703)683-9736

▶ Media Watch

Provides information on: *Women and Minorities: Depiction in the Media*

Media Watch is a group of individuals dedicated to improving the image of women in the media. It believes that women and girls worldwide suffer from a lack of self-esteem that is instilled and maintained by the profusion of sexist, racist, and violent images of women in the media. The group conducts public protests, boycotts, letter writing campaigns, and fundraising events, and maintains a speakers' bureau, biographical archives, and a small library.

Information for free:
Media Watch: Who We Are and What We Do. Describes the organization.
Also offers a brochure of available videotapes.

To find out more, write or phone:

Media Watch
Ann Simonton, Dir.
PO Box 618
Santa Cruz, CA 95061-0618
Phone: (408)423-6355 or *Fax:* (408)423-9119

▶ Motion Picture Association of America (MPAA)

Provides information on: *Film*

MPAA members include producers and distributors of motion pictures in the U.S. It works to establish and maintain high moral and artistic standards in motion picture production by developing the educational as well as the entertainment value and general usefulness of the motion picture.

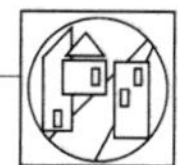

To find out more, write or phone:
Motion Picture Association of America
1600 I St., NW
Washington, DC 20006
Phone: (202)293-1966

▶ MTV

Provides information on: *Television, Music*

MTV, also known as Music Television, is a cable television network and a subsidiary of MTV Networks that provides music videos, news, and special programming. Letters about specific shows will be forwarded to their producers or staff.

To find out more, write or phone:
MTV
1515 Broadway
New York, NY 10036
Phone: (212)258-7800

▶ Naismith Memorial Basketball Hall of Fame

Provides information on: *Basketball, Athletes*

Persons who have performed outstanding services to the game of basketball are elected to the Hall of Fame. They include players, coaches, referees, and contributors in various fields of service to the game. It maintains a museum and a library on basketball related subjects.

Information for a fee:
Naismith Memorial Basketball Hall of Fame: Official Hall of Fame Book. Annual. $10.

To find out more, write or phone:
Naismith Memorial Basketball Hall of Fame
1150 W. Columbus Ave.
PO Box 179
Springfield, MA 01101
Phone: (413)781-6500

▶ National Academy of Television Arts and Sciences (NATAS)

Provides information on: *Television*

The Academy consists of persons engaged in television performing, art directing, cinematography, directing, taping, tape editing, choreography, engineering, film editing, music, production, and writing. It works to advance the arts and sciences of television and promotes creative leadership in the television industry for artistic, cultural, educational, and technological progress. The Academy recognizes outstanding achievements in the television industry by presenting annual Daytime Emmy Awards for excellence.

Information for a fee:
NATAS News. Quarterly. $2.50. NATAS official newsletter.
Television Quarterly. $5. The official journal of NATAS.

To find out more, write or phone:
National Academy of Television Arts and Sciences
111 W. 57th St., Ste. 1020
New York, NY 10019
Phone: (212)586-8424 or *Fax:* (212)246-8129

▶ National Advertising Review Board (NARB)

Provides information on: *Advertising*

The Board aims to keep high standards of truth and accuracy in national advertising by responding to public complaints about national advertising and working to improve advertising performance and credibility.

To find out more, write or phone:
National Advertising Review Board
845 3rd Ave.
New York, NY 10022
Phone: (212)832-1320

▶ National Arts Education Research Center

Provides information on: *Music, Performing Arts, Theater*

The Center conducts research on the arts, with the goal of developing teaching strategies and curricula in arts education. The Center's work focuses on secondary education in music, visual arts, and theater arts.

Information for free:
A Framework for Multicultural Arts Education. 1991. Three-volume set of booklets highlighting the history, issues, and goals of multicultural arts education, and

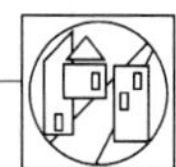

sources of additional information.
Research reports are also available.

To find out more, write or phone:
National Arts Educatiion Research Center
New York University
26 Washington Pl., No. 21
New York, NY 10003
Phone: (212)998-5060 or *Fax:* (212)995-4048

▶ National Baseball Hall of Fame and Museum

Provides information on: *Athletes, Baseball*

The National Baseball Hall of Fame and Museum is designed to honor the significant players, events, and games in the history of professional baseball. The Hall of Fame also houses the National Baseball Library. The library collects and preserves all types of information on baseball and is open to the public.

Information for free:
Baseball Gifts. 29 pages. Catalog of baseball paraphernalia and prices.

Information for a fee:
Baseball's Best Memories. Volume I and II. $10 each. Presents highlights of baseball history from 1927-1969 (Volume I) and 1970-1991 (Volume II).
Baseball's Greatest Quotations. 480 pages. $16. Contains quotations, photographs, and illustrations.
The Great American Baseball Stat Book for 1992. $15. Contains entries for every roster player, team prospects, and other data.
The Major League Way to Play Baseball. 96 pages. $5.95. Provides tips from coaches and players.
The Red Sox Reader. $9.95. Various stories recount the history of the Red Sox.
Sluggers. $16.95. Profiles 27 of the best hitters in baseball.

To find out more, write or phone:
National Baseball Hall of Fame and Museum
PO Box 590A
Cooperstown, NY 13326
Phone: (607)547-9988 or *Fax:* (607)547-5980

▶ National Basketball Association (NBA)

Provides information on: *Basketball*

The NBA consists of 27 teams in major United States cities. These teams are divided into two conferences, the Eastern and Western, which are further divided into two divisions. Each team plays 82 regular season games per year, and then the four division winners qualify for the playoffs. The two conference champions then meet in the NBA finals to determine the final champion.

Information for a fee:
Hoop. Monthly (only during basketball season). $2.95/issue.
NBA Guide. Annual. $11.95.
NBA Register. Annual. $11.95.

To find out more, write or phone:
National Basketball Association
Olympic Tower
645 5th Ave.
New York, NY 10022
Phone: (212)826-7000 or *Fax:* (212)826-0579

▶ National Basketball Players Association (NBPA)

Provides information on: *Basketball*

NBPA is an independent players' union working to improve the performance of NBA players and to represent their interests in collective bargaining with the league. The Association sponsors educational programs and career counseling, and compiles statistics.

Information for free:
Time Out. 6-8/year. Newsletter providing membership activities.

To find out more, write or phone:
National Basketball Players Association
1775 Broadway, Ste. 2401
New York, NY 10019
Phone: (212)333-7510 or *Fax:* (212)956-5687

▶ National Board of Review of Motion Pictures

Provides information on: *Film, Television*

This organization is made up of people interested in all phases of the motion picture industry and specialists interested in the technical and artistic phases of movies. It maintains biographical archives.

Information for a fee:

Films in Review. Bimonthly. $18/year. Journal featuring television, film, video, and book reviews.

How to Judge a Movie. $.50. Pamphlet.

To find out more, write or phone:

National Board of Review of Motion Pictures
PO Box 589
New York, NY 10021
Phone: (212)628-1594

▶ National Cartoonists Society (NCS)

Provides information on: *Cartoons*

A professional society of cartoonists, the group stimulates interest in cartooning by cooperating with established schools and encouraging students. NCS prepares exhibits of original cartoons for schools and museums, assists governmental and charitable institutions, and maintains a hall of fame.

Information for a fee:

The Cartoonist. Annual. $5.

To find out more, write or phone:

National Cartoonists Society
157 W. 57th St., Ste. 904
New York, NY 10019
Phone: (212)333-7606

▶ National Coalition on Television Violence (NCTV)

Provides information on: *Television Violence*

The Coalition is an educational and research organization committed to decreasing the amount of violence shown on television and in film. It provides music video, television, and movie ratings, and conducts toy reviews and updates on aggression and sports violence research. NCTV also sponsors seminars on organizing school programs on nonviolence and seminars on violent entertainment and public action.

Information for a fee:

NCTV News. 8/year. $25. A newsletter covering protests and boycotts, violence research, movie reviews, and listings of television programs and videos containing violence.

Also offers bibliographies covering cartoons, war toys, and boxing and sports violence monitoring for $4 each.

To find out more, write or phone:
National Coalition on Television Violence
PO Box 2157
Champaign, IL 61825
Phone: (310)278-5433

▶ National Collegiate Athletic Association (NCAA)

Provides information on: *Sports, Colleges and Universities, Steroid Use and Effects*

The Association is a group of universities, colleges, and allied educational athletics associations devoted to the administration of intercollegiate athletics. NCAA operates a statistics service for college football and baseball, women's softball, and men's and women's basketball. It maintains 42 sports committees including baseball, ice hockey, men's and women's basketball rules, men's football, men's and women's fencing, men's and women's golf, and more. It also maintains 22 other committees including Academic Requirements, Basketball Officiating Improvement, Communications, Competitive Safeguards and Medical Aspects of Sports; and Eligibility.

Information for a fee:
1992-93 NCAA Manual. $11. Contains all NCAA legislation.
Drug-Testing Program. $1.50. Explains laws regarding drug testing of student-athletes at NCAA championships and postseason bowl games. Also contains a list of banned drugs.
Drugs and the Athlete.a Losing Combination. 1988. $6 for 12 copies. Explains the latest information on the problem of drugs in sports and society.
Foreign Student Handbook. $2. Provides academic eligibility criteria for institutions.
The NCAA News. 46/year. $24. Covers issues concerning college athletics, including legislation, features, and prechampionship and postchampionship reports.
NCAA: The Voice of College Sports. 1981. $18.95 plus $2 handling fee. Official history of the NCAA from 1892 to the 75th convention in 1981.
Official NCAA Division I 1991-92 Graduation-Rates Report. $10. Contains official graduation-rate data for all Division I member institutions.
Sports Medicine Handbook. 1992. $6.50. Contains information on training methods, prevention and treatment of sports injuries, and the use of safety measures.
Sports Participation Survey No. 7. $4. A 1956-87 study of participation in intercollegiate, club, intramural, and physical education programs at member institutions.
Also publishes rule books for more than 10 different sports.

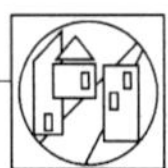

To find out more, write or phone:
National Collegiate Athletic Association
6201 College Blvd.
Overland Park, KS 66211
Phone: (913)339-1906

▶ National Council for Families and Television (NCFT)

Provides information on: *Television*

The Council is a group of people within the television industry and the community who work to enhance the quality of life for families and children by positively affecting the creation and uses of prime time television entertainment. NCFT conducts seminars, symposia, and invitational weekends where television creators meet with experts to discuss ideas for television programming.

To find out more, write or phone:
National Council for Families and Television
3801 Barham Blvd., Ste. 300
Los Angeles, CA 90068
Phone: (213)876-5959

▶ National Football League (NFL)

Provides information on: *Football*

The NFL is made up of 28 teams in major U.S. cities. The League consists of two conferences, the American and National, which are each further divided into three divisions—the Eastern, Western, and Central. Each year, three division winners and three wildcard teams from each conference qualify for the NFL playoffs, which are in late January when the two conference champions meet in the Super Bowl. The League also holds the Pro Bowl, an annual football game featuring the American Conference all-stars versus the National Conference all-stars.

Information for a fee:
NFL Record and Fact Book. $14.95.
NFL and You. $7.

To find out more, write or phone:
National Football League
410 Park Ave.
New York, NY 10022
Phone: (212)758-1500

▶ National Football League Player's Association

Provides information on: *Football*

The Association serves a source of communication between the leagues and players, counsels players concerning a second career, and conducts research and statistics. It maintains a sports library, hall of fame, and specialized education program.

Information for free:
Statistics and studies.

To find out more, write or phone:
National Football League Player's Association
2021 L St., NW, 6th Fl.
Washington, DC 20036
Phone: (202)463-2200

▶ National Hockey League (NHL)

Provides information on: *Ice Hockey*

The NHL is composed of 24 teams, 16 in major United States cities and eight in major Canadian cities. The League consists of two conferences, the Campbell and Wales, each conference further divided into two divisions. The Campbell Conference is comprised of the Norris and the Smythe Divisions; the Wales Conference is made up of the Adams and Patrick Divisions. The NHL regular season begins in October and ends in April with each team playing 84 games. The top four teams from each division qualify for the division playoffs. The division playoff champions play to determine the conference champions, and the two conference champions play for the NHL title and the Stanley Cup. The League holds the NHL All-Star Game annually at mid-season, which features the Campbell Conference all-stars versus the Wales Conference all-stars.

Information for a fee:

Hockey Year in Review. 264 pages. $14. Gives individual and team statistics, regular season and playoffs, from the NHL and other leagues.

NHL Entry Draft Guidebook. 190 pages. $10. Profiles on top North American and European prospects plus draft history and lists. Also includes data on the most recent Entry, Expansion, and Supplemental Drafts.

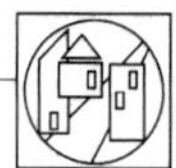

To find out more, write or phone:
National Hockey League
Gary Meagher, Public Relations Dir.
1155 Metcalfe St.
Montreal, PQ, Canada H3B 2W2
Phone: (514)871-9220 or *Fax:* (514)871-1663

▶ National League of Professional Baseball Clubs

Provides information on: *Baseball*

The National League is composed of 11 teams in major United States cities, and one team in Canada. The League is made up of two divisions, the East and the West, each with six teams. The regular season consists of 162 games that are played from early April to early October. Each year the two division winners play a best-of-seven series for the National League pennant, with the winner advancing to the World Series to play the American League pennant winner. The All-Star game held annually in July features the National League all-stars versus the American League all-stars.

Information for a fee:
National League Green Book. Annual. $10.95.

To find out more, write or phone:
National League of Professional Baseball Clubs
350 Park Ave.
New York, NY 10022
Phone: (212)339-7700

▶ National Newspaper Association

Provides information on: *Advertising, Newspapers, Publishing Careers*

The National Newspaper Association is made up of representatives of weekly, semiweekly, and daily newspapers. It has access to experts on issues affecting the newspaper industry and compiles statistics.

Information for a fee:
The Art of Writing Advertising. $9.95. A book of interviews with advertising professionals.
How to Produce a Small Newspaper. $9.95. Provides information on staffing, editing, printing, pasteup, advertising, and circulation.
Journalism Career Guide. 15 pages. $.15. A brochure giving journalism careeer options to secondary school students.

The Marketing Plan—How to Prepare It. What Should Be In It. $19.95. A handbook for preparing the marketing plan.
Media Math. $17.95. Gives instructions on how to calculate and understand media numbers.
The Newspaper. $25. A guide to becoming successful in the newspaper business.
Newspaper in Education. $.15. A guide for ways to get newspapers into the classroom.
Opportunities in Newspaper Publishing Careers. $9.95. Provides an overview of the field, including employment outlook, career advancement, educational requirements, and salaries.

To find out more, write or phone:
National Newspaper Association
1627 K St. NW, Ste. 400
Washington, DC 20006
Phone: (202)466-7200 or *Fax:* (202)331-1403

▶ National Professional Soccer League

Provides information on: *Soccer*

The National Professional Soccer League is made up of 10 teams in United States cities. The teams compete in two divisions, American and National. Six of the teams qualify for post-season play, the two divisional champions and the four teams with the best winning percentages, regardless of division. The League playoffs and championships are held in April.

Information for a fee:
Media Guide. Annual. $7.

To find out more, write or phone:
National Professional Soccer League
229 3rd St., NW
Canton, OH 44702
Phone: (216)455-4625 or *Fax:* (216)455-3885

▶ National Recreation and Park Association

Provides information on: *Travel and Recreation*

The Association is dedicated to improving the human environment through improved park, recreation, and leisure opportunities. Association activities include developing and upgrading leadership in the park, recreation, and leisure field, conducting research, providing information, and giving technical assistance.

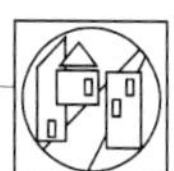

Information for free:
Publications and Videos Catalog.

Information for a fee:
Curriculum Catalog. $15. Provides information on curricula and faculty in the parks, recreation, and leisure studies profession.
Management Planning for Park and Recreation Areas. 1982. 110 pages. $12. Gives background information on what park management is and how it is implemented.
The Information Please Environmental Almanac. Annual. 606 pages. $9.95.
Skateboarding—A New Wave for an Old Game. 1990. 28 pages. $12. Includes discussions of types of skate parks, personnel, who skateboarders are, fees, ramp surfaces, safety, accidents, and liability.

To find out more, write or phone:
National Recreation and Park Association
2775 S. Quincy St., Ste. 300
Arlington, VA 22206-2204
Phone: (703)820-4940 or *Fax:* (703)671-6772

▶ National Soccer Hall of Fame

Provides information on: *Soccer, Athletes*

The National Soccer Hall of Fame was designed to promote a better understanding of soccer in America through maintaining a historical record of soccer in the United States, encouraging the involvement of youth in the game, and defining America's role in international soccer. The campus has an exhibit hall that displays equipment and memorabilia from soccer's greatest players and teams as well as photos, artifacts, and trophies. Clinics and tournaments are scheduled year-round, along with special events, including soccer camps and workshops.

Information for a fee:
National Soccer Hall of Fame News. Quarterly newsletter. $12.50/year.

To find out more, write or phone:
National Soccer Hall of Fame
Victor J. Porto, Public Relations Dir.
11 Ford Ave.
Oneonta, NY 13820
Phone: (607)432-3351

NBC

Provides information on: *Television*

NBC, also known as the National Broadcasting Co., is a major television network and a subsidiary of General Electric that provides news, sports, and entertainment programming. Letters about specific shows will be forwarded to their producers or staff.

To find out more, write or phone:

NBC
30 Rockefeller Plaza
New York, NY 10112
Phone: (212)664-4444

▶ Newspaper Advertising Bureau (NAB)

Provides information on: *Advertising, Newspapers*

The NAB promotes the advantages of newspapers as an advertising medium. The Bureau compiles statistics on newspaper advertising costs and conducts research programs on advertising, editorial content, and reading audiences.

Information for a fee:

Creative Newspaper. Annual. $1. Broadsheet.
Newspaper Advertising Plan Book. Annual. $4.20.

To find out more, write or phone:

Newspaper Advertising Bureau
1180 Ave. of the Americas
New York, NY 10036
Phone: (703)648-1367 or *Fax:* (212)704-4616

▶ Nickelodeon/Nick at Nite

Provides information on: *Television*

Nickelodeon/Nick at Nite is a cable television network and a subsidiary of MTV Networks that provides children's programming and classic television shows. Letters about specific shows will be forwarded to their producers or staff.

To find out more, write or phone:

Nickelodeon/Nick at Nite
1515 Broadway
New York, NY 10036
Phone: (212)258-7800

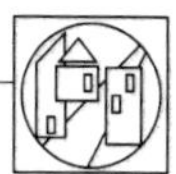

▶ North America Coordinating Center for Responsible Tourism (NACCRT)

Provides information on: *Travel and Recreation*

An educational, nonprofit organization, NACCRT is dedicated to working for responsible travel in developing countries. NACCRT educates North Americans about the negative impact of mass tourism, and is working to change the practices and attitudes of North American travelers. The Center acts as a resource for materials on responsible travel and the economic, political, social, and environmental ramifications of tourism. NACCRT also maintains a 350-volume library on global education, travel, geography, and culture.

Information for a fee:

Caught in Modern Slavery: Tourism and Child Prostitution in Asia. $12. A report of consultation that launched an international campaign.

Challenge of Tourism. $15. Covers such issues as origins of tourism, economic, social, and cultural impact, and case studies.

Contours: Concern for Tourism. Quarterly. $4/single copy, $15/year. Journal.

Guidelines for Planning Travel/Study Experiences. $5. A how-to guide for responsible tours.

Responsible Traveling. Quarterly. $25/year. Newsletter including reports, reviews, and announcements.

Tourism and Ecology: The Impact of Travel on a Fragile Earth. 1989. $7.50. Report and articles.

The group also offers videos, slides, and filmstrips.

To find out more, write or phone:

North America Coordinating Center for Responsible Tourism
PO Box 827
San Anselmo, CA 94979
Toll-free: 1-800-654-7975 or *Phone:* (415)258-6594 or *Fax:* (415)454-2493

▶ PBS

Provides information on: *Television*

PBS, also known as the Public Broadcasting Service, is a major public television network that provides music, drama, documentary, and performing arts programming. Letters about specific shows will be forwarded to their producers or staff.

To find out more, write or phone:

PBS
1320 Braddock Pl.
Alexandria, VA 22314-1698
Phone: (703)739-5000 or *Fax:* (703)739-0775

▶ Pro Football Hall of Fame

Provides information on: *Football, Athletes*

The Hall is an independent, nonprofit organization designed to honor the significant players, events, and games in the history of professional football. It includes exhibition areas covering the history of professional football from 1892 to the present, a movie theater showing football action movies, a research library, and a museum store. The hall sponsors the annual "Pro Football's Greatest Weekend" each summer, which includes a professional exhibition game, hall induction ceremonies, and other festivities.

Information for a fee:
Pro Football Hall of Fame Souvenir Yearbook. Annual. $2.

To find out more, write or phone:

Pro Football Hall of Fame
2121 George Halas Dr., NW
Canton, OH 44708
Phone: (216)456-8207

▶ Professional Bowlers Association of America (PBA)

Provides information on: *Bowling*

The Association works to promote the status of the qualified bowler to the rank of professional and to promote bowling as a major sport. The PBA also works to promote the relationship between the professional bowlers and bowling proprietors, bowling manufacturers, and the communication media. The organization sponsors tournaments, enforces rules and regulations, maintains a small library, and compiles statistics.

To find out more, write or phone:

Professional Bowlers Association of America
1720 Merriman Rd.
PO Box 5118
Akron, OH 44313
Phone: (216)836-5568

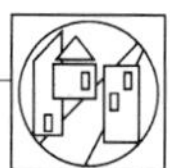

▶ Professional Golfers' Association of America (PGA)

Provides information on: *Golf*

The PGA is an organization established to promote interest in and elevate the standards of professional golf. The PGA sponsors several major professional golf championships throughout the year. The organization maintains the PGA World Hall of Fame, a library, biographical archives, and compilations of annual statistics.

Information for a fee:
PGA Magazine. Monthly. $3/issue.

To find out more, write or phone:
Professional Golfers' Association of America
100 Avenue of the Champions
Palm Beach Gardens, FL 33418
Phone: (407)624-8400 or *Fax:* (407)624-8448

▶ Rock and Roll Hall of Fame Foundation

Provides information on: *Music, Artists*

The Hall of Fame honors artists and industry professionals by inducting those who have made significant contributions to rock and roll music. The organization plans to establish a site for the hall of fame, library and archive department, memorabilia collection, and educational program.

To find out more, write or phone:
Rock and Roll Hall of Fame Foundation
c/o Suzan Evans, Exec. Director
1290 6th Ave.
New York, NY 10104
Phone: (212)484-1755

▶ Role Playing Game Association Network

Provides information on: *Role-Playing Games*

Members of the Role Playing Game Association Network include role-playing and fantasy game players, clubs, and retailers. The group promotes the hobby of fantasy and role-playing games, and encourages continued improvement of games.

Information for a fee:
Polyhedron Newszine. Monthly. Price included in $20/year membership dues. Includes gaming articles, classified ads, and convention listing.

To find out more, write or phone:

Role Playing Game Association Network
Jean Rabe, Pres.
PO Box 515
Lake Geneva, WI 53147
Phone: (414)248-3625

TBS

Provides information on: *Television*

TBS, also known as the Turner Broadcasting System, is a superstation in the cable television industry that provides movies, syndicated television shows, and sports programming. Letters about specific shows will be forwarded to their producers or staff.

To find out more, write or phone:

TBS
Box 105366
1 CNN Center
Atlanta, GA 30348-1947
Phone: (404)827-1700 or *Fax:* (404)827-1947

▶ Television Information Office

Provides information on: *Television*

The Television Information Office seeks to provide a bridge of understanding among the television industry and the public. It commissions research studies and provides members with materials for community education in these fields. It maintains a library collection of 5,000 books, plus material on social, cultural, and programming aspects of television. The group publishes reprints of articles and speeches on social and cultural aspects of television and other materials.

To find out more, write or phone:

Television Information Office
745 5th Ave.
New York, NY 10151
Phone: (212)759-6800

▶ Travel and Tourism Research Association (TTRA)

Provides information on: *Travel and Recreation*

The Association promotes development and marketing within the travel industry by providing professional leadership in travel research. The group sponsors a Travel Research Student Contest, dissertation competition, and two marketing awards. TTRA provides a reference service to assist the travel research and marketing industry in finding information sources and solving business problems.

Information for a fee:
Research Supplier Directory. 1991. $25. Lists and describes travel research suppliers.
First Annual Travel Review Conference Proceedings. 1987. $15. A review of the travel and tourism performance.
Offers many other publications and conference reports.

To find out more, write or phone:
Travel and Tourism Research Association
Mari Lou Wood, Exec.Dir.
PO Box 58066
Salt Lake City, UT 84158-0066
Phone: (303)940-6557 or *Fax:* (801)581-3354

▶ United States Athletes Association (USAA)

Provides information on: *Athletes, Sports*

The Association works to enhance and encourage leadership skills, goal definition, and problem-solving abilities of young athletes. Chapters are organized in high schools and colleges nationwide to encourage academic achievement and promote drug-free lifestyles and community service. Competition among chapters involves and emphasizes academic and community service achievement with success in sports as a secondary goal.

Information for free:
Booklets, brochures, and pamphlets.

Information for a fee:
Beating the Odds. $3.95. Book.

To find out more, write or phone:
United States Athletes Association
3735 Lakeland Ave. N., Ste. 230
Minneapolis, MN 55422
Phone: (612)642-9363

▶ U.S. Gymnastics Federation (USGF)

Provides information on: *Gymnastics*

The USGF is the national governing body for the sport of gymnastics in the United States. It seeks to develop the sport in the U.S. by sponsoring national tournaments and exhibitions, conducting national programs, sponsoring educational sessions on training, safety and coaching techniques, conducting research, and compiling statistics. The Federation is also responsible for selecting and training national teams that represent the United States in international competitions.

Information for a fee:
USA Gymnastics. Bimonthly. $15/year.

To find out more, write or phone:
U.S. Gymnastics Federation
Pan American Plaza, Ste. 300
201 S. Capitol Ave.
Indianapolis, IN 46225
Phone: (317)237-5050 or *Fax:* (317)237-5069

▶ U.S. Hockey Hall of Fame

Provides information on: *Ice Hockey, Athletes*

The Hall of Fame is designed to honor U.S. hockey players, referees, and coaches. Players and referees must be American-born and retired for at least five years, and coaches must be American-born and must have coached predominantly American teams.

Information for free:
Brochure.

To find out more, write or phone:
U.S. Hockey Hall of Fame
801 Hat Trick Ave.
Eveleth, MN 55734
Phone: (218)744-5167

▶ United States Olympic Committee (USOC)

Provides information on: *Olympics, Sports*

The USOC is the governing body in the representation of the United States in the competitions and events of the Olympic and Pan American games. The Association's

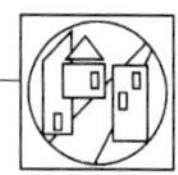

purpose is to support and oversee the activities of the national governing bodies of 41 sports at the games. It supports the the efforts of U.S. cities to host the winter and summer games, and runs Olympic Training Centers in Colorado and New York. The Committee also maintains historical archives, a library on sports and the Olympic games, offers specialized education, and operates a hall of fame.

Information for a fee:
The Olympian. 10/year. $19.92. Magazine.

To find out more, write or phone:
United States Olympic Committee
1750 E. Boulder St.
Colorado Springs, CO 80909
Phone: (719)632-5551 or *Fax:* (719)578-4654

▶ U.S. Olympic Hall of Fame

Provides information on: *Olympics, Athletes*

The U.S Olympic Hall of Fame honors and enshrines outstanding U.S. athletes and teams that have competed in the Winter and Summer Olympics. In addition, one nonathlete who has made a special contribution to the U.S. Olympic movement is selected at each year's induction ceremonies.

Information for a fee:
Olympian Magazine. 10/year. $19.92.

To find out more, write or phone:
U.S. Olympic Hall of Fame
United States Olympic Committee
1750 E. Boulder St.
Colorado Springs, CO 80909
Phone: (719)632-5551 or *Fax:* (719)578-4654

▶ United States Ski Association (USSA)

Provides information on: *Skiing*

The United States Ski Association is the national governing body for the sport of skiing in the U.S. and is the largest sports organization in the U.S. Olympic community. The USSA promotes skiing from children's leagues up to the U.S. Ski Team and even masters and recreation programs. The group also provides support services for athletes in the various competitive skiing programs and selects and trains the U.S. Ski Team that represents the U.S. in international competitions.

Information for a fee:
Ski Racing. 20/year. $19.95.
US Ski Team Media Guide and USSA Directory. Annual. $10.

To find out more, write or phone:
United States Ski Association
PO Box 100
Park City, UT 84060
Phone: (801)649-9090

▶ USA Network

Provides information on: *Television*

USA Network is a cable television network that provides a variety of entertainment programming. Letters about specific shows will be forwarded to their producers or staff.

To find out more, write or phone:
USA Network
1230 Ave. of the Americas
New York, NY 10020
Phone: (212)408-9100 or *Fax:* (212)408-3600

▶ Viewers for Quality Television (VQT)

Provides information on: *Television*

The association promotes the development and supports the continuation of realistic, illuminating, and intelligent television programs. VQT identifies programs that meet their quality standards and commends the major networks for presenting these shows. VQT encourages members to petition networks to continue to present quality television, and campaigns to bring cancelled shows back on the air. The association conducts television viewer surveys.

Information for a fee:
VQT Newsletter. Monthly. $18/year. Includes reviews of programs, rating analyses, and viewer survey results.

To find out more, write or phone:
Viewers for Quality Television
c/o Dorothy Swanson, Pres.
PO Box 195
Fairfax Station, VA 22039
Phone: (703)425-0075

▶ The Weather Channel

Provides information on: *Television, Weather*

The Weather Channel is a cable television network and a subsidiary of Landmark Communications, Inc. that provides international, national, and local weather programming. Letters about specific shows will be forwarded to their producers or staff.

To find out more, write or phone:
The Weather Channel
2600 Cumberland Pkwy.
Atlanta, GA 30062
Phone: (404)434-6800

▶ William Allen White Foundation

Provides information on: *Magazines, Cartoons, Newspapers, Magazines*

The Foundation is a nonprofit research and membership organization concentrating on newspaper commentary, including the investigation of editorial content of given newspapers. It maintains a collection of magazine first-issues, cartoon and comic strip originals, and various journalistic pieces. The Foundation will provide research services.

To find out more, write or phone:
William Allen White Foundation
University of Kansas
200 Stauffer-Flint Hall
Lawrence, KS 66045
Phone: (913)864-4755

▶ Wisconsin Center for Film and Theater Research

Provides information on: *Film, Theater, Performing Arts, Radio*

The Wisconsin Center for Film and Theater Research focuses on performing arts, theater, cinema, radio, and television and their role in cultural history. The Center also serves as a national resource for primary source material available to scholars.

Information for free:

Wisconsin Center for Film and Theater Research. Brochure. Provides an overview of the scope and content of the Center's collections.

To find out more, write or phone:

Wisconsin Center for Film and Theater Research
University of Wisconsin-Madison
6039 Vilas Communication Hall
Madison, WI 53706
Phone: (608)262-9706 or *Fax:* (608)262-2150

▶ Women in Film (WIF)

Provides information on: *Film, Women and Minorities: Job Opportunities in the Media, Television*

The organization's purpose is to support women in the film and television industry and to serve as a network for information on qualified women in the entertainment field. It sponsors screenings and discussions of pertinent issues. Women in Film conducts workshops featuring lectures and discussions on such areas as directing, producing, contract negotiation, writing, production development, acting, and technical crafts.

Information for free:

WIF Reel News. Bimonthly.

To find out more, write or phone:

Women in Film
6464 Sunset Blvd., Ste. 900
Hollywood, CA 90028
Phone: (213)463-6040 or *Fax:* (213)463-0963

▶ World Boxing Organization (WBO)

Provides information on: *Boxing*

The WBO is one of four international organizations that oversees the sport of professional boxing and sanctions championship events. Its membership is composed of the athletic commission or any authorized body legally organized to regulate,

control, or supervise boxing in any country, territorial or political subdivision, province, or city.

To find out more, write or phone:

World Boxing Organization
c/o Nick P. Kerasiotis
412 Colorado Ave.
Aurora, IL 60506
Phone: (708)897-4765

▶ World Wrestling Federation (WWF)

Provides information on: *Wrestling*

World Wrestling Federation is an American professional wrestling organization. The Federation's top wrestlers include Hulk Hogan, Rowdy Roddy Piper, The Natural Disasters, Randy "Macho Man" Savage, Ted "The Million Dollar Man" DiBiase, Sid Justice, and The Bushwackers. Regular events include SummerSlam and Wrestlemania.

Information for a fee:

Spotlight Magazine. Quarterly. $2.50.
WWF Magazine. Monthly. $20/year.

To find out more, write or phone:

World Wrestling Federation
c/o TitanSports Inc.
1241 E. Main St.
Stamford, CT 06902
Phone: (203)352-8600

To Contact People . . .

These books identify individual experts or organizations that can direct you to one.

▶ *The Address Book: How to Reach Anyone Who Is Anyone*

This book can be used to contact more than 3,500 prominent persons including political leaders, business executives, athletes, actors and actresses, artists, musicians, and writers. The book lists name and address. Names are listed alphabetically.
Biennial. Perigee Books.

▶ *American Society of Magazine Photographers—Membership Directory*

This book covers about 5,000 professional photographers for publications. Entries include name, address, phone, and specialty.
Annual. American Society of Magazine Photographers.

▶ *The Athletics Congress of the United States Directory*

This directory provides information on The Athletics Congress of the United States (TAC/USA) and its members. It includes a section listing national, administrative, sports, special, and temporary committees; official bylaws; operating regulations; and an appendix that provides the names, addresses, and telephone and fax numbers of key TAC/USA personnel.
Annual. The Athletics Congress of the United States.

▶ *Authors and Artists for Young Adults*

Use this book to identify authors and artists who create books, movies, television programs, plays, cartoons, and animated features. Entries include name, photograph, contact information, full bibliography, personal and career data, and sources for further information. Each volume in this ongoing series is arranged alphabetically with a cumulative index to the entire series.
Semiannual. Gale Research Inc.

▶ *Baker's Biographical Dictionary of Musicians*

Use this book to identify 13,000 composers, performers, musicologists, and other figures of classical and popular music. Listings include musicians of the past and present worldwide. Entries include name, career data, writings, music composed, and bibliography. Names are arranged alphabetically.
1991. Schirmer Books.

▶ *Baseball Address List*

Use this book to contact some 12,000 baseball players, coaches, and umpires of major league teams. Entries include name and address.
Biennial. Edgewater Book Co.

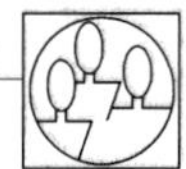

▶ *Billboard's Country Music Sourcebook*

This book contains information on country music artists, songwriters, booking agents, managers, concert promoters, record labels, record promoters, radio stations, organizations, music publishers, and syndicators. Entries list name and contact information. All sections are arranged alphabetically except radio stations, concert promoters, and record promoters, which are arranged geographically.
Annual. BPI Communications, Inc.

▶ *BPI Syndicated Columnists Contacts*

Use this book to contact more than 1,600 major syndicated newspaper columnists in 37 subject categories. Entries include name, address, phone, column format, length, frequency, and lead time. Entries are arranged alphabetically.
Annual with monthly updates. BPI Media Services.

▶ *Broadcast & Cable Market Place*

Use this book to contact television and radio stations in the United States and Canada. Also listed are cable Multiple System Operators (MSOs) and their individual systems; television and radio networks; broadcast and cable group owners; station representatives; satellite networks and services; film companies; advertising agencies; government agencies; trade associations; schools, and suppliers of professional and technical services, including books, serials, and videos; and communications lawyers. Entries include company name, address, phone, fax, and names of executives. Station listings include broadcast power, and other operating details. Stations and systems are arranged geographically; others are alphabetical.
Annual. R.R. Bowker.

▶ *Canadian Who's Who*

This book lists about 12,000 notable Canadians in Canada and abroad based on position or achievement. Entries include name, address, personal and career data.
Annual. University of Toronto Press.

▶ *Cartoonist Profiles*

This publication contains extensive interviews with cartoonists in all branches of the field including comic strips, sports, magazines, greeting cards, movies, politics, etc. Interviews include both biographical and professional information.
Quarterly. Cartoonist Profiles.

▶ *Celebrity Access—The Directory: How and Where to Write the Rich and Famous*

Use this book to contact some 5,000 movie stars, singers, and other noted celebrities. The book lists name, occupation, and contact address. Names are listed in alphabetical order.
Annual. Celebrity Access Publications.

▶ *Celebrity Service International Contact Book*

Use this trade directory to contact producers, agents, and managers. It also lists people associated with motion pictures, television/radio, music, dance, and sports. Additional industries include advertising agencies, recording companies, newspapers, magazines, hotels, restaurants, night clubs, and airlines in New York, Washington, D.C., Los Angeles, London, Paris, Rome, and Toronto. The book lists name, address, phone, and contact. Entries are arranged geographically, then by category.
Annual. Celebrity Service, Inc.

▶ *Cinematographers, Production Designers, Editors and Costume Designers Guide*

This guide covers approximately 2,500 motion picture and television cinematographers, editors, production designers, costume designers, and 11,000 credits. Entries include personal name; name, address, phone of agent or contact; and list of films or shows. Entries are arranged alphabetically.
Annual. Lone Eagle Publishing Company.

▶ *The Complete Hockey Book*

This book contains information on professional and amateur hockey teams. One section includes biographical and statistical data on every player who played in the National Hockey League's previous season. Team entries list name, location, owner, general manager, coaches, past team standings, and playoff records. Player entries list name, team, position, education, personal data, year and round of draft, injuries, awards, and statistics. Information is arranged alphabetically.
Annual. Sporting News Publishing Co.

▶ *Contemporary Artists*

This directory provides contact information and detailed biographical data for 850 artists. Coverage includes painters, sculpture, graphic, and performance artists. Entries

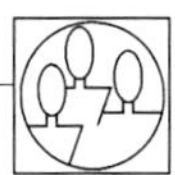

provide biographies, listings of exhibitions or works, bibliographies, critical essay, and photograph. Many entries also contain comments by the artists themselves.
1989. St. James Press.

▶ *Contemporary Authors*

This book provides detailed information on the lives and literary achievements of about 97,000 authors. Entries list name, address, biographical data, description of works, and related information. Names are arranged alphabetically within each volume; the set includes a separate master index.
About six volumes per year; three original and three revised volumes. Gale Research Inc.

▶ *Contemporary Composers*

The directory covers 500 contemporary composers throughout the world. Entries include biography, list of works by category, information about instruments, selective recordings, lists of publications by and about the composer, and more.
1992. St. James Press.

▶ *Contemporary Designers*

This directory provides detailed information on the lives and works of 800 influential designers. Designers profiled work in industry, architecture, furnishing, graphics, publications, theater, fashion, textiles, interior design, and more. Entries provide biography, list of major works, bibliography covering publications by and about the designer, and evaluative essay. Many entries also include personal comments by the designer.
1991. St. James Press.

▶ *Contemporary Musicians*

In six volumes, the book profiles 80-100 popular musicians representing all types of music. Entries include musician name, specialty, address, biographical data, awards and honors, discography, and sources for further information. Names are arranged alphabetically within each volume; a master index classifies names by subject.
Semiannual. Gale Research Inc.

▶ *Contemporary Theatre, Film, and Television*

This ongoing series provides information on more than 5,800 leading and up-and-coming performers, directors, writers, producers, designers, managers, choreographers, technicians, composers, executives, dancers, and critics in the United States and

Great Britain. Entries include name, agent and/or office addresses, personal and career data; stage, film, and television credits; writings, awards, and other information. Names are arranged in alphabetical order within each volume; consult the newest volume for index to the entire set.
Annual. Gale Research Inc.

▶ *Directors Guild of America—Directory of Members*

Use this book to contact over 9,500 motion picture and television directors and their assistants providing films and tapes for entertainment, commercial, industrial, and other non-entertainment fields worldwide. Entries include director name, contact or representative address, phone, speciality, brief description of experience, and credits. Names are arranged alphabetically.
Annual. Directors Guild of America.

▶ *Directory of Music Faculties in Colleges and Universities, U.S. and Canada*

This directory can be used to contact 29,700 music faculty members at about 1,745 colleges and universities. For institutions, the book lists name, address, phone, fax, and degree programs offered. For faculty members, the book lists name, academic rank, highest degree earned, and teaching areas in the field of music. Information is arranged geographically and alphabetically.
Biennial. CMS Publications, Inc.

▶ *Directory of Traditional Music*

The book covers about 1,250 people and institutions interested in "traditional music," primarily folk music. Entries include name, address, and specialty, and are arranged alphabetically.
Biennial. International Council for Traditional Music.

▶ *Editor & Publisher—Directory of Syndicated Services Issue*

Use this publication to contact several hundred syndicates serving newspapers in the United States and abroad with news, columns, features, comic strips, editorial cartoons, etc. Entries include syndicate name, address, phone, and names of executives. Entries are arranged alphabetically.
Annual. Editor & Publisher Co., Inc.

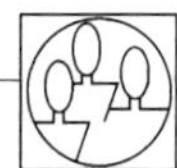

▶ *Fandom Directory*

This directory provides information about some 20,000 fans, fan clubs, fan magazine publishers, and fan events. The book covers television and movies, old radio programs, computer games, comic books, science fiction, fantasy, location of large or rare manuscript collections, and over 4,400 stores that serve fans and collectors. Entries include club, individual, or firm name, address, phone, and special interest(s). Information is presented in geographical order.
Annual. Fandata Computer Services.

▶ *Film Directors: A Complete Guide*

Use this guide to identify more than 2,500 living and primarily active theatrical and television film directors who have made films with running times of one hour or more. Directors of videotaped television dramas are not included. Entries include name, date and place of birth, address and phone (or that of agent), and chronological list of films that meet stated criteria. Directors' names are arranged alphabetically.
Annual. Lone Eagle Publishing Company.

▶ *Guide to Travel Editors, U.S.A. & Canada*

The guide lists approximately 400 travel editors of newspapers and magazines (newspaper coverage includes Canada). Entries include publication name, address, phone, and travel editor name. Entries are arranged geographically.
Biennial. Rocky Point Press.

▶ *Hudson's State Capitals News Media Contacts Directory*

This book provides contact information for about 1,500 media outlets located in or near the state capitals. These include wire services, radio and television broadcasting stations, newspapers, and magazine and newsletter publishers. Entries include name, address, phone, and name of contact. Information is arranged alphabetically.
Annual. Howard Penn Hudson Associates, Inc.

▶ *International Directory of Films and Filmmakers*

This is an illustrated multi-volume set that contains information on 500 directors and filmmakers (Vol. 2), 750 actors and actresses (Vol. 3), and 500 writers and production artists (Vol. 4; Vol. 5 is the index). Both historical and contemporary artists are listed, chosen on the basis of international importance in film history. Entries include name, personal and career data, bibliography, critical essay, illustrations, and other informa-

tion. Names are arranged alphabetically in each volume.
1990-1992. St. James Press.

▶ *International Who's Who*

This book covers 20,000 prominent persons worldwide. Entries include name, nationality, personal and career information, honors, awards, writings, address, and phone. Names are arranged alphabetically.
Annual. Europa Publications Ltd.

▶ *International Who's Who in Music*

This book covers 8,000 composers, critics, managers, publishers, vocalists, instrumentalists, and others in the world of music, primarily classical and semi-classical. Entries include name, profession or musical specialty, personal data, professional career details, principal recordings, current management, writings, address, and phone. Appendixes include lists of orchestras, concert halls and opera houses, musical organizations, music festivals, competitions and awards, and colleges and other institutions offering courses in music. Names are arranged alphabetically.
Biennial. Melrose Press Ltd.

▶ *National Collegiate Athletic Association Directory*

This directory contains an alphabetical listing of NCAA members, a listing of NCAA committees, and the Association's administrative structure.
Annual. National Collegiate Athletic Association.

▶ *National Directory of College Athletics (Men's Edition)*

This directory contains information on men's athletic departments at senior and junior colleges in the U.S. and Canada. It includes school name, address, enrollment, men's athletic director, coaches, tournaments, conferences, records, and other information.
Annual. Ray Franks Publishing Ranch.

▶ *National Directory of College Athletics (Women's Edition)*

This directory contains information on women's athletic departments at senior and junior colleges in the U.S. and Canada. Information includes school name, address, enrollment, women's athletic director, coaches, tournament records, awards, conferences, and other information.
Annual. Ray Franks Publishing Ranch.

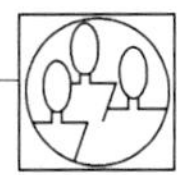

▶ *National Opera Association—Membership Directory*

Use this directory to contact some 300 music and singing teachers, singers, directors, and about 200 schools, colleges, and organizations interested in opera worldwide. Entries include name, address, phone, and activity or occupation. Names are arranged alphabetically within membership divisions.
Annual. National Opera Association, Inc.

▶ *Newsmakers*

This series of biographies contains information on well-known people who are either frequently in the news or deserve media attention. Each paperbound issue covers approximately 50 newsmakers with emphasis on topical issues. Entries include name, photograph, personal data, home and office address, occupation, career, and memberships. Names are arranged alphabetically.
Quarterly. Gale Research Inc.

▶ *O'Dwyer's Directory of Public Relations Executives*

Use the directory to contact about 6,200 corporation and public relations agency executives and private counselors. Entries include name, business affiliation, address, phone; personal, education, and career data. Entries are arranged alphabetically.
Annual. J.R. O'Dwyer Co. Inc.

▶ *Official Baseball Guide*

This book contains lists of baseball teams and their players from the National and American League and their affiliate minor league. Entries for teams include name, location, general manager, owner, names of team members and their statistics. Entries for leagues include batting, pitching, and fielding statistics, and a review of the previous season. Information is arranged alphabetically in American League and National League sections.
Annual. Sporting News Publishing Co.

▶ *Olympic Movement Directory*

This directory provides contact information for the International Olympic Committee and its commissions, 166 National Olympic Committees, upcoming Olympic Games, International Olympic Federations, and other recognized organizations. Entries include address, contact names, telephone, fax, cable, and telex numbers.
Annual. International Olympic Committee.

▶ *Sporting News Football Register*

This book lists about 1,200 National Football League veteran players on the roster for the year covered. Entries include name, teams played for, current position and team location, education and personal data, year and round of draft, injuries, career events and statistics. Entries are arranged alphabetically.
Annual. Sporting News Publishing Co.

▶ *Sporting News Official National Basketball Association Guide*

This source contains lists of National Basketball Association teams and their rosters. Team entries include name, location, general manager and owner, and names of team members. League entries include previous season review, award winners and records, and team statistics from 1946 to present. Entries are arranged alphabetically.
Annual. Sporting News Publishing Co.

▶ *Sports Fan's Connection*

Use the book to find information on sports leagues, associations, teams, conferences, services, fantasy camps, tournaments, bowl games, halls of fame, radio and TV stations, videos, books, magazines, newsletters, and newspapers dealing with professional, collegiate, and Olympic sports in the U.S. and Canada. The entries include name, address, phone, names and titles of key personnel, description, and may include team colors, records, training facilities, minor league affiliates, logos, dates, announcers, frequency, price, or audience. The entries are classified by type of organization or resource.
Biennial. Gale Research Inc.

▶ *Sports Insider's Address Book*

The publication covers approximately 1,000 sports figures, including athletes, coaches, and broadcasters from Major League Baseball, National Football League, and National Basketball League teams. Entries include name, home, agent, or team headquarters address. The entries are arranged alphabetically.
1991. Contemporary Books, Inc.

▶ *Travel Agency Reference & Profile Directory*

North American travel agents, wholesale tour operators, motor coach-sightseeing companies, airlines, steamships, railroads, car rental companies, foreign auto sales, state and foreign government tourist offices, foreign consulates, hotel/motel chains and systems, hotel and travel representatives, and special service companies are listed.

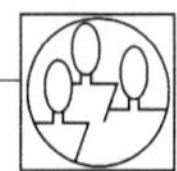

Entries include company name, address, phone, fax, telex, cable address, names of executives, number of employees, association membership, head office location, year established, specialty, and conference appointments. Entries are arranged by type of business.
Annual. Cabell Travel Publications.

▶ *United States Olympic Committee Fact Book*

This directory contains information on the activities and membership of the United States Olympic Committee. It includes a staff directory and information on the history and structure of the committee, USOC programs, Olympic training centers, sports medicine and science programs, drug testing, the International Olympic Committee, the U.S. Olympic Festival, the U.S. Olympic Hall of Fame, and upcoming Olympic games. It also includes a complete directory of national governing bodies for 41 Olympic sports and nine affiliated sports.
Annual. United States Olympic Committee.

▶ *Who's Where in American Theatre*

This book lists more than 3,000 theater artists and scholars in the U.S. Entries include name, title or position, name of organization with which affiliated, address, and phone. Information is arranged in alphabetical order.
Annual. Feedback Theatrebooks.

▶ *Who's Who in America*

This book contains information on 79,000 people, primarily in the U.S., considered to be of current national interest because of achievement or position. Entries include name, address, personal data, career data, memberships, special achievements, and publications. Names are listed alphabetically; a separate volume indexes people by profession and location.
Biennial. Updated quarterly. Marquis Who's Who.

▶ *Who's Who in American Art*

This book lists about 11,500 people active in visual arts, including sculptors, painters, illustrators, printmakers, collectors, curators, writers, educators, dealers, critics, patrons, and museum executives. Entries include name, professional classification, address, preferred media, works in public collections, awards, and other information.
Biennial. R.R. Bowker Co.

▶ *Who's Who of American Women*

This book contains information on more than 30,000 high-profile women in all fields. Entries include name, address, personal, educational, and career data, professional association membership, special achievements, awards, and writings. Names are arranged alphabetically.

Biennial. Marquis Who's Who.

▶ *Who's Who in Canadian Film and Television*

Use this book to contact more than 2,000 writers, producers, directors, art directors, editors, composers, and others involved in the television and film industry in Canada. The book lists name, address, phone; agent name, address, and phone; union or guild affiliation, types and genres of work, biographical data, and filmography. Names are classified by line of business.

Biennial. Academy of Canadian Cinema and Television.

▶ *Who's Who in Entertainment*

Use this directory to contact more than 18,000 notable people in the entertainment industry. Entries list name, company name, address, phone, and biographical data. Names are arranged alphabetically.

Biennial. Marquis Who's Who.

▶ *Who's Who in Music*

Use this book to contact about 20,000 musicians, singers, music associations, broadcasting organizations, record companies, producers, representatives, and others in the Black music industry.

Irregular; latest edition 1987. Women in Broadcast Technology.

▶ *Who's Who in Television*

The publication covers approximately 2,000 studios, production companies, networks, writers, directors, and other professionals involved in cable and network television. The entries include individual or company name, address, phone number, description of projects, names and titles of key personnel, and name and title of contact given for companies. The book is arranged alphabetically.

Annual. Packard Publishing Company.

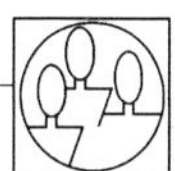

▶ *Who's Who in the World*

This directory covers more than 31,000 people of current international interest because of their achievement or position. Entries include name, address, biographical data, civic activities, awards, writings, and other information. Names are arranged alphabetically.
Biennial. Marquis Who's Who.

▶ *The Writers Directory*

Use this directory to contact over 17,000 writers from the United States, United Kingdom, Canada, British Commonwealth nations, and other countries, whose works are published in English. Entries include name and address; pen names, if any; nature of work; current and past career appointments; and bibliography. Names are arranged alphabetically; a "yellow pages" section also lists names under hundreds of divisions of creative, nonfiction, and other forms of writing.
Biennial. St. James Press.

▶ *Writers Guild Directory*

This directory can be used to identify about 10,000 writers for motion pictures, television, and radio. The book includes listings for members of Writers Guild of America, East. Total listings are about 90% of the combined membership of the two organizations. Entries include name, biographical data, name of agent, and recent work. Names are arranged alphabetically.
Annual. Writers Guild of America, West.

▶ *Yellow Pages of Rock*

This book covers approximately 15,000 music industry professionals at radio stations, music consulting firms, record companies, music retailers, talent buyers, talent agencies, public relations agencies, music publishers, recording studios, and music television networks. Entries include company or personal name, address, phone, and fax. Company names are arranged alphabetically.
Annual. The Album Network.

10

Beliefs, Cults, and Sects

▶ Chapter 10 covers these topics:

Comparative Religions
New Age
Occult
Parapsychology
Religion
Religious Freedom
Satanism/Witchcraft

▶ Related topics appear in chapters on:

Arts and Entertainment; Family Connections and Concerns; Health and Personal Concerns; History and Heritage

▶ Ideas for research topics:

Arguments For and Against the Separation of Church and State
Astrology
The Attraction of Young Persons to Cult Organizations and Behaviors
Beyond the Robes and Dance: The Message of the Hare Krishnas
The Beliefs and Practices of the Presbyterian Church
The Catholic View of Abortion
Compare the Bibblical Story of Genesis with Creation Stories from Other Cultures
The Controversy over School Prayer
The Decline of Religion in Modern America
Differences Between Eastern and Western Religions
Do Rising Interest in Evangelical Christianity and New Age Beliefs Spring From Similar Sources?
The History and Philosophy of Buddhism
How Different Religious Groups Work Together for Common Social Goals
Jewish History, Holidays, and Culture
Major Religious Wars in History
Meditation and Spiritual Healing Practices
Mennonite and Amish Community Practices
The Mormon View of Marriage
Paranormal Phenomena and Psychic Experiences
Parapsychology

▶ Ideas for research topics (continued):

Principles of Canon Law
Religious Ritual as Artistic Outlet
The Religious Unrest in the Middle East
The Role of the Pope in the History of Catholicism
The Role of Women in Various Churches
Scientific Investigations of Mental Telepathy
The Secularization of Modern Society
Should Religious Organizations Be Tax-Exempt?
Similarities and Differences among Jewish, Islamic, and Christian Codes of Behavior
Television Evangelists
The Use of Crystals in Healing Practices
The Use of Tarot Cards, Crystal Balls, and Other Future-Telling Devices
Witches Today—Who Are They and What Do They Do?

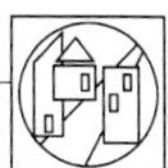

To Contact Organizations . . .

▶ African Methodist Episcopal Church

Provides information on: *Methodist Religions*

The African Methodist Episcopal Church formed after friction developed between blacks and whites of the Methodist Episcopal Church in the 18th Century. In 1981, the church reported that over 2 million members and over 6,000 churches existed. Publishing was seen as an important part of the life of the church, and the items published have had a major impact on the black community. The Church currently operates a publishing house, and a newspaper, magazines, and other resources are offered.

To find out more, write or phone:

African Methodist Episcopal Church
500 8th Ave., S.
Nashville, TN 37203
Phone: (615)256-8548

▶ American Family Foundation

Provides information on: *Child Abuse, Cults, New Age, Satanism/Witchcraft*

The American Family Foundation educates families, professionals, and the general public about cults and psychological manipulation. AFF conducts research on topics such as child abuse and cults, the New Age movement, and satanism. AFF's Victim Assistance Committee helps ex-cult members and their families cope with issues associated with exit from cult groups.

Information for free:

AFF Resource List. Lists mental health professionals, clergy, attorneys, law enforcement professionals, and cult-education organizations around the world.

Cultic Studies Journal, Contents of Back Issues.

Cults and Psychological Abuse. Pamphlet about the AFF. Includes a publications list and order form.

Information for a fee:

Information packets on a group or cult are available for $12. Most packets contain 50-90 pages of newspaper, magazine, and journal articles on such titles as Hare Krishnas, Scientology, the New Age movement, Child Abuse in Cults, Neo-Nazi Cults, the Unification Church (Moonies), and Satanism.

Cultic Studies Journal. Semiannual. Approximately 100 pages. $15. Scholarly journal dealing with cults and psychological manipulation and abuse.
Cults and Mind Control. 6 pages. $1. Educational handout for students and others.
Cults: Questions and Answers. 1988. 13 pages. $3.
Cults: What Parents Should Know. 131 pages. $8. Guidelines for families seeking to help a cultist or ex-cult member.
Easily Fooled: New Insights and Techniques for Resisting Manipulation. $6. A magician explains the deceptions that exist in everyday life.
How Cults Affect Families. 1988. 4 pages. $2.
How to Talk to People Who are Trying to Save You. 4 pages. $1.
Satanism and Satanism-Related Crime: A Resource Guide. 1989. 50 pages. $6.
Young People and Cults: The Newsletter of the International Cult Education Program. Biannual. Available with $25 ICEP membership fee.

To find out more, write or phone:
American Family Foundation
PO Box 2265
Bonita Springs, FL 33959-2265
Phone: (212)249-7693

▶ American Society for Psychical Research (ASPR)

Provides information on: *Parapsychology*

The Society investigates and distributes information about telepathy, visions and apparitions, dowsing, precognition, psychokinesis (mind over matter), automatic writing and other forms of automatism, psychometry, psychic healing, dreams, clairvoyance, clairaudience, predictions, the physical phenomena of mediumship (such as materialization, telekinesis, rapping, and other sounds), and other unclassified parapsychological phenomena. ASPR works to collect, classify, study, and publish firsthand reports of these phenomena. It also maintains a library on psychical research.

To find out more, write or phone:
American Society for Psychical Research
Donna L. McCormick, Dir. of Admin.
5 W. 73rd St.
New York, NY 10023
Phone: (212)799-5050 or *Fax:* (212)496-2497

▶ American Society for the Study of Religion

Provides information on: *Comparative Religions*

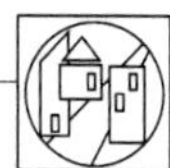

The Society is composed of scholars doing research in religion, often a religion other than their own. The group promotes the scholarly study of religion in its various forms and fosters communication among those engaged in such study.

Information for a fee:
Newsletter. Periodic. $10/year. Price includes membership.

To find out more, write or phone:
American Society for the Study of Religion
c/o Dr. Willard G. Oxtoby, Pres.
University of Toronto
Trinity College
Toronto, ON, Canada M5S 1H8
Phone: (416)978-2156

▶ Amistad Research Center

Provides information on: *Religious History, Religion, Ethnic Americans, Civil Rights and Liberties*

The Amistad Research Center collects materials on the history of American ethnic minorities, race relations, civil rights, and various religions. The Center provides research services.

Information for a fee:
Amistad Reports. Quarterly.

To find out more, write or phone:
Amistad Research Center
Tulane University
6823 St. Charles Ave.
New Orleans, LA 70118
Phone: (504)865-5535

▶ Borderland Sciences Research Foundation

Provides information on: *Occult, Parapsychology*

Members of the Foundation are individuals who take an active interest in unconventional sciences, including the fields of parapsychology, the occult, psychic research, hypnosis, dowsing, radiesthesia, radionics, flying saucers, electricity and the evolving soul, hollow earth mysteries, telepathy, and other phenomena. The Foundation explores phenomena that orthodox science cannot or will not investigate.

Information for free:

Borderland Sciences Catalog. Lists available publications, videos, and other material.

Information for a fee:

Color—Its Manifestation and Value. 40 pages. $5.95. Explores the importance of color in our lives.

Cosmic Music. 255 pages. $12.95. Approaches music as a path to cosmic knowledge.

The Crystal Book. 92 pages. $15.95. A look at crystals as powerful tools to heal, inspire, and create energy.

Flying Saucers and Harmony with Nature. 50 pages. $7.50. A report on the occult and etheric connections of the UFO phenomena.

Handbook of Unusual Natural Phenomena. 431 pages. $12.95. Includes nocturnal lights, unexplained mirages, cloudless rain and snow, strange hums and hisses, freak whirlwinds, and more.

The Journal of Borderland Research. Bimonthly. $3/sample copy; $15/student membership. Alternative scientific magazine containing listings of researchers and research sources.

Koch Treatment for Cancer and Allied Allergies. 68 pages. $9.95. Outlines non-traditional treatments for cancer focusing on blood purifying remedies.

Metal Power. 99 pages. $8.95. Examines connections between the Earth, human consciousness, and the cosmic energies of the planets.

To find out more, write or phone:

Borderland Sciences Research Foundation
Thomas Joseph Brown, Dir.
PO Box 429
Garberville, CA 95440
Phone: (707)986-7211 or *Fax:* (707)986-7272

▶ Center for Philosophy of Religion

Provides information on: *Comparative Religions*

The Center promotes, supports, and distributes scholarly work in Christian philosophy, philosophical theology, and philosophy of religion. The Center deals with such topics as the rationality of belief in God, the problem of evil, and the nature of religious language.

Information for free:

The Center publishes its research in collections of conference papers.

The Autonomy of Religious Belief. 1981.

The Existence and Nature of God. 1983.

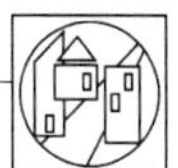

Rationality and Religious Belief. 1980.
A general information brochure, and fellowships factsheet are also available.

To find out more, write or phone:

Center for Philosophy of Religion
University of Notre Dame
Notre Dame, IN 46556
Phone: (219)239-7339

▶ Center for the Study of Contemporary Society

Provides information on: *Religion*

The Center focuses their studies on contemporary society, including studies of social histories of American Catholicism, evaluation of moral philosophy, business ethics, journalism ethics, perception and artificial intelligence, minorities in the U.S., family studies, gerontology, and the sociology of education. Specific activities of the Center include a study of American institutions, a program on multinational corporations and poverty in developing countries. The group maintains a data archive on the social sciences.

Information for free:
Newsletter. Annual.

To find out more, write or phone:

Center for the Study of Contemporary Society
University of Notre Dame
G123 Memorial Library
Notre Dame, IN 46656
Phone: (219)239-7212

▶ Center for the Study of World Religions

Provides information on: *Comparative Religions*

The Center for the Study of World Religions is a focal point for comparative and historical research in religion, with an international emphasis. The Center sponsors an international seminar, conferences, and public lectures.

To find out more, write or phone:

Center for the Study of World Religions
Harvard University
42 Francis Ave.
Cambridge, MA 02138
Phone: (617)495-4495 or *Fax:* (617)495-9489

▶ Christian Research Institute (CRI)

Provides information on: *Cults, New Age, Satanism/Witchcraft, Occult*

CRI is a clearinghouse for current information on cults, the occult, the New Age movement, and unconventional or non-traditional Christian teachings. It provides answers in defense of the gospel through an international team of researchers and missionaries, public speaking, publications, and counseling. Researchers are available to answer questions and assist people in situations regarding cults, the occult, and unconventional or nontraditional Christian teachings. Reseachers schedule speaking engagements, seminars, and intensive studies on cult-awareness and responses to popular false teachings.

Information for free:

CRI Resource Catalogue. A collection of resources providing information on cults, the occult, unconventional approaches to Christianity, and the New Age Movement.

Christian Research Newsletter. Bimonthly. Highlights information about cults and the occult.

Information for a fee:

Christian Research Journal. Quarterly. $14. Evaluates the religious movements of today and equips Christians to better share their faith.

Jehovah's Witnesses. $4.

The Mind Sciences. $6.

Scripture Twisting: Twenty Ways the Cults Misread the Bible. $10.

Sun Myung Moon and the Unification Church. $4.

"TEARS" of Scientology. $6.

Where Does It Say That? . $3.

Whom Can You Trust? $6.50.

To find out more, write or phone:

Christian Research Institute
17 Hughes St.
Irvine, CA 92718
Phone: (714)855-9926 or *Fax:* (714)855-9623

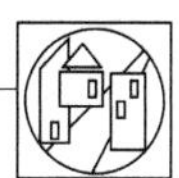

▶ Christian Science Publishing Society

Provides information on: *Christian Science*

The Christian Science Publishing Society is a nonmembership organization that publishes and distributes Christian Science books and periodicals. It also produces news and religious programs for radio, television, and distribution.

Information for a fee:
The Christian Science Journal. Monthly. $20/6 months. Magazine.
The Christian Science Monitor. Daily. $.50/issue.
Christian Science Quarterly. $3/issue.
World Monitor-The Christian Science Monitor Monthly. $18/year. News magazine.

To find out more, write or phone:
Christian Science Publishing Society
1 Norway St.
Boston, MA 02115
Toll-free: 1-800-225-7090 or *Phone:* (617)450-2000

▶ Christian Solidarity International, USA (CSIUSA)

Provides information on: *Religious Freedom*

The organization is made up of Christians seeking to protect the rights of individuals worldwide to worship and believe in God and to act according to their religious beliefs. It concentrates its efforts in communist, Islamic, authoritarian, and politically unstable nations. Christian Solidarity publicizes information concerning oppression and discrimination suffered by Christians and files written protests against violating governments, and encourages supporters to mail written protests. CSI provides legal counsel for arrested Christians and offers material aid for prisoners and their families. It monitors compliance with international law concerning religious freedom, sends attorneys to visit officials of violating governments, and holds human rights briefings with members of the U.S. Congress. The group maintains biographical archives and compiles statistics.

Information for free:
Action Reports. Monthly.
Mission to the Persecuted. Periodic. Newsletter of CSI.

Information for a fee:
Shining in the Darkness. 168 pages. $25. A story of four Christians devoted to their faith.
Trajectories of Despair. $15. Report.

To find out more, write or phone:

Christian Solidarity International, USA
Steven L. Snyder, Pres.
PO Box 70563
Washington, DC 20024
Phone: (301)989-0298 or *Fax:* (301)989-0398

▶ Church of the Brethren

Provides information on: *Brethren Religion*

The Church of the Brethren have a German cultural background, an Anabaptist theology, and a commitment to peace and simplicity. They have been best known for their efforts in relief and rehabilitation work in Europe after World War II. The Brethren has programs in the areas of parish ministries, disaster response, and publishing.

Information for free:

FaithQuest: The Official Trade Imprint of Brethren Press. 1991. 23 pages.

Information for a fee:

Creation on Crisis. 173 pages. $9.95. A book offering a biblical perspective on solutions to prevent the degradation of our environment.
Computer Ethics. 120 pages. $9.95.
Helping the Homeless: God's Word Into Action. 96 pages. $9.95.
Home Care: Alternatives to the Nursing Home. 128 pages. $9.95.
The New Abolitionists: The Story of Nuclear Free Zones. 288 pages. $14.95.
Repairing Christian Lifestyles. 1991. 80 pages. $24.95. A book to help young people develop a sound Christian lifestyle based on sound faith.
Reaching Out in Word and Deed. 1991. 90 pages. $7.95. Contains practical information on how to actively plan and execute a commitment to personal faith.
Teenage Sexuality: Local Church and Christian Home Program Guide. 160 pages. $10.95.
Worship Resources for Youth. 140 pages. $12.95.
Youth Workers' Handbook. 192 pages. $16.95. Provides practical strategies for fellowship groups, retreats, camps, Sunday school classes, evangelism, Bible study, music, and fund raising.

To find out more, write or phone:

Church of the Brethren
1451 Dundee Ave.
Elgin, IL 60120
Phone: (708)742-5100

▶ Church of God in Christ

Provides information on: *Adventist Religions*

Church of God in Christ is a religious denomination whose doctrine focuses on the Trinity, holiness, healing, and the pre-millennial return of Christ. The denomination recognizes three ordinances: baptism by immersion, the Lord's Supper, and foot-washing.

Information for free:

Church of God in Christ Bookstore General Catalog. Catalog of religious publications and equipment.

Information for a fee:

Church of God in Christ History, Theology, and Structure. $8.50.

Church of God in Christ Official Manual. $10. Guidelines dealing with the tenets of faith, the doctrine, discipline and liturgy.

Doctrinal Statement and Statement of Faith. $1.50. Lists basic doctrine and contains Statement of Faith and meaning of Church Seal.

The History and Life Work of Bishop C. H. Mason. $5. Contains information on the early life and ministry of church founder Bishop C. H. Mason.

Membership Manual For Laymen. $2.95. Practices and principles of the denomination in concise form.

To find out more, write or phone:

Church of God in Christ
272 S. Main St.
Memphis, TN 38103
Phone: (901)578-3803

▶ Committee for Public Education and Religious Liberty (PEARL)

Provides information on: *Religious Freedom*

PEARL's purpose is to protect the constitutional principle of separation of church and state in education and to preserve the democratic system of free public schools. The group researches, and offers data, facts, and other information in connection with its purpose.

Information for free:

Public Education and Religious Liberty. Brochure giving PEARL's purpose, goals, and membership organizations.

Information for a fee:

PEARL Newsletter. Bimonthly. $25. Newsletter reporting the efforts and activities of PEARL's committee for Public Education and Religious Liberty. Covers legislative actions, court decisions, and the attempts of other organizations to introduce religion into public schools.

To find out more, write or phone:

Committee for Public Education and Religious Liberty
9 E. 69th St.
New York, NY 10021
Phone: (212)730-2250

▶ Committee for the Scientific Investigation of Claims of the Paranormal (CSICOP)

Provides information on: *Parapsychology*

The Committee is made up of psychologists, philosophers, astronomers, science writers, and others interested in the field of the paranormal, including UFOs, astrology, and psychic phenomena. Members are concerned about biased, media presentations of claims of paranormal occurrences, fearing that the ready acceptance of such claims erodes the spirit of scientific skepticism and opens the public to gullibility in other areas. The Committee encourages evaluative research in the paranormal and provides a "dissenting scientific point of view" through aggressive challenge.

Information for a fee:

Skeptical Briefs. Quarterly. $15/year.

The Skeptical Inquirer. Quarterly. $25/year. Includes articles on paranormal occurrences and trends, news and comments, book reviews, and letters from readers.

To find out more, write or phone:

Committee for the Scientific Investigation of Claims of the Paranormal
PO Box 703
Buffalo, NY 14226
Phone: (716)636-1425 or *Fax:* (716)834-0841

▶ Council of Societies for the Study of Religion (CSSR)

Provides information on: *Religion*

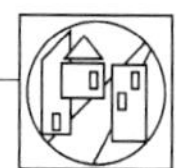

To find out more, write or phone:
FOCUS
c/o C.A.N.
2421 W. Pratt Blvd., Ste. 1173
Chicago, IL 60645
Phone: (312)267-7777

▶ Friends United Meeting

Provides information on: *Quaker Religion*

Friends United Meeting, a Quaker organization, believes in true religion as a personal encounter with God rather than ritual and ceremony. Other beliefs include individual worth before God, worship as an act of seeking, concern for the suffering and unfortunate, and Christian virtues of moral purity, integrity, honesty, simplicity, and humility.

Information for free:
Friends United Press Catalog 1992-1993. Resource catalog listing books, pamphlets, prints, and curriculum materials.

Information for a fee:
An Introduction to Quakers. Pamphlet. $.45.
Friends in East Africa. 263 pages. $13.95. Introduction to people and events in East Africa.
Laughing Out Loud and Other Religious Experiences. 133 pages. $5.50. Describes the value of laughter in everyday life.
A Living Faith. 217 pages. $13.95. A historical study of Quaker beliefs.
A Quaker View of Ministry. Pamphlet. $.45.
Reminiscences of Levi Coffin. 390 pages. $15.95. Contains historical information on the underground railroad.
We Would Not Kill. 263 pages. $13.95. Details the lives of conscientious objectors during World War II.

To find out more, write or phone:
Friends United Meeting
Friends United Press
101 Quaker Hill Dr.
Richmond, IN 47374-1980
Toll-free: 1-800-537-8838 or *Phone:* (317)962-7573 or *Fax:* (317)966-1293

▶ General Council of Assemblies of God

Provides information on: *Pentecostal Religions, Religious History*

The Council was formed when a publisher called for a convention to be held to decide upon some doctrinal standards; a policy of cooperation; missionary, ministerial, educational, and publishing interests; and government religious requirements for business. In 1986, the Council reported over 16 million members worldwide. The group operates the Gospel Publishing House, which offers a wide variety of bibles, sermon materials, church supplies, bulletin and newsletter references, bible study materials, children's books, filmstrips, parenting aids, and more.

Information for free:

Gospel Publishing House 1992 General Catalog.

Information for a fee:

Abortion: Pro-Life by Conviction, Pro-Choice by Default. $5.95. Answers questions that pro-choice advocates raise.

Changing the Way America Thinks. $14.99. A discussion about the secularization of America, and its effect on pornography, abortion, science, government, race relations, sex roles, the family, and more.

Dating and Waiting for Marriage. $2.95. Offers biblical guidelines to help young people maintain spiritual integrity through friendship, dating, engagement, and preparation for marriage.

Making the Most of Single Life. $7.95. Provides Christian counsel for the single person.

Medical Ethics, Human Choices. $9.95. Addresses questions relating to medical care from a Christian perspective.

Smart Kids, Stupid Choices. $7.95. Deals with issues of the 90s, including drugs, teenage pregnancy, and peer pressure.

The Story of the Christian Church. $12.95. Tells the story of the 20th Century growth of the Christian church.

When Divorce Happens. $5.95. Helps readers understand divorce.

The Youth Leader Magazine. 8/year. $13.50. Features articles, programming ideas, and information on successful youth ministry programs.

To find out more, write or phone:

General Council of Assemblies of God
1445 Boonville Ave.
Springfield, MO 65802
Phone: (417)862-2781

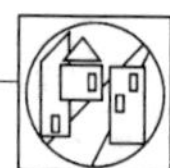

▶ Greek Orthodox Archdiocese of North and South America

Provides information on: *Orthodox Religions*

The Greek Orthodox Church has seven districts, each headed by a bishop. An Archbishop acts as a spokeperson for the community to the outside world. The Archdiocese has reported almost two million members, over 500 churches, and over 600 priests. The group publishes a newsletter and maintains two educational facilities.

To find out more, write or phone:

Greek Orthodox Archdiocese of North and South America
8-10 E. 79th St.
New York, NY 10021
Phone: (212)570-3500

▶ Haunt Hunters (HH)

Provides information on: *Parapsychology*

Haunt Hunters serves as a clearinghouse for experiences and information on ghosts, hauntings, extrasensory perception, and other psychic phenomena. The group seeks to improve the public image of psychic research. It also maintains a file of over 300 case histories of psychic phenomena.

Information for a fee:

Haunt Hunters Handbook for the Psychic Investigator. $19.95. Available from Superior Travel Service, 1-800-875-8747.

To find out more, write or phone:

Haunt Hunters
2188 Sycamore Hill Ct.
Chesterfield, MO 63017
Phone: (314)831-1379

▶ Individual Freedom Federation (IFF)

Provides information on: *Cults*

The Federation is made up of individuals united to aid victims of destructive cults, and to provide support to victims' friends and families. According to IF, a cult is destructive when it uses mind control and psychological coercion to gain and hold converts. IFF conducts educational campaigns stressing the nature and dangers of destructive cults, and teaches ways to prevent conversion of susceptible individuals. The organization maintains a library and bibliography of books on destructive cults.

To find out more, write or phone:
Individual Freedom Federation
Edward M. Mielock, Pres.
4545 Wagon Wheel Dr.
Bloomfield Hills, MI 48301
Phone: (517)738-7496

▶ Institute for Advanced Studies of World Religions (IASWR)

Provides information on: *Comparative Religions, Buddhism*

The Institute provides research facilities and information services to people, institutions, and organizations interested or involved in the academic study and social role of world religions. It collects and preserves religious materials, and works to translate and publish Asian religious texts and studies. The institute maintains an extensive research library in 32 Asian and 11 non-Asian languages.

Information for a fee:
Buddhist Text Information. Quarterly. $16/year. Journal providing a bibliography of Buddhist texts.
IASWR Library Catalog. $10.

To find out more, write or phone:
Institute for Advanced Studies of World Religions
RD 2, Rte. 301
Carmel, NY 10512
Phone: (914)225-0447 or *Fax:* (914)225-1445

▶ Institute on Religion and Democracy

Provides information on: *Religious Freedom*

The Institute focuses on religious liberty and church support of political extremist organizations. It monitors the publications and actions of U.S. church bodies and assists reform and renewal movements in several denominations. The Institute serves as a clearinghouse for old line, Roman Catholic, and evangelical churches in order to promote Christian involvement in international affairs.

Information for a fee:
Religion and Democracy Newsletter. Monthly. Available with $25 membership.

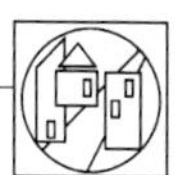

To find out more, write or phone:
Institute on Religion and Democracy
1331 H St. NW, Ste. 900
Washington, DC 20005
Phone: (202)393-3200 or *Fax:* (202)638-4948

▶ International Religious Liberty Association (IRLA)

Provides information on: *Religious Freedom*

The association seeks to "publish and proclaim the principles of the universal right to religious liberty, promote respect for the religious rights and freedoms of all humankind, minorities as well as majorities, and secure worldwide recognition of and respect for the basic human right to freedom of conscience and belief."

Information for a fee:
Liberty. Bimonthly. $1.50/single copy, $6.95/year. Magazine covering issues of religious freedom.

To find out more, write or phone:
International Religious Liberty Association
c/o B.B. Beach, Sec.Gen.
12501 Old Columbia Pike
Silver Spring, MD 20904-6600
Phone: (301)680-6680 or *Fax:* (301)680-6695

▶ Islamic Information Center of America

Provides information on: *Islam*

The Islamic Information Center of America provides information on Islam to the general public and the media. Its objectives include fostering awareness of Islam in the American people and helping Islamic Americans to bring Islam to non-Muslims.

Information for free:
The Invitation. Quarterly. Newsletter that contains articles on the Islamic perspective of contemporary social problems.
The group also offers pamphlets, booklets, and flyers.

To find out more, write or phone:
Islamic Information Center of America
PO Box 4052
Des Plaines, IL 60016
Phone: (708)541-8141 or *Fax:* (708)824-8436

▶ Jehovah's Witnesses

Provides information on: *Adventist Religions*

Jehovah's Witnesses is a unitarian, separatist group that agrees upon the Bible as a source of belief, but denies the Trinity and the divinity of Christ. Ethics and lifestyle are important aspects of the Witnesses' life, and each member sells and distributes Witness literature.

Information for free:
The Awake. Only written requests accepted.
The Watchtower.

To find out more, write or phone:
Jehovah's Witnesses
25 Columbia Heights
Brooklyn, NY 11201
Phone: (718)625-3600

▶ Lutheran Church-Missouri Synod

Provides information on: *Lutheran Religions*

The Missouri Synod is a conservative faction of the Lutheran bodies. The group is involved with evangelism, youth services, parish services, and other ministry work.

Information for free:
Black Ministry Support Brochure. A brochure to be used for local celebrations connected with support for LCMS Black Ministry.
A Christian Will. Discusses why Christians should write a will, what happens if you don't, and what Christian purposes can be served by writing a will.
Foundation News. Quarterly. Newsletter containing information on financial matters, reports on tax law changes, and guidelines for writing wills.
Guardians and Minor's Trusts. Brochure describing the importance of naming guardians for minor children.
The Harvesters. Quarterly. Newsletter covering world mission stations, personnel, and projects supported by TIM congregations.
LCMS World Relief Today. Brochure describing LCMS World Relief, its programs, and projects.
Sharing Newsletter. Bimonthly. Describes the work of LCMS World Relief and Social Ministry.
World Hunger/World Relief Resources. A packet of resources for LCMS World Relief and Social Ministry.

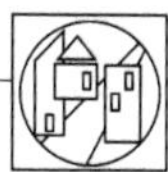

Information for a fee:

Assimilation: The Church Involving and Keeping its Members. 169 pages. $10. Information on how to develop an effective way to incorporate new members.

Concordia Historical Institute Quarterly. $20/year. Contains articles, book reviews, news, and editorials covering Lutheranism in America.

Mission Blueprint for the Nineties. $2.50. A report of the President's Task Force on Mission covering all areas of mission activities.

Seventy-Seven Ways of Involving Youth in the Church. $4.95. Book to help congragations put together a youth ministry program.

Teaching Disabled Students in the Sunday School. $2. Discusses needs, goals, and techniques for teaching disabled students in Sunday school.

Young Adolescent Kit. $8.50. Provides tips, program ideas, and information for ministry with the young adolescent.

To find out more, write or phone:

Lutheran Church-Missouri Synod
International Center
1333 S. Kirkwood Rd.
St. Louis, MO 63122
Phone: (314)965-9000

▶ Mennonite Church

Provides information on: *Mennonite Religions*

The Mennonite Church is a Christian group that grew out of the Anabaptist movement of the 16th century. Mennonites place high value on the family, world peace, and voluntarism.

Information for free:

About the Mennonite Church. Pamphlet.
Biblical Basis of a Peace Witness. Pamphlet.
Biblical Basis on Justice. Pamphlet.
When You Disagree.It's Okay to Ask for Help. Pamphlet on mediation services.
Who are the Mennonites? Pamphlet.

Information for a fee:

Caring Enough to Confront: How to Understand and Express Your Deepest Feelings Towards Others. 1973. 142 pages. $6.95. Describes a lifestyle for Christians who care to confront others when differences become important, and discusses the feelings of trust, anger, prejudice, blame, and guilt.

Christ and Violence. 1979. 104 pages. $4.95. A book that uses Jesus as an example for how to respond to violence in the world.

Communication Skills and Conflict Resolution. 1983. $4.95. A ten-session curriculum for Christian youth and adults.

Crime and Reconciliation: Creative Options for Victims and Offenders. 1985. 141 pages. $7.95. Describes a program where offenders are "restored to society" through a wholistic system of justice and reconciliation.

Darkening Valley: A Biblical Perspective on Nuclear War. 1989. 256 pages. $14.95. Calls for Christians to resist militarism.

A Lay Person's Guide to Conflict Management. 1979. 15 pages. $6.50. An introduction to managing conflict using Christian methods.

Mediation for Troubled Marriages. 1989. 144 pages. $9.95. Makes the case for churches to offer mediation services to members.

The Peacemaker. 1987. 208 pages. $8.95. Addresses such issues as war and peace, relationships between the sexes, world hunger, and evangelism.

Slavery, Sabbath, War, and Women: Case Studies in Biblical Interpretation. 1983. 368 pages. $15.95. Shows how the Bible has been used to justify opposing viewpoints in the past, and how it can be used for guidance on social issues today.

To find out more, write or phone:

Mennonite Church
528 E. Madison St.
Lombard, IL 60148
Phone: (708)627-5310 or *Fax:* (708)627-9893

▶ MENSA Pagan/Occult/Witchcraft Special Interest Group (POWSIG)

Provides information on: *Satanism/Witchcraft, Occult*

This organization is made up of people who are interested in witchcraft, nature religions, mythological traditions of various cultures, or related topics. The group promotes communication and contact among members, offers information about paganism and related topics, fosters spiritual exploration with a view to a "healthy community on a healthy planet." POWSIG provides consultation to law enforcement and other public officials and maintains archive of pagan periodicals published worldwide.

Information for a fee:

Pagana. 8/year. $12/year. Newsletter featuring reviews, poetry, how-to materials, and obituaries.

What are Paganism and Witchcraft? $1.

To find out more, write or phone:
MENSA Pagan/Occult/Witchcraft Special Interest Group
Valerie Voigt, Coordinator
PO Box 52010
Palo Alto, CA 94303
Phone: (415)856-6911

▶ Mormon History Association

Provides information on: *Mormon Religion*

The Mormon History Association is an organization of professional historians, students, and others interested in the history of Mormonism. The group encourages research and writing in the field of Mormon history.

Information for a fee:
Journal of Mormon History. Biannual. Included in $15 membership dues.
Mormon History Association Newsletter. Quarterly. Included in $15 membership dues. Contains notices of new books and bibliographies.

To find out more, write or phone:
Mormon History Association
University Sta.
PO Box 7010
Provo, UT 84602
Phone: (801)378-4048

▶ Mormonism Research Ministry

Provides information on: *Mormon Religion*

Mormonism Research Ministry is a nonprofit Christian organization that distributes information on the teachings of the Mormon Church and "how those teachings differ from biblical Christianity."

Information for free:
Mormonism Researched. Quarterly. A magazine that contains articles concerning the Mormon Church.

To find out more, write or phone:
Mormonism Research Ministry
PO Box 20705
El Cajon, CA 92021-0955
Phone: (619)447-3873

▶ Orthodox Church in America

Provides information on: *Orthodox Religions*

The Orthodox Church in America is a multi-ethnic Orthodox community headed by an archbishop. There are nine dioceses in the United States, one in Canada, and one in Mexico. The church offers several periodicals.

Information for free:
The Russian Orthodox Messenger. Includes a list of publications.

To find out more, write or phone:
Orthodox Church in America
c/o Most Blessed Theodosius
Box 675
Syosset, NY 11791
Phone: (201)694-5782 or *Fax:* (201)365-1478

▶ Parapsychology Institute of America

Provides information on: *Parapsychology*

The Institute investigates ghosts, psychic phenomena, haunted houses, and other aspects of parapsychology. It is currently researching psychic abilities to read information stored in computers.

Information for a fee:
Amityville Horror Solved. $3.99.
True Tales of the Unknown. $3.99.
True Tales of the Unknown: Beyond Reality. $3.99.
The Uninvited. $3.99.
We Don't Die. $5.
We Are Not Forgotten. $5.

To find out more, write or phone:
Parapsychology Institute of America
PO Box 252
Elmhurst, NY 11373
Phone: (718)894-6564

▶ Presbyterian Church (USA)

Provides information on: *Presbyterian Religion*

The Presbyterian Church focuses on the reconciling work of Christ through the grace of God, with a significance on the mission of the Church in society. It is concerned with personal growth, social issues, racial-ethnic studies, and health and wellness.

Information for free:

Presbyterian Publishing House Books and Supplies Catalog. 1992-1993. 120 pages.

Information for a fee:

Alcoholics and Their Families: A Guide for Clergy and Congregations. $17.95. Shows how to use caring, love, and grace to help alcoholics and their families.

Christians and the Art of Caring. $8.99. Suggests ways to create a caring ministry.

Cry Softly! The Story of Child Abuse. $10. Covers sexual, physical, and emotional abuse. Provides hotline numbers and other resources.

Hospice and Ministry. $12.95. Discusses the role of the pastor, ministry with dying persons, working with families, children, and working with AIDS patients.

Ministry of Love: A Handbook for Visiting the Aging. $3.95. Practical advice for visiting the aging, suggestions for group programs, and resources for prayers.

Pastor, Our Marriage is in Trouble. $11.99. A guide to short-term counseling.

Pastoral Care with Adolescents in Crisis. $12.99. Outlines the pressures faced by today's youth and offers methods for responding to crisis in the areas of family, school, sex, substance abuse, and depression/suicide.

Sex in the Parish. $14.99. Examines issues such as setting boundaries between clergy and parishioners, ethics issues, and the sexuality of women pastors, single pastors, and gay, lesbian, or bisexual pastors.

Where Does God Live? Questions and Answers for Parents and Children $11.95. Explains the similarities and differences between religions for readers of all ages.

Why Should I Care? Honest Answers to the Questions that Trouble Teens. $8.95.

To find out more, write or phone:

Presbyterian Church (USA)
475 Riverside Dr.
New York, NY 10115
Toll-free: 1-800-554-4694

▶ Protestant Episcopal Church in the U.S.A.

Provides information on: *Protestant Religions*

The Protestant Episcopal Church represents the Anglican tradition in the United States. The Church is identified by its liberalism in matters of discipline, doctrine, and Biblical interpretation. In 1976, the ordination of women was approved and a revised "Book of Common Prayer" was introduced. The Church makes available several periodicals.

To find out more, write or phone:

Protestant Episcopal Church in the U.S.A.
815 2nd Ave.
New York, NY 10017
Phone: (212)867-8400

▶ Reasons to Believe

Provides information on: *Religious History*

Reasons to Believe seeks to explain the theory of creation in a biblically sound and scientifically valid manner, in an effort to "remove the doubts of skeptics" and strengthen the faith of Christians. The organization also conducts research and educational programs and maintains a library.

Information for free:

Reasons to Believe Materials Catalog. Listing of publications, audiotapes, and videotapes offered.

Information for a fee:

Encyclopedia of Bible Difficulties. 1982. $21.95. Presents arguments for the unity and integrity of the Bible in an attempt to explain the seeming discrepancies in Scripture.

The New Testament Documents: Are They Reliable? 1987. $3.95. Presents results of modern research into the realiability of the New Testament.

Scaling the Secular City. 1987. $13.00. Offers defense of the Christian faith, including arguments for the existence of God and the resurrection of Jesus Christ.

Reasons to Believe also offers a number of short papers priced from 25 cents to $3.00. Some of these include:

Astrology—Help, Hoax, or Harm?,
Barriers to Faith,
Biblical Forecasts of Scientific Discoveries,
New Astronomical Proofs for the Existence of God.

To find out more, write or phone:

Reasons to Believe
Hugh Ross, Pres.
PO Box 5978
Pasadena, CA 91117
Phone: (818)335-1480 or *Fax:* (818)852-0178

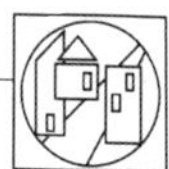

▶ Reform Judaism

Provides information on: *Judaism*

The Reform Judaism church broke away from the traditional Jewish community to modernize. They revised prayer books for those who spoke no Hebrew, abolished the practice of covering the head during worship, and advocated an openness among the general religious community.

Information for a fee:

Drugs, Sex, and Integrity: What Does Judaism Say? $10. A learning tool for young adults about Jewish law. It covers such issues as alcoholism, sex, integrity, and Jewish religious values.

Every Person's Guide to Judaism. $8.95. Provides the basics of Jewish life.

Israel: Covenant People, Covenant Land. The history of the land of Israel, its people, and its faith.

The Jewish Wedding Book. A how-to book on the ceremony and an explanation of the heritage and symbolism in the Jewish wedding.

Love in Your Life: A Jewish View of Teenage Sexuality. $9.95. A book providing young adults with a Jewish perspective on issues concerning teenage sexuality. Covers such topics as infatuation, love, premarital sex, AIDS, abortion, sexually transmitted diseases, homosexuality, dating, sexual abuse, and maturity.

One People: A Study in Comparative Judaism. $6.95. Explores the similarities and differences among the major movements of Judaism.

Reform Judaism/Focus On. Quarterly. $10/year. Magazine.

Tough Choices: Jewish Perspectives on Social Justice Issues in the 21st Century. 1992. $11. Confronts racial justice, church and state relations, civil liberties, Israel, bio-medical ethics, world peace, environmental issues, gay rights, and abortion.

Understanding Judaism. Looks at the history of Judaism while exploring personal and ethical responsibility in the areas of sex, drug and alcohol use, and marriage and divorce.

What Happens After I Die? $8.95. Jewish views of life after death.

To find out more, write or phone:

Reform Judaism
Union of American Hebrew Congregations
838 5th Ave.
New York, NY 10021
Phone: (212)249-0100

▶ Religion and Ethics Institute (REI)

Provides information on: *Religious History*

The Institute promotes the discovery and distribution of historical and scientific knowledge in the fields of religion and ethics. Its work focuses on promoting an accurate understanding of religion and ethics of the past and developing new directions in which these fields should move in the future. The Institute also conducts research, sponsors educational programs, and maintains a library and slide collection on the history of religion.

Information for free:
REI Catalog. Lists publications, slides, and video lectures.

Information for a fee:
The Historical Approach to the Bible. 1982. 334 pages. $10. Presents a survey of the history and methodological approach to understanding the Bible.
I Started to be a Minister: From Fundamentalism to a Religion of Ethics. 1990. 265 pages. $19.95. An autobiography that relates the author's 50 years of research on the Bible and religion.
The Literary Origin of the Gospel of John. 1974. 297 pages. $7.50.
The Noah's Ark Nonsense. 1978. 156 pages. $10. Looks at the biblical account of a universal flood, and a report of the unsuccessful search for Noah's Ark on Mount Ararat in an effort to defend the Bible.

To find out more, write or phone:
Religion and Ethics Institute
PO Box 5510
Evanston, IL 60204
Phone: (708)328-4049

▶ Research Center for Religion and Human Rights in Closed Societies

Provides information on: *Religious Freedom, Human Rights*

The Center translates and analyzes official and underground documents and articles regarding religious life in communist, formerly communist, and other totalitarian societies, focusing attention on the violation of religious freedom and human rights. RCDA makes available translations of documents and articles. It maintains a private library of material from various communist countries.

Information for a fee:
RCDA (formerly Religion in Communist Dominated Areas). Quarterly. $25/year. Journal including case histories, book reviews, research reports, and translated documentation.

 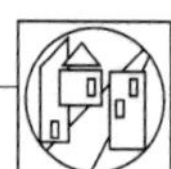

To find out more, write or phone:
Research Center for Religion and Human Rights in Closed Societies
Olga S. Hruby, Exec.Dir. & Editor
475 Riverside Dr., Ste. 448
New York, NY 10115
Phone: (212)870-2481

▶ Roman Catholic Church

Provides information on: *Catholicism*

The Roman Catholic Church is a Christian religious community whose members are "baptized and incorporated in Christ, profess the same faith, partake of the same sacraments, and are in communion with and under the government of the successor of St. Peter, the pope, and the bishops in union with him."

Information for a fee:

Catholic Campaign for Children and Families. 1992. 84 pages. $4.95. A manual that includes practical planning and support materials, bulletin quotes, liturgal and preaching guides and models.

The Challenge of Peace. 1983. 142 pages. $3.95. Gives the views of U.S. Catholic bishops on nuclear weapons and the arms race.

Economic Justice for All. 1986. 208 pages. $3.95. Addresses the issues of poverty, unemployment, food, and the economic relationship that the U.S. has with developing nations.

Faith and Culture: A Multicultural Catechetical Resource. 1987. 96 pages. $5.95. Explores the cultural aspects brought to Catholic worship by African Americans, Native Americans, Hispanics, and Asians.

A Family Perspective in Church and Society. 1988. 60 pages. $7.95. Addresses the plight of today's American family.

Human Sexuality. 1991. 127 pages. $9.95. Provides educational and informational guidance on the questions and problems involved with human sexuality.

Live the Faith, Share the Story. 1992. 64 pages. $8.95. A resource designed to help celebrate youth as important in the parish and school community and encourage family involvement in all 1993 World Youth Day plans.

Many Pilgrims, One Family God. 1992. 52 pages. $7.95. A book designed to emphasize the integration of migrants, immigrants, and refugees into the community.

Putting Children and Families First. 1992. 24 pages. $1.95. Examines the needs of all children in an increasingly difficult world.

Renewing the Earth. 1992. 20 pages. $1.95. Discusses environmental problems, including global warming, ozone depletion, deforestation, and toxic and nuclear waste.

To find out more, write or phone:
Roman Catholic Church
National Conference of Catholic Bishops
1312 Massachusetts Ave., NW
Washington, DC 20005
Toll-free: 1-800-235-8722 or *Phone:* (202)541-3000

▶ Shi'a Muslims

Provides information on: *Islam*

The Shi'a Muslim community is one of the two orthodox branches of Islam, and includes Iranian-Americans, Lebanese, Pakistani, and Yemini-Americans. Publications are available at little or no cost.

To find out more, write or phone:
Shi'a Muslims
Islamic Center of Detroit
15571 Joy Rd.
Detroit, MI 48228
Phone: (313)582-7442

▶ Southern Baptist Convention

Provides information on: *Baptist Religions*

The Southern Baptist Convention has a strong belief in Jesus Christ, the Bible, and experiencing believer's baptism by immersion.

Information for free:
Meet Southern Baptists! An information brochure on the Church, their beliefs, and missions.

To find out more, write or phone:
Southern Baptist Convention
c/o Executive Committee
460 James Robertson Pkwy.
Nashville, TN 37219
Phone: (615)244-2495

▶ Sunni Muslims

Provides information on: *Islam*

The Islamic community is one of the two orthodox branches of Islam, and is organized into a number of independent centers. Each center tends to be dominated by one ethnic community. Many of the major centers offer a periodical. The mosque, headed by the Imam (minister-teacher) is the basic center of Islam.

To find out more, write or phone:

Sunni Muslims
Islamic Center
2551 Massachusetts Ave., NW
Washington, DC 20008
Phone: (202)332-8343

▶ Unarius Academy of Science

Provides information on: *New Age*

The organization promotes the teaching of past life therapy and works to liberate people from what it defines as the "psychic amnesia" of the past. The Academy believes all humans have lived on other worlds in the past and will do so again, and that everyone functions at "half-potential" until psychic awareness is achieved. Unarius is an acronym for Universal Articulate Interdimensional Understanding of Science.

Information for a fee:

Facts About UFOs. 57 pages. $6.95. Addresses questions about UFOs and their purpose in landing on Earth.

Have You Lived on Other Worlds Before? Volume 1: 367 pages. $10.95. Volume 2: 268 pages. $8.95.

History of the Universe. 450 pages. $17.95. Examines the cause for the decline of man's intelligence, evidence of extraterrestrial heritage, and how the reader fits into the world.

Infinite Contact. 199 pages. $10.95. Follows the evolution of man, and offers answers about questions of life on other planets.

A Newsletter for the 21st Century. 6/year. $15.

The Proof of the Truth of Past Life Therapy. 212 pages. $10.95. A Unarius book demonstrating how to teach others to heal themselves of the emotional blocks left from negative past-life experiences.

Unarius Light. Quarterly. $24. Newsletter.

Also offers a publications booklet, audio and videotapes, and educational materials.

To find out more, write or phone:

Unarius Academy of Science
145 S. Magnolia Ave.
El Cajon, CA 92020-4522
Phone: (619)444-7062 or *Fax:* (619)447-6485

To Contact People . . .

These books identify individual experts or organizations that can direct you to one.

▶ *American Buddhist Directory*

Use this directory to find Buddhist temples; meditation groups, study groups and organizations; Zen, Theravada, Mahayana, and Tantric centers. Entries are arranged geographically. Coverage includes Canada.

1992. American Buddhist Movement.

▶ *American Jewish Organizations Directory*

This directory lists Jewish organizations, synagogues, and schools. Listings include name, address, phone, rabbi or key person for some listings, denomination, and key indicating whether school, synagogue, or organization. Arranged geographically.

1987. H. Frenkel, Publisher.

▶ *Canadian Who's Who*

This book lists about 12,000 notable Canadians in Canada and abroad based on position or achievement. Entries include name, address, personal and career data.

Annual. University of Toronto Press.

▶ *Directory of African American Religious Bodies*

Listed are some 1,000 Afrian American religious denominations; resource and service agencies that serve the African American community; religious educational institutions; African American colleges and universities founded by religious bodies; and African American religious scholars. Entries are grouped into separate sections by organization type.

1991. Howard University School of Divinity Research Center.

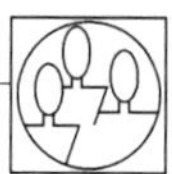

▶ *Directory of the American Baptist Churches in the U.S.A.*

The directory provides names and addresses for Baptist denominational boards, regional and state groups, churches, pastors and other professional leadership. Entries are classified by membership type.
Annual. American Baptist Churches in the U.S.A.

▶ *Directory of Faculty in Departments and Programs of Religious Studies in North America*

The faculty directory covers more than 3,200 individuals involved in the teaching of religious studies. Entries include personal name, address, phone, educational background, degrees earned, publications, honors received, employment history, fields of specialty, and other biographical data. Arrangement of the book is alphabetical.
First edition spring 1988, new edition expected 1992. Council of Societies for the Study of Religion (CSSR).

▶ *Encyclopedia of American Religions*

This book contains information on approximately 1,700 religious and spiritual groups in the United States and Canada, including Roman Catholic, Judaic, Protestant, Eastern, and Middle Eastern religions. It includes other beliefs and practices, such as occultism, magic, Satanism, and communes. The first part of the book contains an essay on the development of religion in the U.S., a historical survey of religion in Canada, and historical essays grouped by broad religious family. The second part contains corresponding directory sections listing individual churches and groups constituting the religious families discussed in the historical essays. Entries include group name, address (if group is still active); description of group's history, beliefs, and organization; membership data, educational facilities, periodicals, and bibliography of additional information sources. Both sections are arranged by general religious family.
1992. Gale Research Inc.

▶ *Episcopal Church Annual*

The directory covers the churches and clergy of the Episcopal Church; seminaries, training schools, retreat centers, and social service agencies; and dioceses and provinces of Anglican Communion. It includes information and statistics on dioceses, the structure of the church, and its institutions.
Annual. Morehouse Publishing.

▶ *Guide to the American Occult: Directory and Bibliography*

This directory provides information on about 1,200 organizations and periodicals concerned with occult and paranormal groups and movements. Coverage includes astrology, psychics, biorhythm, extrasensory perception, faith healing, fortune telling, magic, metaphysics, palmistry, mysticism, numerology, parapsychology, pyramid power, reincarnation, spiritualism, unidentified flying objects, voodoo, witchcraft, etc. The book lists name, address, and area of interest. Entries are arranged alphabetically.
Annual. Laird Wilcox: Editorial Research Service.

▶ *International Directory of Persons Granted Degrees for Work in Parapsychology*

The directory covers 434 persons granted advanced degrees in part for a thesis or dissertation on a parapsychological topic, and institutions conducting research in the field of parapsychology. The entries include individual name, degree, date conferred, name of granting institution, title of thesis, and languages used in thesis. Entries are arranged alphabetical1y.
Parapsychology Sources of Information Center.

▶ *International Who's Who*

This book covers 20,000 prominent persons worldwide. Entries include name, nationality, personal and career information, honors, awards, writings, address, and phone. Names are arranged alphabetically.
Annual. Europa Publications Ltd.

▶ *Lutheran Annual*

Lists congregations, pastors, teachers, and other professionals of the 38 districts of the Lutheran Church Missouri Synod and Lutheran Church-Canada. The book includes affiliated educationsl institutions, auxiliary organizations, and health and welfare agencies. Arranged alphabetially.
Annual. Concordia Publishing House.

▶ *Mennonite Yearbook*

This book lists individual Mennonite churhes and groups of congregations, church boards, colleges and seminaries, secondary schools, elementary schools, members of councils and committees, mission programs at home and overseas, historical societies,

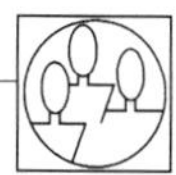

mutual aid organizations, publishers, camps, health and human service institutions, service organizations, Mennonite world conferences, and ministers of the Mennonite Church. Entries are arranged by activity.
B Annual. Mennonite Publishing House.

▶ *National Association of Congregational Christian Churches—Yearbook*

Congregational Christian churches are listed, including associate and affiliate churches. The yearbook also lists ministers, officers, congregational associations, and fellowships. It is arranged into separate sections for churches, ministers, committees and their officers, and associations.
Annual. National Association of Congregational Christian Churches.

▶ *National Evangelical Directory*

Listed in this directory are more than 4,000 evangelical denominations, missions and service organizations, Christian schools and camps, and religious broadcasting stations. The book is arranged by type of organization.
Biennial. National Association of Evangelicals.

▶ *National Spiritualist Association of Churches—Yearbook*

Use this listing to find chartered churches and state associations, ordained ministers and licentiate ministers, commissioned spiritual healers, certified mediums, and state lyceum superintendents. Listings include church, association, or personal name, address, phone, name of contact, and category of certification. Listings are in separate geographical sections.
Annual. National Spiritualist Association of Churches.

▶ *New Age Almanac*

The almanac is primarily an encyclopedia that lists concepts, individuals, and organizations related to the New Age movement, giving descriptions of their significance. Some entries for organizations give the group's address and phone, and the book also includes several directory-type lists of educational institutions and groups associated with New Age topics.
1990. Visible Ink Press.

▶ *New Marketing Opportunities*

Use this book to locate over 8,000 New Age and metaphysical publishers, events, retailers, distributors, services, publications, reviewers, catalogers, media connections, associations, and other resources. Entries include company name, address, phone, date established, percentage of products devoted to New Age/metaphysical topics, and description of products and services. Entries are arranged alphabetically.
Biennial. First Editions.

▶ *Official Catholic Directory*

The directory lists more than 60,000 clerical and lay leaders of the institutions, organizations, and possessions of the Catholic Church in the U.S. and Vatican. For official bodies and organizations the book includes name, address, names and titles of key personnel, and may include phone and brief description and/or statistics. Listings for priests include name, order, diocese, and address. The book is arranged geographically.
Annual. Reed Reference Publishing.

▶ *Parapsychology Organizations: A Directory*

The directory covers approximately 45 parapsychology organizations worldwide. Entries include organization name, address, phone, name and title of contact, and are arranged by type, then alphabetically.
1991. Parapsychology Sources of Information Center.

▶ *Who's Who in America*

This book contains information on 79,000 people, primarily in the U.S., considered to be of current national interest because of achievement or position. Entries include name, address, personal data, career data, memberships, special achievements, and publications. Names are listed alphabetically; a separate volume indexes people by profession and location.
Biennial. Updated quarterly. Marquis Who's Who.

▶ *Who's Who of American Women*

This book contains information on more than 30,000 high-profile women in all fields. Entries include name, address, personal, educational, and career data, professional association membership, special achievements, awards, and writings. Names are arranged alphabetically.
Biennial. Marquis Who's Who.

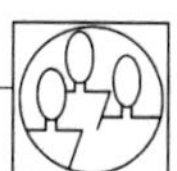

▶ *Who's Who in Religion*

Coverage includes more than 16,000 men and women worldwide who have made an impact on spiritual life and principles. Individuals listed are clergy, bishops, executive officials and administrators, heads of religious associations, rabbinical organizations, religious educators, publishers, broadcasters, and lay leaders.
1992. Marquis Who's Who.

▶ *Who's Who in the World*

This directory covers more than 31,000 people of current international interest because of their achievement or position. Entries include name, address, biographical data, civic activities, awards, writings, and other information. Names are arranged alphabetically.
Biennial. Marquis Who's Who.

▶ *Yearbook of American and Canadian Churches*

Listed are over 500 established religious groups in the United States and Canada. Also included are lists of local church councils, theological seminaries, church-related colleges and universities, and religious periodicals. The publication also includes statistical information on denominations, membership, finances, clergy, and more.
Annual. Academic & Reference Books Division of Abingdon Press.

Alphabetical and Subject Index

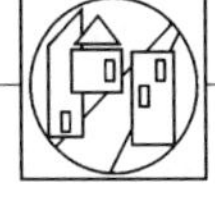

The Alphabetical and Subject Index is an A-Z listing of all organizations, agencies, and publications included in SCB. These resources are also listed under their subject specialties, which appear in boldface type below. Consult "How to Use This Book" for more detailed information about the index.

A

B

C

D

E

H

Immigration and Naturalization (continued)

Incest

J

N

P

S

Travel and Recreation (continued)

U

V

W

Y